Teaching Anglophone South Asian Women Writers

Teaching Anglophone South Asian Women Writers

Edited by
Deepika Bahri
and
Filippo Menozzi

Modern Language Association of America
New York 2021

Library of Congress Cataloging-in-Publication Data

Names: Bahri, Deepika, 1962- editor. | Menozzi, Filippo, editor.
Title: Teaching Anglophone South Asian women writers / edited by Deepika Bahri and Filippo Menozzi.
Description: New York : Modern Language Association, 2021. | Series: Options for teaching, 10792562 ; vol 52 | Includes bibliographical references.
Identifiers: LCCN 2021004691 (print) | LCCN 2021004692 (ebook) | ISBN 9781603294898 (hardcover) | ISBN 9781603294904 (paperback) | ISBN 9781603294911 (EPUB)
Subjects: LCSH: South Asian literature (English)—Women authors—Study and teaching (Higher) | English literature—South Asian authors—Study and teaching (Higher) | South Asian literature (English)—Women authors—History and criticism. | Feminism and literature—South Asia.
Classification: LCC PR9410.A53 T43 2021 (print) | LCC PR9410.A53 (e-book) | DDC 820.9/92870954—dc23
LC record available at https://lccn.loc.gov/2021004691
LC ebook record available at https://lccn.loc.gov/2021004692

Options for Teaching 52
ISSN 1079-2562

Cover illustrations (left to right):

Jamawar length (detail). Courtesy of the RISD Museum, Providence, RI.

Fragment of a lampas (detail). Virginia Museum of Fine Arts, Richmond. Gift of the Friends of Indian Art and the Robert A. Ruth W. Fisher Fund. Photo: Katherine Wetzel. © Virginia Museum of Fine Arts.

Woman's wrapped dress (detail). Courtesy of the RISD Museum, Providence, RI.

Tree-of-Life palampore (detail). Virginia Museum of Fine Arts, Richmond. Arthur and Margaret Glasgow Endowment, along with gifts by exchange from Mrs. M. N. Blakemore, in memory of her late husband, Major Maurice Neville Blakemore, Estate of Miss Lizzie Boyd, Russell O. and Lucille T. Briere, Mrs. Harvey Archer Clopton, Dr. and Mrs. Robert A. Fisher, Mr. and Mrs. Eric M. Lipman, George C. and Cecilia D. McGhee, Dr. Brooks Marsh, Dr. Leigh A. Marsh, Mrs. Oliver F. Marston, Dr. William M. Patterson, Miss Anne Rowland, Mr. Charles B. Samuels, Dr. George N. Thrift, Mrs. M.S. Wightman, Mrs. Nellie L. Wiley, Mr. and Mrs. Erwin Will, and the Virginia Museum of Fine Arts Foundation. Photo: Travis Fullerton. © Virginia Museum of Fine Arts.

Textile fragment (detail). Courtesy of the RISD Museum, Providence, RI.

Published by The Modern Language Association of America
85 Broad Street, Suite 500, New York, New York 10004-2434
www.mla.org

Contents

Chronology

Chronology of historical events and of significant works published in English by South Asian women writers

Year	Literary Works	Historical Events
1813		East India Company Act
1829		Bengal Sati Regulation
1857		Indian Mutiny
1876	Raj Lakshmi Debi, *The Hindu Wife*	
1878	Toru Dutt, *Bianca; or, The Young Spanish Maiden*	
1885		Foundation of Indian National Congress
1895	Shevantibai Nikambe, *Ratanbai* Krupabai Satthianadhan, *Saguna*	
1896		Indian famine
1901	Cornelia Sorabji, *Love and Life behind the Purdah*	
1905	Sarojini Naidu, *The Golden Threshold*	Partition of Bengal
	Rokeya Sakhawat Hossain, *Sultana's Dream*	
1907		Establishment of monarchy in Bhutan
1928	Alice Maud Sorabji Pennell, *The Begum's Son*	
1942		Quit India movement
1947		Independence and partition of India and Pakistan
1951		Revolution of 1951 in Nepal
1954	Kamala Markandaya, *Nectar in a Sieve*	
1955	Ruth Prawer Jhabvala, *To Whom She Will*	
1958	Nayantara Sahgal, *A Time to Be Happy*	
1961	Attia Hosain, *Sunlight on a Broken Column*	
1962		Sino-Indian War
1963	Anita Desai, *Cry, the Peacock*	
1965	Kamala Das, *Summer in Calcutta*	Indo-Pakistani War; Independence of Maldives
1971		Bangladesh Liberation War
1976	Meena Alexander, *The Bird's Bright Ring*	
1977	Anita Desai, *Fire on the Mountain*	The Emergency in India; Muhammad Zia-ul-Haq takes power in Pakistan
1978	Bapsi Sidhwa, *The Crow Eaters*	

(continued)

Chronology (continued)

Year	Literary Works	Historical Events
1979	Gita Mehta, *Karma Cola*	
1980	Anita Desai, *Clear Light of Day*	
1981	Suniti Namjoshi, *Feminist Fables*	
1983		Sri Lankan civil war (Black July) begins
1984	Jean Arasanayagam, *Apocalypse '83* Anita Desai, *In Custody*	Assassination of Indira Gandhi
1985	Suniti Namjoshi, *The Conversations of Cow* Nayantara Sahgal, *Rich Like Us*	Shah Bano case
1987	Chitra Divakaruni, *Dark Like the River*	
1988		Benazir Bhutto prime minister in Pakistan
1989	Bharati Mukherjee, *Jasmine* Imtiaz Dharker, *Purdah and Other Poems* Sara Suleri, *Meatless Days*	
1991	Bapsi Sidhwa, *Cracking India*	Assassination of Rajiv Gandhi
1992	Gita Hariharan, *The Thousand Faces of Night*	Demolition of Babri Masjid
1993	Meena Alexander, *Fault Lines*	
1994	Imtiaz Dharker, *Postcards from God*	Rise of *Bharatiya Janata Party* in Indian elections
1997	Arundhati Roy, *The God of Small Things* Chitra Divakaruni, *The Mistress of Spices*	
1998	Kiran Desai, *Hullabaloo in the Guava Orchard*	
1999	Jhumpa Lahiri, *Interpreter of Maladies*	
2000	Shashi Deshpande, *Small Remedies*	
2001	Arundhati Roy, *The Algebra of Infinite Justice*	Indian Parliament attack
2002	Meena Alexander, *Illiterate Heart* Kamila Shamsie, *Kartography*	Gujarat riots
2003	Monica Ali, *Brick Lane* Jhumpa Lahiri, *The Namesake*	
2004		Indian Ocean tsunami
2005	Choden Kunzang, *The Circle of Karma* Manjushree Thapa, *Forget Kathmandu*	
2006	Kiran Desai, *The Inheritance of Loss* Yasmine Gooneratne, *The Sweet and Simple Kind* Bapsi Sidhwa, *Water*	
2007	Tahmima Anam, *A Golden Age*	Assassination of Benazir Bhutto
2008		Mumbai attacks
2009		End of Sri Lankan civil war
2013	Sonali Deraniyagala, *Wave*	
2014	Arundhati Roy, *Listening to Grasshoppers* Meena Kandasamy, *The Gypsy Goddess*	Narendra Modi prime minister in India
2017	Arundhati Roy, *The Ministry of Utmost Happiness*	

Map

Afghanistan
Nepal
Bhutan
Pakistan
Bangladesh
India
Sri Lanka
The Maldives

Deepika Bahri and Filippo Menozzi

Introduction

Anglophone South Asian women's writing is a complex formulation, referring simultaneously to a language (English), a geographical and historical context (South Asia), and a gendered literary tradition. Each of the key units of this compound expression invites further scrutiny of the histories involved in its production and currency today. In their introduction to the 2004 edition of *Modern South Asia: History, Culture, Political Economy*, the historians Sugata Bose and Ayesha Jalal note that the term *South Asia* is a relatively "recent construction—only about five decades old" (2). Michael Mann locates the first use of the term in a nineteenth-century German school atlas and notes its increasing currency after World War II. Modern South Asia commonly refers to the nation-states of India, Pakistan, Sri Lanka, and Bangladesh and "the transformation of the monarchies of Afghanistan, Bhutan, Maldives, and Nepal into modern republics," as Kamala Visweswaran explains, although Myanmar and Tibet are occasionally included in the region (1). What makes South Asia a meaningful unit of analysis? Bose and Jalal observe that "it is a commonplace in any introduction to South Asian history to expound on the cliché about the region's unity in diversity. It may be more appropriate to characterise South Asia and its peoples as presenting a picture of diversity in unity, indeed of immense diversity" (2). We suggest that a literary map of South Asian women's writing in English nonetheless points to shared coordinates alongside diversity and difference.

The routine use of the modifier *modern* in histories of the region functions as implicit reference to colonial imperialism, capitalism, and the independence movements of decolonization, elucidating the prevalence of *nation* and *colonialism* as key terms in this literature. Even if the modifier *anglophone* invokes vernacular languages and cultures and glimpses of premodern histories and literary traditions, colonialism and modernity explain the choice of English by many writers. Modern South Asia's postcolonial legacy also includes intraregional conflict, civil war, and religious strife, topics treated with sensitivity by South Asian women writers. At the same time, these writers also address the more recent phenomena of globalization, diaspora, and markets for anglophone writers at home and abroad. In her pivotal study of modernism, Jessica Berman claims that texts by Indian women writers "ask us to reconsider the role of women in the development of Indian modernity and to recognise the powerful ethical and political engagement their texts evidence" (141). Although Ian Talbot notes the synonymous use of the terms *South Asia*, *the Indian subcontinent*, and *India* by many commentators on the region, the extension of Berman's claims about Indian women writers' engagement with modernity to women from other parts of South Asia is not a conflation but a recognition of parallel concerns and aesthetic developments in anglophone South Asian women's writing. This body of writing is distinguished by the confident emergence of women's stakes in responding to global and local currents of history; the exploration of emergent genres such as the graphic novel, chick lit, or Instapoetry; the engagement with pressing issues such as ecological devastation, war culture, and growing inequality; and representations of postcolonial South Asian women, whether in the homeland or the diaspora.[1]

As creative participants in the ethical and political challenges of modern history, South Asian women writers have long sought a place in the world republic of letters as equal claimants to what Pascale Casanova calls "literary legitimacy" in the international marketplace (15). Literary legitimacy, however, should not be limited to recognition of these writers through awards such as the Booker Prize; equally important, we would argue, is the need to recognize multilingual writers such as Toru Dutt with implicit claims to the cosmopolitan sphere from the very beginnings of anglophone writing. More recently, writing by poets such as Meena Alexander, Imtiaz Dharker, and Raman Mundair confidently appropriates multilingual and multicultural frames of reference as markers of global citizenship in what Salman Rushdie calls "the unfettered republic of the tongue," where the writer may move freely, "needing no passport or visa" ("Declaration" 92). In *Home Truths: Fictions of the South Asian Diaspora in Britain*, Susheila Nasta also suggests that writers like Sunetra Gupta and Attia Hosain articulate "a sensibility which may stem from a specific location, but which nonetheless creates an imaginative facility to live freely in the world at large" (221). Nasta claims that Gupta resists both the "migrant camp" and the registers of "Western modernity." Gupta also strives to reconnect home and diaspora by claiming membership in "an ancient Bengali diaspora" characterized by its "literary eclecticism," long before more recent contexts of migration and diaspora (213). Instead of the fetters of national and geographic belonging, the idea of the literary home reflects an affinity for belonging in a world of letters. Apart from the world of letters and language, these writers occasionally locate themselves in a broader planetary context. Because the realpolitik of the literary industry, academic disciplinarity, and canon patrol accords limited space to these writers in the world republic of letters, the task of criticism and pedagogy—for reading and teaching are sometimes mirrored activities—is to reclaim space for more South Asian women writers in a bid to counter regimes of inequality and "unequal advantages" of other writers (Casanova 40). Finally, the emergence of the Internet republic of letters and Instapoet celebrities like Rupi Kaur continue to demand a reexamination of the *world* in *world literature* and the print-bound imaginary of the world republic.

There is a long and prolific tradition of literary production by women in South Asia, dating at least from the second millennium BCE, with writing in English starting to appear in the second half of the nineteenth century. The latter cannot be approached without considering the complex entanglements of the English language both in the history of colonialism and in the subcontinent's cultural heritage. Our use of the term *anglophone* should be understood as a strategic one in that it simultaneously acknowledges the global dominance and currency of English as well as its coexistence in a polyphonic context alive with the presence of other languages and traditions. *Anglophone*, the *Oxford English Dictionary* clarifies, is coined etymologically after the term *francophone* as a compound of *Anglo* (relating to England or English) and *phone* (making or relating to sound). It designates an English-speaking person in countries such as Canada and India, where English is not the only language spoken. In the study of literature, *anglophone*, as opposed to *English*, is used to describe literature in English written by authors from countries outside Britain and the United States.[2] The term signals the history of the global dissemination of English as a dominant language as well as a reminder that, in anglophone contexts, English is often only one of other languages in use. The tactical inclusion in this volume of essays on key South Asian texts translated into English gestures overtly at this imbricated history, one that also surfaces in anglophone novels that include debates about languages in the subcontinent.

Anglophone South Asian women's writing flourishes in multiple genres and locations, reflecting its enduring engagement with "modern" history and the associated phenomena of globalization, migration, and the geopolitics of cultural encounter. No less significant, therefore, is the need to contextualize the work of resident and diasporic writers of South Asian origin while also recognizing the import of teaching these works in different locations (India, Finland, Germany, Spain, the United Kingdom, and the United States). What are the challenges of teaching writing by Muslim women from South Asia in the North American classroom in the age of terror? How best to engage with the "politics of stereotyping" as well as the location and circumstances of students in countries outside South Asia (Morey and Yaqin)? How to approach this body of writing in the nonanglophone classroom in Germany or Finland? How do we understand war, history, or meaningful citizenship through the contributions of South Asian women writers? How do we approach that which resists translation in this writing? These are among the questions raised by contributors to this volume. The following discussion is intended to guide teachers through the main currents in the evolution of a rich and lively tradition of writing by South Asian women writers through key contextual debates about history, language, location, and emergent horizons for writing and teaching. Essays in this volume offer a wide range of pedagogical contexts including elite universities as well as public institutions at different levels, and they emphasize the specificity of teaching South Asian women's writing in contexts marked by national, regional, and economic diversity.

Historical Contexts: Colonialism, Partition, Neoliberalism

Women have been producing literature in South Asia since 600 BCE. So abundant is this corpus and so varied its contexts, media, and forms that

Susie Tharu and K. Lalita's *Women Writing in India* spans two volumes (1,200 or so pages) and includes texts translated from eleven languages—even Persian and Pali, which are no longer used in India—into English and 140 authors, culled from an early list of more than six hundred writers. Despite its expansive scope, the exclusion of prominent writers for a variety of reasons—duplication, logistical concerns about the sheer number of works, and the struggle to gather expertise in languages such as Assamese, Punjabi, Rajasthani, Kashmiri, and Sindhi, which had to be omitted—caused the editors much regret. The earliest anthology of women writers in India, and arguably in the world, appears in *Therigatha*, a collection of songs in the Pali language, committed to writing by Buddhist nuns around 80 BCE. Against a long and rich tradition of writing in vernacular languages over twenty centuries, writing in English in the nineteenth century begins to take shape in part as a consequence of and in part as a response to colonialism and anticolonial movements.

Anticolonial national consciousness began to gather momentum with the Indian Mutiny of 1857, which signaled the start of an organized struggle against British rule in then undivided India. Rooted in history, the beginning of a tradition of literary writing in English by women can be traced to the 1870s after the Mutiny.[3] In this late nineteenth-century historical context, important authors who adopted English for literary expression and representation emerged from a variety of contexts and backgrounds and included women such as Raj Lakhsmi Debi, Toru Dutt, Shevantibai Nikambe, Krupabai Satthianadhan, Pandita Ramabai, Cornelia Sorabji, Sarojini Naidu, and Rokeya Sakhawat Hossain. These writers were part of a native middle class seeking "greater access to English-language education and civil service jobs" and aimed to gain recognition "by turning toward, not away from, the British" (Brinks 7). The use of English in the second half of the nineteenth century, therefore, needs to be understood as part of a political project that was middle class and reformist, aiming at recognition from the colonial government. This project, however, also involved heightened awareness of the reality of colonial domination and the birth of a national consciousness, leading eventually to the formation of the National Congress in 1885. As Ellen Brinks writes in her important study of anglophone women writers in the period 1870–1920, this was "a pivotal time in modern Indian history," because it coincided with a transition from the belief that the Raj was an unquestionable, seemingly enduring fact to the conviction that an independent nation must be the goal (6).[4] Women writers took an active role in the beginnings of anticolonial resistance while participating in debates on tradition and modernity, women's education and social condition. As Padma Anagol suggests, nineteenth-century Indian women developed "an awareness of women as a specific group—*stri jati* and a concept of sisterhood—*bhaginivarg*. . . . This was a crucial step in the formation of a feminist consciousness whereby women began to perceive themselves as a collective. This solidarity cut across caste and religion" (219). In this context, Shevantibai Nikambe's *Ratanbai: A Sketch of a Bombay High Caste Hindu Young Wife* tells the story of a Hindu Brahman child wife who gains an education, thanks to the encouragement of her liberal father, while retaining a "traditional" way of life. Although the author had converted to Christianity, the novel does not explicitly criticize tradition or call for conversion. It deals instead with the ambivalence between the possibilities of emancipation enabled by access to Western-style education and the demands of tradition. Indrani Sen notes that the novel proposes a docile, reformist vision, while also dealing with the issue of high-caste Hindu widowhood, which was hotly debated at the time. Sen observes that "the text carries resonances of Pandita Ramabai's reformist tract *The High-Caste Hindu Woman* with its sharp indictment of the treatment of high-caste widows" (8).

The centrality of what Partha Chatterjee and others call the "women's question" (116) during colonial times is evident in debates concerning widow immolation, or *sati*, a practice abolished in 1829. In her examination of the issue, Lata Mani demonstrates that debates on women and tradition occupied a central role in the colonial public sphere not because they concerned the ending of a "barbaric" tradition but rather because they offered the possibility of a "rearticulation" of the traditional idiom essential to colonial governmentality. As Mani remarks, "These debates are in some sense not primarily about women but about what constitutes authentic cultural tradition. . . . Contrary to the popular notion that the British were compelled to outlaw *sati* because of its barbarity, the horror of the burning of women is, as we shall see, a distinctly minor theme" (122; see also Loomba; Viswanath).

Often positioned as placeholders of authenticity and objects of appropriation in both colonial and nationalist politics, South Asian women, however, were not just passive subjects of these contentious debates but rather active agents who contributed to the making of nineteenth-century history. Most important, women started to claim rights by addressing a variety of audiences in South Asia and beyond. The activist Pandita Ramabai, for example, condemned Hindu nationalist celebration of *sati* and British imperialism, suggesting that both neglected the rights of women (Brinks 91–122). Similarly, the autobiographical novel *Saguna: A Story of Native Christian Life*, by Krupabai Satthianadhan, offers a vocal critique of patriarchy by narrating the story of a woman's struggle to become a medical doctor. The quest for female education also played a crucial role in the life and writing of Toru Dutt, one of the most important South Asian writers of the nineteenth century. Dutt was, in Brinks's description, "an Indian who loved European literature, adopted some English customs and liberal, modernising attitudes and . . . though converted, remained proudly connected to Hindu traditions" (27). Dutt was a cosmopolitan writer who combined "hybrid cultural leanings with a strong desire to improve social and political injustices in Bengal stemming directly from colonialism" (27). Along with poems and letters, Dutt was the author of an unfinished novel, *Bianca, a Spanish Maid*; an epistolary novel in French, *Le Journal de Mademoiselle d'Arvers*; and translations of tales and legends from the Sanskrit, published in a posthumous volume, *Ancient Ballads and Legends of Hindustan*. In spite of her conversion to Christianity and liberal education in Europe, Dutt did not achieve literary success or social mobility in her lifetime. As Alpana Sharma writes, "[E]xcluded by orthodox Hindu society on account of her family's conversion, yet not wholly included in the British social order on account of her Indian/'native' origin, Toru traversed the improvisational space in between these two positions" (102; see also Bagchi). Dutt's cosmopolitan location, at the same time central and marginal in the rearticulation of Indian culture at the end of the nineteenth century, is emblematic of the life and writing of other important upper-class, Western-educated authors, including Sarojini Naidu and Cornelia Sorabji.

Late nineteenth-century South Asian women writers reveal themes that will remain central in the twentieth and early twenty-first centuries: colonial modernity, women's rights and participation in public life, and a cosmopolitan sensibility merging different traditions. They have been, since the beginnings of this literary history, concerned with the effect of colonial rule on their societies and, in particular, the possibilities of women's emancipation through Western or liberal values, while defining their position at the intersection of different cultural formations. Writers like Qurratulain Hyder and Rokeya Sakhawat Hossain were simultaneously anglophone and *bhasha* (vernacular) writers, comfortable in Urdu and Bengali in addition to English, or like Dutt, engaged in translation from

Sanskrit to English. South Asian women's writing today continues to draw on a variety of literary and cultural traditions, with Dutt's nineteenth-century francophone epistolary novel and Jhumpa Lahiri's 2015 italophone memoir serving as eloquent examples of a diversely cosmopolitan inheritance.

Trends identified above continue as writers respond to subsequent developments in South Asia's political and cultural history. Historical events in the subcontinent have long served as a textured backdrop for South Asian women's writing: the independence and partition of India and Pakistan in 1947 after a long anticolonial struggle; the 1971 Bangladesh Liberation War resulting in a new partition as Pakistan split into two separate countries; the 1983 riots against Tamil communities, which gave rise to a violent civil war in Sri Lanka that lasted for more than twenty years; decades of postpartition sectarian violence in India, followed by the destruction of the Babri Masjid in Ayodhya by right-wing Hindu fundamentalists in 1992; and the rise of political formations combining hegemonic Hindu nationalism and aggressive neoliberal policies of privatization and dispossession. The events of 1857, 1947, 1971, 1983, and 1992 have been registered by women writers who engage with the evolving sociopolitical landscape in South Asian countries.

The trauma of partition, Ritu Menon and Kamla Bhasin note, had a profound impact on women in South Asia, particularly in the border regions of the nations that emerged from it. In their milestone analysis of women's testimonies of the events of 1947, they document unspeakable violence toward women, including rape, displacement, mass abduction, forced conversion, and migration, suggesting that "the issue of gendered identities is central to any discussion on the interplay of community, class and caste with wider political, economic and social forces" (21; see also Butalia and Talbot). Menon and Bhasin also note that the violence endured by women during the events shows not only "their particular vulnerability . . . but an overarching patriarchal consensus that emerges on how to dispose of the troublesome question of women's sexuality" (20).

Many twentieth-century South Asian women writers have documented partition through memoir, poetry, and narrative. Some of the most important works on the gendered history of partition have been authored by Sara Suleri, Ismat Chughtai, Bapsi Sidhwa, Deepa Mehta, Anita Desai, Meera Syal, Qurratulain Hyder, Amrita Pritam, and Attia Hosain. Sidhwa's novel *Cracking India* is one of the most widely discussed texts in relation to women's experience of partition. Set in 1947 Lahore, the novel narrates the escalation of violence as seen through the eyes of a young Parsi girl. The novel provides a vivid description of the violence directed toward women during partition, and through the central character of Shanta, the girl's *ayah* (nanny), who is abducted by Muslim men, including a former admirer, the narrative envisages their status as, according to Kavita Daiya, "other to both social spaces of kinship: nation and patriarchal community" (74). Novels by women authored in the decades after 1947 testify to the continuing relevance of partition. Anita Desai's novels, in particular *Clear Light of Day* and *In Custody*, document its effects on places, families, and communities and the dialectic of loss and retrieval in postcolonial India.

While partition mainly refers to the events of 1947, it could be argued that the historical process of partitioning the subcontinent did not end with the collapse of the British Empire but rather continued—and somehow still continues—to affect the history of South Asia. The 1971 war of independence of Bangladesh from Pakistan too was marked by genocide and violence both gendered and communal. As Cara Cilano explains, conflicts related to the events of 1971 "remained (and remain) unresolved. . . . 'Stranded Pakistanis,' the citizens of the united nation who were unable to evacuate Bengal and return to the west, exist in a national limbo as they are barred from repatriation in what is now Pakistan." Cilano speaks of a lacuna in official national discourse, a "narrative vacuum, which implicitly facilitated a national amnesia on the subject" (64). The voices of women writers have addressed this vacuum and countered this amnesia, narrating the events through memoir and fiction. For example, the events of 1971 form the basis of Shahbano Bilgrami's novel *Without Dreams* and Tahmima Anam's novel *A Golden Age*. Similarly, women writers have addressed the aftermath of the civil war in Sri Lanka. In this context, the work of Jean Arasanayagam has shown the trauma and crisis of identity that ensued after the riots of 1983 (Salgado). As Ananya Jahanara Kabir notes,

> The novels of the women authors . . . represent attempts to re-create and recuperate, through narrative, a life anterior to trauma whose loss formed the fabric of post-partition life. However nostalgic or recuperative, such narratives compulsively return to the moment of violence and rupture. . . . Whose partition do we then talk about? Sikh, Hindu, or Muslim? Pakistani, Indian, Bangladeshi, diasporic? (177–90)

While the 1947 partition, the 1971 Bangladesh liberation, and the 1983 riots represent dramatic events in postcolonial South Asia, the 1990s signaled a radical transformation in the history and economy of the subcontinent. In particular, the emergence of a new global economic order during the 1990s coincided with the rise of Hindu fundamentalism in India, the escalation of violence in Sri Lanka, and the beginning of aggressive capitalism in Prime Minister Benazir Bhutto's Pakistan. In this context of intensifying violence and economic exploitation, the demolition of the Babri Masjid in Ayodhya in 1992 epitomized the beginning of a new era of religious extremism and neoliberalism, described by the writer Shashi Deshpande in her novel *Small Remedies.* In 1996 the Hindu nationalist Bharatiya Janata Party (BJP) emerged as a leading political force. Since then, the BJP has been a key player in this new phase of South Asian history, in which increasing sectarian violence and neofascism coexist with the alignment of India and Pakistan with the global economy through policies aimed at attracting multinational corporations and foreign investments (R. Desai). Women writers have addressed the emergent political and economic regimes, critical of the rising inequality and violence in contemporary South Asia. In a skillful mix of history, reportage, memoir, and travel writing, the Nepali writer Manjushree Thapa, for instance, explores her nation's quest for democracy and the implications of the Maoist war in *Forget Kathmandu: An Elegy for Democracy*, while Nandini Sundar explores the violence of the repression of the Maoist guerrillas in her moving and informative *The Burning Forest.*

In this new era of hegemonic nationalist ideologies and neoliberal power, women writers have assumed the role of producers of counter-histories that oppose both hegemonic nationalism and neoliberal capitalism. As the leading critic Susie Tharu explains in her comments on the rise of right-wing Hinduism after Ayodhya:

> The real, and most durable, power of the Hindu communal Right lies not in its shocking excesses. . . . It does so in its hold over the normative structuring of subjectivities and the institutions and practices of everyday life: in the stories that move us, the characters we identify with . . . indeed in the casteism, communalism and sexism of the "humanity" we share as Indians. ("Rendering Account" 88)

Vandana Shiva notes, in her reflections on a case of gang rape in Delhi in 2013, that violence against women has increased since the 1990s, because "traditional patriarchal structures have hybridized with the structures of capitalist patriarchy . . . the economic model focusing myopically on 'growth' begins with violence against women by discounting their contribution to the economy" (see also Oza). Arundhati Roy has emerged as one of the most vocal critics of the violence of global capitalism and hypernationalism. Roy won the Booker Prize in 1997 for her novel *The God of Small Things*; Kiran Desai won it in 2006 for *The Inheritance of Loss*. Disseminated and commodified in a global marketplace, literary works by South Asian women writers in English have taken part in a growing global cultural industry of postcolonial literature, mirroring and interrogating the logic of late capitalism. These writers have been central to the agenda of postcolonial literature and have prompted questions about the "postcolonial exotic." As Graham Huggan notes, "*The God of Small Things* . . . is a novel partly *about* (media) promotion. It both displays and implicitly ironises its own lushly romantic images, its metaphor-laden language, its transferred Conradian primitivist myths. . . . Roy's novel shows the continuing presence of an imperial imaginary lurking behind Indian literature in English" (77).[5]

Huggan's comments can be linked to Deepika Bahri and Mary Vasudeva's remark that "the branch of academic inquiry referred to as South Asian studies carries the undeniable legacy of the political and economic maneuvers of colonialism, themselves buffered by orientalist scholarship . . . [and] the tradition of study about South Asia in colonial India" (3; see also Viswanathan). While novels like *The God of Small Things* and *The Inheritance of Loss* cannot be detached from a neocolonial, neoliberal context of production and circulation, close reading and thoughtful pedagogy of many chapters in the volumes could prove potentially decommodifying gestures that challenge shallow models of consumption common in the reading of non-Western literature. South Asian women's writing thus constitutes a thriving literary market that partly mirrors wider economic dynamics at the heart of global capitalism but also offers literary representations of dispossession, social struggle, and inequality that articulate possibilities of critique and resistance. Contemporary authors offer politically conscious, critical interventions in the form of nonfiction, prose, and poetry. After the publication of her first novel, Roy devoted herself to frontline journalism and political writing, returning to the novel form in 2017 but to continue this vein of criticism through her second novel. A new generation of writers, including the Chennai-based poet and writer Meena Kandasamy and the Sri Lankan writer Sonali Deraniyagala, investigate questions of gender roles, caste discrimination, environmental damage, and sectarian violence (Gajarawala; Tharu, "Impossible Subject").

Resident and Diasporic Geographies: Mapping the Literary Landscape

This volume puts resident and diasporic writers into dialogue, because major stylistic, thematic, and aesthetic commonalities connect writers of South Asian ancestry inhabiting different regions of the globe. While some of the most successful postpartition anglophone writers, including Arundhati Roy and Anita Desai, live or lived in South Asia for an important part of their writing careers, and while the number of popular writers resident in South Asia has grown exponentially since 2000, a good number of important writers are or have been based in Europe and North America, including Kiran Desai, Bapsi Sidhwa, Jhumpa Lahiri, Sara Suleri, Meena Alexander, Attia Hosain, Chitra Divakaruni, Bharati Mukherjee, Kamila Shamsie, Monica Ali, and Imtiaz Dharker. Other diasporic sites, in particular Australia, are the location of work by important writers such as Yasmine Gooneratne and Michelle de Kretser.

The experience of migration, diaspora, and relocation in the centers of the global capitalist system emerges powerfully in writing by this group, though this does not mean that there are no continuities with resident writers and earlier forms of South Asian literature. As indicated in the previous section, South Asian women's writing in English has been global and cosmopolitan since the late nineteenth century, and it has engaged with colonial modernity and multiple literary traditions since the very start. Peter van der Veer notes that, notwithstanding historical differences, South Asian communities have been on the move for a long time and that migration is an "old phenomenon" not reducible to the novelty of neoliberal globalization and the postcolonial condition (3–4). Diasporic communities from India, in particular, experienced an earlier phase in which, as Vijay Mishra observes in his compelling study of the diasporic imaginary, South Asians interacted with other colonized peoples and relocated as indentured labor. The "new" late twentieth-century phase of migration has witnessed the emergence of a highly educated, mobile, upper-class intelligentsia, benefiting from dual citizenship and new technologies in mediating relationships with the home country (Mishra). The exchange between diasporic communities and home countries has been a central factor in recent history, and the diaspora has been an active player in South Asian politics. More recently, ecological concerns seem to be an increasingly important element connecting diasporic and home writers, mirroring the realities of climate change, and debates on the Anthropocene and the capitalocene offer points of connection globally.

With particular reference to this second wave of migration, diasporic South Asian women writers have offered substantial interventions into the literary landscape of both their nations of provenance and their host nations, in particular Britain and the United States. In this regard, Joel Kuortti observes that diasporic writers "are not merely assimilating to their host cultures but they are also actively *reshaping* them through their own, new voices bringing new definitions of identity" (6). South Asian women writers have claimed an important role in different literary traditions and have represented the complexities of gender, community, class, and racial subjectivities in the contemporary world. Furthermore, they have contributed to the representation of what Avtar Brah calls the "diaspora space," which is defined as "a point of confluence of economic, political, cultural, and psychic processes. It is where multiple subject positions are juxtaposed, contested, proclaimed or disavowed" (208).

The representation of this diasporic space of confluence and contestation emerges in works such as the poetry of Imtiaz Dharker, who was born in Pakistan, raised in Glasgow, and married in Wales and now divides her time between London and Mumbai. In her 1997 poem "Minority," Dharker writes:

> There's always the point where
> the language flips
> into an unfamiliar taste;
> where words tumble over
> a cunning tripwire on the tongue;
> were the frame slips,
> the reception of an image
> not quite tuned, ghost-outlined,
> that signals, in their midst,
> an alien.

This stanza reveals the concern with unfamiliarity and alienation and the dilemmas faced by subjects framed by histories of displacement and minority status. The use of English becomes, for the diasporic writer, a material expression of stories of longing, displacements, and impossible returns. In "Minority," Dharker cannot inhabit the English language fully but has to confront constant communicative slippage caused by a sense of nonbelonging.

The relation between place, language, and belonging also recurs in literature by resident South Asian writers. Both diasporic and resident writers reveal common themes, experiential echoes, and stylistic resonances. Thus, in her poem "An Introduction," collected in her 1965 volume *Summer in Calcutta*, the Indian poet Kamala Das offers a provocative and embattled proposition on the sense of self that can be acquired through poetic creation. Das writes:

> Why not let me speak in
> Any language I like? The language I speak,
> Becomes mine, its distortions, its queernesses
> All mine, mine alone. It is half English, half
> Indian, funny perhaps, but it is honest,
> It is as human as I am human, don't
> You see? and it is useful to me as cawing
> Is to crows or roaring to the lions. (59)

While Dharker addresses the question of foreignness and alienation by exploring the slipperiness of the English language, Das appropriates the language as a medium for self-expression through distortions and queerness.[6] Both poets show their creative engagement with literary language as a way of redefining the position of the writer and the displacements that constitute the quest for identity in South Asia and its diasporas. The resonance between authors like Dharker and Das reveals lines of intersection, overlap, and transmission of South Asian women's writing across historical and geographical distances. Instead of approaching the work of resident and diasporic writers as two separate sets, this volume suggests that the category of South Asian women's writing needs to be placed in a resident-diasporic cultural and geographical continuum. While recognizing differences and displacements, shared South Asian ancestry and common stylistic and thematic preoccupations make this body of writing a common space of circulation, cross-pollination, and influence.

Anglophone Writing and Its Others

South Asia presents a multitude of languages and literary traditions, and an encompassing view of this rich heritage seems an arduous, if not impossible, task. In the introduction to a volume titled *The Guarded Tongue: Women's Writing and Censorship in India*, a group of South Asian writers tell of an "unusual conclave of women" meeting for a national conference on the outskirts of Hyderabad in July 2001: "The interactions at the meeting could have amounted to no more than Babel: the 65 women writers from different parts of India spoke in as many as 11 tongues. But they made eminent sense to each other and to everyone else who had the privilege of listening to them at this unique literary event, a National Colloquium of women writing in India" (qtd. in Nadotti).

In spite of the diversity of language and background, the meeting of South Asian women through literature can create a space of unity and belonging, while recognizing the plurality of voices and experiences marking this body of writing. There is, indeed, a vast production of literary works by South Asian women writers in languages other than English. Hindi, Urdu, Tamil, Marathi, Odia, Telugu, Kannada, Bengali, and Malayalam, for example, have long, rich, and diverse traditions of literary writing by women. Some of these writers have been extremely influential and widely taught in South Asia and beyond; among them are Mahasweta Devi (Bengali), Ismat Chughtai (Urdu), Qurratulain Hyder (Urdu), Amrita Pritam (Hindi and Punjabi), Krishna Sobti (Hindi), Geetanjali Shree (Hindi), and Kamala Das, who wrote some of her works in Malayalam as well as English. It should be recognized that English coexists with a multiplicity of languages and literary traditions that are often in competition with anglophone fiction. As Francesca Orsini notes in her critique of the concept of "world literature" in the context of Indian literatures, it is not English but Hindi that plays a dominant role in the contemporary literary scene in India, thanks to the influence of the national academy of letters, Sahitya Akademi, and the "hostility to the hegemony of English" shown by Hindi literary institutions ("India" 84).

However, while Indian institutions promote the use of Hindi as postcolonial lingua franca, the market of fiction is still dominated by English-speaking publishers and public spheres. Orsini acknowledges that the "filters that determine what a world-fiction best-seller will be effectively exclude Indian vernacular literatures" (86). International publishers such as Penguin Random House, Longman, Heinemann, HarperCollins, and Picador have had a strong impact on literary production: the publishing industry ensures the continuing privilege of English and, importantly, the availability of anglophone texts, which is a crucial factor in determining the options available for creating syllabi and curricula in higher education. The current hegemonic role of English, alongside its connection to the history of colonial modernity, suggests that anglophone South Asian women writers have carved out a significant space in many higher education programs worldwide, though it should also be recognized, following Feroza Jussawalla and Deborah Fillerup Weagel, that for many emergent South Asian women writers, access to publishing in English remains fraught with difficulties.

While it is important to recognize the uneven global public sphere and the existence of other important literary traditions, the term *anglophone* highlights the dominance of English and the fact that South Asia cannot be detached from the history of global capitalism constitutive of modernity. Furthermore, anglophone South Asian writers themselves have justified, explained, and reflected upon their use of English as literary language, making linguistic choice a primary subject for discussion. Bapsi Sidhwa declares her claim to English forcefully in these terms:

> [T]his useful language, rich also in literature, is no longer the monopoly of the British. We the excolonized have subjugated the language, beaten it on its head and made it ours! Let the English chafe and fume. The fact remains that in adapting English to our use, in hammering it sometimes on its head, and in sometimes twisting its tail, we have given it a new shape, substance, and dimension. ("Creative Processes" 231–32)

In her response to a question about her use of English, Anita Desai states, "I did not feel I was confronted with a choice but a heritage," and yet she also observes, "I've been interested in finding ways of bending or expanding the language, so that it includes the tones and accents and rhythms of other peoples" (Desai et al. 84). Anglophony, the very condition of the popularity of this literature, is nonetheless subject to *chutnification*, to use Salman Rushdie's term (*Midnight's Children* 642), pointing to its local inflections and regional histories.

This volume treats anglophony, translation, and cultural translatability as related concerns in the teaching of South Asian women's writing. The inclusion of a handful of translated texts for discussion in this volume is a symptom of the ways in which our syllabi de facto extend and problematize the anglophone as a linguistic and literary category. In response to what is being read and discussed at a particular time, a translated text occasionally surfaces on a syllabus otherwise dominated by anglophone writing. Far from dislodging its dominance, however, texts by nonanglophone writers such as those by the tribal and Dalit advocate Mahasweta Devi, the prominent Muslim feminist Ismat Chughtai, and the Dalit poet Bama underscore the reliance on English as a means of access to vernacular writing in the wake of a long imperial history that lodges

English squarely not only in the national imagination but also in educational curricula and practice.[7]

As some of the essays in the volume make abundantly clear, however, literary language resists transparent readings even in English. Gayatri Chakravorty Spivak's translation of Mahasweta Devi's volume *Imaginary Maps*, discussed in Henry Schwarz's essay in this volume, makes an important case for exploring the role of the translator and the teacher when dealing with the incommunicable. Spivak's thoughts on translation explore the ways in which literary texts yield as well as resist transparent meaning, emphasizing the need to explore the ethical and political implications of acts of translation. In her engagement with the concept of an enlarged sense of the term *translation*, Spivak writes, "Translation in this general sense is not under the control of the subject who is translating. Indeed the human subject is something that will have happened as this shuttling translation, from inside to outside, from violence to conscience: the production of the ethical subject" (*Aesthetic Education* 242). Translation should be seen as a creative event that produces new subjects and redefines the ethical dimension of reading. This question has recently emerged as a key concern in debates on the notion of "world literature," in particular after the formulation of the idea of the "politics of untranslatability" discussed by the critic Emily Apter. While it is important to recognize the difficulties and unevenness of the transition from one language to another, references to untranslatability and the incommunicable should not result in reiterating social and political divisions but in promoting recognition of the political, social, and cultural aspects involved in the linguistic transactions that define this literary corpus.

Interestingly, some of the writers considered in this volume have rethought and reframed the opposition between English and vernaculars by engaging with the complexity of the act of translating. For example, Jhumpa Lahiri, after a successful career as a novelist and short fiction writer in English—including her best-selling books *Interpreter of Maladies* and *The Namesake*—decided to move to Italy, learn Italian, and publish a diary of her experience in a bilingual text, *In Other Words*, in which the English translation is not by Lahiri but by Ann Goldstein. Lahiri's work is indicative of the contested role of English for South Asian women writers, showing a constant tension and need for self-translation that complicates the sense of belonging to a tradition of writing in English. The inclusion of Lahiri, Dharker, and others in the canons of the national literatures of their adopted countries (the United States, the United Kingdom, and, in the case of Lahiri, Italy) reveals the problematic positioning of these writers and limits the extent to which the term *anglophone* can capture the complications and nuances of the relation of writers to languages. Similarly, in her collection of poetry *Poppies in Translation*, the Germany-based poet Sujata Bhatt includes resonances from the German language and influences from the German literary canon. The task of translation is unfinished, subtle, and complex, yet it inhabits the work of many writers in English and in other languages, posing crucial questions about the aesthetic dimensions of this body of literature. As Tahira Naqvi, the writer and English translator of Ismat Chughtai's works, puts it, "[T]here is not just a story that requires retelling; there is also the question of metaphor and figure of speech that has to be grappled with."

The authors analyzed in this volume adopt, expand, and interrogate the anglophone as a category and means of expression, while testifying to the permanence of English as dominant in a world determined by global capitalism and information technologies.

Writing across Genres

The choice of apt literary form repeatedly confronts South Asian woman writers. In the early years of the emergence of anglophone writing, women were negotiating the demands of self-representation alongside representation of the social world being shaped by empire, or what the fiction writer Krupabai Satthianadhan, in her novel *Saguna*, calls "the new order of things . . . spreading its influence . . . over the whole of her native land" (1). As Jessica Berman writes, "[M]any of the narratives written by Indian women in the late-colonial period engage in complex ways with the conventions of narrative fiction and autobiography, developing an intersecting critique of gender and genre" (139–40). Berman's study of modernism shows how writers like Cornelia Sorabji experimented with form in the late nineteenth and early twentieth centuries, giving rise to "hybrid genres" through which women writers were able to engage with history, politics, and gender (141).

Form, content, and context in dialogue generated varieties of experimental realism through mixed genres involving autobiography, biography, oral elements, and epistolary narrative in ways that challenged conventions of realism based on British models and expressing the complexities of what Ulka Anjaria thought-provokingly defines as "realism in the colony." Likewise, in the poetry of the sisters Aru and Toru Dutt, local scenery, narrative elements, the ethos of Romantic poetry, and the blending of Indian, French, and English cultural references might be understood as an experimental quest for form rather than evidence of postcolonial literary hybridity. Whether in poetry or prose, questions of form and genre in this early period were entangled with direct or displaced representations of social agency. In later years the tradition of radical realism continues but now as a confident choice rather than tentative exploration, whether depicting the excesses of the Emergency (1975–77),[8] as in Nayantara Sahgal's *Rich Like Us*, or what Anjaria calls the "aesthetic of the ordinary," as in writing by Shashi Deshpande. Meanwhile, the staples of literary modernism—temporal rupture, change, alienation, and the injunction to make it new—also appear in forms of realism employed by South Asian women writers. The persistence of fable and vernacular modes of storytelling, moreover, challenges any formulaic understanding of either realism or modernism in prose fiction. Forays into newer genres such as chick lit or graphic literature seem to represent nods toward globally emergent forms, while this claim is belied by a complementary turn toward local contexts and audiences. In each case, South Asian women writers want to capture the new order of things from colonialism to modernity and globalization while claiming social agency through the act of writing.

Any discussion of the genres used by South Asian women writers must contend with the overwhelming dominance and curricular representation of prose forms, especially the novel and, to a lesser extent, short stories. As Rosinka Chaudhuri explains in the introduction to a recent volume on the subject, "Indian poetry in English is an indissoluble component of India's existence in modernity, yet this is a tradition without a proper history, an unclaimed tradition for much of its beleaguered and secret existence" (3). By contrast, the long-standing emphasis on the novel is also mirrored in the proliferation of award-winning and internationally acclaimed South Asian women novelists since at least Anita Desai's *Clear Light of Day*, which was shortlisted for the Booker Prize in 1980. As Jahan Ramazani remarks in his book *The Hybrid Muse*, "contemporary poetry is typically limited to the United States, Britain, and Ireland. . . . Yet a rich and vibrant poetry has issued from the hybridization of the English muse with the long-resident muses of Africa, India, the Caribbean, and other decolonizing territories of the British empire" (1). South Asian women writers nonetheless await fuller recognition of their contributions to the canon of anglophone world poetry.

Building on the increasing recognition of poetry as a postcolonial, global, and hybrid genre, important volumes such as Chaudhuri's edited collection suggest that new and future directions in the study of South Asian women's writing are likely to redress this "unclaimed tradition." We share Chaudhuri's concern about a "proper history" of the poetic tradition of South Asia, and, indeed, while some essays in this volume address the teaching of poetry by writers such as Sujata Bhatt, Kamala Das, Meena Alexander, Raman Mundair, Meena Kandasamy, and Rupi Kaur, these are fledgling efforts that invite further scholarship and pedagogic reflections on a range of contemporary and earlier writers such as Eunice de Souza and Sarojini Naidu.

Alongside poetry, future scholarship and pedagogy will need to engage with South Asian women writers adopting nonfiction and noncanonical forms of expression, such as frontline and online journalism, chick lit, and essays. Given the increasing prominence of women as public intellectuals and activists in South Asia, future teaching practices, arguably, will deal substantially with the intersections between aesthetics and politics. As the work of Sorabji and Roy, among others, shows, teaching South Asian women's writing means exploring the intersections of genre, gender, and politics that highlight the creative and critical dimensions of this body of writing.

Canon, Structure, and Resources

A fundamental principle underlying this volume is a concern with recognizing and emphasizing the key contexts and debates that inform the field of anglophone South Asian women's writing and the spectrum of options for teaching this literature. Twenty-first-century pedagogy must continue to be informed by knowledge of historical contexts past and present even as we encounter new genres, methodological approaches and concerns, and tools for teaching that now routinely include digital resources, as well as the changing composition of the student demographic. More recently, the contestation of normative gender categories on the grounds of biological being in addition to the familiar one of social construction suggests that we need to remain aware of new challenges in teaching South Asian women's writing.

The preceding discussion on debates and contexts is mirrored to some extent in the organization of the volume as a useful guide for teachers invested in teaching South Asian women writers or those who might be considering the inclusion of these writers in existing courses on other topics. Essays in this volume offer a wide range of pedagogical contexts including elite universities as well as public institutions at different levels, and they emphasize the specificity of teaching South Asian women's writing in contexts marked by national, regional, and economic diversity. While this volume aims to serve as a guide and introduction for all teachers, experienced teachers will find new directions in teaching and scholarship in each section of the book, organized on the basis of the contexts and debates that have shaped this field of study: "Narrating History and Identity," "Language, Form, and Translation," "Feminism, Gender, and Sexuality," and "Situated Pedagogy." Part 5 contains a variety of resources for teaching anglophone South Asian women's writing.

The first section includes essays that discuss the ways in which writers have responded to and represent major historical events in South Asia, such as the partition of British India, the rise of Hindu fundamentalism, the destruction of the mosque in Ayodhya in 1992, and the civil war in Sri Lanka. Long-standing traditions such as the caste system in India, the complexities of Christian identity, and the newly salient context of globalization also appear in the texts discussed by the contributors. While events such as the partition and the horrific history of gendered violence bear directly on the identity and position of women as national subjects, women writers have also responded to the larger question of history through a turn to the intimate space of the self as constructed by national and regional histories but also in retreat from them. This section provides teachers with tools for negotiating the historical contexts that inform women's writing and the way in which history has shaped the aesthetic narration of identities and subjectivities.

The second part of the volume centers on the interrelated topics of language, form, and translation. Distinctive elements of this relationship concern the problem of translation and the untranslatable, the relation of English and anglophone writing to vernacular languages and traditions, and the interaction between verbal and visual forms of communication, especially through a consideration of the language and politics of images. The general theme of translation also refers, in an expanded frame, to the question of translating popular visual cultures into print and text, which emerges through an engagement with noncanonical forms such as graphic novels and chick lit, emerging areas in the study of South Asian women writers (Mehta and Mukherji; Varughese). Although a discussion of the rise of a "Hindi public sphere" (Orsini, *Hindi Public Sphere*; Nijahwan) in the subcontinent is not overtly mentioned in any of the essays in this section, the politics of language nonetheless surfaces as a potent zone of struggle and articulation of the self. As some of the essays demonstrate, *bhasha* languages and traditions constitute an implicit subtext in anglophone writing, whether in the original or in translation.

The third section offers resources for exploring central debates on feminism, gender, and sexuality in the classroom. Alongside introductions to teaching gender issues within a historically informed perspective, the section also includes new trends in discussion, research, and social activism; in particular, the current agendas of queer studies, intersectional disability studies, and Dalit feminism are emerging as vital terms for negotiating gendered subjects in South Asia in the twenty-first century. South Asian women writers review these new modes of subjectivity against traditional forms of gendered identity. This volume hints at future developments in this area, as writers engage further with queer and transgender identities as well as intersectional ways of negotiating religion and gender in South Asia.[9]

In the fourth section, a sense of place or location surfaces as a concern in the writing and teaching of authors discussed by contributors. The term *situated pedagogy* captures the imperative to ground teaching practice into the material specificities of institutional and national contexts, reshaping, adapting, and situating South Asian women's writing in relation to local concerns that could speak to students in countries like Finland and Germany. While two of the essays in this section take the situational aspect of teaching South Asian women's writing to mean the natural world, in ways we associate with ecocritical concerns and the environmental humanities, others engage with place and location through a discussion of specific teaching contexts or the interweaving of local and global concerns or, indeed, through a turn to the reception of this body of writing in the classroom by South Asian students. The concluding essay examines the notion of world literature, a debate currently animating the fields of English studies, comparative literature, and critical theory, with significant repercussions for what and how we teach.

A quick glance at the table of contents will undoubtedly appear to suggest an implicit canon in the field of anglophone South Asian women's literature. Indeed, teachers will find in this volume many essays dealing with writers who are unlikely to occasion surprise because they appear routinely in the research agenda of those who work in the field. Instead of construing the table of contents as tacit endorsement of an established canon, however, readers should take note of the extent to which the essays in the volume discuss the particular circumstances informing their choices, including questions of availability of both primary texts and resources for teaching them. Teachers describe their attempts to combat these challenges through the use of digital alternatives, Skype meetings with authors, and, on occasion, teacher-sourced materials unavailable in the Anglo-American academy. Contributors also note that their use of canonical texts furnishes opportunities for engaging with newer rather than more traditional issues, through an emphasis on, for instance, disability and public health, human rights and sexual trafficking, or the salience of an altered student demographic.

Finally, essays on emergent writing, new genres, and born-digital writing using social media problematize the idea of a stable canon. Readers will find a variety of creative responses to the rubric of anglophone South Asian women's writing through two important interventions. The first concerns the inclusion of post-2000 emergent writers and forms of writing, which should be seen as a commitment to exploring the function and value of the new text or mode of writing in the moment when it appears at the recognizable margins of the canon. Therefore, even if chick lit generated for a local audience in South Asia is unlikely to find widespread circulation outside its intended target demographic, a sampling of this material through excerpts in courses on global literature, women's writing, or romance fiction or the place of the marriage plot in the rise of the novel can create valuable teaching moments. At the same time, this kind of literature, and indeed work by younger writers, often challenges the field's traditional preoccupation with colonialism and its immediate history, issues related to migration, or the relation of gender to national history by exploring more eclectic themes, ways of writing, and thematic concerns. The second major intervention concerns the inclusion of translated texts that coexist in a field that explores the relation of anglophone to *bhasha* writing and culture and that illuminate debates about a variety of global and local issues in anglophone classrooms through nonanglophone literary voices. The plight of marginal populations, growing inequalities, and the devastation of the ecological habitat of Fourth World peoples, for instance, can enrich the discussion on issues that have begun to command more space in the civic university.

The expansion of digital technologies and resources is likely to exert increasing influence on the shape of the canon in the future, particularly if digital space sports a more inclusive and adventurous stance than that taken by traditional print media and publishing houses. At the same time, it is clear that the disappearance of Web sites and the exercise of censorship and algorithmic choices can also constrain its potential for a revolutionary expansion of the canon. Moreover, in the face of direct marketing to readers, as in Rupi Kaur's use of social media platforms such as *Instagram*, *Facebook*, and *Tumblr*, it may be students who bring to teachers' attention material that speaks to their concerns. In recognition of the canon to come and pedagogies of the future, the final section of this volume furnishes a dynamic list of online resources along with published resources, including special issues and significant articles in peer-reviewed journals with relevant secondary readings. This gesture toward a future beyond the volume draws its inspiration from what Spivak calls "nonexhaustive taxonomies," in recognition of a heterogeneous and dynamic field of creative expression by South Asian women that keeps the door open for what is to come (*Death* 6).

Notes

1. As Hiro has shown, millions of South Asians migrated to countries like the United Kingdom and North America in the years following partition.

2. See, for example, the English professor Donna V. Jones's syllabus for her course Graduate Readings: The Anglophone Novel, where the term is defined as referring "specifically to literature written in English from former British colonies (excluding the United States)" (english.berkeley.edu/courses/4539).

3. The fight against colonialism had already started before the 1857 Mutiny, especially through peasant revolts such as the Matale rebellion of 1848 (Bates; Guha).

4. On the leading role of women in anticolonial struggle, see, for example, Devi's *The Queen of Jhansi*, which narrates the story of Lakshmibai, one of the most important actors in the 1857 rebellion.

5. For more in-depth discussions of the novel in the context of a postcolonial critical aesthetic, see Bahri; Tickell; Boehmer.

6. Queerness is a central theme in both resident and diasporic women's writing, explored by resident authors like Ismat Chughtai as well as diasporic writers like Suniti Namjoshi and Bapsi Sidhwa (on this topic, see Gopinath).

7. On the question of the "vernacular," see Ramanathan.

8. The Emergency was enacted by Indira Gandhi in 1975 and lasted until 1977. This is a very controversial period in the history of India, in which Gandhi enforced the restriction of civil liberties and the establishment of a neoliberal economic regime (Tarlo).

9. On transgender identities by emerging authors, see, for example, the visual artist Tejal Shah's 2006 installation *Hijra Fantasy Series*.

Works Cited

Anagol, Padma. *The Emergence of Feminism in India, 1850–1920.* Routledge, 2016.

Anam, Tahmima. *A Golden Age.* 2008. Canongate, 2012.

Anjaria, Ulka. *Realism in the Twentieth-Century Indian Novel: Colonial Difference and Literary Form.* Cambridge UP, 2012.

Apter, Emily. *Against World Literature: On the Politics of Untranslatability.* Verso, 2014.

Bagchi, Barnita. "'Because Novels Are True, and Histories Are False': Indian Women Writing Fiction in English, 1860–1918." *A History of the Indian Novel in English*, edited by Ulka Anjaria, Cambridge UP, 2015, pp. 59–72.

Bahri, Deepika. *Native Intelligence: Aesthetics, Politics, and Postcolonial Literature.* U of Minnesota P, 2003.

Bahri, Deepika, and Mary Vasudeva, editors. *Between the Lines: South Asians and Postcoloniality.* Temple UP, 1996.

Bates, Crispin. *Subalterns and Raj: South Asia since 1600.* Routledge, 2007.

Berman, Jessica. *Modernist Commitments: Ethics, Politics, and Transnational Modernism.* Columbia UP, 2012.

Bhatt, Sujata. *Poppies in Translation.* Carcanet, 2015.

Bilgrami, Shahbano. *Without Dreams.* HarperCollins, 2007.

Boehmer, Elleke. "East Is East and South Is South: The Cases of Sarojini Naidu and Arundhati Roy." *Women: A Cultural Review*, vol. 11, nos. 1–2, 2000, pp. 61–70.

Bose, Sugata, and Ayesha Jalal. *Modern South Asia: History, Culture, Political Economy.* 4th ed., Routledge, 2017.

Brah, Avtar. *Cartographies of Diaspora: Contesting Identities.* Routledge, 1996.

Brinks, Ellen. *Anglophone Indian Women Writers, 1870–1920.* Ashgate, 2013.

Butalia, Urvashi. *The Other Side of Silence: Voices from the Partition of India.* Penguin, 1998.

Casanova, Pascale. *The World Republic of Letters.* Harvard UP, 2004.

Chatterjee, Partha. *Empire and Nation: Selected Essays.* Columbia UP, 2010.

Chaudhuri, Rosinka, editor. *A History of Indian Poetry in English.* Cambridge UP, 2016.

Cilano, Cara N. *Contemporary Pakistani Fiction in English: Idea, Nation, State.* Routledge, 2013.

Daiya, Kavita. *Violent Belongings: Partition, Gender, and National Culture in Postcolonial India.* Temple UP, 2011.

Das, Kamala. *Summer in Calcutta.* Rajinder Paul, 1965.

Desai, Anita. *Clear Light of Day.* 1980. Vintage, 2001.

———. *In Custody.* Heinemann, 1984.

Desai, Anita, et al. "The Other Voice." *Transition*, no. 64, 1994, pp. 77–89.

Desai, Kiran. *The Inheritance of Loss.* Atlantic Monthly, 2006.

Desai, Radhika. *Slouching towards Ayodhya: From Congress to Hindutva in Indian Politics.* Three Essays, 2004.

Deshpande, Shashi. *Small Remedies.* Penguin, 2000.

Devi, Mahasweta. *The Queen of Jhansi.* Translated by Sagaree Sengupta and Mandira Sengupta, Seagull, 2010.

Dharker, Imtiaz. "Minority." *Poetry by Heart*, www.poetrybyheart.org.uk/poems/minority/.
Dutt, Toru. *Ancient Ballads and Legends of Hindustan*. Kegan Paul / Trench, 1882.
———. *Le Journal de Mademoiselle d'Arvers*. Didier, 1879.
———. *Toru Dutt's* Bianca; or, The Young Spanish Maiden. 1878. Edited by Subhendu Mund, Prachi Prakashan, 2001.
Gajarawala, Toral Jatin. *Untouchable Fictions: Literary Realism and the Crisis of Caste*. Fordham UP, 2012.
Gopinath, Gayatri. *Impossible Desires: Queer Diasporas and South Asian Public Cultures*. Duke UP, 2005.
Guha, Ranajit. *Elementary Aspects of Peasant Insurgency in Colonial India*. Oxford UP, 1983.
Hiro, Dilip. *Black British, White British: A History of Race Relations in Britain*. Updated ed., Paladin, 1992.
Huggan, Graham. *The Postcolonial Exotic: Marketing the Margins*. Routledge, 2001.
Jussawalla, Feroza, and Deborah Fillerup Weagel, editors. *Emerging South Asian Women Writers: Essays and Interviews*. Peter Lang, 2015.
Kabir, Ananya Jahanara. "Gender, Memory, Trauma: Women's Novels on the Partition of India." *Comparative Studies of South Asia, Africa and the Middle East*, vol. 25, no. 1, 2005, pp. 177–90.
Kuortti, Joel. *Writing Imagined Diasporas: South Asian Women Reshaping North American Identity*. Cambridge Scholars, 2009.
Lahiri, Jhumpa. *In Other Words*. Translated by Ann Goldstein, Alfred A. Knopf, 2016.
———. *Interpreter of Maladies*. Houghton Mifflin Harcourt, 1999.
———. *The Namesake*. Harper Perennial, 2004.
Loomba, Ania. "Dead Women Tell No Tales: Issues of Female Subjectivity, Subaltern Agency and Tradition in Colonial and Post-colonial Writings on Widow Immolation in India." *History Workshop*, no. 36, Autumn 1993, pp. 209–27.
Mani, Lata. "Contentious Traditions: The Debate on Sati in Colonial India." *Cultural Critique*, no. 7, Autumn 1987, pp. 119–56.
Mann, Michael. *South Asia's Modern History: Thematic Perspectives*. Routledge, 2015.
Mehta, Binita, and Pia Mukherji, editors. *Postcolonial Comics: Texts, Events, Identities*. Routledge, 2015.
Menon, Ritu, and Kamla Bhasin. *Borders and Boundaries: Women in India's Partition*. Rutgers UP, 1998.
Mishra, Vijay. *The Literature of the Indian Diaspora: Theorizing the Diasporic Imaginary*. Routledge, 2007.
Morey, Peter, and Amina Yaqin. *Framing Muslims: Stereotyping and Representation after 9/11*. Harvard UP, 2011.
Nadotti, Anna. "In the Infinite Labour of Translation an Impossible Map Emerges: The Other Walking Alongside Us Takes Shape." Translated by

Helen Ferguson. *Transversal Texts*, Apr. 2007, transversal.at/transversal/1107/nadotti/en.

Naqvi, Tahira. "To Be a Gentle Coloniser." *Kindle Magazine*, 4 Aug. 2015, kindlemag.in/to-be-a-gentle-coloniser/.

Nasta, Susheila. *Home Truths: Fictions of the South Asian Diaspora in Britain*. Palgrave, 2002.

Nijhawan, Shobna. *Women and Girls in the Hindi Public Sphere: Periodical Literature in Colonial North India*. Oxford UP, 2012.

Nikambe, Shevantibai. *Ratanbai: A Sketch of a Bombay High Caste Hindu Young Wife*. Marshall Brothers, 1895.

Orsini, Francesca. *The Hindi Public Sphere, 1920–1940: Language and Literature in the Age of Nationalism*. Oxford UP, 2009.

———. "India in the Mirror of World Fiction." *New Left Review*, vol. 13, Jan.–Feb. 2002, pp. 75–88.

Oza, Rupal. *The Making of Neoliberal India: Nationalism, Gender, and the Paradoxes of Globalization*. Routledge, 2012.

Ramabai, Pandita. *The High-Caste Hindu Woman*. J. B. Rodgers, 1887.

Ramanathan, Vaidehi. *The English-Vernacular Divide: Postcolonial Language Politics and Practice*. Multilingual Matters, 2005.

Ramazani, Jahan. *The Hybrid Muse: Postcolonial Poetry in English*. U of Chicago P, 2001.

Roy, Arundhati. *The God of Small Things*. IndiaInk, 1997.

———. *The Ministry of Utmost Happiness*. Hamish Hamilton, 2017.

Rushdie, Salman. "A Declaration of Independence." International Parliament of Writers, 14 Feb. 1994. *Autodafe: The Journal of the International Parliament of Writers*, vol. 1, 2001, pp. 92–95.

———. *Midnight's Children*. 1981. Vintage, 2006.

Sahgal, Nayantara. *Rich Like Us*. Heinemann, 1985.

Salgado, Minoli. *Writing Sri Lanka: Literature, Resistance and the Politics of Place*. Routledge, 2007.

Satthianadhan, Krupabai. *Saguna: A Story of Native Christian Life*. 1895. Edited by Chandani Lokugé, Oxford UP, 1998.

Sen, Indrani. "Writing English, Writing Reform: Two Indian Women's Novels of the Nineteenth Century." *Indian Journal of Gender Studies*, vol. 21, no. 1, 2014, pp. 1–26.

Sharma, Alpana. "In-Between Modernity: Toru Dutt (1856–1877) from a Postcolonial Perspective." *Women's Experience of Modernity, 1875–1945*, edited by Ann L. Ardis and Leslie W. Lewis, Johns Hopkins UP, 2003, pp. 97–110.

Shiva, Vandana. "Our Violent Economy Is Hurting Women." *Yes!*, 19 Jan. 2013, www.yesmagazine.org/peace-justice/violent-economic-reforms-and-women.

Sidhwa, Bapsi. *Cracking India*. Milkweed, 1991.

———. "Creative Processes in Pakistani English Fiction." *South Asian English: Structure, Use and Users*, edited by R. J. Baumgardner, U of Illinois P, 1996, pp. 231–40.

Spivak, Gayatri Chakravorty. *An Aesthetic Education in the Era of Globalization.* Harvard UP, 2012.

———. *Death of a Discipline.* Columbia UP, 2003.

Sundar, Nandini. *The Burning Forest: India's War in Bastar.* Verso, 2019.

Talbot, Ian. "Literature and the Human Drama of the 1947 Partition." *South Asia: Journal of South Asian Studies*, vol. 18, no. 1, 1995, pp. 37–56.

Tarlo, Emma. *Unsettling Memories: Narratives of the Emergency in Delhi.* U of California P, 2003.

Thapa, Manjushree. *Forget Kathmandu: An Elegy for Democracy.* Penguin, 2005.

Tharu, Susie. "The Impossible Subject: Caste and the Gendered Body." *Economic and Political Weekly*, vol. 31, no. 22, 1 June 1996, pp. 1311–15.

———. "Rendering Account of the Nation: Partition Narratives and Other Genres of the Passive Revolution." *Oxford Literary Review*, vol. 16, no. 1, 1994, pp. 69–91.

Tharu, Susie, and K. Lalita, editors. *Women Writing in India: 600 B.C. to the Present.* Feminist Press, 1993. 2 vols.

Tickell, Alex. *Arundhati Roy's* The God of Small Things. Routledge, 2007.

Varughese, Emma Dawson. *Reading New India: Post-Millennial Indian Fiction in English.* Bloomsbury, 2013.

Veer, Peter van der, editor. *Nation and Migration: The Politics of Space in the South Asian Diaspora.* U of Pennsylvania P, 1995.

Viswanath, C. K. "Sati, Anti-Modernists and Sangh Parivar." *Economic and Political Weekly*, vol. 34, no. 52, 25–31 Dec. 1999, p. 3648.

Viswanathan, Gauri. *Masks of Conquest: Literary Study and British Rule in India.* Columbia UP, 1989.

Visweswaran, Kamala, editor. *Perspectives on Modern South Asia: A Reader in Culture, History, and Representation.* Wiley-Blackwell, 2011.

Part I

Narrating History and Identity

Stephen Morton

History and Story in South Asian Women's Writing

One of the pedagogical challenges facing students and teachers of anglophone South Asian women's fiction is how to make sense of the ways in which history is mediated in literary texts. Students approaching South Asian women's writing for the first time may find the experience of reading references to historical events such as independence and partition or to the legacy of colonialism daunting. At the same time, a consideration of the significance of such historical references can distract new readers from the aesthetic form of the texts themselves. This essay addresses the task of encouraging students to build on their knowledge and understanding of literary methodologies to reflect on the ways in which women's experiences of modern South Asian history have been fictionalized in literary texts. To clarify how this approach enhances engagement with South Asian women's writing, I draw on my experience of teaching an upper-level undergraduate course, comprising chiefly English literature majors, on postcolonial literatures at the University of Southampton. A detailed consideration of the British Empire's historical involvement in South Asia lies beyond the scope of this essay, focused as it is on literary representations of modern South Asia written by women. I mention this history here in order to emphasize how teaching South Asian women's writing can also help students to unlearn their schooling in colonial amnesia and to begin to ask questions about the relation between the histories of modern South Asia and the British Empire.

In Salman Rushdie's controversial novel *The Satanic Verses*, a peripheral character named Whisky Sisodia declares that the "trouble with the Engenglish is that their hiss hiss history happened overseas, so they dodo don't know what it means" (343). In British high schools, the history of the British Empire, and its specific involvement in the history of modern South Asia, is sanitized, if it is taught at all; similarly, English literature is often taught according to the principles and procedures of close reading, with a narrow focus on plot, character, language, and imagery, with little more than a gesture toward critical reception and cultural and historical context (if these are discussed at all). This situation seems particularly ironic when one considers that English was first taught as a university subject in British colonial India (Viswanathan). Yet unless individual teachers or schools have a particular interest in teaching the subject, it is unlikely that many undergraduate students reading literature in British universities will have encountered any formal education in the history of modern South Asia and its relation to the legacy of British imperialism.

If, as Whisky Sisodia suggests, the English are schooled in colonial amnesia, it is also true that the national project of secondary-level education in the United Kingdom has overlooked the specific connection between the legacy of the British Empire, India's partition, and the patriarchal formations of nationalist violence partition engendered. The fiction of Rushdie, again, can help to shed light on this problem. The incessant sound of "Mountbatten's ticktock" (123) in Rushdie's *Midnight's Children* clearly draws readers' attention to the association between Mountbatten as a figure of colonial sovereignty and the movement toward India's independence. And yet, as Rushdie makes clear in *Shame*, the promise of national freedom is overshadowed by the divide-and-rule policy of the British partition plan. In this later novel, the narrator recounts how the character Bilquìs Kemal flees India for Pakistan in the wake of partition in order to escape from the gangs of men who seek to redraw the map of India on the bodies of women along communal lines. Carried along by a "tide of human beings," the narrator discloses how Bilquìs "passed out" in a cinema after being "overwhelmed by the humiliation of her undress." He goes on to explain how, in "that generation many women, ordinary decent respectable ladies of the type to whom nothing ever happens, to whom nothing is ever supposed to happen except marriage children death, had this sort of strange story to tell" (65).

The "strange story" to which Rushdie's narrator alludes speaks volumes about the unspeakability of South Asian women's historical experience of partition. Through this rather elliptical account of what actually happened to Bilquìs, the Rushdie narrator uses the literary conventions of fiction to foreground the ways in which women's historical experience is either elided or ignored. The cited extract is also an example of Rushdie's historiographic metafiction—historical fiction that draws attention to the process of writing history and the ways in which all history is necessarily partial. Earlier in this chapter, the voice of the author interrupts the main narrative to announce that many Muslims in Delhi had been locked up in the red fortress during the partition riots, including his own relatives. As he puts it, "It's easy to imagine that as my relatives moved through the Red Fort in the parallel universe of history, they might have felt some hint of the fictional presence of Bilquìs Kemal, rushing cut and naked past them like a ghost . . . or vice versa" (65). The point here is that the commonsense distinction between literary fiction and history, or text and context, is destabilized. In times of social and political turbulence, such as India's partition, historical truth is revealed to be particularly partial and unreliable. There is a clear gap between dominant, official narratives of historical events such as partition and the historical experience of such events from the perspective of the marginalized, the oppressed, or the subaltern.

Gayatri Spivak has written of how the writing of subaltern histories in the context of modern South Asia entails reading or interpretation that is similar to the practice of literary interpretation (243). Recent attempts to commemorate women's historical experiences and memories of South Asia's partition can be seen to draw on the narrative strategies of fiction to account for the ways in which women's histories had been overlooked in elite national narratives of South Asian history. At the same time, South Asian women writers have developed narrative techniques and rhetorical strategies to recover the buried histories of gendered violence and brutalization associated with partition.

The gap between the promise of India's national sovereignty and the communalist violence that followed partition is foregrounded in Bapsi Sidhwa's novel *Cracking India*. After the official announcement of partition, the child narrator, Lenny, describes how the relationships between the adult characters in her everyday life start to change and people become defined in terms of religious identities:

> Gandhi, Jinnah, Nehru, Iqbal, Tara Singh, Mountbatten are names I hear.
>
> And I become aware of religious differences.
>
> It is sudden. One day everyone is themselves—and the next day they are Hindu, Muslim, Sikh, Christian. People shrink, dwindling into symbols. Ayah is no longer just my all-encompassing Ayah—she is also a token. A Hindu. (101)

Employing the device of a child narrator, Sidhwa intimates that there is a connection between the decision of the political elite "to break a country" and the production of communal identities (101). The metonymic list of names that Lenny hears highlights the privileging of dominant political figures, including "Gandhi, Jinnah, Nehru, Iqbal, Tara Singh, Mountbatten," in public discourse and histories of partition. Yet Lenny's repetition of these names also foregrounds the distance between these elite political figures and the subsequent production of ethnic identities along religious lines. In doing so, Lenny highlights the gap between the official discourse of the state and the lived experience of genocide, violation, and displacement that constituted partition. What's more, Lenny's observation that her friends "shrink" and "dwindle" into symbols or communal identities exposes the vulnerability of the people to the ethnic and communal violence that followed the abdication of colonial sovereignty. To be thought of in the exclusive terms of a communal identity is not only reductive; it is also to think of the other as a disposable form of life, who can be mutilated, tortured, raped, or killed in the name of a patriarchal notion of national honor.

Against this patriarchal logic of communal violence, Sidhwa registers the traumatic histories of partition from the standpoint of South Asian women who were victims of sexual violation perpetrated by men against women of different ethnicities. Indeed, as the historians Ritu Menon and Kamla Bhasin note, "[T]he reconfiguration of relationships between communities, the state and women in the wake of a bitter and violent conflict amongst Hindus, Muslims and Sikhs took place in part around the body and being of the abducted woman of all three communities" (109). By emphasizing the connections between Sidhwa's goal of making public women's historical experiences and recent historical scholarship that attempts to do justice to women's experiences of partition in my classes, I try to encourage students to reflect on the historical value of South Asian women's fiction, while also maintaining a focus on the novel's organizing metaphors and narrative techniques. The concern with the body of the violated and abducted woman, for instance, is a motif that recurs throughout *Cracking India*. Near the beginning of the novel, which is set during the end of British colonial rule, the child narrator describes how her Hindu *ayah* (nanny), Shanta, is the object of the masculine gaze during their walks in a local park in Lahore; Lenny emphasizes that Shanta's Hindu, Sikh, and Muslim admirers are "unified around her" (105). Such passages foreshadow Shanta's status as a symbolic figure that embodies the gendered dynamics of communal violence in the text, for later in the narrative, Shanta is abducted and raped by her former Muslim admirer Ice-Candy-Man, who forces her to change her name to Mumtaz and work as a sex worker in Lahore's red-light district.

It is primarily through the character of Shanta that Sidhwa reveals the ways in which women were at the center of communalist violence during and after the partition of India. In a related discussion, Menon and Bhasin note how the "range of sexual violation explicit in [many women's testimonials] . . . is shocking not only for its savagery, but for what it tells us about women as objects in male constructions of their own honour" (43). In light of this observation, the abduction and violation of Shanta at the end of the novel can be interpreted as an act of communal violence, which foregrounds the ways in which the bodies of women refugees became a sign of dispossession and disposability in the violent reordering of South Asia's political geography.

In *Cracking India* it is generally Lenny who mediates the representation of sexual and physical violence against women, and this narrative device clearly distinguishes the text from the testimonials and interviews that constitute much recent scholarship on women's partition narratives. For instance, the child narrator describes the massacre of Muslims on a train from Gurduspur and the monstrous spectacle of a gunny sack full of dismembered women's breasts through the reported speech of Ice-Candy-Man. Such a representation of violence and bodily dismemberment may seem distanced from the events themselves. Indeed, for the critic Ambreen Hai, Sidhwa's representation of women's sexual violation in this passage and others "reveals a narrative inability to recuperate a national and ethnic past too violent, shameful, and traumatic to be told except through the distancing of a child's censored vision" (413). Lenny's second- or third-hand account of historical events as they happened also foregrounds the role of rumor in the transmission of historical events. Her description of the ways in which Ice-Candy-Man understands the significance of a rumor about the mutilated bodies of Muslim women demonstrates how the errant speech of rumor aids and abets the patriarchal and communal logic of revenge and honor underpinning the looting, rioting, murder, and rape associated with partition.

In times of crisis such as India's partition, fiction can encourage readers to reflect on the partiality and unreliability of historical fact. In *Cracking India*, the effect of focalizing the events of India's partition through the consciousness of a Parsi minority character in Lahore is that the narrator and her family seem to inhabit a relatively secure and privileged perspective that "insists on ethnic neutrality as a basis for contesting both Indian and Pakistani nationalist discourses founded upon religious identity" (Hai 389). Yet Sidhwa also highlights the complicity and responsibility of Lenny and her family in partition and communal violence. When Shanta is apprehended by a mob of angry Muslim men, Lenny feels guilty for inadvertently revealing Shanta's hiding place to the mob. Furthermore, as the critic Sangeeta Ray has suggested in an illuminating reading of the novel, the involvement of Lenny's mother and aunt in the project of recovering women refugees from the camp for fallen women and returning them to their home where they may not be welcomed is a highly dubious one (126–47). Although their involvement in the recovery process might seem like a worthy cause that counteracts the abduction and violation of women refugees, it is also complicit in the maintenance of national boundaries and discourses of ethnic purity.

By focusing on the gendered dimensions of home, with its connotations of national belonging and private property, South Asian women's texts such as *Cracking India* raise important questions about how to represent and commemorate the specific historical experiences of homelessness, displacement, and dispossession that have marked the bodies of women. Indeed, it is precisely the ruins of nationally bound concepts of home and property that are foregrounded in many women's testimonial narratives and fictional accounts of India's partition. In her essay "Telling Tales," the critic Deepika Bahri asks, "[W]hat kind of home can women hope to have in the structures the subcontinent supports, why do these structures fail repeatedly, and why are women fair game at the first hint of the suspension of the usual civic norms?" (289). A provisional answer to this question can be found in Amrita Pritam's novella *Pinjar* (*The Skeleton*). Pritam is a celebrated Punjabi author of fiction and poetry who moved from Punjab to Delhi following India's partition; Pritam's writing is also profoundly marked by the experience of partition. Since an English translation of *Pinjar* is regularly reprinted and the story is often referred to in critical scholarship on South Asian women's writing, I teach the translation of this story to provide students with a broader understanding of the cultural landscape of South Asian women's writing. In a lament for her daughter, the mother states, "To sons are given homes and palaces; / Daughters are exiled to foreign lands" (5). In Pritam's story, the concepts of home, property, dignity, and belonging associated with national independence are bound up with patriarchal discourses of ethnicity, cultural purity, and possessive individualism—discourses that frame women's bodies as a sign of property, honor, and territory rather than as an embodied human subject. Puro, the female protagonist of *Pinjar*, is kidnapped by a Muslim neighbor as an act of vengeance and forced to convert to Islam and change her name. The narrative trajectory of the story traces the ways in which Puro comes to terms with her new identity as Hamida after the birth of her child. While Pritam's representation of Hamida's maternal body in the story may seem to rehearse certain essentialist or biologically determined ideas of femininity, it is possible to read this trope as an instance of what Spivak calls "strategic essentialism" (205). In other words, if we read Hamida's bond with her child as a refusal of patriarchal discourses of honor and purity, we can begin to see how this framing of Hamida's maternal body functions as a strategy that encourages readers to imagine a more inclusive and progressive idea of the nation—one that questions patriarchal discourses of honor and shame.

It is important to remember too that South Asian women's fiction is also implicated in the histories of violence, dispossession, and displacement it fictionalizes. At the end of Sidhwa's *Cracking India*, Lenny describes how her godmother helps Shanta to return from Lahore to her family in Amritsar in the violent aftermath of partition. In response to Shanta's demand to return to her family in India, Lenny's godmother questions whether her family will take her back (274). By asking this question, Lenny's godmother foregrounds how, in the violent aftermath of South Asia's partition, the founder of Pakistan Muhammad Ali Jinnah's secular promise of national belonging for all is haunted by a patriarchal communalist discourse of cultural purity and honor. The godmother's question also emphasizes how Shanta's understanding of her home as a place of refuge is inextricably bound to gendered narratives of national belonging and ethnic identity. In the aftermath of partition, the Abducted Persons Act of 1949 defined *home* in terms of religious affiliation and cultural purity rather than a place of habitation. As Menon and Bhasin explain, "The Abducted Person's Act was remarkable for the impunity with which it violated every principle of citizenship, fundamental rights and access to justice" (125). More specifically, the practice of recovering abducted citizens from either India or Pakistan centered on the "proper regulation of women's sexuality" within patriarchal communalist discourses of national honor and cultural purity (108).

If the aesthetic codes and narrative techniques of literary fiction can help to elucidate the ways in which the writing of modern South Asian history is always partial and unreliable in certain ways, it can also help to give form to the histories of state oppression that are rendered invisible and unspeakable by elite national narratives. The short fiction of the Bengali writer Mahasweta Devi is an exemplary case in point. Devi's short story "Draupadi" combines the writing of history and epic to foreground the marginalized place of women, the rural peasantry, and the tribals in India. The main character of "Draupadi" is Dopdi Mejhen, an illiterate, uneducated tribal woman who doesn't have a voice or a place from which to speak in elite Indian society. She is an instance of what Spivak has called the "gendered subaltern" (241). Dopdi is not considered a part of mainstream Indian society and occupies the lowest rung in a class-based society. In this sense, the story is both a feminist story and a story concerned with tribal people and their rights (or lack of rights). It is also important to say that the story takes place in the context of the Naxalite uprising of the late 1960s in West Bengal. The Naxalite movement started off as a landless peasant movement against landlords, but it also inspired radical students in Calcutta (now Kolkata) to engage in acts of militant violence against the state. The Naxalites waged a class war against the reformist Communist Party and against people who were perceived to be representatives of the state. These actions led to a brutal state repression of Naxalites and Maoists. It is with the framing of the Naxalites as terrorists that Devi's short story is in part concerned.

As Spivak has noted in her translator's foreword to "Draupadi," the story is written in part from the narrative point of view of the police inspector Senanayak (Devi 179). Senanayak is a figure of state authority: he writes the script that frames the Naxalites as dangerous individuals or insurgents. Indeed, it is significant that the first part of the story is presented as a series of police reports that are written in a rather telegraphic style: "Name Dopdi Mejhen, age twenty-seven. Husband Dulna Majhi (deceased) . . ." (187). This form of writing seems to reinforce the point made by Spivak and others that the subaltern is always spoken for by the historical records and archives of the elite. The histories and perspective of the subaltern—the illiterate peasant or the tribal—cannot be easily recovered from those archives, since these figures do not have access to representation. The critical task, therefore, is to treat such archives with suspicion and to pay attention to the gaps and silences in those dominant archives, records, and sources. By including this police report in the narrative as a historical source, Devi draws our attention to the process of writing history, and, in doing so, she encourages us to question the representation of these Naxalite insurgents in the police report and the official national archives that these reports represent. In this sense, Devi's story can be seen to contribute to the writing of a subaltern history by staging the police techniques of counterinsurgency in order to expose their shortcomings. In order to more effectively counter the Naxalite insurgent, Senanayak feels he needs to understand them better. Senanayak is an intellectual figure who tries to imagine the Naxalite movement from the perspective of the insurgents themselves (189). These literary references evoke a sense of an all-powerful figure and of a state that is able to control or counter threats to its authority, including its narrative authority.

Senanayak's narrative authority is, however, interrupted by the spectacle of Dopdi's bloodied and naked body following her torture and sexual violation during police interrogation. Dopdi's refusal to cover her naked, bruised body and her demand that Senanayak "counter" (196) her functions as a powerful and disarming symbolic act that defies the elite, patriarchal authority of the postcolonial state. In this way, the story recalls the histories of women's participation in acts of insurgency against different forms of state oppression in South Asia before and after colonialism—a history that also deconstructs metaphors of the gendered nation that frame women as passive objects of an elite national history.

An approach to South Asian women's writing that is informed by an engagement with the history of decolonization and partition that is specific to modern South Asia can certainly help students of literature in Britain understand the historical and political significance of reading postcolonial literatures. But more than this, by engaging with the insights of postcolonial feminist theory and criticism, students can also begin to formulate more nuanced and sophisticated readings of the narrative techniques, tropes, and imagery of South Asian women's writing.

Works Cited

Bahri, Deepika. "Telling Tales: Women and the Trauma of Partition in Sidhwa's *Cracking India*." *Interventions*, vol. 1, no. 2, 1999, pp. 217–34.

Devi, Mahasweta. "Draupadi." Translated by Gayatri Chakravorty Spivak. Spivak, pp. 179–96.
Hai, Ambreen. "Border Work, Border Trouble: Postcolonial Feminism and the Ayah in Bapsi Sidhwa's *Cracking India*." *Modern Fiction Studies*, vol. 46, no. 2, Summer 2000, pp. 379–426.
Menon, Ritu, and Kamla Bhasin. *Borders and Boundaries: Women in India's Partition*. Rutgers UP, 1998.
Pritam, Amrita. The Skeleton *and* That Man. Translated by Khushwant Singh, Oriental UP, 1987.
Ray, Sangeeta. *Engendering India: Women and Nation in Colonial and Postcolonial Narratives*. Duke UP, 2000.
Rushdie, Salman. *Midnight's Children*. Picador, 1981.
———. *The Satanic Verses*. Picador, 1988.
———. *Shame*. Picador, 1983.
Sidhwa, Bapsi. *Cracking India*. Milkweed Editions, 1991.
Spivak, Gayatri Chakravorty. *In Other Worlds: Essays in Cultural Politics*. Routledge, 1988.
Viswanathan, Gauri. *Masks of Conquest: Literary Study and British Rule in India*. Columbia UP, 1989.

Kavita Daiya

Reframing Partition: Gender, Migration, and Storytelling in Postcolonial Conflict

Partition heralded the dawn of independent nationhood for India and Pakistan after centuries of British colonial rule, but it also entailed unprecedented violence and the displacement of millions. Outside the subcontinent, this history is little known. Women's writing on the subject invites dialogue on the translation of historical events into art and on the role of literature in rendering legible the gendered experience of war, freedom, migration, and citizenship in the nation. The inclusion of these works in a course on global anglophone literature or South Asian literature presents the experience of empire from the viewpoint of the female colonized subject. Many of these works have a fractured aesthetic: they are narratives in which the dominant literary form, whether realist or modernist, is marked by breaks and interruptions that signal the limits of that formal convention in the aesthetic project of capturing women's experiences during partition. In this sense, the fractured narratives enact the ruptures of decolonization to which they bear witness. I argue that in its reflections on women's experiences as migrants, refugees, and citizens in nation-states and conflict zones, this archive resonates in urgent ways for our time, given ongoing mass migrations or expulsions across the world today stemming from war, economic violence, and conflict.

By unofficial counts, the partition left two million people dead, between twelve and sixteen million displaced as refugees, millions of women and children raped and assaulted, and between 83,000 and 110,000 Hindu, Muslim, and Sikh women abducted (French). The literature about this historical trauma includes a vast body of Hindi, English, Urdu, Punjabi, Bengali, and Sindhi fiction, prose, and poetry. This archive includes writers based in the subcontinent as well as those settled in the diasporas in the United Kingdom and North America. The latter's immigrant experiences often inflect their textual exploration of the 1947 partition. Many important women writers have contributed to the literary archive of decolonization and partition. Spanning both the subcontinent and the diaspora, this literature can be seen as reframing partition; it is a critical archive of women's perspectives on and experiences of war, violence, and displacement that marked decolonization in South Asia.

A chronological approach to teaching women's writing on partition could be organized into two parts: the first would include writing by women authors in India and Pakistan from the early national period (roughly between 1947 and 1970) in English, Hindi, Urdu, Punjabi, Sindhi, and Bengali. This would include realist writers like Krishna Sobti, Ismat Chughtai, Amrita Pritam, Attia Hosain, Anita Desai, Jyotirmoyee Devi, and others. The second would focus on anglophone South Asian writers, from the subcontinent and the diaspora alike, who return to this event after 1990; their aesthetically experimental novels and short stories depict women entrapped in what Judith Butler has called "frames of war," even as they sometimes index partition's legacies of regional conflict and discrimination for contemporary South Asia. These authors would include Shauna Singh Baldwin, Manju Kapur, Bapsi Sidhwa, Jhumpa Lahiri, and Beena Sarwar, among others.

Three dominant themes connect these diverse works about 1947, suggesting potential frameworks for different courses on postcolonial literature, South Asian literature, gender and sexuality studies, as well as world literature. Courses on modern South Asian fiction, world literature, or postcolonial anglophone writing should ideally include and address the following themes: nationalism and gender; caste, class, and gender; and global migration and displacement. A comparative juxtaposition of texts from both historical moments under one of these themes allows us to consider both the continuities and discontinuities in women's experiences of citizenship and power in post-1947 South Asia. This approach engages questions about the politics of form in depicting the ethnic, gendered, and socioeconomic relations that shape women's subjectivity and citizenship. What emerges then, in the classroom, is a dialogue about power, subalternity, and knowledge during British colonialism, as well as about who gets represented as the normative citizen-subject in the postcolonial nation in South Asia.

Nationalism and Gender

If decolonization and nation formation constitute the most pervasive political changes of the global twentieth century, as European empires were dismantled and new nations emerged across Asia, Africa, and the Caribbean, then the literature of decolonization becomes one of the most powerful windows into how many experienced the nation as an "imagined" community, in Benedict Anderson's words. Because the political materialization of the imagined nation in India was also accompanied by a division that created two new nations, the literary representation of empire's end and the attainment of political freedom in much South Asian women's writing depicts this dual and contradictory experience of liberation and violence. Novels such as Attia Hosain's semiautobiographical *Sunlight on a Broken Column*, Bapsi Sidhwa's *Cracking India*, and Shauna Singh Baldwin's *What the Body Remembers* all depict partition in narratives that begin well before 1947. Moreover, they follow minority female protagonists, youths and adults, who witness and experience the transformations wreaked by partition on ordinary people in urban and rural India and Pakistan. While Sidhwa narrates partition from the perspective of Lenny (a wealthy, disabled Parsi girl), Singh Baldwin's novel presents Sikh women's experiences, and Hosain depicts the politics of partition from the perspective of women from elite, landowning, upper-caste, upper-class Muslim families in the United Provinces.

These novels describe the fierce passions that drove the desire for freedom from British oppression. Girls and women in these stories at times embrace anticolonial nationalism; yet, at other times, they recognize its complicity with patriarchal norms and criticize gender discrimination. Sidhwa's and Hosain's novels show the slow dissolution of cultural hybridity and peaceful interethnic relations in India as partition becomes a certainty. They also represent middle- and working-class characters who had an ambivalent relationship to elite nationalism and were critical of partition. Without idealizing prepartition India or the interwoven lives of its different minority communities, then, these writers poignantly depict how partition shatters interethnic friendships and intimacies, with violent consequences for women. These novels are aesthetically varied: for instance, Hosain's *Sunlight on a Broken Column* emblematizes what Ulka Anjaria has called the critical, aspirational energy of "realism in the colony" (1), rooted in a "detachment from and continuing skepticism toward the nationalism of the public sphere" (127). Singh Baldwin and Sidhwa experiment with modernist and realist modalities, presenting fractured narratives that present multiple narrators and points of view as empire unravels. Singh Baldwin's novel moves back and forth between a linear realist narrative and stream-of-consciousness monologues representing the female protagonists Satya's and Roop's interiority. Sidhwa's *Cracking India* also vividly depicts the fractured aesthetics discussed earlier: as partition violence increases in Lahore, its first-person realism at times gives way to narratives representing the points of view of other characters, interrupting its temporal continuity. This hybrid narrative allows Sidhwa to depict the complex social and psychic fractures generated by decolonization from multiple perspectives—Parsi, Sikh, Hindu, and Muslim.

Krishna Sobti's short story "Where Is My Mother?," Amrita Pritam's poem "Ode to Waris Shah," and Ismat Chughtai's story "Roots" depict traumatic communal divisions alongside women's experiences of losing homes and families. They interrogate the colonial and nationalist elite's great game of division by raising ethical questions about the loss of lives and the treatment of women. In this literature, we meet women who are anticolonial subjects swept up in the energy of the freedom movement. Often they are also women navigating the tension between tradition and modernity, between family constraints and political participation in the context of patriarchal dominance. Manju Kapur's novel *Difficult Daughters* describes the unequal gender norms of romantic and familial intimacies, as well as the dehumanizing violence meted out to women and children in conflict zones. Similarly, the Bengali writer Jyotirmoyee Devi's novel *The River Churning*, set in 1946, bears powerful witness to history's erasure of women and to patriarchal discourses about women's sexual purity as women are subjected to sexual violence. Anita Desai's novel *In Custody* offers a poignant account of postpartition India that intertwines the decay of Urdu literary culture with the disempowerment of Muslim women in the decades that followed 1947.

These works can be engaged productively in classroom conversations about different aesthetic strategies in depicting women's negotiations with postcolonial modernity. Importantly, they unveil how women's bodies become symbolic of community in the modern rhetoric of nationalism, turning them into objects of ethnonationalist violence during partition and unequal citizens in the new nation-state. The work of vernacular writers like Devi, Chughtai, and Sobti is easily available in translation and hence is included in this discussion. In these stories, girls and women bear the brunt of the process of violent decolonization, yet are complex, agentive political subjects. In their representations of female disempowerment, silencing, and agency, many of these works gesture to the long history of oppressive gender norms that South Asian women negotiate as well as resist, both at home and in the nation, before and after decolonization.

Caste, Class, and Gender

Any course on caste, class, and gender in South Asia would benefit from including women's writing on the 1947 partition. Through the Muslim protagonist Laila and her elite, aristocratic *zamindar* (landholding) family, Hosain's *Sunlight on a Broken Column* tracks how religion, class, and caste relations change as the Indian independence movement intensifies. Its critical realism foregrounds how the British instigated Hindu-Muslim animosity in a hybrid, secular culture, even as it is equally critical of how Laila's family treats Hindu servants. More recently, the Bangladeshi author Taslima Nasreen's experimental novel *Lajja* (*Shame*) represents the ongoing persecution of the Hindu minority in Bangladesh through a persistent invocation of the 1947 partition. In a realist narrative repeatedly fractured by excerpts from newspaper articles enumerating incidents of ethnic and sexual violence, Nasreen offers a complex picture of how language, region, religion, class, poverty, caste, and gender are interwoven in the gendered experience of unequal citizenship for Bangladesh's largely poor Hindus.

Likewise, Devi's extensive writings also illuminate how class, poverty, and caste shape women's experiences of abduction, displacement, and forcible repatriation. From her story "The Crossing" to her novel *The River Churning*, Devi's explicitly feminist representations give voice to the inequity and injustice that shape women's experience of sexual violence and social dispossession during and after partition. These texts encourage students to raise questions about women's rights and agency as political subjects. They also invite students to consider how the power relations instituted by decolonization, capitalism, and partition have profoundly violent implications for girls and women as precarious members of the new national communities.

Even when preoccupied with middle-class experience, partition literature by women attempts to aesthetically translate and bear witness to the intimate, everyday oppressions of the lived experience of caste and class. For example, in Sidhwa's *Cracking India*, Lenny often describes the physical and emotional abuse suffered by the girls and female servants in her parents' elite, bourgeois household. Lenny's portrayal of her beloved nanny Shanta, who is forcibly abducted and raped by her friend Ice-Candy-Man during partition, is an intimate and heartbreaking glimpse into the precarious status of working-class women like Shanta in this time. Through Lenny's perceptive eye, we are confronted with the female experience of the intertwined institutions of class, caste, and patriarchy in the conflict zone of partition. Similarly, in Desai's novel *Clear Light of Day*, the experience of partition is reflected in the internal divides that surface in a middle-class Hindu family via different economic conditions and responsibilities. Both before and after 1947, the novel shows Bim negotiating tradition and modernity—her thwarted aspirations for marital intimacy and a teaching career—as she is repeatedly cast as a caretaker for her brother Raja; their alcoholic aunt, Mira; and, later, her autistic brother, Baba. Through the story of her economically and emotionally riven family, the novel both mourns Bim's gendered disappointment in the newly divided Indian nation, even as it inscribes respect for her professional and intellectual independence as a college lecturer in history. It thus invites us to see Bim as strong, precisely in her willingness and ability to take responsibility for the rest of the family.

Global Migration and Displacement

As Lisa Lowe demonstrates, the migration and circulation of people and goods in the form of slavery, indentured labor, war, and postwar migration point to the "intimacies of four continents" in modern history (3). Given that the twentieth century has seen the largest displacement of people, courses on migration profit from attention to women's experiences as migrants and refugees. Yet scholarly discussions of South Asian migration often focus on immigration north, to the United Kingdom and North America. This elides the experience of millions who migrated within South Asia at different points of political upheaval, like the 1947 partition. The noted filmmaker Deepa Mehta, who directed *Earth 1947* (an adaptation based on Sidhwa's *Cracking India*), has argued, "This was our Holocaust."

South Asian women's writing on this traumatic displacement then allows us to recast the history of modern South Asian migrations by displacing the dominant frame that focuses on immigration north. For instance, Paromita Vohra's script for the Pakistani filmmaker Sabiha Sumar's film *Khamosh Pani* (*Silent Waters*) revolves around the life of Ayesha, a Punjabi Muslim widow and mother in rural Pakistan in the 1970s, who was a young Sikh girl at the time of partition. The cinematic narrative foregrounds how her partition-era experience of abduction and rape surfaces as a memory when Islamization sweeps the Pakistani countryside under General Muhammad Zia-ul-Haq, at the same time that her Indian Sikh brother arrives in her village on a pilgrimage. In the film's fractured aesthetics, its neorealism is interrupted by sepia-toned flashback sequences, in which we learn that her father, prior to fleeing to India, had asked her to jump into the village well like her mother in order to avoid the threat of rape at the hands of Muslims in 1947. Rejecting this death, Ayesha chooses life: she runs away. Unfortunately, she is caught and raped by some men. She eventually marries one of her rapists, converts to Islam, and bears a son. The film's script thus syntagmatically links, across time, the intimate violence of men (father and son) in the family, of men in the "other" community, and of the contemporary Pakistani state for a nonmigrant haunted by the impossibility of escape from a home that is rendered foreign by partition. Ayesha insists on living, and she rebuilds her life and relationships in her village community; the film shows her vulnerable yet "stubborn life" alongside the threat of growing political extremism in the nation (Butler 62).

In her Hindi novel *Pinjar* (*Skeleton*), readily available in translation, Amrita Pritam offers a moving representation of a Hindu girl's experience of abduction and forced marriage to a Muslim during partition. Adapted in 2003 into an eponymous film in Hindi, this realist novel addresses caste and class animosities, as well as the controversial efforts of the Indian and Pakistani governments to forcibly retrieve and return abducted women, often to families who disowned them, and without the children they had borne. The experience of return as unwilling migration during partition offers a unique perspective on the customary understanding of displacement. Simultaneously, the nonnormative choice of the abducted Hindu protagonist Puro to stay with her Muslim abductor in Pakistan and not return to her natal family in independent India creates a new discursive space for rethinking women's agency and rights in the nation. This text can be taught in conjunction with selections from Ritu Menon and Kamla

Bhasin's landmark historical work *Borders and Boundaries*, which documents oral accounts of the Indian and Pakistani governments' traumatic and forcible repatriation of abducted women in the early 1950s. Another important text for a comparative consideration of trauma and memory is Urvashi Butalia's *The Other Side of Silence*, which presents powerful oral histories of partition refugees in Delhi, along with new digital humanities initiatives like *1947Partition.org* and *1947 Partition Archive* (1947PartitionArchive.org), both of which record voices and memories of partition migrants and refugees across South Asia, the United Kingdom, and North America.

Crucially, this cultural archive not only illuminates the trauma of sexual and familial violence often erased from historiographical accounts but also bears witness to the fractured texture of everyday life for migrant women as they struggle economically and socioculturally to hold on to safety, find a home and work, and rebuild life. Relatedly, Samina Ali's novel *Madras on Rainy Days* powerfully sutures an elite Muslim family's forced displacement *within* India during partition with the story of Indian American immigrant experience and contemporary gender-based violence during communal riots. This, Nazia Akhtar suggests, enacts "an aesthetics of postmemory" (a term theorized by Marianne Hirsch), not unrelated to other ethnic American writings that address immigrant women's experiences of genocide, conflict, and war (16). Taken together, these writings have profound political consequences: as Butler notes in a different context, "emerging from scenes of extraordinary subjugation, they remain proof of stubborn life, vulnerable, overwhelmed, their own and not their own, dispossessed, enraged, and perspicacious" (62).

Literary representation of refugee experience can be important in contemporary European and American classrooms in the context of the widespread and often negative media coverage of refugees' arrival in Europe and at the United States–Mexico border. Engaging Butler's analysis of cultural representations of war trauma in *Frames of War* with the aesthetic translation of refugee women's psychic, material, and embodied trauma in literary works like Singh Baldwin's *What the Body Remembers* can incite a humanist, ethical regard for the refugee often othered in our mainstream media discourses. The literary archive of women's writings about the 1947 partition also speaks to the experience of division that marked many communities across Asia, from Korea to China to Vietnam, during the post–World War II period—even when it was not named "partition."

A pathbreaking work of graphic narratives ties together the above themes: the anthology *This Side, That Side: Restorying Partition*, curated by Vishwajyoti Ghosh, which includes poetic and moving experimental pieces by many women writers, activists, illustrators, and photographers from Pakistan, Bangladesh, and India (like Beena Sarwar, Bani Abidi, Mehreen Murtaza, Syeda Farhana, Priya Sen, and others, some in collaboration with their male counterparts). This volume experiments with the conventions of comics and photography to comment on media, memory, gender, and war. In its narratives about fractured communities, relationships, and memories, a fractured aesthetic dominates: for instance, panels are often unevenly sized and spaced, and the borders between them are fluid or, at times, missing. More than any other work, this anthology vividly addresses the links across South Asia's history of war and conflict, from the memory and trauma of 1947, the refugee experience, the 1971 war, and Indo-Pakistani hostilities to contemporary joblessness in Dhaka's Geneva Camp, the multigenerational poverty of millions of refugees, and state violence. This latter dimension resonates urgently today, as the world witnesses what Saskia Sassen has called the systemic mass "expulsion" of people by war, environmental degradation, state and corporate land grabbing, and poverty around the world (1). Urban experience and media appear here in radical new ways: Delhi, Karachi, and Dhaka are recast as refugee cities. Sonya Fatah and Archana Sreenivasan's collaboration "Karachi-Delhi Katha" is especially moving as it contemplates the complexities of Indo-Pakistani identity and the experience of migration in Delhi and Karachi. When taught along with other popular postcolonial graphic narratives about migration and war, like the French Iranian Marjane Satrapi's *Persepolis*, this anthology eloquently animates partition's transnational legacies for contemporary South Asia.

Contemporary South Asian women's writing also joins the subcontinent and diaspora. The 1947 migrations haunt this literature in suggestive ways, shaping identities, conversations, and lives. From the Pakistani American Kamila Shamsie's novel *Salt and Saffron* to the Indian American Jhumpa Lahiri's short story "When Mr. Pirzada Came to Dine" in *Interpreter of Maladies* to the Indian American Sudha Koul's *The Tiger Ladies: A Memoir of Kashmir*, South Asian women's narratives of migration also mark how the 1947 decolonization of India resonates today in the region and abroad. This literature traces how the submerged history of partition inhabits contemporary South Asian and South Asian American citizenship and belonging.

Together these texts urge us to reconsider the relation between literature and history and between art and our received narratives of official political and national history. By juxtaposing literary works with chapters from historiography about partition (Sarkar; Pandey) and oral histories (Butalia; Menon and Bhasin), one can foreground for students the stakes involved in engaging literature to apprehend historical experiences. Read alongside Walter Benjamin's seminal essay "The Work of Art in the Age of Mechanical Reproduction" on the relation between aesthetics and politics, these works also generate new conversations about the role of storytelling in world conflict. A historical approach to this body of writing enables us to incite classroom conversations about realist, modernist, postmodernist, and graphic forms that dominate recent revisionist fiction about the partition, allowing for an appreciation of the mirroring of experiences of rupture and of a fractured aesthetic. Finally, this archive of migration in the context of conflict is important in one more way: it represents a hidden or subaltern history of women's experiences that often have no other official archive.

Works Cited

Akhtar, Nazia. "Rape and the Imprint of Partition in Samina Ali's *Madras on Rainy Days*." *Postcolonial Text*, vol. 9, no. 2, 2014, pp. 1–20.

Ali, Samina. *Madras on Rainy Days*. Farrar, Straus and Giroux, 2004.

Anderson, Benedict. *Imagined Communities: Reflections on the Origin and Spread of Nationalism*. Revised ed., Verso, 2016.

Anjaria, Ulka. *Realism in the Twentieth-Century Indian Novel: Colonial Difference and Literary Form*. Cambridge UP, 2012.

Benjamin, Walter. "The Work of Art in the Age of Mechanical Reproduction." *Illuminations*, edited by Hannah Arendt, Schocken Books, 1969, pp. 217–52.

Butalia, Urvashi. *The Other Side of Silence: Voices from the Partition of India*. Duke UP, 2000.

Butler, Judith. *Frames of War: When Is Life Grievable?* Verso, 2009.

Chughtai, Ismat. "Roots." Translated by M. Asaduddin. *India Partitioned*, edited by Mushirul Hasan, vol. 2, Roli Books, 1995, pp. 279–89.

Desai, Anita. *Clear Light of Day*. 1980. Vintage, 2001.

———. *In Custody*. Heinemann, 1984.

Devi, Jyotirmoyee. "The Crossing." *Bengal Partition Stories: An Unclosed Chapter*, edited by Bashabi Fraser, translated by Sheila Sen Gupta et al., Anthem Press, 2006, pp. 247–54.

———. *The River Churning*. 1968. Translated by Enakshi Chatterjee, Kali for Women, 1995.

French, Patrick. *Liberty or Death: India's Journey to Independence and Division*. HarperCollins, 1997.

Ghosh, Vishwajyoti, compiler. *This Side, That Side: Restorying Partition*. Yoda Press, 2013.
Hosain, Attia. *Sunlight on a Broken Column*. Chatto and Windus, 1961.
Kapur, Manju. *Difficult Daughters*. Penguin, 1998.
Koul, Sudha. *The Tiger Ladies: A Memoir of Kashmir*. Beacon Press, 2002.
Lahiri, Jhumpa. "When Mr. Pirzada Came to Dine." *Interpreter of Maladies*, Houghton Mifflin, 1999, pp. 23–42.
Lowe, Lisa. *The Intimacies of Four Continents*. Duke UP, 2015.
Mehta, Deepa. Interview. Conducted by Richard Phillips. *World Socialist Web Site*, 6 Aug. 1999, www.wsws.org/articles/1999/aug1999/meh-a06.shtml.
Menon, Ritu, and Kamla Bhasin. *Borders and Boundaries: Women in India's Partition*. Rutgers UP, 1998.
Nasreen, Taslima. *Lajja* [*Shame*]. Penguin, 1994.
Pandey, Gyanendra. *Remembering Partition: Violence, Nationalism, and History in India*. Cambridge UP, 2001.
Pritam, Amrita. "Ode to Waris Shah." *Punjab Research Group*, theprg.co.uk/2008/08/06/amrita-pritam/. Accessed 14 Sept. 2020.
———. *Pinjar* [*Skeleton*]. 1950. Translated by Khushwant Singh, Tara India Research Press, 2009.
Sarkar, Sumit. *Modern India, 1885–1947*. St. Martin's Press, 1989.
Sassen, Saskia. *Expulsions: Brutality and Complexity in the Global Economy*. Belknap Press of Harvard UP, 2014.
Satrapi, Marjane. *Persepolis: The Story of a Childhood and The Story of a Return*. Vintage, 2008.
Shamsie, Kamila. *Salt and Saffron*. Bloomsbury, 2000.
Sidhwa, Bapsi. *Cracking India*. Milkweed Editions, 1991.
Singh Baldwin, Shauna. *What the Body Remembers*. Doubleday, 1999.
Sobti, Krishna. "Where Is My Mother?" Translated by Alok Bhalla. *Stories about the Partition of India*, edited by Bhalla, vol. 2, Indus Publishing, 1994, pp. 135–40.
Sumar, Sabiha, director. *Khamosh Pani* [*Silent Waters*]. Vidhi Films, 2003.

Gurleen Grewal

Gender, Caste, and Capital in *The God of Small Things*

In "Reading Arundhati Roy Politically," a controversial essay published in 1997, the Marxist critic Aijaz Ahmad starkly criticizes Arundhati Roy's first novel, *The God of Small Things*, for its apparent reduction of the political to the personal in a love story revolving around the sexual transgression of caste boundaries in contemporary India. According to Ahmad, Roy's novel is a deeply problematic reduction of the public space of politics to the private realm of the individual and desire. In this essay, I suggest that teaching *The God of Small Things* could show how the novel also enacts the opposite move, turning the realm of the personal into a politically engaged literary form. For this reason, teaching *The God of Small Things* should emphasize the multiple ways in which the personal and the political are entwined and interconnected in the novel. Indeed, in the past decades, Roy has emerged as a socially committed writer and activist mainly devoted to frontline journalism and nonfictional work. The interspersion of her second novel, *The Ministry of Utmost Happiness*, with highly politicized authorial intrusions further indicates that her literary writing has never been detached from political engagement with ongoing realities of caste and gender oppression and social inequality. Roy's representational strategies charge literary expression with a vocal denunciation of everyday violence against the environment, the poor, women, Adivasi, and Dalits. *The God of Small Things* highlights forms of oppression often repressed in the triumphalist narrative of postcolonial India as a neoliberal state and a developing economy. This essay focuses especially on the intersections of oppression along caste and gender lines and the denunciation of predatory capitalism in the novel. If Roy's novel deals with individual stories of loss and pain, these individual stories cannot be restricted to the realm of the singular and the specific, but rather capture and epitomize wider social and political tendencies at work in postcolonial India.

Because of the entanglement of the big and the small, the political and the personal, this richly layered novel enables students to understand quintessential concerns that are at the center of debates and research in postcolonial criticism, in particular the intersectional dimension of caste, class, race, and gender oppression and its effects on ordinary life in postcolonial nations. Accordingly, I ask my students to consider Roy's important novel from the point of view of characters undergoing different kinds of trauma and loss. Can Roy's writing also suggest ways of working through traumatic experiences, giving literary writing the important social function of countering dominant single stories about social and economic development in contemporary India? The novel's narrator wryly acknowledges a distinction between the "Small God" that is "personal turmoil" and the "Big God" that is the "public turmoil of a nation"—the former knows its "inconsequence" before the latter (20). Yet the small and the unequal can resist. And out of the turmoil that is seemingly personal, private, and unspeakable, this antibildungsroman novel registers a scathing critique that is public, collective, national, and global in its implications.

The bildungsroman novel typically depicts the self-formation of a protagonist whose coming of age, though marked by conflict or struggle, is ultimately resolved by the character's assimilation into the social order. For postcolonial writers such as Roy, along with other important writers such as Tsitsi Dangarembga and Jamaica Kincaid, the bildungsroman is often an antibildungsroman when it criticizes the project of *bildung* (development), both at the personal and at the national level, drawing parallels between the small gods of fictional characters and the continuing injustice at the national level. In terms of content as well as genre, Roy's postcolonial coming-of-age narrative is a radical critique of the violence sanctioned by ruling classes and castes in contemporary India. This essay will hence explore the representation of caste, gender, and capital in the novel, offering some possible suggestions for classroom debates.

The Politics of the Personal

The first aspect of the novel to consider concerns the representation and working through of traumatic experience, which enables Roy to charge individual stories with wider political valences. The novel is structured by a trope familiar in postcolonial and American novels such as Tayeb Salih's *Season of Migration to the North*, Leslie Marmon Silko's *Ceremony*, and Toni Morrison's *Beloved*: the working through of repressed memories of traumatic experiences that drives the narrative and makes it possible. As Cathy Caruth notes, traumatic experience is "an experience that is not fully assimilated as it occurs" (5); to narrate such a story is thus an "attempt to master what was never fully grasped in the first place" (62). The traumatic story of two of the main characters in the novel, Ammu and Velutha, becomes the emblem of persisting caste and gender violence in contemporary India.

Velutha, a Dalit, engages in a romantic relationship with Ammu Ipe. After a series of vicissitudes concerning Velutha; Ammu's twins, Rahel and Estha; and their cousin Sophie, Velutha is brutally beaten and killed by the police for his alleged involvement in Sophie's death and his transgression of caste discrimination. In the classroom, I ask students to ponder how Roy locates the "sober, steady brutality" (292) of the policemen, Velutha's punishment for his transgression, within the long-term history of repression and marginality impelling the violence:

> Feelings of contempt born of inchoate, unacknowledged fear—civilization's fear of nature, men's fear of women, power's fear of powerlessness. . . . If they hurt Velutha more than they intended to, it was only because any kinship, any connection between themselves and him . . . had been severed long ago. They were not arresting a man, they were exorcising fear. (293)

Velutha poses a threat to existing communal, caste, and class hierarchies: it is not simply a question of restricting the possibility of agency to the realm of desire. A potential classroom question concerns whether it is possible to read Velutha on an allegorical level, as a stand-in for a wider social and political history, rather than simply an individual character, trapped in the singular and the unverifiable. This remarkable passage anticipates Roy's increasing and abiding concern with minority, caste, and class discrimination in both India and the world in the two decades following the novel's publication.

When teaching these themes in the American classroom, students may respond to parallels between caste violence in India and documented police violence on black bodies in the United States. Accordingly, the novel invites us to consider the following questions for discussion in the classroom: What are the wider social and political structures and forms of inequality that preclude solidarity across gender, caste, race, community, and class? What perceptions of otherness prevent empathy and reinforce instead the legitimation of existing inequality? These are some questions that the novel allows teachers and instructors to ask and to connect to experiences closer to the everyday lives of our students. Can the personal and the domestic be framed as highly politicized spaces?

One of the key questions raised in the classroom concerns the relation between the familial, domestic sphere and the wider historical and social problems addressed, especially gender and caste politics. From this point of view, it could be argued that the novel offers a feminist critique of the ideological function of the bourgeois domestic sphere of home and the family. Conventionally thought of as women's space, the home in Roy's novel emerges as an ambivalent or even inhospitable place where patriarchal social hierarchies are practiced and policed. In Susan Strehle's words, the home is "a space where national discourse speaks and reproduces itself" (2). In the familial and domestic space of the Ipe family house, women and children are taught their status as subordinate subjects. Pappachi, a retired colonel and government officer, vents his frustration by beating Mammachi with a brass vase. The twins' mother, Ammu, marries an alcoholic tea-plantation manager, who is ready to act as his English boss's pimp to save his job and beats Ammu. When she leaves him and returns to her parental home, she is ostracized for her various transgressions: for marrying outside her community and religion (a Syrian Christian, she speaks Malayalam, while her husband is a Bengali Hindu) and for her subsequent divorce. If "a married daughter had no position in her parents' home," a divorced woman has no locus standi ("Locusts Stand I" in the twins' lingo), no place to stand (45, 56). Ammu works at the family's pickle factory alongside her brother without a claim to a share in it; after disgracing the family by her affair with Velutha, she is banished by her enraged Marxist brother Chacko, who, by patriarchal code, claims their parental home as exclusively his own and sends Estha away to a distant father in Calcutta. That Ammu dies at age thirty-one alone and impoverished in an alien hotel room at the Alleppey Bharat Lodge—*Bharat* is the Sanskrit name for India—signifies woman's space of unbelonging in the Indian nation.

Imbuing domestic spaces and encounters with the trauma of violence thus links women's disenfranchisement within the nation with the politics that inhere at home. Rahel and Estha's is not the only incestual relationship in the novel. Emotional incest may be at the heart of patriarchy when thwarted women turn to intervening sons who question the law of the father even as they take his place: witness Mammachi and Chacko. We learn that ever since Chacko rescued Mammachi from Pappachi's beatings, "Mammachi packed her wifely luggage and committed it to Chacko's care. . . . [H]e became the repository of all her womanly feelings. Her Man. Her only Love." The hostile mother-in-law scenario made popular by Bollywood films and sitcoms comes to mind as Mammachi hates Margaret "for being Chacko's wife" (160). Mammachi is both victim of patriarchal power and its upholder.

Feminist thought provides a framework for understanding the complicated relationship of women to power—a simple solidarity based on gender identity is a myth, since identity is complicated by caste and class. Students may ponder the various kinds of abuse perpetuated *by* female characters. That Mammachi condones and accommodates Chacko's "Man's Needs" (160)—he uses his position as a landlord to seduce female workers—is reflective of women's complicity in patriarchal, class, and caste hegemony. Accordingly, Mammachi, enraged by her daughter's flaunting the "morality of motherhood and divorcee-hood" and transgressing caste taboos (43), locks Ammu in her bedroom. The inspector at the police station who taps Ammu's breast with his phallic baton and calls her a whore shares Mammachi's worldview. The spinster grandaunt Baby Kochamma, embittered by the narrow prospects of her own life, has no solidarity or empathy with Ammu or the hapless twins. The Ayemenem House's proscriptions and prohibitions around caste are amplified by the state police.

Further to the intersections of gender and caste oppression, Roy's novel shows the commodification of personal space determined by the neoliberal economic regime of postcolonial India. In the transformation of the History House, one of the most significant locations of the story, to Heritage Hotel, the novel charts the trajectory of capitalist imperialism from colonialism to the neoliberal economy of the 1990s. The transformation may be read as a potent allegory of capitalism's empire: as a result of India enlisting in the neoliberal free market enterprise in the 1990s, the colonial economy of plantations extracting rubber, symbolized by Kari Saipu's house, is replaced by the neoliberal economy of globalization, where land and culture are again usurped and commodified: a "five-star hotel chain had bought the heart of Darkness" (119), and for the short attention span of "rich tourists" the "ancient stories" of the Kathakali dancers "were collapsed and amputated" (120–21); in the private Ayemenem home and the public space of the Heritage Hotel arrived "[b]londes, wars, famines, football, sex, music, coups d'etat"—random invasions of American popular culture (*The Bold and the Beautiful*, etc.) and the media detritus of an imperial neoliberal economy of consumerism. The five-star hotel had not only bought the History House but also older ancestral homes, including that of Comrade E. M. S. Namboodiripad: "Toy histories for rich tourists to play in. . . . Kurtz and Karl Marx joining palms to greet rich guests as they stepped off the boat" (120). The devastating commodification of history and culture is observed with trenchant irony.

This subordination of postcolonial culture to the demands of capital is related to the devastation of the environment. The commodification of life stinks: the wild Meenachal River of the twins' childhood is "no more than a swollen drain" (118); polluted, its banks "smelled of shit and pesticides bought with World Bank loans" (14). We learn that "a saltwater barrage had been built, in exchange for votes from the influential paddy-farmer lobby," so that they had "two harvests a year instead of one," at the expense of the fisherfolk whose livelihood is gone (118). The transnational complicity of exploiting natural resources and cheap labor at the expense of the environment and the poor has earned the most stringent critiques of the postcolonial Indian nation-state from Roy in her essays, which I introduce into the classroom as companion pieces. A powerful amalgam of green and red politics and environmental, class, and caste issues find unfettered expression in Roy's advocacy for the fisherfolk and farmers displaced by the damming of the Narmada River in *The Greater Common Good*.

Teaching *The God of Small Things*: Beyond the Single Story

The God of Small Things connects the personal to the political by telling the narrative of one family from many angles, as many stories overlap, underscoring the novel's epigraph, from John Berger: "Never again will a single story be told as though it's the only one." Roy's novel seeks accountability on behalf of the "fragments" of the Indian nation as theorized by the postcolonial historian Partha Chatterjee—those marginalized by the nation-state and its ordering of history. The novel achieves this by connecting the private and public spheres and interrogating the politics of both the home (the middle-class Ayemenem family house) and the History House. Roy's questioning of the "single story" of the postcolonial nation emphasizes the failures of many forms of belonging and mobilization: from Christianity to the Communist Party, the novel denounces the underlying patriarchy and casteism dominating Indian society. The novel compels us to ask the question "Who belongs to the space of the nation?" (Nayar 141). Whose identity is marginal to it? Whose footprints have been completely erased? On a syllabus that includes it, the class may recall Morrison's *Beloved*, as it poses these literal and metaphoric questions regarding slavery in America.

If Velutha and Ammu epitomize the oppressive and violent effects of caste and gender inequality on private lives and romantic relations, religion and the economy operate in the novel as multiple levels of political struggle in which these forms of oppression and marginalization are constantly reproduced but also challenged. Thus, while Christianity was imposed upon the colonies as a civilizational upgrade, Marxism was adopted as an emancipatory ideology by both the working class and the intelligentsia within postcolonial society. However, Roy's novel undercuts and complicates both these understandings, as neither Christianity nor Marxism ameliorates caste oppression. Interestingly, the Syrian Christian community of Kerala predates by fifteen centuries the Christianity the British brought to India. Saint Thomas the Apostle is said to have converted several Brahman families in the first century CE. In the fifteenth century the Portuguese imposed Roman Catholicism on a section of the native Syrian Christians. In the 1830s another sect, influenced by Anglican missionaries, created a reform movement that eventually became known as the Mar Thoma Church, the one the Ipe family belongs to, the twins' great-grandfather being a priest of this community (Tickell 21). After this lesson in the history of Christianity in India, students may contemplate the ways in which Christianity and conversion, precolonial or postcolonial, failed to overcome the problems of entrenched caste oppression. When those of the oppressed castes converted to Anglicanism, they merely constituted a segregated church of the pejoratively termed "Rice-Christians" (Roy, *God* 71). Conversion only ensured that they were now officially casteless and no longer eligible for compensations by the postcolonial state. In legal terms, we discuss how they had no "footprints" at all. The feudal hierarchy and systemic inequality of the caste system, constitutionally abolished in 1947 with India's independence, continue.

The complicity of Christianity and the Communist Party shows the continuation of caste oppression throughout the passage from colonial to postcolonial moments in Indian history. Consider the special status of Kerala as a Communist state. The novel accounts for the success of a democratically elected Communist government in Kerala as follows: "The Marxists worked *within* the communal divides, never challenging them, never appearing not to" (64). The Communist Party's doublespeak and its entrenchment in the culture of gender and caste hierarchy receive the novelist's most scathing criticism. As I explain to students, what happened to Velutha echoes the fate of the Naxalites in West Bengal.[1] Samik Bandyopadhyay writes of their "organized massacre" in 1970–71 as "perpetrated by the police, the party in power, . . . and even parties of the Left Establishment acting in unholy collusion" (xv).

Finally, no discussion of the novel would be complete without noticing the lyric force of the prose that matches that of Kerala's tropical environs, conjures the exuberant imagination of childhood, and evokes the freedom that contracts in the face of social strictures and hierarchies. *The God of Small Things* can offer productive openings for discussing with students the complex intersections of archaic and modern forms of oppression in contemporary India. Roy's novel shows how the personal is always mediated by the political, and teaching it captures its ongoing relevance for linking literary studies to the struggle for social justice in the twenty-first-century classroom.

Note

1. The only other state in India that elected a Communist government was West Bengal, which began the Maoist-inspired Naxalite rebellion of 1969. The rebellion has been fictionalized in several novels by South Asian women writers, among them Bharati Mukherjee's *The Tiger's Daughter*, Mahasweta Devi's *Mother of 1084*, Nayantara Sahgal's *A Situation in Delhi*, and Jhumpa Lahiri's *The Lowland*.

Works Cited

Ahmad, Aijaz. "Reading Arundhati Roy Politically." *Frontline*, vol. 8, 1997, pp. 103–08.

Bandyopadhyay, Samik. Introduction. *Mother of 1084*, by Mahasweta Devi, Seagull Books, 1997, pp. vii–xx.

Caruth, Cathy. *Unclaimed Experience: Trauma, Narrative, and History.* Johns Hopkins UP, 1996.

Chatterjee, Partha. *The Nation and Its Fragments: Colonial and Postcolonial Histories.* Princeton UP, 1993.

Nayar, Pramod K. *Postcolonialism: A Guide for the Perplexed.* Continuum, 2010.

Roy, Arundhati. *The God of Small Things*. HarperCollins, 1997.
———. *The Greater Common Good*. India Book Distributor, 1999.
Strehle, Susan. *Transnational Women's Fiction: Unsettling Home and Homeland*. Palgrave Macmillan, 2008.
Tickell, Alex. *Arundhati Roy's* The God of Small Things. Routledge, 2007.

Josna E. Rege

Small Remedies: Shashi Deshpande Treats Political Violence

In this essay, from my position in a classroom in the twenty-first-century United States—post-9/11, post-onset of the so-called war on terror—I explore responses to politicized religious violence in Shashi Deshpande's novel *Small Remedies*. Here, instead of fear and anger, revenge and retribution—often the reactions to acts of terrorism—there is introspection, self-scrutiny, and a search for healing. A number of contemporary South Asian women have written about political violence, and their treatment of the subject has been quite different from the prevailing discourse. While works by globally celebrated writers such as Kiran Desai, Jhumpa Lahiri, Arundhati Roy, and Kamila Shamsie are arguably more accessible to readers outside the Indian subcontinent, the particular challenges posed by Deshpande offer important pedagogical opportunities. As one of India's foremost writers in English, Deshpande belongs in a wide range of courses, her works usefully exploring themes such as life writing, history and memory, the public and private spheres, and the politics of language. For a writer as prominent and prolific as Deshpande—to date, her works include eleven novels, two crime novellas, four children's books, several short story collections, an essay collection, and, most recently, an autobiography—her works are less frequently taught outside of

India because their language and references are unfamiliar, they are not always readily available,[1] and they complicate assumptions about the South Asian woman.

With regard to language, although Deshpande writes exclusively in English, her novels can read more like translations. This is because they are resolutely—though never exclusively—regional (almost always set in western India) and addressed to an Indian audience rather than to a global one; as such, they use idioms, convey a multilingual context, and involve complex kinship relationships that may initially be difficult to grasp for a non-Indian reader. With regard to stereotypes, as the critic Meenakshi Mukherjee has noted, Deshpande refuses to fulfill expectations of Third World female abjection or of herself as a "Champion of Oppressed Women." Instead, readers will find "an uncompromising toughness . . . insistence on being read on her own terms and a refusal to be packaged according to the demands of the market." They will also find a refusal to employ the polarized discourse of global terrorism, on either side of that bloody binary.

I teach *Small Remedies* through three basic teaching modules. In the first, I examine the novel's use of language, structure, and narrative style and its basic stance with regard to the originary act of violence. In the second, I trace its key themes and their exposition, asking how they relate to one another and to violence. In the third, I explore the meanings of "small remedies" as a treatment for the trauma of political violence. At the outset, I review and discuss the terms *terrorism* and *political violence* and define *communalism* in its uniquely subcontinental sense, which refers to the differences among religious communities and the fomentation of conflict between them for political ends. Instead of *terrorism*, I use the rather ungainly *political violence*, because *terrorism* is nowhere to be found in Deshpande's novel and, as many have pointed out, its meaning is exceptionally vague. Jonathan Barker defines *terrorism* as including "three elements: violence, threatened or employed; against civilian targets; for political objectives" (27). He discusses terrorism by nation-states as well as by nonstate actors and notes that Reuters eschews the unqualified use of the word *terrorist* because of its emotive nature, a point discussed in the classroom. In "Terrorism: Theirs and Ours," Eqbal Ahmed suggests that the definition is deliberately kept vague to heighten its emotive force. When an act of violence is isolated and labeled in this way it can resist reasoned analysis, becoming shorthand for anything that is sought to be attached to or associated with it: hence *9/11* or, in India, *Ayodhya*, referring to the December 1992 destruction of the sixteenth-century Babri Masjid and all that followed (Das). If we allow that "everything changed" after such an event, it becomes exceptional rather than the logical culmination of a number of identifiable forces or factors that can be understood and remedied (Keeble). I also remind my American students that the rest of the world would use the shorthand *11/9*, not *9/11*, and then ask whether anyone can think of another significance that that date might hold. A reference to 9/11 as the anniversary of the 1973 CIA-backed coup d'état in Chile helps to reframe their view of political violence in a global historical perspective.

In the same vein, *Small Remedies* is pedagogically valuable precisely for its decentering effect, inducting readers into an entirely different sociolinguistic environment, albeit one rendered in English. Deshpande approves of the fact that Indian writing in English "no longer seems to shrink from the hard-for-the-outsider-to-understand particularities, the 'local uniqueness' as Sonita Sarker calls it," noting that some "earlier writers . . . offered what Meenakshi Mukherjee called an 'India-made-easy' . . . picture" ("Where Do We Belong" 51). Readers must work to enter the novel's regionally specific, multilingual world and, in so doing, open themselves up to it on its own terms: a small remedy for literary-cultural homogenization. Take, for example, the protagonist Madhu Saptarishi's aunt Leela, whose second husband, Joe, a lover of English literature, often says, in response to the children's complaints, "Think of the Brontës." Aunt Leela, who is fluent only in Marathi, "thought Brontë was a Maharashtrian name—like Kale or Gore, you know" (52)—since Maharashtrian surnames frequently end with an *e*, like *Brontë*, and are pronounced as such. This domestication of the Brontës is greeted with hilarity by Leela's more worldly relatives and may similarly amuse readers who are used to English names—and literary texts—as the norm; but from Leela's perspective, it was only natural to slot them into a familiar pattern of naming.

Small Remedies, Deshpande's sixth novel (eighth if you count her crime fiction), navigates skillfully between the personal and the political. Madhu, paralyzed by grief at the loss of her teenage son, Aditya (Adit), wakens alone in an unfamiliar setting with an unfamiliar identity, "the writer from Bombay" (16). To escape her painful memories, she has accepted an assignment to write the biography of Savitribai Indorekar (Bai), an eminent (and now elderly) classical vocalist who lives in Bhavanipur, a provincial town similar to the one in which Madhu grew up. During her sojourn in Bhavanipur she must find a way to live with the death of her son and to heal the rift that has developed between her husband and herself. We eventually learn that both Adit and Madhu's childhood friend

Munni were random victims of the violence that ripped through Bombay and other cities across India in the months following the December 1992 destruction of the Babri mosque in Ayodhya by right-wing Hindu nationalists.[2]

During Madhu's childhood Bai, her lover Ghulam Ahmed, and their daughter Munni had been her neighbors for a time. Bai, having dared to flout convention to become a classical singer and having left her Brahmin marital home to live with her Muslim tabla player, was a subject of scandal. She has now recovered her respectability, but at a cost. Although Bai has a well-rehearsed narrative that is the authorized biography that she wants Madhu to write, it is immediately clear to Madhu that Bai's story is full of omissions, most notably Ghulam Ahmed and Munni, neither of whom she will now acknowledge. As Madhu struggles to get at the truth of Bai's life story, she cannot help seeing her own denials and evasions in Bai's. A second act of violence finally triggers her memories of the events surrounding her son's death, but she refuses to succumb to fear. In a series of quiet endings, she finds "small remedies" that will enable her to survive and begin to heal.

Students are encouraged to explore the political and historical framework of the novel. Madhu's maternal aunt Leela, a social activist and union organizer, participated in the 1942 Quit India movement, the 1972–75 women's anti-price-rise movement, and the 1974 railway strike and was jailed for a year during the 1975–77 State of Emergency imposed by Prime Minister Indira Gandhi. She chose to live in a working-class Bombay *chawl* (tenement) until she was driven out by shadowy, menacing forces. Deshpande is clearly referring to the Shiv Sena, a militant Hindu nationalist political party founded in 1966 that now exercises a great deal of control over the politics of the city and, indeed, the region. The class considers the function of these historical markers, reflecting upon who and what might be threatened by the changing climate in Bombay, soon to become Mumbai in the 1993 of the novel.[3]

Against this backdrop of personal trauma and historical change, Madhu seeks the elusive truth of Bai's story and her own. I ask students to trace three intertwined themes at the levels of narrator, narrative, and metanarrative: exclusions and inclusiveness, the personal and the political, memory and forgetting.

Even as Deshpande registers a social and political climate becoming more exclusive and less tolerant of difference, she continues to affirm diversity and inclusiveness wherever she finds it. For instance, students can readily contrast Bai's desire for respectability in her erasure of Ghulam Ahmed and Munni with Aunt Leela's utter disregard for social status. Likewise, both Madhu and Munni maintain the facade of respectability, Madhu making no attempt to challenge Bai when she refuses to recognize her as her daughter's childhood friend and Munni remaking herself in the image of a conventional Hindu housewife, disavowing her mixed parentage. Ironically, conformity cannot save Munni; she is killed anyway.

Deshpande demonstrates the invisibility and the normalization of power in her description of the rise of the Shiv Sena in Bombay without once mentioning the organization by name. She presents the pervasive threat of violence for those who fail to toe the line, but presents a very different Bombay from the one being fashioned by the Hindu right. Shirley Chew notes that although Deshpande does not challenge the Shiv Sena explicitly, Madhu's depiction of the facility with which the various characters switch between languages can be seen as "Deshpande's implicit criticism of the 'nativist agenda' which [it] has been pursuing since the mid-1960s" (85).

Where Bai has recovered her reputation by excluding difference, Aunt Leela, a Hindu widow, opens her heart and home to Joe, a Catholic widower, and his children, Paula and Tony. This is the home into which the newly orphaned Madhu enters, and the resulting blended family can be seen as a microcosm of Bombay's exuberant linguistic and literary-cultural diversity. Tony consciously makes himself her brother, performing the Hindu *bhau-bij* ceremony with her at Diwali that is generally carried out only by biological siblings. As Caroline Herbert observes, "Presenting familial bonds as self-conscious acts that cross religious and linguistic boundaries, Madhu's affiliative community performs a secular inclusivity that challenges notions of cultural purity" (74). Until Madhu is mistaken for Bai's Muslim disciple Hasina and injured in a hit-and-run attack by forces seeking to prevent a Muslim singing at a Hindu temple, she avoids public or political engagement; but after the attack she takes a public stand in support of religious pluralism, and Hasina's performance is a transcendent experience for all who attend it.

In a feminist text, it may seem axiomatic that the personal is political. Here, as in all her works, Deshpande refuses to engage in blaming: her female protagonists must take personal responsibility for their complicity with the prevailing political climate. Removed from the domestic roles by which she has long defined herself and struggling to shut out thoughts of her son, Madhu initially judges the choices Bai has made in her life ("What kind of a mother would deny her own child?"), but then, rather than projecting blame outward, she reflects upon her own abuse of motherhood. In Bhavanipur, Madhu seeks to escape the most painful identity of all: "*Aditya-chi-Aai*, Aditya's mother, the identity . . . I've drowned myself in for nearly eighteen years" (153). Given that motherhood is a socially sanctioned, almost sacrosanct role, what can be wrong with Madhu having given it her all? Although she has left home to forget, she finds herself subjecting all her years of motherhood to scrutiny. Pregnancy had given her permission to resign from her job at *City Views* magazine and withdraw into the domestic sphere; motherhood absolved her of any responsibility for the social and political forces that were transforming the city. As the political climate worsened, she focused anxiously on her son. When Aunt Leela was imprisoned during the Emergency, Madhu remembers with shame that she was afraid to visit Leela in case she herself got into trouble and could no longer protect Adit. Wholly absorbed in motherhood, she remembers similarly turning her back on her dear friend Ketaki in her time of need. Although she denied it strenuously at the time, she now acknowledges that there was something wrong with her mother's love: "a small centre, a vast exclusion—I thought this was love" (144). Her "*putra moha* (son-obsession)" had caused Adit to pull away from her, trying to protect himself from her love (188). She realizes, with a quiet horror, that she had lost her son through her grasping love even before she lost him to the anonymous forces of hate.

Earlier still, Madhu remembers her failure to protect Bai's daughter. As a girl, Munni was repeatedly tormented by schoolmates trying to get her to confess to her Muslim parentage, all her denials falling on deaf ears. Madhu reflects: "The cruelty of children making fun of children. . . . Is this where they came from, those people who ran amok through the streets, hurting, maiming, killing? . . . People so ensconsed in their cruelty that they are impervious to human grief" (35–36). The scene of Munni's bullying is the only place in the novel where the word *terror* is employed—"I think of it now, her terror, her distress and her grief" (77)—not in reference to the post-Ayodhya communal violence or the subsequent bomb blasts in the financial and business districts, but much closer to home, in the relentless Muslim-baiting of a small Indian girl by her Hindu classmates. Significantly, the violence is presented as an internal dis-ease, not as the work of an evil outsider.

What does one make of a novel about political violence that resists even naming the tragic event? What is the function of this deferral? I ask students to take note of the various roles of memory and forgetting over the course of the novel. Upon arrival in Bhavanipur, Madhu is in full retreat, unable to face her grief and desperate to forget that terrible time when her son went out and never came home again. But her very displacement, discussed usefully by Caroline Herbert, precipitates self-examination. Madhu notes, "We remember the wrongs done to us, but we forget our sins" (107). Over the course of her often frustrating interviews with Bai, in which she despairs of learning the whole truth of Bai's story, she comes to accept that "there are ellipses in all stories" (171) and to recognize memory in all its partiality as self-deception, as self-protection, and as a precious gift.

The arc of the novel does not simply encompass the usual stages of grief—denial, anger, and, finally, acceptance; it also recognizes that as memory is highly selective on the individual level, so is it on the collective level, for families, communities, and nations. Thus recovery becomes a collective as well as an individual task. As the first anniversary of Adit's death approaches, Madhu opens a letter from her husband, Som: "Come home. We need to be together at this time" (323). At last, Madhu embraces memory as that small remedy that makes life possible after tragic loss: "How could I have ever longed for amnesia? Memory, capricious and unreliable though it is, ultimately carries its own truth within it. As long as there is memory, there's always the possibility of retrieval, as long as there is memory, loss is never total" (324).

As we conclude our discussion, I invite consideration of the eponymous "small remedies." Deshpande uses the term directly in two different contexts, both of them referring to the fragility of happiness and the transience of life, human conditions for which there is no remedy. There are the rituals of superstition (knocking on wood, crossing one's fingers) and of religion ("the Ganeshas in niches, the decorated thresholds . . . the charms and amulets—all to keep disaster at bay") performed, ultimately, to no avail; death comes anyway. "Such small remedies, these, to counter the terrible disease of being human . . . mortal and vulnerable," reflects the grieving Madhu (81). When Adit was a baby, *Small Remedies* was a handbook of home remedies (a book within a book of the same name) that the anxious young mother swore by, consulting it at every turn, holding on to its assurances for dear life; but again, ultimately, all in vain.

Students brainstorm the meanings of small remedies as theme and as metacommentary. Are they stopgap measures, timid compromises, gestures of the powerless? Are they confined narrowly to the domestic sphere? They are surely not guns-blazing shows of force, shock-and-awe tactics, politics of blame or revenge. Small remedies can be compared with home remedies, in contrast to those powerful but crude allopathic medicines whose collateral damage may kill the patient along with the disease. On the contrary, small remedies involve self-examination and self-healing, slow but sure responses to political violence that attend to its root causes. Encouraging students to identify the repertoire of responses to political violence in this and other South Asian women's novels offers them another set of tools that are quietly constructive, a different kind of Homeland Security that offers long-term solutions.

On 5 September 2017 the journalist and newspaper editor Gauri Lankesh was shot dead outside her Bengaluru (formerly Bangalore) home by two unidentified hit-and-run assailants. The day after her funeral, *The Indian Express* ran an opinion column by Deshpande (also based in Bengaluru) on the growing intolerance in India toward those who uphold secularism or speak out against the Hindu right: "If you are not with us you are against us, President George W. Bush told the world after 9/11. This is exactly the way it is in India today. If you don't agree with us, you are the enemy . . ." ("From Silence"). Deshpande noted that learning of Lankesh's murder was "like watching the replay of a movie I'd seen before," the latest in a number of recent drive-by killings of writers and journalists by right-wing Hindu nationalists and mob lynchings of Muslims. In 2015 she had resigned from the Sahitya Akademi's General Council in protest of its silence after the killing of the Kannada writer M. M. Kalburgi. Readers of *Small Remedies* will recall the hit-and-run attack that finally prompted Madhu to break her silence and note its prescience in light of what was to follow. Deshpande closed by reiterating "how important it is to speak out, to refuse to be afraid." Such attacks create a pervasive threat of violence—everyday terror. Here again the most effective responses may be those that resist the fear and seek to understand the problem. Far from being weak or passive, they require great personal courage. Such are the small remedies that Deshpande prescribes in her treatment of political violence.

Notes

1. The Feminist Press at the City University of New York has issued editions of two of Deshpande's novels, *A Matter of Time* and *The Binding Vine*, each with a glossary of terms and an explanatory afterword. However, no such edition ex-

ists for *Small Remedies*. Teachers can order the Penguin India paperback edition from www.dkagencies.com.

2. Post-Ayodhya violence in Bombay in December 1992 and January 1993 killed more than nine hundred people, the majority of whom were Muslims; injured more than two thousand; and displaced many more. Subsequently, on 12 March 1993, a series of twelve bomb blasts killed 257 and injured more than seven hundred people (Sengupta; Suri).

3. The name change took place in 1995 after the Shiv Sena gained control of the Bombay Municipal Corporation.

Works Cited

Ahmed, Eqbal. "Terrorism: Theirs and Ours." *Geopolitics Review*, vol. 2, no. 3, Oct. 2001, pp. 1–7, 16.

Barker, Jonathan. *The No-Nonsense Guide to Terrorism*. Verso, 2003.

Chew, Shirley. "'Cutting Across Time': Memory, Narrative, and Identity in Shashi Deshpande's *Small Remedies*." *Alternative Indias: Writing, Nation and Communalism*, edited by Peter Morey and Alex Tickell, Rodopi, 2005, pp. 71–88. Cross/Cultures 82.

Das, Krishna N. "Factbox: Ayodhya Temple Dispute." *Reuters*, 21 Nov. 2018, in.reuters.com/article/india-election-religion-factbox-ayodhya/factbox-ayodhya-temple-dispute-idINKCN1NR03I.

Deshpande, Shashi. "From Silence to Speech." *The Indian Express*, 8 Sept. 2017, indianexpress.com/article/opinion/columns/from-silence-to-speech-gauri-lankesh-journalist-murder-4833497/.

———. *Small Remedies*. Viking, 1999.

———. "Where Do We Belong: Regional, National, or International?" *Writing from the Margin and Other Essays*, Penguin, 2003, pp. 30–60.

Herbert, Caroline. "Music, Secularism, and South Asian Fiction: Muslim Culture and Minority Identities in Shashi Deshpande's *Small Remedies*." *Imagining Muslims in South Asia and the Diaspora: Secularism, Religion, Representation*, edited by Claire Chambers and Caroline Herbert, Routledge, 2014, pp. 70–85.

Keeble, Arin. "Why the 9/11 Novel Has Been Such a Contested and Troubled Genre." *The Conversation*, 9 Sept. 2016, theconversation.com/why-the-9-11-novel-has-been-such-a-contested-and-troubled-genre-64455.

Mukherjee, Meenakshi. "On Her Own Terms." *The Hindu*, 7 May 2000, www.thehindu.com/todays-paper/tp-miscellaneous/tp-others/on-her-own-terms/article28015042.ece.

Sengupta, Ananya. "What About Us, Ask Bombay Riot Victims." *The Telegraph*, 30 July 2015, www.telegraphindia.com/india/what-about-us-ask-bombay-riot-victims/cid/1479868.

Suri, Manveena. "India: Five Sentenced in 1993 Mumbai Blast Case." *CNN*, 7 Sept. 2017, www.cnn.com/2017/09/07/asia/india-sentenced-mumbai-blast/index.html.

Nilufer E. Bharucha

Teaching Parsi Women Writers in Mumbai

This essay offers a brief history of the evolution of the Indian English literature curriculum at Mumbai University, the place of Parsi women writers within it, and the pedagogical strategies I have used in recognition of the local political and sociocultural context in which I teach. Following an introduction to the history of the Parsis in India, I focus on two novels by Parsi women writers, Bapsi Sidhwa's *Ice-Candy-Man* (published in the United States as *Cracking India*) and Dina Mehta's *And Some Take a Lover.* I contextualize these novels in relation to the historical backgrounds of colonialism and partition as well as the more recent rise of fundamentalism. References to these contexts show how teaching Parsi women writers can lead students to reconsider questions about the representation of gender, violence, and nationalism from a minority perspective.

Indian Literature in English in India

The teaching of English literature in India was a colonial construct steeped in the belief articulated by T. B. Macaulay, in his 1835 "Minute on Indian Education," that "a single shelf of a good European library was worth the whole native literature of India." When the first modern Indian universities were established in 1857 in Calcutta, Bombay, and Madras, the curriculum featured English literature, a subject not taught at British universities until the first quarter of the twentieth century. The Indian colonial education system became the laboratory in which the experiment of teaching English literature was carried out in the belief that the natives would benefit from the moral values inherently inscribed in the literature of the colonial master race. The educated Indian classes were hence exposed to English literature, especially writers of the evolving canon: Shakespeare, Milton, Austen, and Dickens. Interestingly enough, English literature was also thought to be a fit subject to be taught to women and the working classes in the newly established colleges of the University of London (Viswanathan).

The introduction to English writers through the colonial educational curriculum resulted in creative writing in English by Indians; the first Indian novel in English, *Rajmohan's Wife*, by the Bengali writer Bankim Chandra Chatterjee, was published in 1864. Chatterjee was followed by novelists such as Mulk Raj Anand, Raja Rao, and R. K. Narayan and poets such as Nissim Ezekiel and A. K. Ramanujan. Only a few women writers, like Kamala Markandaya, Nayantara Sahgal, and, later, Shashi Deshpande, featured in the emerging canon of Indian writing in English. Notwithstanding the rich cultural and literary production in English by Indian authors, its inclusion in Indian universities took a long time. Even after decolonization, a Eurocentric view of the curriculum endured in the Indian education system. Only in the 1970s did some Indian universities established after independence introduce these writers into the curriculum. Older universities such as Bombay (now Mumbai) University took much longer. In the 1990s Indian writing was eventually introduced at Bombay University as an optional course in the English literature curriculum. The emergence of a tradition of Parsi writing in the subcontinent needs to be placed within this context marked by the influence of a colonial education. Indeed, the Parsis, who were colonial elite like the Bengalis, also produced literature in English, while many of the nineteenth-century Parsi writers like Behramji Malabari were bilingual and wrote both in English and Gujarati. During the colonial period none of these writers was included in the school or university curricula (Bharucha, "Forging Identities").

The mid-1990s saw the entry of the Parsi novelist Rohinton Mistry into the consciousness of the Indian academia. Focused as they were on the Bombay Parsis, Mistry's novels found ready entry into the bachelor's and master's curricula at Bombay University and elsewhere in India. The fact that Mistry was based in Canada, had acquired international visibility, and had also won several awards made it easier for academics to introduce his novels into the curriculum. Another Parsi writer gaining influence in the 1990s was Bapsi Sidhwa. Her first novel, *The Crow Eaters*, had upset Bombay Parsis with what they considered an irreverent portraiture of their community. Her second novel, *The Bride*, was based entirely in Pakistan. Her third novel, *Ice-Candy-Man*, set in Pakistan but within the context of the partitioning of India, shot her into international fame when it was adapted into the film *Earth 1947* by the director Deepa Mehta in 1998. This period also saw two Parsi women journalists becoming novelists: Dina Mehta with *And Some Take a Lover* and Meher Pestonji with *Pervez*. The latter was a response to the demolition of the Babri Masjid in Ayodhya. The resultant communal riots that engulfed the city of Bombay from December 1992 to January 1993 culminated in a series of blasts that shook the city in March 1993. These are traumas from which the city of Bombay, renamed Mumbai in 1995, has yet to recover. During the 1990s only two Parsi writers, Mistry and Sidhwa, started to be included in the canon of South Asian writing in English and in university courses.

By the end of the 1990s Mumbai University had introduced several more relevant courses as electives in the English literature master's degree program: Contemporary Indian Writing in English, Postcolonial Theories and Literatures, and Gender Studies, among others. This was a serious breach in the bastions of canonical British-literature-oriented courses; these new electives became core classes, displacing courses in Elizabethan, Restoration, Romantic, and Victorian literatures. Canonical Literature was retained but under the title Re-reading the Canon. More recently, the master's degree program in English literature was converted into a more research-driven honors program. Sidhwa's *Ice-Candy-Man* and Mehta's *And Some Take a Lover* became prescribed texts in such new courses. The remainder of this essay focuses on these two writers and my pedagogical experience in the context of the increasing dominance of the Hindutva ideology in India and the marginalization of minority communities including not just the Muslims but also the Parsis.

Parsi Writing: Historical Contexts

Teaching Sidhwa and Mehta requires contextualization of their texts within their ethnoreligious background. In my courses, classroom engagement with *Ice-Candy-Man* and *And Some Take a Lover* begins with readings, images, and lectures on the Parsi Zoroastrians in India. Without this, even students in Mumbai would not be able to grasp fully the identity issues foregrounded in both novels. Although the majority of Parsis in the world today live in Mumbai, most of my English literature students at Mumbai University would know little other than the stereotypical image of a community of rather eccentric, quaint, and mainly elderly people. Very few of them know that the Parsi Zoroastrians are a tiny ethnoreligious minority who came to India between 756 CE and 936 CE from Persia (Iran), having repeatedly been attacked from the seventh century onward by Arabs bearing the flag of their new religion, Islam. With the collapse of the Persian Empire, the ancient, monotheistic Zoroastrian religion was replaced by Islam. While most Persians accepted the new religion so they would not suffer economic and social disadvantages, some continued to adhere to Zoroastrianism. The more adventurous among them escaped to India, settling largely in the state of Gujarat in India. They brought their belongings, including the urns containing their sacred fire, a symbol of purity and their one god, Ahura Mazda, for the Zoroastrians.

The Zoroastrians were given refuge in India on the condition that they adopt the local language and customs. They in turn bargained to retain their religion. So they stayed in India, where they became known as Parsi Zoroastrians. Another condition enjoined upon the ancestors of the present-day Parsis was that they would not convert anyone from their host population. In order to safeguard their future survival, they in turn imposed endogamy upon themselves, thus ensuring their unique ethnic identity well into the twenty-first century, 1,300-odd years after their arrival in India. Parsi, the ethnic marker, refers to either Farsi, the dialect of Persian they had spoken when they came to India, or Pars, an Iranian province. So this compound ethnic and religious identity uniquely distinguishes the Parsis of India. However, many of the other standard identity markers provided by sociologists like M. Bulmer, such as language, is missing among them. Since their arrival in India, they have spoken the local language, which was then Apbhransh or Old Gujarati but is now modern Gujarati. With the way back to Iran blocked by the increasing Islamization of their old homeland, Parsis lost the longing to return home of most diasporas. Ethnically they might belong to the present Islamic Iranian grouping, but civilizationally they are closer to their Hindu Indian hosts.[1]

Bapsi Sidhwa and Dina Mehta: Teaching Parsi Women Writers

Alongside an introduction to Parsi history, teaching Parsi women writers in India offers an opportunity to address how these writers engaged with major political events such as the struggle for independence and partition and violent twentieth-century episodes such as the 1992 demolition of Babri Masjid and the 2008 Mumbai attacks. Teaching Sidhwa in Mumbai presents an additional challenge: although she is a Parsi writer and hence considered eligible for being taught in the Indian writing in English course, she is also a Pakistani. Like many Parsis at the time of the partitioning of India, Sidhwa's family found itself on the other side of the new border in Pakistan. Today, the Parsis are a tiny minority in Pakistan, and although Sidhwa now lives mainly in the United States, she sees herself as a "Punjabi-Parsi-Pakistani" ("Bapsi Sidhwa") and was awarded the Sitara-i-Imtiaz, Pakistan's highest national honor in arts, in 1991. The Parsis, as neither Hindus nor Muslims, did not have to deal with dislocations and relocations as did the Hindus, Sikhs, and Muslims on both sides of the border. Sidhwa's *Ice-Candy-Man*, however, is not just a book about Parsis but about all those affected by the partition of India, and is thus taught alongside other partition texts like Khushwant Singh's *Train to Pakistan*.

The majority of Parsis in Pakistan settled in Karachi when the British added Sindh to their Indian possessions in 1843 and it became part of the Bombay Presidency. Parsi communities in Bombay and Pakistan are closely connected. After her first marriage, Sidhwa, born in Karachi in 1938, lived in Bombay for five years before relocating to Lahore and marrying her second husband. She was, like her hero Lenny in *Ice-Candy-Man*, nine years old when the subcontinent was ripped apart to create two new nations. In Deepa Mehta's film version of the book, *Earth 1947*, the authorial connection is made very clear in the last few scenes where Sidhwa herself appears. The movement of the Parsis as entrepreneurs and professionals has been dealt with by many writers including Sidhwa in her first novel, *The Crow Eaters*. This hilarious novel encapsulates wonderfully the famed Parsi humor and irony. It also introduces one of the main strands of *Ice-Candy-Man*: a tiny minority's need for sociopolitical neutrality. In 1947 Parsi Zoroastrians did not take sides between the two new nations in order to survive the violence of partition. I often follow background readings on the Parsis with a viewing of *Earth 1947*. The film's images of violence, bloodshed, and brutality often shock my students, who, as third-generation postcolonial Indians, have no connection with the partition except through history books or jingoistic Bollywood films. Moreover, Bombay did not experience communal Hindu-Muslim riots in 1947; the partition did not impact this part of India as much as it did the north of the country.

For Mumbai students, what is more immediate are the aforementioned post–Babri Masjid riots. What also resonates with them are the terrorist attacks on the city in the last decade of the twentieth century and the first decade of the twenty-first century, peaking in November 2008 with the siege of Mumbai. These events have polarized this otherwise cosmopolitan, tolerant city. This is reflected in the fact that after decades of rule by the centrist Congress Party, Hindu right-wing parties have been able to form governments in the state of Maharashtra, of which Mumbai is the capital. I therefore link the communal riots, violence, and rape of women in *Ice-Candy-Man* to these events, mindful of the fact that classroom discussions and presentations can be difficult for many students, especially those from religious minorities. The novel, indeed, does not have a mere historical value, representing the events of partition, but also can be taught in order to explore and interrogate disturbing continuities between the partition and contemporary forms of violence in India.

The fragmentation of the tolerant social fabric of Lahore in 1947 into communal violence by militant Hindu, Sikh, and Muslim groups can sound familiar to young Mumbaikars who have either seen or heard about similar experiences from their parents. These events have also restricted the freedom of movement of my female students, as each community guards its women from the men of other communities. My students can thus empathize with little Lenny in *Ice-Candy-Man* when she complains, "My world is compressed . . ." (1). Lenny's femaleness is linked to the disability of her right foot from polio, and her world becomes an enclosure that she escapes in the company of her Hindu *ayah* (nanny), Shanta, but their halcyon days are short-lived, as Shanta becomes a trophy for Muslim rioters who bay for her outside the gates of Lenny's Parsi parents' house. Shanta is stoutly defended by Lenny's mother and the family's servants, most of whom are either Muslim or newly converted Christian (who, like the Parsis, were seen as neutral). It is, however, Lenny's "truth infected tongue" (239) that betrays Shanta, as she is unable to deny Shanta's presence in the house when asked about her by their once mutual friend the Ice-Candy-Man.

Shanta is dragged away, raped, and confined to a brothel like hundreds of Hindu and Muslim women during not only the partition but the creation of Bangladesh and, more recently, the Bombay riots of 1992–93. Shanta is raped and incarcerated in retaliation for murdered Muslim women; gunny sacks full of their breasts are found on the train to Lahore from India by Muslims in Pakistan. These acts of unspeakable gendered violence express, as Kate Millet has said, a logic whereby "rape is an offence one male commits upon another—a matter of abusing 'his woman'" (36). In this brutal game of one-upmanship—a rape for a rape, a murder for a murder—the two newly created countries burned as Hindus, Sikhs, and Muslims, driven by fear and anxiety, brutalized and killed one another. Amid these killings, minorities belonging to religions other than Hinduism or Islam tried their best to remain neutral and not draw the attention of what Rushdie has called the "Majority, that Mighty elephant and her side kick, Major-Minority" (87). Likewise, the Lahore Parsis in Sidhwa's novel try to ensure their survival in the new country by reassuring themselves that no harm will come to them as long as they remain neutral. As one character, Colonel Bharucha, says, "Ahura Mazda had looked after us for 1300 years, he will look after us for another 1300 years" (38).

In spite of the neutrality maintained by most Parsis, as Mehta's *And Some Take a Lover* demonstrates, they are nonetheless haunted by anxiety. Mehta's novel is also set in colonial India but against the backdrop of the nationalist struggle and the Quit India movement of 1942. In the colonial context, the Parsis occupied an elite space but were not actually empowered. Mehta's female hero Roshni is a girl from a rich Parsi family who gets caught up in these historical events because of her involvement with one of Gandhi's Hindu followers, Sudhir. Roshni, in spite of her prosperous background and education, is in her female enclosure.[2]

Roshni's love for Sudhir meets with strong resistance from her family, which also looks disdainfully at the handwoven khadi saris she wears to please her Gandhian friend. Unfortunately, Sudhir too is not impressed at this flaunting of Roshni's nationalistic fervor. Embracing celibacy, Gandhi had frowned upon sexuality as a hindrance to the higher goals of the independence of India. Roshni's femaleness, even if disguised under layers of coarse khadi cloth, upsets the young man. The nationalist imaging of India as a mother, Bharat Mata, denies or underplays female sexuality. Sudhir rejects Roshni in favor of a fellow Gandhian, Lajwanti, a desexualized, nonthreatening woman who, unlike Roshni, will not distract him from his nationalist goals. In Byronesque retaliation, Roshni takes Rustom, a fellow Parsi, as a lover, but then she turns away from him. Free of male control now, she daringly plunges into wider sociopolitical spaces and tries to lead a life faithful to her past, present, and future in the imminently independent India. This book resonates powerfully with students of English literature who, like Roshni, come mainly from the upper class. Yet, in spite of their education and relative financial prosperity, they, like her, have limited autonomy when it comes to leading their own lives.

Teaching these texts, written by women from a tiny ethnoreligious minority spread out across the contested borders of India and Pakistan, thus requires an engagement with both politics and pedagogy. The contemporary turmoil within India in the context of contested notions of patriotism and nationalism makes these novels what Homi K. Bhabha calls "the literature of recognition" (9). In the context of the competing nationalisms of India and Pakistan, there is also the question of how the minor minorities such as the Parsis view themselves vis-à-vis these nation-states. In the present political climate, it is important for students to know that minorities are as nationalistic and patriotic as the majority and have as much right to the nation space as the majority, whether in India or in Pakistan.

Notes

1. The history of the Parsis and their diaspora is available in the writings of Kamerkar; Kamerkar and Dhunjisha; Kulke; Bharucha, "Imaging." Select readings from these books and articles form the precourse reading package, reinforced in the classroom through PowerPoint presentations and discussions leading to the target texts.

2. Seventy thousand Parsis remain in India today, with a few thousands more around the world in a Western diaspora, plus the approximately twenty thousand in Iran (Axelrod; Shroff and Castro). For students who are interested in reading more on the condition of women and patriarchy among the Parsis, I suggest Bharucha, "Inhabiting Enclosures"; Palsetia; Sharafi. Though Parsi women appear to be more emancipated and free compared with their Hindu or Muslim sisters, they are also bound by patriarchal laws.

Works Cited

Axelrod, Paul. "Cultural and Historical Factors in the Population Decline of the Parsis of India." *Population Studies: A Journal of Demography*, vol. 44, no. 3, 1990, pp. 401–19.

"Bapsi Sidhwa a Punjabi Parsi Pakistani." *ParsiNews.net*, 18 Dec. 2015, www.parsinews.net/bapsi-sidhwa-a-punjabi-parsi-pakistani/253577.html.

Bhabha, Homi K. *The Location of Culture*. Routledge, 1994.

Bharucha, Nilufer E. "Forging Identities, Initiating Reforms: The Parsi Voice in Colonial India." *South Asian Review*, vol. 25, no. 1, 2004, pp. 177–99.

———. "Imaging the Parsi Diaspora: Narratives on the Wings of Fire." *Shifting Continents/Colliding Cultures: Diaspora Writing of the Subcontinent*, edited by Ralph J. Crane and Radhika Mohanram, Rodopi, 2000, pp. 55–82.

———. "Inhabiting Enclosures and Creating Spaces: The Worlds of Women in Indian Literature in English." *ARIEL*, vol. 29, no. 1, Jan. 1998, pp. 93–107.

Bulmer, M. "Race and Ethnicity." *Key Variables in Sociological Interventions*, edited by R. G. Burgess, Routledge, 1986, pp. 54–75.

Chatterjee, Bankim Chandra. *Rajmohan's Wife*. 1864. Rupa Publications, 2008.

Kamerkar, Mani. "Parsees in Surat from the Sixteenth to the Middle of the Nineteenth Century: Their Social Economic and Political Dynamics." *Journal of the Asiatic Society of Bombay*, vol. 70, 1995, pp. 71–88.

Kamerkar, Mani, and Soonu Dhunjisha. *From the Iranian Plateau to the Shores of Gujarat: The Story of Parsi Settlements and Absorption in India*. Allied, 2002.

Kulke, Eckehard. *The Parsees in India: A Minority as Agent of Social Change*. Vikas, 1978.

Macaulay, T. B. "Minute on Indian Education." 1835. www.columbia.edu/itc/mealac/pritchett/00generallinks/macaulay/txt_minute_education_1835.html.

Mehta, Deepa, director. *Earth 1947*. Cracking the Earth Films, 1998.

Mehta, Dina. *And Some Take a Lover*. Rupa Publications, 1992.

Millet, Kate. *Sexual Politics*. Doubleday, 1969.

Palsetia, Jesse S. *The Parsis of India: Preservation of Identity in Bombay City*. Brill, 2001.

Pestonji, Meher. *Pervez*. HarperCollins, 2003.

Rushdie, Salman. *The Moor's Last Sigh*. Jonathan Cape, 1995.

Sharafi, Mitra. *Law and Identity in Colonial South Asia: Parsi Legal Culture, 1772–1947*. Cambridge UP, 2014.

Shroff, Zubin C., and Marcia C. Castro. "The Potential Impact of Intermarriage on the Population Decline of the Parsis of Mumbai, India." *Demographic Research*, vol. 25, July–Dec. 2011, pp. 545–64.

Sidhwa, Bapsi. *The Bride*. St. Martin's Press, 1983.

———. *The Crow Eaters*. 1978. Sangam, 1980.

———. *Ice-Candy-Man*. Heinemann, 1988.

Singh, Khushwant. *Train to Pakistan*. 1956. Penguin, 2016.

Viswanathan, Gauri. *Masks of Conquest: Literary Study and British Rule in India*. Oxford UP, 1998.

Ruvani Ranasinha

Contemporary Anglophone Sri Lankan Women Authors

Teaching contemporary anglophone Sri Lankan women's writing to predominantly European and American undergraduates and postgraduates at King's College, London, presents several challenges that make the selection of writers taught particularly significant. First, Sri Lankan writing is especially marginalized in discussions of South Asian and diasporic literature, with Indian writers dominating the curriculum. It has not reached the international visibility of Indian writing in English in part because of smaller literary output and comparatively nascent anglophone publishing culture. A key preliminary pedagogical task, then, is to pay careful attention to Sri Lanka's distinct sociohistorical contexts and their implications for women's writing.[1] In addition to the importance of context-sensitive approaches to teaching noncanonical courses on Sri Lankan women's writing, this essay emphasizes the perspectives of resident Sri Lanka writers alongside diasporic voices and outlines the ways in which the resident writer Ameena Hussein and the diasporic Sri Lankan writers Minoli Salgado and Roshi Fernando allow the teacher to illuminate Sri Lanka's distinctive contextual history alongside "the many cross-border issues that are pertinent to . . . [the nation's] women's movements" in "a South Asia intimately connected through geography and history," as the critic Neloufer de Mel reminds us (47).

My courses include at least one novel focused on educating students about the nuances of Sri Lanka's history, long overlooked in Western classrooms. Sri Lanka's experience of war and terrorism (decades before 9/11) and protracted civil war cost Sri Lanka between eighty thousand and one hundred thousand lives. However, the brutal ending of twenty-six years of war, culminating in the death of thousands of civilians in May 2009, attracted much controversy and began to change the world's awareness of this small island nation. Recent anglophone Sri Lankan fiction appears haunted by the ghosts of the nation's warring past. The outbreak of a fully fledged civil war between the Sinhala majority-led government and the Liberation Tigers of Tamil Eelam (LTTE), fighting for a separate Tamil state, dates back to the horrific anti-Tamil violence of July 1983. The funeral of thirteen Sinhalese soldiers ambushed and killed by the LTTE in Jaffna in July 1983 sparked a horrific spate of state-sanctioned murder of Tamil citizens and burning of Tamil-owned homes and businesses in the capital and elsewhere. "Black July" marked a defining turning point in the conflict and for Sri Lankan creative writing, searing the creative sensibilities of a generation of authors writing in its aftermath.

Although July 1983 marked a pivotal turning point, the eruption of civil war was a culmination of previous events, among them the contentious Sinhala Only Act passed by the Sinhala majoritarian government less than ten years after independence from Britain in 1956. This made Sinhala the official state language and elevated Buddhism to a state religion. This ill-judged constitutional act was intended to placate Sinhala nationalists by redressing both the perceived overrepresentation of Tamils under British rule and the balance of influence of the minute English-speaking elite who controlled much of the power. However, although seen by some as a democratizing move because of the displacement of the English-speaking elite, it alienated and discriminated against Tamil speakers; anti-Tamil riots followed in 1958. Although Tamil remained an official language (enshrined in the Tamil Official Act of 1958) and Tamil speakers continued to be able to study and work in Tamil, the Sinhala Only Act transformed Sri Lanka's sociopolitical and cultural landscape. It also prompted a questioning of the role of English, the English-educated, and the English-language creative writer.

A Little Dust on the Eyes, the 2014 debut novel by the United Kingdom–based Sri Lankan writer Minoli Salgado, can be usefully explored in terms of its participation in and interrogation of a longer history of cultural and literary representation of Sri Lanka. Given Sri Lanka's little understood violent past, it is important to choose a literary text that engages with and offers some insight into the complexity of the civil strife in order to complicate hegemonic representations of Sri Lanka that naturalize dominant accounts of the country as a homogenized place of violence where conflict is both deplorable and inevitable. Such dehistoricized, exoticized treatments of Sri Lanka's ethnopolitical crises often overlook its entanglement with the brutal Sinhala Marxist Janatha Vimukthi Peramuna (JVP) insurrection and vicious countersuppression in the south: they simplify the conflict in terms of an endemic Sinhala-Tamil binary.[2] Therefore, my classroom emphasizes the novel's engagement with this critical juncture in Sri Lanka's history: the state's counterterrorism and the rise of the Sri Lankan state as violent and corrupt. Set on the southern coast of Sri Lanka in the 1980s, the novel explores lives "enmeshed in this hidden war that failed to make international news . . . masked by the shrieking headlines on the larger war between the government and the LTTE . . . that lacked the comfortable logic of race and ethnicity, religious, cultural difference, easy distinctions favoured by those who liked to keep things simple and clean" (76). Like Michael Ondaatje's novel *Anil's Ghost*, Salgado's novel contextualizes the role of the Sinhalese JVP insurgency in the larger war between government forces and the LTTE fighting for a separate state. The JVP first came to prominence in the late 1960s with the aim of establishing a socialist state. It was founded by Rohana Wijeweera, who had been educated at a Soviet university and brought a rural revolutionary attitude to this antigovernment rebellion. The JVP's first period of insurrection (April–June 1971) was crushed by the then socialist government (this is explored in the fiction of Ediriweera Sarachchandra, among others). The background to Salgado's novel, however, is the second, more brutal insurgency: the "bloodletting" on the southern coast during the mid- to late 1980s that almost brought down the Sinhalese government (99). This later insurgency's intimidation and violence, and the government's even more vicious repression, resulted in the death and disappearance of an estimated sixty thousand people.

A Little Dust on the Eyes explores loss, trauma, and the scarring psychosis of the abductions and disappearances through the intersecting lives of Bradley Sirisena, who witnesses his father's abduction and torture and for whom "the word for father had been torn out of him when he saw him pulled into the van" (78); Renu, who documents the details of hundreds disappeared for an NGO; and her cousin Savi, long based in the United Kingdom, who is researching Sri Lanka's conflict. Self-conscious about its migrant perspective and the familiar story of the expatriate returned, the novel interrogates the gulf between the experiences of those affected by trauma and the academic discursive field: the different names for memory—"field, observer, collective, cultural, textual"—"that made sense only in closed seminar rooms" (82). For Renu, Savi discusses the violence in "a language so clouded that it spun out of meaning" (99). Salgado juxtaposes these abstract ideas with the unofficial human stories behind headlines, notably the impact of the island's conflicts on the most vulnerable: the Muslim boy who witnessed his father's abduction and the murder of his mother and sister by the LTTE, but insists they are safe in the forest "even though we had found the bodies of them all" (165). Salgado includes real historical events recognizable to readers familiar with contemporary Sri Lankan history. These include the murders of the poet and journalist Richard de Zoysa by government forces in 1990 and the human rights activist Rajani Thiranagama, gunned down by the LTTE for criticizing the group in 1989. At the same time these inclusions provide European and American students insight into the trauma and loss that haunt Sri Lanka.

Furthermore, the novel interleaves ethnic and political violence within a broader critique of patriarchal violence. Detailing Renu's assault and the domestic violence experienced by the family's long-serving cook, Josilin, whose "bruises . . . swelled into unnamed shades of damage," the author notes Josilin's employers' complicity with her "silence" in their "acceptance that there was nothing to be done" (182). This is linked to the novel's critique of Buddhism. It suggests the emphasis on karma inculcates the acceptance of violence and hinders civil society. The novel links familial and national violence through the willed amnesia of karma deployed to buttress the lie that "there was no point trying to enforce earthly mechanisms of justice" (183).

The Moon in the Water, a novel by the Sri Lanka–based writer Ameena Hussein that was long-listed for the Booker Prize, similarly complicates nationalist, essentialized binaries of Sinhalese versus Tamils, with its insights into a Sri Lankan Muslim family seldom explored in Sri Lankan fiction, even though Muslims constitute the island's second-largest ethnic minority. The novel constructs an affectionate portrait of the contradictions of a privileged Colombo Muslim family, the members of which see themselves as modern and broad-minded even as "they bundled up [their daughter Khadeeja's] sleeveless dresses and shoved them to the back of her cupboard" and arranged her engagement. Through a trigenerational structure comparing the subversive Khadeeja (who breaks off the betrothal organized by her parents, initiates a relationship with the Malawian Abdullah, and further defies convention by living with her fiancé) with her mother, RaushenGul, and her grandmother Sara, Hussein traces a minority community in transition and explores her Islamic heritage from a feminist perspective.

Set in Sri Lanka in 2005, Hussein's unconventional novel, part bildungsroman and part love story, scrutinizes ethnicity, family ties, and patriarchal interpretations of Islam; it lends itself for discussion in a range of courses on feminism, including postcolonial feminism, and literature. The novel's feminist critique of rigid, authoritarian, and patriarchal interpretations of Islam begins with the *iddah*, the widow's compulsory mourning period of four months and ten days. It highlights Sara's and the wider community's "insensitivity and haste to rush [RaushenGul] into secluded widowhood" soon after the trauma of losing her husband to a violent, sudden death when caught up in an LTTE bomb attack (25). RaushenGul questions the premise of *iddah* and the need to ascertain the father's identity should the widow be pregnant and wish to marry again quickly. RaushenGul reasons "if a woman who has just been widowed desires to contract another marriage immediately on her husband's death . . . and if her new husband to be is willing to accept the financial responsibility of looking after the child . . . then who cares about paternity? Secondly, what about women like me, who are past the age of child-bearing?" (37). RaushenGul values individual discernment and belief above blind allegiance to some of her community's dogmatic imperatives. She tells her mother, Sara, who internalizes and reproduces dogmatic interpretations of Islamic codes, "[E]verything about Islam is interpretation. So you keep to your interpretation and I shall keep to mine." Sara insists, "It is *not* interpretation it is Islam. We have our ways of doing things, ways that have been in existence for generations. Who do you think you are to change them to suit your convenience?" (38).

The novel clearly promotes Islamic revisionism. RaushenGul's interrogation of Islamic customs is a deliberate revival of the spirit of inquiry and the tradition of respected Muslim women philosophers during the early decades of Islam, as discussed by feminist scholars, most notably Leila Ahmed. This self-conscious revival of Islamic traditions of rational inquiry is underscored by the symbolic naming of the protagonist Khadeeja after the prophet Muhammad's first wife, an iconic figure of feminist agency in

Muslim historiography, as Ahmed's invaluable study makes clear. Economically independent Khadeeja proposed to the much younger Muhammad and remained his only wife until her death. This allusion to the revival of progressive Islamic traditions also serves to counter received ideas that Islam requires modernization by Western influences. This is an important but subtle part of the text's politics. RaushenGul self-arranges her marriage contrary to customs revolving around family obligation. Moreover, RaushenGul's feminist agency and decisiveness are emphasized above her husband's as she "pounces inelegantly" and pronounces Muhammed Rasheed "my husband" (32). The novel further avoids tired, binary contrasts between liberated women in the Global North and their oppressed counterparts in the Global South. It juxtaposes female oppression within this extended family, with Christine, Khadeeja's brother's German girlfriend, recollecting her mother's regrets and advice to her daughter to lead a more empowered life than hers: "Be a somebody in life. Don't settle for being a nobody. Don't be like me, Christine, don't be like me" (81). The novel privileges RaushenGul's and Khadeeja's interpretations of Islam that embody how the future ideally should be, with possibilities for greater freedoms for women and men above Sara's outdated interpretation. However, it skillfully avoids caricature or schematic generational differences by probing these characters' complexity with nuance, texture, and context, presenting Sara as a "daunting" matriarchal figure "who could be silenced only by her husband and that too with difficulty" (26). Yet Sara accepts and perpetuates the gendered burden of transmitting cultural values, an ambivalence characteristic of many matriarchs in South Asia. The novel thus interleaves issues of Islamic culture and female emancipation by suggesting that Muslim women have agency in nonobvious ways and could derive a feminist political theory specifically from their own cultural histories, background, and experience. Such a reading can encourage students to consider not only the limitations of reading from a Western perspective but also from a Eurocentric feminist one.

Homesick is the finely structured debut collection of linked short stories by the British Sri Lankan writer Roshi Fernando. It gives voice to four generations of a Sri Lankan family living in South London and challenges expectations of female-authored diasporic writing. The collection centers on Preethi and her extended Sri Lankan family and their circle of friends. The tales unfold in loose, chronological progression over thirty years or so, moving from Preethi's childhood and delineating her teenage romances and her marriage in middle age. While Sri Lanka's civil war hovers in the background, Fernando's most powerful and moving stories exceed questions of identity and belonging. Instead they explore marital unease ("The Barn Dance"), teenage sexual drama, adult sexual and gender politics, and the challenges of parenting children with disabilities ("The Turtle"), as well as the dark, tragic topics of the murder of beloved sons ("A Bottle of Whisky") and of mothers ("Mumtaz Chaplin") and child abuse ("The Fluorescent Jacket").

Fernando invites the reader to reflect on the relation between personal and sociohistorical realities and on the self-perpetuation of different forms of violence, most powerfully in her award-winning story "The Fluorescent Jacket," which innovatively fuses the political and the personal. It is narrated through the eyes of Kumar, a newly arrived immigrant from Sri Lanka to 1960s Britain who speaks very little English. Housed unwillingly by his cousin Shamini in an environment hostile to migrants, he works illegally and finally performs unpaid labor as a park gardener; the fluorescent jacket provided to him gives him a sense of pride, for it is the only thing he owns. Yet this voluntary work makes him a suspect when the bodies of young murdered girls are discovered in the park and he is wrongfully imprisoned. Although innocent of these murders, he has begun to sexually abuse Shamini's eight-year-old daughter, Louisa. The abuse is anticipated subtly early on in the story before it is revealed. His nieces "are like puppies, he thinks, watching their bottoms wobble" (40). Later we learn that he too had been abused as a child: "He enjoys [Louisa's] fear. . . . He remembers feeling how she feels" (47). The repetition of abuse within this familial context is mapped onto a wider politics. In a masterful delayed plot development, right at the close of the story we learn that at the age of twelve Kumar was sold to a German tourist for a summer, recalling a history of white pedophiles visiting Sri Lanka, a notorious spot for neocolonial sex tourism particularly in 1970s and 1980s. Moreover, the money Kumar "earned" that summer paid for "Shamini's life in England" (53); "she owes [Kumar's] father money and that is why she continues to have him under her roof" (44). The circulation of capital at the expense of the exploited is succinctly conveyed. For Fernando, Kumar represents "a symbol of colonialism repeated over and over: Sri Lanka is an abused country, battered out of colonialism" (Fernando, "Undateable" 27:00–27:22). Earlier, the story alerts us to the unequal, neocolonial valuation of lives in the First and Third Worlds partly internalized by the Global South. In the outcry over the missing British girls, Kumar observes, "[C]hildren go missing all the time in Sri Lanka. I went missing for a time. No one cried for me" (44).

Fernando's intervention is also a feminist one that focuses explicitly on the gendered politics of sex and agency. In "Sophocles' Chorus," teenager Preethi tastes the "eroticism of becoming a woman, the eroticism of making a choice to kiss Ollie, not being chosen from the pack of girls at a party, like a boy taking a Top Trump card" (104). "The Comfort, the Joy" voices the still inadmissible desires of older women, with the middle-aged widow expressing desire for "sex in [her] *head*" (162), while "Honeyskin" explores sexual desires and orientations that are not easily labeled or confined to a category. Dorothy, an elderly widow, misses sex with her husband of forty-five years, whom she loved intensely even though her fantasies were always lesbian. She wants to tell her daughter Stella, "I loved your father but . . ." (261). Like all the characters in the collection "homesick" for something, Dorothy is yearning for her own sexual identity, but the story also weaves in questions about genealogy. Her father was the son of a British headmaster in Colombo who married a local Sri Lankan schoolteacher. However, mixed-race Dorothy does not know much about her past. She tries to decipher her gendered, sexual identity from photographs of a maiden aunt in Sri Lanka. She wonders if her daughter's gay sexuality and her own is hereditary: "genealogy and genetics are peculiar sciences . . . and I hold no truck with them. And yet, Stella?" (261). In this regard, Fernando's works are radical and variegated, in terms of her exploration of alternative sexualities and her inhabitation of narratorial perspectives rarely addressed in fiction, as in Kumar the child abuser and Mumtaz Chaplin's heartbreaking story of why he refuses to speak (he fears he will sound like his father, who murdered his mother when pregnant with a second child).

Hussein, Salgado, and Fernando could be taught in a range of courses and fields, including South Asia studies, postcolonial literary and globalization studies, and contemporary, transnational feminisms, as well as those focused on war, conflict, and memory. These authors amplify students' understanding of issues peculiar to Sri Lankan history and experience in diverse, nuanced ways that often transcend specificities.

Notes

1. Important country-specific contexts include universal franchise in 1931, a high literacy rate in vernacular Sinhala and Tamil, and higher levels of female education in comparison with other subcontinental nations. English—only one strand of Sri Lanka's rich literary and linguistic heritage—is spoken as a first language by less than one percent of the population. Although proficiency levels

exceed this, access to English remains classed; anglophone writing in Sri Lanka is therefore haunted by questions about the extent to which it is circumscribed within the interests and viewpoints of the privileged.

2. For a fuller discussion of literary representations that naturalize a certain colonialist understanding of Sri Lanka as a place of endemic violence, and the apparent fixity of the violent present, see Ranasinha.

Works Cited

Ahmed, Leila. *Women and Gender in Islam: Historical Roots of a Modern Debate.* Yale UP, 1992.

de Mel, Neloufer. *Women and the Nation's Narrative: Gender and Nationalism in Twentieth-Century Sri Lanka.* Kali for Women, 2001.

Fernando, Roshi. *Homesick.* Bloomsbury, 2012.

———. "The Undateable." *Woman's Hour*, BBC Radio 4, 3 Apr. 2012, www.bbc.co.uk/programmes/b01f5lcj.

Hussein, Ameena. *The Moon in the Water.* Perera-Hussein, 2009.

Ondaatje, Michael. *Anil's Ghost.* Vintage Books, 2000.

Ranasinha, Ruvani. "Writing and Reading Sri Lanka: Shifting Politics of Cultural Translation, Consumption, and the Implied Reader." *The Journal of Commonwealth Literature*, vol. 48, no. 1, 2013, pp. 28–39.

Salgado, Minoli. *A Little Dust on the Eyes.* Peepal Tree Press, 2014.

Maryse Jayasuriya

War and Identity: Writing the Sri Lankan Ethnic Conflict

The United States–Mexico border may seem an unlikely space for spirited discussion of anglophone Sri Lankan literature. El Paso, Texas, is a long way from South Asia and a long way even from the major tech sector hubs in Austin and Houston that have attracted numerous South Asian immigrants. Yet I have found that writing by Sri Lankan women on matters of war, violence, and identity have proved tremendously resonant for many of my students in this region, resulting in research into these matters that goes well beyond the classroom.

Questions of war, violence, and identity compose a significant part of my classes, from undergraduate surveys of postcolonial literature to graduate seminars in South Asian literature, the literature of decolonization, and the literature of war, violence, and terrorism. A cluster of women who have written about the Sri Lankan ethnic conflict that lasted from 1983 to 2009 provides a particularly valuable set of insights into how issues of war and identity are mobilized in South Asian women's writing. Jean Arasanayagam, Vivimarie VanderPoorten, Anne Ranasinghe, and V. V. Ganeshananthan have written about the conflict from various minority vantage points within Sri Lankan society, revealing what the conflict has meant from a variety of subject positions, particularly for Sri Lankan women who in one way or another have been involved in or affected by the war.

My department does not have any classes specifically on South Asian women writers. Therefore, I try to include the work of as many such writers as I can into the framework of each class that I design. My department's course offerings are built around English and American literature, with cultural studies functioning as a loosely defined category for everything that doesn't seem to fit within those two national literatures. South Asia figures largely as a subset of postcolonial literature for our curriculum; ensuring that the voices of the writers I have mentioned above can be heard often calls for creativity in course design. I have worked these authors into a graduate class on genre; a graduate class on literature and culture; undergraduate classes on theory, postcolonial literature, and world literature—classes that I cross-list with women's and gender studies or with Asian studies—and even a graduate class on British literature from 1832 to the present, which I have designed as a course on empire and postcolonial literatures in English. As a result, students at the University of Texas, El Paso, now frequently have the opportunity to encounter writing by South Asian, and particularly Sri Lankan, women that might otherwise be inaccessible to them.

Sri Lanka's ethnic conflict had its origins in 1956, when a law was passed making Sinhala, the language of the majority ethnic group, the only official language of the newly postcolonial country. When the largest minority group, the Tamils, protested, riots ensued. In 1972 other laws—including one that limited educational opportunities for ethnic minorities—were passed that disenfranchised the Tamils even further. This led to the ethnic conflict, which started with riots targeting Tamils in 1983 and continued in various permutations until the defeat of the dominant Tamil militant group, the Liberation Tigers of Tamil Eelam (LTTE), by the government in 2009. Arasanayagam, Ganeshananthan, Ranasinghe, and VanderPoorten all provide opportunities to explore how this conflict has intersected with Sri Lankan women's lives and writings.

Identity, Language, and Postcoloniality

In my undergraduate postcolonial literature class, I have used the poetry of Arasanayagam, VanderPoorten, and Ranasinghe to help my students understand the intersections of identity and postcoloniality, drawing upon my scholarly work on anglophone Sri Lankan literature in *Terror and Reconciliation*. Arasanayagam is a Burgher—a descendant of Dutch colonizers who settled in Sri Lanka—and writes about what it means for her to have pride in her bold seafaring Dutch ancestors even as she feels guilt at the thought that those same ancestors might have raped Sri Lankan women in addition to exploiting the country's land and resources:

> The blood of the colonizer that runs
> In my veins is also the blood of the
> Colonized, an island invaded
> An island raped. ("Colonizer/Colonized," lines 1–4)

Arasanayagam is living proof of her country's colonial past and does not find it easy or even possible to subsume one part of her identity for another, in the same way that the speaker in Derek Walcott's "A Far Cry from Africa" emphasizes being "divided to the vein" (27) because of his mixed ancestry.

VanderPoorten, the daughter of a Burgher father and a Sinhalese mother, is marked both by her appearance and her Western name and is quizzed about her identity. In "Doppelganger," she writes about her first brush with racism at ten years old, when a schoolmate calls her *para lansiya*, a derogatory Sinhala epithet that literally means "outsider from Holland":

> the shock stained
> like
> ink
> on fingers
> the first time
> with a fountain pen (lines 9–14)

The speaker in the poem writes about being thus singled out "to bear the collective blame / for my foreign sounding name" (lines 25–26). The speaker says that she didn't realize how traumatic this moment had been for her until

> years later
> in a foreign land
> it found its doppelganger:
> —"Paki bitch." (lines 33–36)

The racist remark that is hurled at her in a host land brings back to her the shame and embarrassment of the earlier insult she experienced in her homeland; the pejoratives underscore the fact that she is perceived as belonging in neither place.

The poetry of Arasanayagam and VanderPoorten helps my students understand the full complexity of Homi Bhabha's concept of hybridity: the "interstitial passage between fixed identification opens up the possibility of a cultural hybridity that entertains difference without an assumed or imposed hierarchy" (4). As Neloufer de Mel has asserted, hybrid identities are called into question particularly during times of war and conflict when opposing sides resort to originary myths of purity in order to validate their respective claims. By insisting on the existence and value of hybridity in their poetry, Arasanayagam and VanderPoorten use their own complex identities as a means of resisting these myths of purity. As a Christian Burgher married to a Tamil Hindu, Arasanayagam has to respond to questions about her identity as well as her loyalty during the ethnic conflict:

> The talk comes up
> In odd places
> Who are you?
> What are you? ("Question" lines 1–4)

Her attempts at explaining and classifying her ethnic and religious affiliations do not prevent her from being viewed with suspicion: eventually she is compelled to flee with her family to a refugee camp in the midst of mob violence. As Arasanayagam writes in "Aftermath," "I didn't know this country, I didn't know / That I didn't belong until I was surrounded / Hunted out and forced to disclose my identity" (lines 91–93). This sense of exclusion and threat translates powerfully into the context of the United States–Mexico borderlands, where immigration status can be a matter of constant anxiety for those without documents.

The Kenyan writer Ngugi wa Thiong'o has argued that language is a carrier of culture and that postcolonial writers need to turn their backs on the colonizer's language and enrich the literatures of their respective mother tongues, while Salman Rushdie has claimed the English language as a tool that postcolonial writers have at hand to use as they will. Since language was an important factor in the Sri Lankan ethnic conflict, I teach VanderPoorten's poem "Diplomatic" in the unit about language and postcoloniality. In the poem, a British woman—seemingly oblivious about English being a colonial legacy that was imposed on and then appropriated by the colonized—is surprised that the speaker is a creative writer, a poet, in English. In response, the speaker's

> smile turns
> apologetic
> for a reason that can't find its voice
> in poetry or prose. (lines 18–21)

At this moment the speaker realizes—somewhat like Stephen Dedalus in James Joyce's *Portrait of the Artist as a Young Man*—that despite her mastery of English, the language is not considered hers and that perhaps she has internalized this idea, which is why she nods "a diplomatic yes" (line 22) instead of challenging her interlocutor's assumption. My students, the majority of whom identify as Hispanic, have much to say about their experiences with language issues on the border between the United States and Mexico. In their daily journal responses to reading assignments, which provide a springboard for class discussions, some students mention their difficulties as native Spanish speakers having to use English in the classroom, while others discuss stories that their parents or grandparents have told them about being forced to learn English in school in earlier decades and being penalized if they lapsed into Spanish.

War, Violence, and Terrorism

Matters of language and identity are necessarily threaded into any discussion of Sri Lanka's ethnic conflict and the terrorism by state and nonstate actors that it involved. At a time when global terrorism is a major concern, I have found it useful to consider the complexities of conflict through literature. I have designed a course built around just these themes, concentrating on contemporary depictions of war, violence, and terrorism in fiction, nonfiction, poetry, film, and theoretical works. Students explore a variety of questions, including the purpose of focusing on war, violence, and terrorism in a literary work—whether war is merely a plot device, a voyeuristic and exploitative exercise, or whether there is an attempt to depict a specific reality. Students consider whether such writing distorts reality and whether it affects people's perceptions, thereby creating an impact on real-life situations. A particular concern is how terrorist acts and the aftermath of such violence are depicted and if it is ethical to humanize terrorists, particularly suicide bombers. Other issues examined include how we retrieve hidden or forgotten histories of war, how women participate in war, the role of humor in depictions of war, the rhetoric associated with concepts like heroism and terrorism, the relation between trauma and memory, and the significance of grieving and mourning. I begin the class with literature dealing with 9/11 and its aftermath, followed by literary works dealing with conflicts in different regions. For the unit on Sri Lanka, I assign novels like Michael Ondaatje's *Anil's Ghost*, Shyam Selvadurai's *Funny Boy*, and Ganeshananthan's *Love Marriage* along with poetry. I pair the assigned primary sources with theoretical discussions on violence, trauma, and mourning, including excerpts from Frantz Fanon's *The Wretched of the Earth*, Cathy Caruth's *Unclaimed Experience*, and Judith Butler's *Precarious Life*.

My students and I discuss the poetry of Arasanayagam and VanderPoorten, which records the violence of a constantly evolving war situation. In her collection *Apocalypse '83*, Arasanayagam has written poignantly about her experience during the pogrom of July 1983, when Sinhalese mobs targeted Tamil homes and businesses, destroying property and killing the owners. She also writes about what it means to be compelled to leave one's home and seek safe haven in a refugee camp. Arasanayagam conveys how much everything has changed for her as a result of this trauma: what she would previously have considered sacred or beautiful are now merely reminders of violence. In "If the Gun Speaks," for example, the scarlet hibiscus that decorate a statue of the Hindu god Ganesh look like "gouts of blood" (7). In the poem "Flamboyants in July—from a Refugee Camp," the speaker gazes at the flamboyant trees in bloom, "scarlet as if the clouds / were pricked with blood" (lines 3–4). Seeing the clouds framing the profusion of red flowers on the trees, the speaker thinks of bruises and welts covering the body of a tortured, unnamed "you" that she is apostrophizing, while the "scarlet pools of fallen flowers" (line 25) only bring to mind the blood that has been spilled in such careless abundance in the streets.

VanderPoorten has recorded experiences of the conflict from many different perspectives. She writes very personal poems about living through daily reports of violence ("Haiku: War"; "Diary of Bombs"; "Explosion"), the trauma of such violence on victims and survivors ("Vadani in Our Hostel"), internally displaced persons in camps ("Love, Displaced"), and journalists assassinated in broad daylight ("Death at Noon"). Many of my students are familiar with or have witnessed the drug violence that occurred in El Paso's sister city, Ciudad Juárez, from 2008 to 2012 and are able to relate to the experience of living with violence on a daily basis. Both the analogies and the differences between the Sri Lankan and Mexican contexts for violence become important in our class discussions.

In the same class I teach Ganeshananthan's novel *Love Marriage*, which explores collective trauma and how a conflict raging in the homeland continues in a host land within a diasporic community, making an impact on the lives of second- and third-generation immigrants. Ganeshananthan, born and raised in the United States, explores how Yalini, the daughter of Sri Lankan Tamil immigrants, moves—as Kachig Tololyan has put it—from being "ethnic" to being "diasporic" by becoming more involved with the original homeland (13). The arrival of her uncle, who has long been a member of the LTTE, prompts Yalini to learn more about what led to the ethnic conflict in Sri Lanka by reading scholarly material on the topic and by interviewing family members and collecting their stories. Yalini is adamant about the need for preserving experiences through stories but uses fragmentation, multiple perspectives, and even blank pages as narrative strategies to emphasize the inevitability of omissions, elisions, lapses in memory, and competing and contradictory narratives.

In order to enable students to get some context about the Sri Lankan conflict and also explore how ethnicity, gender, and activism intersect, I show my students the documentary *No More Tears Sister*, which deals with the Sri Lankan medical doctor, university professor, and human rights activist Rajani Thiranagama, who was a critic of both the Sri Lankan government's ethnic chauvinism and the LTTE's atrocities; she was assassinated by the LTTE for being a dissident. The documentary includes letters written by Thiranagama, which provide an additional dimension about a woman's competing imperatives as a professional, a mother, and an activist. If Thiranagama emerges as a martyr for human rights, tolerance, and freedom of expression, my courses also try to take account of less admirable ways in which martyrdom has been invoked in Sri Lanka. The intersections of ethnicity, gender, and violence are also evident in the figure of the female suicide bomber, which has received much attention in recent years but has also frequently been sensationalized. I assign Amila Weerasinghe's poem "Suicide Bomber" along with the film *The Terrorist*, which explore, in a nuanced way, the motivations of women who make the choice to become suicide bombers. Considering these works helps to encourage thoughtful discussions about the complexities and role of women within the conflict in Sri Lanka.

Throughout my classes, I try to make connections between Sri Lankan literature and wider South Asian and postcolonial contexts. The German-born Jewish Sri Lankan poet Anne Ranasinghe lost her entire family in the Holocaust; she later married a Sri Lankan doctor and moved to his homeland. Her poetry, which deals with collective trauma, allows me to establish a still wider context for the violence in Sri Lanka. She focuses on seeing the ethnic conflict in Sri Lanka through the Holocaust in poems such as "July 1983." She begins the poem by wondering whether former Nazis and those complicit in their crimes are haunted by guilt. For decades she has been attempting to understand why people chose to do what they did—both those who carried out the atrocities of the Holocaust and the bystanders who passively observed the horrors without stepping forward to intervene. The focus of the poem changes to memory and guilt in a Sri Lankan context.

> Forty years later
> once more there is burning
> the night sky bloodied, violent and abused
> and I—though related
> only by marriage—
> feel myself both victim and accused. (lines 19–24)

In "Memory Is Our Shield, Our Only Shield," Ranasinghe examines the significance of memorials and mourning as a stay against atrocities:

> A memorial is the final seal
> Upon the grief
> It is a link
> Between past and future
> . . . .
> It is evil to forget
> It is necessary to remember.
> For memory is our shield, our only shield.
> The memorial warns:
> Six million Jews. (lines 22–25, 28–32)

Ranasinghe's call to mourn, to memorialize, and to remember is not for the purpose of finding a way out of guilt but to ensure, by means of a full awareness and understanding of reality, that history does not repeat itself. I play for my students recordings of Ranasinghe's poetry, which are available through the Library of Congress.

A challenge facing anyone trying to teach Sri Lankan women's literature is the limited availability of important texts. Although Ganeshananthan's *Love Marriage* is readily available in stores, many other texts by women about the Sri Lankan ethnic conflict are not. I have dealt with this problem in part by purchasing books in Sri Lanka myself and bringing them back so I can provide readings to students (I post short readings on *Blackboard*), but this may not be an option for everyone. I am pleased that some of the more recent books by Sri Lankan women are becoming more available through commercial venues in the United States. The works of Arasanayagam and VanderPoorten can be purchased online and have been anthologized in collections such as Sukrita Paul Kumar and Malashri Lal's *Speaking for Myself* and Selvadurai's *Many Roads through Paradise.*

My students have benefited from reading these works because they have had the opportunity to engage broadly and deeply with Sri Lankan cultural and political histories that would otherwise be unfamiliar. Their understanding of South Asia is enriched by their reading of Sri Lankan women's writing alongside more visible writing from India and Pakistan, and the graduate classes have produced papers that are more nuanced and ambitious because they take in a wider range of literary materials. Sri Lanka is certainly a long way from the United States–Mexico border, but the issues raised in the fiction and poetry that I teach by Sri Lankan women undoubtedly have global resonance.

Works Cited

Arasanayagam, Jean. "Aftermath." Arasanayagam, *Apocalypse*, pp. 86–89.

———. *Apocalypse '83.* International Centre for Ethnic Studies, 2003.

———. "Colonizer/Colonized." *Colonizer/Colonized: Poems from a Postcolonial Diary*, Writers Workshop, 2000, pp. 16–17.

———. "Flamboyants in July—from a Refugee Camp." Arasanayagam, *Apocalypse*, p. 78.

———. "If the Gun Speaks." Arasanayagam, *Apocalypse*, p. 74.

———. "A Question of Identity." *Reddened Water Flows Clear*, Forest, 1991, pp. 82–85.

Bhabha, Homi K. *The Location of Culture.* Routledge, 1994.

Butler, Judith. *Precarious Life: The Powers of Mourning and Violence.* Verso, 2004.

Caruth, Cathy. *Unclaimed Experience: Trauma, Narrative, and History.* Johns Hopkins UP, 1996.

de Mel, Neloufer. *Women and the Nation's Narrative: Gender and Nationalism in Twentieth-Century Sri Lanka.* Rowman and Littlefield, 2001.

Fanon, Frantz. *The Wretched of the Earth.* 1961. Translated by Richard Philcox, Grove Press, 2004.

Ganeshananthan, V. V. *Love Marriage.* Random House, 2008.

Jayasuriya, Maryse. *Terror and Reconciliation: Sri Lankan Anglophone Literature, 1983–2009.* Lexington, 2012.

Kumar, Sukrita Paul, and Malashri Lal, editors. *Speaking for Myself: An Anthology of Asian Women's Writing.* Penguin Enterprise, 2009.

No More Tears Sister: Anatomy of Hope and Betrayal. Directed by Helene Klodawsky, National Film Board of Canada, 2005.

Ondaatje, Michael. *Anil's Ghost.* Knopf, 2000.

Ranasinghe, Anne. *At What Dark Point.* English Writers Cooperative of Sri Lanka, 1991.

———. "July 1983." Ranasinghe, *At What Dark Point*, p. 171.

———. "Memory Is Our Shield, Our Only Shield." Ranasinghe, *At What Dark Point*, pp. 156–57.

Rushdie, Salman. "Commonwealth Literature Does Not Exist." *Imaginary Homelands: Essays and Criticism, 1981–1991*, Granta, 1991, pp. 59–70.

Selvadurai, Shyam. *Funny Boy.* Harcourt Brace, 1994.

———, editor. *Many Roads through Paradise: An Anthology of Sri Lankan Literature.* Penguin, 2014.

The Terrorist. Directed by Santosh Sivan, performance by Ayesha Dharkar and K. Krishna, Movie Gallerie, 1998.

Tololyan, Khachig. "Rethinking *Diaspora*(s): Stateless Power in the Transnational Moment." *Diaspora: A Journal of Transnational Studies*, vol. 5, no. 1, Spring 1996, pp. 3–36.

VanderPoorten, Vivimarie. "Death at Noon." VanderPoorten, *Stitch*, pp. 38–39.

———. "Diary of Bombs." VanderPoorten, *Stitch*, p. 59.

———. "Diplomatic." VanderPoorten, *Stitch*, p. 71.

———. "Doppelganger." VanderPoorten, *Nothing*, pp. 60–61.

———. "Explosion." VanderPoorten, *Nothing*, p. 35.

———. "Haiku: War." VanderPoorten, *Nothing*, p. 73.

———. "Love, Displaced." VanderPoorten, *Stitch*, pp. 10–11.

———. *Nothing Prepares You.* Zeus, 2007.

———. *Stitch Your Eyelids Shut.* Akna, 2010.

———. "Vadani in Our Hostel." VanderPoorten, *Stitch*, pp. 5–6.

Walcott, Derek. "A Far Cry from Africa." *Collected Poems, 1948–1984*, Farrar, Straus and Giroux, 1998, pp. 17–18.

wa Thiong'o, Ngugi. *Decolonizing the Mind: The Politics of Language in African Literature.* J. Currey / Heinemann, 1986.

Weerasinghe, Amila. "Suicide Bomber." *Channels: A Compendium of Creative Writing, 1989–2001*, English Writers Cooperative of Sri Lanka, 2001, p. 63.

Harleen Singh

Interior Spaces in Tahmima Anam's *A Golden Age*

How should the political be framed in teaching South Asian women's writing? The following analysis reconfigures the space of interiority—often read as women's disengagement from tumultuous national moments—in the Bangladeshi writer Tahmima Anam's *A Golden Age* as a complex literary representation that imparts agency to the individual while elaborating upon the contested histories and antagonisms of the national political location. Instead of demarcating the interior, psychological, and domestic narrative as a mere retreat from the public space, the inner lives described by Anam offer significant insights about the so-called externalized phenomenon of nation, culture, and politics. This essay engages a feminist analysis of nationalism through a reading of the domestic and psychological, to provide a productive frame of reference for the wider historical processes that define nations and their narratives in South Asian women's writing.

Rethinking the political dimension of the interior can also impact the teaching of South Asian women's writing: instead of relegating family and personal stories to the domain of the private, my approach suggests that these texts can provide a pedagogical lens to reimagine the boundaries of politics in the classroom. Through these novels, students might be encouraged to reflect on these questions: What counts as politics? Should we, following Aijaz Ahmad's famous essay on Arundhati Roy, read (and teach) South Asian writers politically? But how should teachers circumscribe the space of the political? How do introspective narratives become endowed with political values? Drawing on my experience of teaching South Asian women's writing in a university environment in the United States, I propose that Anam's novel be considered a compelling meditation on the intersections between life writing and the historiographical document, a shifting terrain ultimately leading students to reflect on the gendered dimension of the narratives of nation, class, and culture. While the internalized first-person, personal narrative in women's writing is often read as limiting, if not enfeebling, I suggest instead that these inner voices expound as easily on the broader political arguments determined by the frames of nation, culture, and politics as on the personal.

These voices provide a productive way of countering monolithic readings of the national, which is often identified by large-scale political movements or the personages who constitute the pantheon of the nation's leaders; the inner lives depicted in this novel offer a salient representation of the dilemmas of the postcolonial citizen. Thus, I focus on those moments and passages where the narrative is centered on a female character peripheral to the large politics of the nation, in order to show that even these "small" spaces allow for a more nuanced reading of women's texts in relation to the political. These passages postulate a more complex vision that gestures toward an alternative reading of women as fluid, contradictory, and purposeful in questioning the boundaries between private and public, memory and history, individual and collective. Anam's *A Golden Age* depicts events placed roughly in the 1970s and features characters who do not take part in the center stage of national history. In the classroom, this text can be used to challenge students to displace and redraw the borders between political and literary discourses and to question the arbitrary binary between the personal and the political. While feminist theorization in the United States, at least in second-wave feminism, was built on the "personal is political" adage, Anam complicates that as her protagonist Rehana loses her children precisely because the personal is political under the Pakistani judiciary's interpretation of Islamic law. *A Golden Age* negotiates between a strict separation of the domestic and the national, the personal and the political, and also the difficulty in creating these separate spheres in the lives of postcolonial citizens. In the following sections, I propose a reading that restructures politics at the juncture between history and narration and outline a pedagogical vision that could stimulate further debate in the classroom.

Reading Anam's *A Golden Age*

Anam, who currently lives in London, was born in Dhaka and raised in New York City, Paris, and Bangkok. *A Golden Age*, her debut novel published in 2007, has gained great critical success since its publication and was shortlisted for various literary prizes, including the Costa Book Award for First Novel. In an interview for *The Guardian*, Anam explains the origins of her first novel:

> After graduating from university I started a PhD in social anthropology, but really I was dreaming of writing a novel. . . . It was when I started doing the research that it became more real. I travelled back to Bangladesh and met survivors of the Bangladesh war. After hearing their stories, I felt that I really ought to take the project more seriously, and that's when I began writing the novel in earnest. ("First Look")

The novel builds, as Anam reveals in this interview, on fieldwork research with survivors of the Bangladesh war, one of the most violent episodes of twentieth-century South Asian history. As Willem van Schendel observes in his *History of Bangladesh*, to tell "the story of the war is not easy because so many things were happening at the same time—and so much is still fiercely contested" (161). Indeed, alongside the main struggle between the Pakistani army and the Bangladeshi nationalists, there is a multilayered history including the partitioning of the Bengal region, the victimization of ethnic and religious minorities, the displacement of thousands of people, the "local vendettas and the settling of personal scores" (161), and the links between the civil war and larger dynamics such as the antagonism between India and Pakistan and the Cold War. The tensions and complexities of the history of Bangladesh have their roots in the aftermath of partition. As Nazneen Ahmed writes in a pivotal essay, the creation of Pakistan as a bilateral state presented "a unique cultural challenge," because "the two wings of the state . . . were separated by 700 miles of Indian territory. Culturally and linguistically, the two wings had little in common, except religion" (257).

The legacy of the 1971 war still affects contemporary politics in Bangladesh. In 2013 a massive national protest erupted as a response to the disputed sentencing of a war criminal by the International Crimes Tribunal of Bangladesh, a war tribunal instituted in the country in 1998 and still at work to shed light on the crimes committed in the 1970s. During the events of 2013, known as the Shahbag protest, an atheist blogger was killed, an episode followed by the killing of other bloggers in 2015 and the rise of fundamentalist tendencies in the country. In 1971, while the majority of the East Pakistanis supported the war effort against West Pakistan, certain Islamic political parties continued to support the established government and collaborated in war crimes. And though these parties, specifically the Jamaat-e-Islami party, are now allied with other political parties in power in Bangladesh, the International Crimes Tribunal convicted some members of the Jamaat-e-Islami for war crimes. While most protesters demanded harsher sentences for the convicted persons, a sizable group also turned out to protest against the convictions. Political engagements reframing the unstable and conflictual situation in contemporary Bangladesh can be traced back to the wounds and unresolved tensions left over by the 1971 conflict, the partition of India, and earlier attempts to partition Bengal by the British in 1905. As Salil Tripathi writes, these conflicts derive from "two forms of identity struggling within the Bangladeshi soul—Muslim and Bengali" (vii).

A Golden Age brings recognition to a period of history that remains neglected in larger narratives of decolonization and that still affects the political landscape of the region. Set at the onset of the 1971 civil war, the novel charts a trajectory of revolution and instability in the life of the protagonist Rehana Haque. A widowed mother, Rehana loses custody of her children to her husband's family in a court decree that declares, "She was too young to take care of the children on her own. She had not taught them the proper lessons about *Jannat* and the afterlife" (5). Islamic, patriarchal dictates rupture Rehana's family, and it is a decision that pronounces Rehana unfit owing to her inexperience, age, and lack of dedication to religious education. As Clemency Burton-Hill notes in a review of the novel published in *The Guardian*, for the protagonist of the novel, "born in the western 'horn' but living in 1971 in the Bengali East, the chasm dividing Pakistan has long been metaphorical as well as geographic." The division between East and West Pakistan, which led to the formation of Bangladesh in 1971, redefines Rehana's sense of belonging and distances her from her own family. The novel shows how political divisions cut through families, communities, and, in the end, the very sense of subjectivity of the protagonist of this important novel.

At the onset, Rehana is defined as an unsuitable mother who cannot nurture a proper citizen; she is, as an ethnic Bengali, an educated woman and one not averse to Western books or culture, at a distance from what constitutes the right national narrative. Yet, it is, as Anam points out, a deeply political moment that exhorts the reader to reassess how domestic lives are traversed by the state: "we need to expand our notion of the political. It isn't just writing about revolutions or armed struggles, it can also be about the politics of the family or relationships" ("Interview"). The "politics of the family" are navigated often in postcolonial contexts through the contradictory dictates of the nation-state, and it is imperative to read "revolutions" alongside "relationships" in South Asian women's writings.

Rehana eventually manages to regain custody of her children, and the novel begins at this juncture where the individual's happiness is punctuated by unrest in the country: a reminder that no sense of the personal can exist outside a conjunction with the particularly volatile postcolonial politics of South Asia. Bookended by the compelling use of the epistolary mode in Rehana's letters to her dead husband, the novel creates an interior monologue that seems to privilege the anxious reflections of the maternal. When her children—ideologically committed young college students—find themselves in the middle of the war, Rehana is dedicated to retrieving and keeping them and cannot bring herself to participate in their political fervor. It is a scalar comparison juxtaposing the individual's political fight against the state and the larger struggle of the Bengali people against West Pakistan, but Anam hints at the slippage between the two and does not pose them as opposing narratives. As the war arrives in Dhaka, Rehana turns more inward, more detached from the cause, while her children move inexorably outward into the world of violence and danger. While the third-person contrapuntal narrative depicts her in contrast to her children—the spirit of insurrection inspires them, while she longs for the simple rhythms of her domesticity—it is through Rehana and her peripheral observation of the war that the novel conveys the true horror of the times and a trenchant analysis of the context:

> Lately, the children had little time for anything but the struggle. It had started when Sohail entered the university. Ever since '48, the Pakistani authorities had ruled the eastern wing of the country like a colony. First they tried to force everyone to speak Urdu instead of Bengali. They took the jute money from Bengal and spent it on factories in Karachi and Islamabad. One general after another made promises they had no intention of keeping. (33)

Rehana's maternal monologue remains focused on her children and their well-being, and a note of resentment creeps in as the mother realizes her children "had little time for anything but the struggle." But the usual expectations of maternal preoccupation are deftly expanded to include the growing sense of oppressive policies, political disenfranchisement, economic exploitation, and eventually military violence and rape that finally culminated in the rebellion against West Pakistan. The maternal, in this reading, is a capacious rendering of the citizen: Rehana's fight to keep her children, to claim their time and energy for her own, is refracted through the struggle of the Bengali people. That should not, however, be taken as a negation of the mother or an attempt simply to recuperate her as a political figure. First, the maternal as revolutionary has a long cultural history in South Asia in the non-Muslim Bengali sociocultural context, and one must account for the dominance of that tradition, which has often foisted the "mother goddess nation" imagery onto non-Hindu cultures. Second, Rehana's resistance toward the national conflict in order to protect her domestic bliss is an entirely legitimate response of the individual against the overarching concerns of the national context, especially when the national and the political have been instrumental in separating a widowed Rehana from her children in the past.

But, try as she must, Rehana is unable to keep conflict and violence outside her home. Her children bring it in every day, and the anxieties expressed by Rehana push the narrative closer to the larger political context:

> But in 1970, when the cyclone hit, it was as though everything came into focus. Rehana remembered the day Sohail and Maya had returned from the rescue operation: the red in their eyes as they told her how they had waited for the food trucks to come and watched as the water rose and the bodies washed up on the shore; how they had realized, with mounting panic, that the food wouldn't come because it had never been sent. (33)

While Rehana's narrative is focused on her children's trauma, it performs a dual function by bridging their grief to the totality of devastation in East Pakistan. It is through Rehana's perspective that the novel encapsulates the political environment of the time, but most important, it is through her eyes as a mother that the reader can glimpse what the Bengali Pakistani citizen might have felt: a complete denial of her humanity. At first reading, the sole focus on the maternal objectives of the female protagonist in the midst of the turmoil seems to imply a refusal to engage with the wider dynamics of social conflict and a retreat from perspectival points that would allow a systemic, holistic grasp of the social situation. And yet, Rehana's struggle as a widowed mother, as a woman in a patriarchal, Islamic society, and as a Bengali in undivided Pakistan mounts a personal, interior revolution that reflects the wider, historical culmination of a revolt against the state.

The individual's struggle in *A Golden Age*, a brutal separation of a mother from her children and her quest to recover them, serves as a metaphoric rendering of the Bengali citizen's distance from the promises of the postcolonial state. It is through these distinct concerns of one person, which may appear petty in the larger scheme of culture, nation, language, and borders, that the reader can get a more substantive sense of the weight of the historical moment in individual lives. The life story, however, is not simply detached from the wider scheme of things, but it recapitulates it, mirrors it, and reframes it, without losing its specificity. The personal is not merely absorbed by the political but emerges as a narrative perspective that displaces the very meaning of the political as an exterior, public space to be segregated from the invisible spaces of interiority and individual suffering. What the novel requires, ultimately, is a nuanced reading able to consider politics as a contested, more elastic form, which the novel itself asks us to redefine and to reimagine.

Literature, Politics, Pedagogy

Reading *A Golden Age* as a complex novel in which the personal and the political intersect and recapitulate each other may respond to a pressing pedagogical question at the heart of teaching South Asian women's writing in North America: are all postcolonial novels national stories? While students need to engage with the political context of the novel, reading closely also entails not reducing the complex forms and relations in the novel to predefined grand narratives of nation and partition. This essay suggests that the classroom become the space for interrogating the political dimension of the novel. Instead of giving students a rigid binary of text and context, an informed pedagogical practice needs to be attentive to the multiple ways in which the literary representation weaves and reframes contextual information. This is especially important when teaching contentious accounts such as the history of Bangladesh, which is still marked by unreconciled social antagonisms. For these many reasons, I suggest a strategy of reading that seeks to foreground the introspective, feminine voice as an insightful tool for political and cultural analysis without necessarily privileging the state over the individual. Marred by a default collapsing of the female voice into the personal, the domestic, or even the sexual, literary analysis often reads these individual stories as emblematic of women's segregation from political space. By categorizing women's voices as personal, private, and internal, even if they are represented as such, we run the risk of rationalizing an overt political and historical commentary as the sole arbiter of national analysis. However, this essay argues for an alternative interpretation in which this supposed exclusion, often demarcated in the novel as a deeply withdrawn, internalized voice for the female protagonist, may serve instead to reimagine the very meaning of the space of the political, which contests the national but also renders it more comprehensible.

Rather than reading these novels simply as narratives of women's disenfranchisement in South Asia, I would include them in a course of study that seeks to discuss political and national imaginaries. Relegated often to simply being personal stories, women authors and their characters offer a rich repository of political analysis that is of worth precisely because it is deemed distant from the nuts and bolts of political machinations. One may ask students to consider, for instance, how novels, specifically those by South Asian women writers, offer a particular historical empathy. How could characters such as Rehana, at a remove from active politics and yet never entirely distanced from it, offer up readings of South Asian female characters as not simply foreclosed options of marginalization but rather historical possibility?

Courses on South Asian women writers are often faced with the challenge of conveying the nuanced intricacies of women's writing and their lives alongside the diverse imaginary of the postcolonial social and political milieu. How does one, as a teacher, convey the existence of facts and practices that severely discriminate against women while also ensuring that students understand the integral role, both actual and analytic, women play in South Asian history? How can a textual analysis navigate between stereotypical expectations and representational complexity? The issues discussed in this essay can help stimulate further thoughts on the question of politics in the classroom. Instead of treating history as mere background or context that students need to know in order to approach the novels,

I require students to reflect on how the novels contest and redefine political, social, and historical narration through the lives of female protagonists.

Works Cited

Ahmad, Aijaz. "Reading Arundhati Roy Politically." *Frontline*, 8 Aug. 1997, pp. 103–08.

Ahmed, Nazneen. "The Poetics of Nationalism: Cultural Resistance and Poetry in East Pakistan/Bangladesh, 1952–71." *Journal of Postcolonial Writing*, vol. 50, no. 3, 2014, pp. 256–68.

Anam, Tahmima. "First Look: Tahmima Anam." *The Guardian*, 24 Nov. 2007, www.theguardian.com/books/2007/nov/24/featuresreviews .guardianreview24.

———. *A Golden Age*. John Murray, 2007.

———. "An Interview with Tahmima Anam." Conducted by Amy Finnerty. *Wasafiri*, vol. 30, no. 4, 2015, pp. 43–46.

Burton-Hill, Clemency. "And Ne'er the Twain Shall Meet." Review of *A Golden Age*, by Tahmima Anam. *The Guardian*, 21 Apr. 2007, www.theguardian .com/books/2007/apr/22/fiction.features.

Schendel, Willem van. *A History of Bangladesh*. Cambridge UP, 2009.

Tripathi, Salil. *The Colonel Who Would Not Repent: The Bangladesh War and Its Unquiet Legacy*. Yale UP, 2016.

Alpana Sharma

Intimations of Modernity: The Legacy of Toru Dutt

In the genealogy of South Asian women's writing in English, the works of the nineteenth-century Bengali poet and translator Toru Dutt play a vital role. Dutt was among the first Indian women to negotiate in aesthetic terms the divided legacy of colonialism for the modern anglophone colonial subject. As such, she helped lay the foundation for South Asian women's writing in English, which, even in its present-day postcolonial articulations, remains structurally and ideologically entangled with the West, owing to, in large part, its historical moorings in British colonialism. Dutt's body of work, consisting of English translations of French poetry and Sanskrit epic verse as well as original English-language poetry and prose (recently collected in Chandani Lokugé's handsome anthology *Toru Dutt: Collected Prose and Poetry*), is remarkable for its linguistic fluency and cultural range. Published primarily during the last three years of Dutt's short life, with the Sanskrit translations, miscellaneous poems, and two novels appearing posthumously, it dramatizes the cultural politics of a certain in-between cosmopolitan space, one that is neither properly European nor properly Indian but is, instead, a hybrid produced from the encounter between these two worlds. When read as an example of a rich and proliferating hybridity, then, Dutt's writing becomes a fruitful challenge to the kinds of binary thinking that underpin exclusionary ideas about nations, national cultures, and, by extension, literary canons. Literary canons in particular reproduce nationalisms and nationalities in problematic ways for students of literature, for whom the required survey courses are typically classified as British, American, or "other" (or postcolonial). Compounding the problem, British and American surveys are also typically periodized, whereas it would appear that the "other" survey courses fall outside history altogether, being characterized neither by period nor by nation. Dutt offers a useful corrective to such curricular practices because her work belongs equally in the Victorian and the postcolonial survey, hence critically interrupting for students the reproduction of national and historical categories.

I begin with an introduction to the life and work of Dutt, situating her in the historical context of the mid- to late nineteenth century, a period of political and cultural upheaval for a region that was by then well and truly under British imperial rule. Following a brief overview of current critical scholarship on Dutt, I direct readers' attention to her poem "Savitri," Dutt's free English translation of the legend of the mythic woman featured in the ancient Hindu epic the *Mahabharata*. Dutt's rendition of Savitri exemplifies for readers unfamiliar with her work the hybrid, experimental, and transnational quality of Dutt's writing. The source of her characteristic style lies not in a unitary literary tradition conceived along national lines but in her wide reading of diverse texts, made available to her through the emerging transnational circuits of modern textual production and reception during that historical period. Because she underwent no formal training and was largely self-taught and home tutored, Dutt's approach to writing was readerly; that is to say, her choice of subject, selection of words, and literary influences were driven by and improvised out of her reading pleasures and thus were unencumbered by the weight of any particular convention or tradition, limited only by what was available to her through the Calcutta Public Library, the family's private library, and the occasional parcel of books ordered from England. Accordingly, I show that "Savitri" reflects the poet's idiosyncratic approach to one of the most pressing issues of her time: the negotiation of modernity by early Indian nationalists and the construction of Indian womanhood that emerged as a result of that negotiation. I conclude by suggesting that Dutt's pedagogical value lies precisely in her refusal to be assigned a fixed position on either side of the colonizer-colonized dyad. Modernity in the colonies did not have to mean a slavish imitation of European literary examples by early South Asian women writers in English; nor, by the same token, did it have to produce noncompliant, purely anticolonial, essentially Indian subjects.

Dutt was born into an affluent Bengali family in 1856. Her father, Govin Chunder Dutt, may well have counted among "Macaulay's minutemen," Salman Rushdie's playful term for the "class of persons Indian in blood and colour, but English in tastes, in opinions, in morals and in intellect" that the Anglicist administrator Thomas Babington Macaulay wished to create with his infamous "Minute on Indian Education" in 1835 (Rushdie 165; Macaulay 171). Govin Chunder was employed by the colonial government and, upon retiring, became honorary magistrate, justice of the peace, and a fellow of the University in Calcutta. He and his brothers converted to Christianity, and the entire Dutt family was baptized in 1862. An avid admirer of William Wordsworth, Govin Chunder raised his two daughters, Aru and Toru (a son, Abju, died young), on a steady diet of French and British Romantic poetry. The most formative experience in the young sisters' lives occurred when the Dutts traveled to Europe in 1868, where they stayed for four years. Lokugé points out that with this visit they had "once again transgressed the borders of Hindu religious and social mores," claiming that they were "the first Bengali (if not Indian women) [sic] to cross the 'black waters,' considered a blasphemous act in Hinduism as it meant pollution and loss of caste" (xvii). Just one year after the family's return to Calcutta, Aru died of tuberculosis.

Toru would outlive her sister by only three years, dying in 1877, but during these years she read widely and wrote prolifically. Her letters to her English friend Mary Martin, which constitute most of what we know about Dutt's private life, testify to the range of her voracious reading: William Shakespeare, Victor Hugo, Molière, George Eliot, the Brontë sisters, George Sand, Edward Bulwer-Lytton, William Makepeace Thackeray, all the Romantics, and countless lesser-known authors who appeared in *Revue des deux mondes*. She began publishing essays in *The Bengal Magazine*, and in 1876 her book of verse translations from French to English, *A Sheaf Gleaned in French Fields*, was published by Kegan Paul & Co. in London; it was received favorably in France and England, thanks in large part to its first European reviewers, André Theuriet in France and Edmund Gosse in England. Gosse had happened upon the book's original Indian publication ("a hopeless volume . . . with its queer type") and was won over by its freshness and lyricism; he subsequently wrote a glowing review for it in the *Examiner* in August 1876 (see Das 291–92). Dutt embarked on a study of Sanskrit in 1875 with her father and was working on a collection of translated verse from Sanskrit to English when she died of tuberculosis in 1877; it was published posthumously in 1882 under the title *Ancient Ballads and Legends of Hindustan* and included Gosse's introductory memoir. Two novels also appeared posthumously: *Bianca, a Spanish Maid*, an unfinished novel written in English, and *Le Journal de Mademoiselle d'Arvers*, a French novel.

The nineteenth century was a period of great political unrest and social change in India. From the early to mid-1800s, nationalist reformers, sensitive to British intervention in areas hitherto governed by Indian social codes and customs, looked askance at some of their backward-seeming patriarchal traditions (Tharu 258; Lokugé xv). They sought to improve the lot of Hindu women with a range of social reforms addressing *sati* (widow immolation), widow remarriage, child marriage, purdah, and women's education (Sharma 99–101). Much of this reformist effort was led by progressive associations like the Brahmo Samaj and popularized by the *bhadralok*, the "respectable" Bengali middle classes (Lokugé xlv). In the wake of the 1857 Mutiny (referred to by Indians as the first war of independence), the East India Company was dissolved and British rule was enforced militarily. This in turn added fuel to the nationalist struggle for independence and political self-determination. But, as the historian Partha Chatterjee has shown, by the last few decades of the nineteenth century, reformist debates about the "women's question" left the public sphere and effectively disappeared. This disappearance occurred because nationalists began to enforce a strict dichotomy between the material and spiritual spheres of Indian life, selecting which features of modernity to adopt and which to reject. They did not abandon modernity but rather attempted "to make modernity consistent with nationalism" (Chatterjee 240). As a result, while nationalists were more than willing to concede the public sphere to the British and to modernize accordingly, the home—the "inner sanctum" of the national culture over which women were seen to preside—had to remain pure and untouched by outside influence (239).

While Dutt's class status and her father's progressive views on education lifted her condition above that of other Bengali women, by no means was she liberated from the domestic chains that bound most women of the time. The rare English-educated Bengali woman was the object of much derision (Mukherjee 93), and, in Dutt's case, her confinement indoors was also due to her family's conversion, which had ostracized it from the orthodox Hindu society of Calcutta. Dutt makes a matter-of-fact reference to this in her letter to Mary Martin, writing, "The day before yesterday my mother's *cousine* was married. She is a Hindu and so is her family, so of course we were not invited" ("Letters" 261). Unaccepted by the orthodox folds of Hindu society, Dutt was not fully embraced as a foreign poet either; the reception of her first book of translated verse proves that European reviewers saw her as irrevocably Indian, and their praise was tempered by their paternalistic attitude toward the "Hindu poetess [who] was chanting to herself a music that is discord in an English ear" (Das 300). Gosse, who penned these words in his introductory memoir for Dutt's posthumously published *Ancient Ballads*, called *Sheaf* "a wonderful mixture of strength and weakness, of genius over-riding great obstacles and of talent succumbing to ignorance and inexperience" (qtd. in Das 300). Thus, it becomes clear that Dutt cannot be placed squarely in either Indian (nationalist) or European (colonial) frames of reference. It is no wonder, then, that her poetry and prose are charged through and through with hybrid, cross-pollinating figures: lotuses growing among roses and lilies in "Psyche's bower" ("Sonnet—The Lotus" 210); tamarinds and mangoes in a tropical "primeval Eden" in which the seemul flower is "Red,—red, and startling like the trumpet's sound" ("Sonnet—Baugmaree" 210); the "dirge-like murmur" of her native casuarina tree heard abroad in concert with the waves of "the classic shore of France or Italy" ("Our Casuarina Tree" 211–212); and, finally, the heroine of her unfinished eponymous novel *Bianca*, who, being Spanish, is not quite white, not quite brown, but a near other: "pale olive," with "dark brown eyes," "long black curls," and "warm southern blood" (93, 103).

Since the 1990s there has been a revival of critical interest in Dutt; not surprisingly, it coincides with the growing prevalence of theories in the related fields of postcolonialism, transnationalism, translation, and cosmopolitanism, among others. For instance, Meera Jagannathan draws on Elleke Boehmer's *Empire Writing* to make the point that Dutt "sits at the entry point between colonial literature, which could be interpreted as writing dominated by the metropole, and postcolonial literature, which is the free expression of the indigenous populations"; for Jagannathan, she is "a comparative writer who spoke in the transnational, multi-lingual voice of a unique Indian modernity" (14). Meenakshi Mukherjee writes of Dutt's "double ventriloquism" in her French-to-English translations and the "hyphenated space" that allows her, in *Ancient Ballads*, to infuse the Hindu folktales passed on to her from her mother "with the cadence of Wordsworth and Shelly [sic]" (96, 111). Critics have remarked on her "interstitial position" between "fixed binaries" (Sharma 108), her "strategic singularity" (Phillips), and her "ethical inventiveness of . . . fragile communities" within the economy of "gift exchange" (Ekman 27, 35). Some, like Alison Chapman, have argued for Dutt's place in the canon of Victorian literature, showing how a poem like "Sonnet—Baugmaree" reinvents the classical form of the Petrarchan sonnet, rendering it "part Petrarchan and part Shakespearean, part Italian and part English, [challenging] the homogeneity of the form as it implicitly questions the nationality of the sonnet" (602). And finally, Tricia Lootens shows how *Sheaf* is best read "as a many-layered critical and creative exploration of cultural mimicries" (582).

Students encountering Dutt for the first time might fruitfully address the following kinds of questions: as one of the very first anglophone (and francophone) women writers from South Asia and certainly the first known Indian female novelist in English, how does she complicate any easy attribution of national identity or colonial affiliation? By Dutt's writing not from the heart of the European metropole but from the place of textual improvisation and experimentation within the confines of her city and country homes in Bengal, what habits of reading led her to both assume and create a convivial community of readers outside her immediate frame of reference? How did her writing embody a particular gendered form of early modernity in the colonies? A reading of her poem "Savitri" provides an entry point to some of the answers.

Savitri is the heroine in the *Mahabharata* who selflessly and ingeniously rescues her husband, Satyavan, from the clutches of the dreaded god of death, Yama. Satyavan's death was foretold before Savitri married him, but neither his fated death nor the fear of widowhood deterred Savitri from marrying him. At the appointed time, when the young Satyavan grew faint and Yama came to claim his soul, he was moved by Savitri's pure wifely devotion and granted her the wish to bring Satyavan back to life. In traditional Hindu culture, Savitri is venerated for the feminine ideals that she represents; like Sita, the character in the *Ramayana* who similarly devotes herself wholeheartedly to her wifely duties, she is the archetype of the ideal Hindu woman. In Dutt's retelling of the legend, while this ideal aspect of Savitri is preserved, what is extolled at least as much are her freedom, mobility, and inherent right to self-determination. Dutt's Savitri "wandered where she pleased / In boyish freedom" (132), and her "sweet simplicity and grace" persuade her parents to allow her to choose her own mate. As the poet puts it:

> In those far-off primeval days
> Fair India's daughters were not pent
> In closed zenanas. On her ways
> Savitri at her pleasure went
> Whither she chose. . . . (131)

In contrast to the poem's present, in which Indian women are "pent / In closed zenanas," Dutt evokes the free-spiritedness of the Vedic women of "those far-off primeval days." Quite strikingly, she sees fit to insert an authorial commentary on her own time, inflecting it with what appears to be a very modern Enlightenment ideology of the sovereign individual subject.

These lines present a kind of puzzle for Dutt critics, just as *Ancient Ballads* itself poses somewhat of an enigma: how are we meant to read these translations from the Indian vernacular and Sanskritic traditions, when the author in question was an unabashed Europhile, a devout Christian who was convinced of the false idolatry of Hinduism?[1] According to Susie Tharu, Dutt's portrayal of Savitri was intended to counter the negative images of Indian women projected by the British with positive ones. The Bengali *bhadralok* were highly sensitive to colonial stereotypes of Indian women as backward and oppressed. Influenced by nationalist social reformers' zeal to counteract perceived deficiencies of Hindu culture evidenced in such practices as the *zenana* (segregated women's quarters), child marriage, *sati*, and so on, Dutt creates a Savitri who reproduces the Victorian ideal of chaste femininity even as she helps to combat Victorian stereotypes about Indian femininity (Tharu 258–60). But this double gesture, according to Jagannathan, does not make Dutt "an anti-colonial rhetorician" (21). Nowhere in Dutt's poetry and personal letters does Jagannathan find Dutt aligning with the nationalists; indeed, her interest in the Hindu myths about Indian women was sparked by her transnational epistolary friendship with the French orientalist Clarisse Bader, who had written a book on women of ancient India that Dutt had read and admired. Jagannathan reads in this relationship a "remarkable cross-fertilization of diverse ideas brought on by European colonization of India" (21). For Jagannathan, then, "Savitri" is proof that Dutt's sympathies actually lie with the orientalists, who lamented the degeneracy of contemporary Hindu practices and lauded India's glorious Vedic past as idyllic and the ancient Hindu religion as in fact a close cousin to Christianity (23).

Yet Jagannathan's reading of Dutt as a Christian orientalist who was contemptuous of Indian society does not fully account for the outrage Dutt increasingly expresses in her letters to Mary Martin at the unfair balance of power in colonial Bengal. She provides Martin with excerpts from police reports published in the local newspapers that illustrate everyday examples of random brutality directed against Indians by British officers, British soldiers' callous murders of Indian subjects, and unfair legal sentences passed down by British judges (see, for instance, "Letters" 282, 294). Some of her publications for *The Bengal Magazine* indicate to Lokugé "her subversive effort to create awareness amongst her compatriots of the regular injustices" suffered by Indians under the British (xxiii). While hardly anticolonial in sentiment, these texts suggest that Dutt's affiliations and identifications were multidirectional and fluid, implying trajectories that would never be completed and hence never be known because of her early death. In her unfinished novel *Bianca*, for example, she was beginning to forge a genuinely new style of writing in English, having little precedent for what an Indian novel in English was or should look like. While experimental, in its very experimentation it articulated an early form of South Asian modernism, inflected and produced by the textual crosscurrents of the transnational world in which Dutt lived and wrote.

Toru Dutt provides a significant historical precedent for South Asian women writers, who are beginning to be included in the college English curriculum. Her pedagogical value lies in her refusal to fit within narrowly conceived national categories of race, gender, religion, culture, and language, categories that, while strategically necessary in some ways, in other ways also limit critical thinking and serve only to further marginalize those others whom we would seek to understand.

Note

1. See, for instance, "Letters to Miss Martin," where Dutt expresses sadness at the Hindu worship of "graven image[s]" and wishes that India would "turn to the true and loving God, who is alone able to save us and cleanse us from our sins" (313).

Works Cited

Chapman, Alison. "Internationalising the Sonnet: Toru Dutt's 'Sonnet—Baugmaree.'" *Victorian Literature and Culture*, vol. 42, no. 3, 2014, pp. 595–608.

Chatterjee, Partha. "The Nationalist Resolution of the Women's Question." Sangari and Vaid, pp. 233–53.

Das, Harihar. *Life and Letters of Toru Dutt.* Oxford UP, 1921.
Dutt, Toru. *Bianca; or, The Young Spanish Maiden.* Dutt, *Toru Dutt*, pp. 91–125.
———. "Letters to Miss Martin." Dutt, *Toru Dutt*, pp. 222–345.
———. "Our Casuarina Tree." Dutt, *Toru Dutt*, p. 211.
———. "Savitri." Dutt, *Toru Dutt*, pp. 131–158.
———. "Sonnet—Baugmaree." Dutt, *Toru Dutt*, p. 210.
———. "Sonnet—The Lotus." Dutt, *Toru Dutt*, p. 210.
———. *Toru Dutt: Collected Prose and Poetry.* Edited by Chandani Lokugé, Oxford UP, 2006.
Ekman, Gabriella. "Gifts from Utopia: The Travels of Toru Dutt's Poetry." *Victoriographies*, vol. 3, no. 1, May 2013, pp. 23–45.
Jagannathan, Meera. "The Enigma of Toru Dutt." *Dalhousie French Studies*, vol. 94, Spring 2011, pp. 13–25.
Lokugé, Chandani. Introduction. Dutt, *Toru Dutt*, pp. xiii–xlviii.
Lootens, Tricia. "Bengal, Britain, France: The Locations and Translations of Toru Dutt." *Victorian Literature and Culture*, vol. 34, no. 2, 2006, pp. 573–90.
Macaulay, Thomas Babington. "Document Fourteen." *The Great Indian Education Debate: Documents Relating to the Orientalist-Anglicist Controversy, 1781–1843*, edited by Lynn Zastoupil and Martin Moir, Routledge, 2013, pp. 162–72.
Mukherjee, Meenakshi. "Hearing Her Own Voice." *The Perishable Empire: Essays on Indian Writing in English*, Oxford UP, 2000, pp. 89–116.
Phillips, Natalie. "Claiming Her Own Context(s): Strategic Singularity in the Poetry of Toru Dutt." *Nineteenth-Century Gender Studies*, vol. 3, no. 3, Winter 2007, ncgsjournal.com/issue33/phillips.htm.
Rushdie, Salman. *The Moor's Last Sigh.* Vintage, 1996.
Sangari, Kumkum, and Sudesh Vaid, editors. *Recasting Women: Essays in Colonial History.* Kali for Women, 1993.
Sharma, Alpana. "In-Between Modernity: Toru Dutt (1856–1877) from a Postcolonial Perspective." *Women's Experience of Modernity, 1875–1945*, edited by Ann L. Ardis and Leslie W. Lewis, Johns Hopkins UP, 2003, pp. 97–110.
Tharu, Susie. "Tracing Savitri's Pedigree: Victorian Racism and the Image of Women in Indo-Anglian Literature." Sangari and Vaid, pp. 254–68.

Part II

Language, Form, and Translation

Indrani Mitra

(Re)membering the Past: Linguistic Dislocation in Anita Desai's *Clear Light of Day*

Some years ago, at a reading by Anita Desai, I overheard a youthful member of the audience confessing that she had come to the event curious about "the mother of Kiran Desai," winner of the 2006 Booker Prize. The casual dismissal of Anita Desai, whose novels of female quests had once stirred the imagination of many women born in independent India, gave me pause. The remark, in my view, spoke to the coming of age of a generation of anglophone writers of Indian origin whose works recognize the growth of a bilingual readership in India and in the diaspora, a new confidence in the English language as a vehicle for the expression of cross-cultural experience, and, above all, the secure situation of India in the marketplace of multinational print capitalism. This new age would seem to have put to rest the tired question of whether the English language can indeed communicate Indian experience and whether the writer in English can legitimately claim an Indian identity.[1] Anita Desai's *Clear Light of Day*, published in 1980, appeared at the dawn of this new age of English literature in India.

In my Literature of Modern India course, taught at a liberal arts institution on the East Coast of the United States, I examine how an idea of

India is constructed within colonial, nationalist, postindependence, and diasporic contexts. Gender is a running thread through the course as I invite students not only to understand the ways in which all social experience is gendered but also to examine the availability or unavailability of women's voices at particular historical moments. Desai's *Clear Light of Day*, with its metalinguistic subtext, allows us to confront important questions of writing in English in contemporary India and writing as a woman.

By the 1960s, when Desai's first novels were published, the era of nationalist exuberance was over and the age of disillusionment had begun. Of 15 August 1947, the day of India's independence, Desai has said, "[It was] probably the most traumatic event of my childhood" ("Sense" 153). Her perspective on that historic moment has the uniqueness of her multicultural experience: the German, Bengali, and anglicized influences of her home; her childhood in the linguistic mosaic of Old Delhi, where Hindi was the language of the streets, English the language of school and of official discourse, and Urdu the language of poetry; and the ambiguities of her formation as a woman writer in patriarchal Indian society and as a writer in English at a time when the debates of language and national culture were especially fraught.

In the early decades of her literary career, Desai's reflections on her predicament as an artist echoed the anxieties she depicts in *Clear Light of Day*. The English language, Desai said in an essay in 1982, is "at best an immigrant in India." Not having any roots, it has no literary tradition, leaving the writer in English "with a fearful time of it, picking and choosing his way amongst thorns, pot holes and booby-traps" ("Indian Writer's Problem" 224). In a 1970 essay on Indian women writers, Desai had dismissed the groping attempts of her predecessors to carve out a space in the existing Western tradition by "exchanging primroses for oleanders and church spires for temple bells." The alternative of gleaning through "a welter of languages, of regional literatures," Desai had found even more daunting ("Women Writers" 41). Desai has since changed much of her thinking on the possibilities of English-language literature in India; indeed, she no longer retains that sweeping dismissal of literature in the regional languages ("Sense" 160). However, the unawareness of regional literatures in her formative years as a writer may explain the linguistic predicament she presents in her novel.

Clear Light of Day is the story of the Das family: two sisters, Tara and Bim; Raja, the romantic older brother; and Baba, the autistic younger brother. The novel moves through a series of recollections from a present in the 1970s back to the troubled years of 1947 and 1948 (the years of independence as well as the partition riots) and further back to the childhood of the Das children in the 1930s. The past that individual characters reach into, familial or national, is contingent on class, gender, social, and psychological situations. I point my students to Homi Bhabha's description of postcolonial subject formation: "It is a painful *re-membering*, a putting together of the dismembered to make sense of the trauma of the present" (qtd. in Gandhi 9).[2] For the gendered subject, as much as for minorities, lower castes, and other disempowered populations in India, the past is mediated not only by colonialist distortions but also by the elitist, patriarchal formulations of nationalism, with their multiple erasures and selective recall. From here it takes only a slight nudge for students to note that in Desai's narrative 1947 does not mark the triumphant birth of a sovereign nation. The actual hour of independence, on 15 August 1947, is conspicuously absent in *Clear Light of Day*. The novel records instead the grim other face of the historic moment: the partition of the subcontinent and the mass hysteria and genocide that accompanied the transfer of populations. In fact, the only historic event mentioned in the text is the assassination of Mohandas K. Gandhi, the architect of the new nation; the event testifies to the sectarian hysteria raging through the country.

Desai's ambivalent representation of the nation's birth may be understood in terms of the disenchantments of the 1960s and 1970s. By the mid-1960s, the almost religious aura of nationalism was quite obviously past, as was the enthusiasm surrounding nation-building manifest in the 1950s. Serious flaws in Prime Minister Nehru's economic as well as foreign policies had become apparent. Through the 1960s, a mood of militancy was evident in the organized sectors of labor, spreading through sections of the countryside (Frankl 340–42). More fundamentally, the original secular ideology, the foundational consensus of the Indian nation, had begun to erode following repeated conflicts with Pakistan, and various sectarian and linguistic nationalisms periodically challenged the basis of national integrity.[3] The death knell of nationalist idealism would be the declaration of a state of emergency in 1975.

The novel's setting in "the great cemetery" of Old Delhi is a reminder of cultural violence and historical amnesia in the nation's birth (5). The Civil Lines, where the Das house is situated, carries its own connotations of an ambivalent past. Once the secluded residential neighborhood for the officers of the British imperial civil service, the Civil Lines provides the setting for Desai's protagonists drawn from the class of brown *sahibs* (gentlemen, which came to imply "white men"), a class created and left behind as a legacy of British rule.[4] Through the lives of the three families on Bela Street, the text draws attention to the cultural palimpsest of Old Delhi. On the eve of national independence in the 1940s, the three houses represent diverse strands in the multilayered formation of the native elite. The Hyder Ali mansion embodies the vestiges of a Muslim feudal class, recalling the aristocratic elegance of Old Delhi. The Misras, on the other side, bear the mark of a newly prosperous Hindu bourgeoisie, the *banya*, whose lack of refinement would naturally be held in contempt by anglicized Indians like the Dases. In the Das household one encounters the cultural neurosis of the brown *sahib*, struggling to keep up appearances with "curtains at the windows, carpets on the floors, solid pieces of furniture placed at regular intervals, plates that matched each other on the table, white uniforms for the house servants and other such appurtenances" (137).

In the 1970s the three houses on Bela Street reflect three stages of decay. The Hyder Ali mansion stands abandoned, signifying the erasure of the old Muslim aristocracy in contemporary India. For the Misras, the encounter with modern India has not been free from ironic tensions. Beneath the veneer of changelessness, the traditional Hindu joint family faces a pervasive decay, figuratively extending from the supine figure of the old patriarch to the last of his idle, alcoholic sons. My students note the ironic "re-membering" of a Hindu cultural past, implicit in the old father's memories of Rakshabandhan (the Hindu festival of brotherly affection), and an imagined era of benign patriarchal care of women, juxtaposed with the middle-aged Misra sisters' tired dance demonstrations of the love of Radha for Krishna to a group of perspiring students in order to pay for the whiskey their brothers consume liberally. Beyond the ironic improbability in the situation of the Misra sisters, I ask students to reflect on what the iconic status of the Radha-Krishna story (expressions of medieval Hindu devotionalism in the regional dialects of Hindi, especially Braj Bhasha) means for the preeminence given to particular sociolinguistic and religious traditions and the marginalizing of others.[5] The novel reminds us, however tentatively, of the cultural and linguistic politics of postcolonial India—the tortuous process by which one language comes to embody the national culture of a linguistically diverse population while others acquire the markers of regionalism, communalism, and even antinational foreignness. The most profound irony in the Indian situation is the process by which English came to be naturalized and Urdu, at one point the lingua franca of North India, came to acquire the mark of alienation. In order to understand the language politics of India, my class follows the linguistic negotiations of Raja and Bim Das, especially the latter.

In the Das children's youth, their imaginative world had been mapped within the semantic boundaries of the English language and its literature. Where Bim stumbled in her articulation of a heroic female destiny in the paths of Joan of Arc and Florence Nightingale, the tubercular Raja languished in his sick bed "hop[ing] like Byron to go to the rescue of those in peril" during the partition riots (60). The novel's most humorous depiction of linguistic alienation is through Bim's disastrous visit with her Bengali suitor, Dr. Biswas, who inhabits, with his mother, a culturally coded world of Rabindrasangeet (Songs of Tagore) and homemade sweets. I point out to students the gendered implications of linguistic choices, so while Bim's failure to understand Rabindrasangeet ends the prospects of a romance with Biswas, the English language empowers her to enter the male-dominated arena of college teaching. Nonethcless, hungry for a more obvious feminist resolution, my students express frustration at the novel's quiet end, as the self-reliant and reflective Bim accepts her place as her family's anchor, inviting her estranged siblings to return home as they wish. I, on the other hand, ask them to view the novel's conclusion as the most radical kind of re-membering.

In a particularly evocative passage at the novel's end, Bim listens to the music of a young disciple and his aged guru:

> She saw before her eyes how one ancient school of music contained both Mulk, still an immature disciple, and his aged, exhausted guru. . . . With her inner eye she saw how her own house and its particular history linked and contained her as well as her whole family with all their separate histories and experiences—not binding them within some dead and airless cell but giving them the soil in which to send down their roots. . . . The soil contained all time, past and future, in it. It was dark with time, rich with time. It was where her deepest self lived, and the deepest selves of her sister and brothers and *all those who shared that time with her.* (182; my emphasis)

The passage evokes cognates *gharana* (Hindustani music schools, conceived as familial traditions) and *ghar* (home or family), bringing to Bim the lasting ties incarnated in her home. The Hindustani or North Indian classical music tradition, with its origins in the ancient Sanskrit texts but developed under Moghul-Muslim patronage, is an outstanding example of cultural syncretism. In addition, the passage invites a metaphoric reading of *ghar/gharana* as nation. Time and place, the two coordinates of nationhood, are both here as well as the terms of kinship and fraternity with which nations are imagined. The last line gestures prominently beyond Bim's biological family to a shared cultural community.

But at this point textual implications become provocative. In the following moments, Bim reclaims her lost ties with her brother through her recognition of the verses of Muhammad Iqbal, sung by the old musician. "Raja's favorite," she whispers (182). A few pages earlier in the book, Bim uncovers a forgotten moment from their past in which Bim translated a collection of Urdu poems written by a youthful Raja. The poems unlock a memory of their youth that Bim has long suppressed. Elsewhere in the novel, Urdu is the sign of fragmentation. In Bim's embittered memory, Raja's discovery of Urdu had been the beginning of his eventual abandonment of her. It had ended their shared love of the English Romantics and Victorians. In her youth, she had found (reactively perhaps) Urdu poetry incredibly monotonous. Yet, she had translated Raja's poems. One wonders if she might have grown to love Urdu literature with comparable zest if the possibility of such a bilingual cultural world had not been tragically disrupted by the events of the partition. In the context of the 1940s' sectarianism, the Hindu boy Raja's choice of Urdu had meant betrayal of family, community, and nation. But in a different time, Urdu might even have been the sign of a truly national culture. Therefore, Bim's recognition of Iqbal's voice at the novel's end is loaded with meaning, from the personal to the political.

So why Urdu over any other subcontinental language with which Desai might have explored the language politics of postcolonial India? A language born in the Muslim courts of India, Urdu came to be the national language of Pakistan and, in India, in recent times, almost exclusively associated with the minority Muslim population. Yet of Raja's choice to study Urdu in college, we learn that "it was a natural enough choice to make for the son of a Delhi family" (47). Here, Desai recognizes the pervasive influence through much of the twentieth century of Urdu language and literature on the educated, upper-class milieu of North India. Delhi was one of the centers of Urdu culture, but it had others scattered around the country. Of this cultural and linguistic community of North India, Aijaz Ahmad has said that "its ideas of a composite Indian culture were derived from the world of *taluqdars* and ICS officers which Hindus and Muslims of that class relished *with remarkable lack of mutual friction*" (7; emphasis added). Urdu, the linguistic sign for this "composite Indian culture," had no clear identification with being Muslim even a decade after partition.

In fact, claims Ahmad, "a secularist belief in a composite culture of Hindus and Muslims in India was the predominant ideological position of this community. . . . [D]ecisive shifts came later" (11–12). In the 1970s this cultural world of Urdu was in decline; its loss Desai narrates in her elegiac novel *In Custody*. Therefore, the novelistic closure of *Clear Light of Day* constitutes a radical kind of postcolonial re-membering of a moment of human connectedness made impossible by the sectarian interests fueled during independence and subsequent developments in India and Pakistan.

Yet one more vexing issue lingers at the novel's closure. Iqbal, a controversial figure, is associated with Islamic revival in India in the first half of the twentieth century; in fact, he is widely credited with the foundational idea of Pakistan, of a separate state for the Muslims of India. Yet it is also Iqbal who in his youth framed the ditty "*sarey jahan se achha, Hindustan hamara*" (Of all the countries in the world, the best is our Hindustan) that even today rings on many lips as the real anthem of the Indian nation, more popular by far than the official one. Admittedly, the song was a product of his youth, and in his mature years, Iqbal became the proponent of a transnational Islam. In 1930 he would give the now famous or notorious presidential address at the Twenty-Fifth Annual Session of the All India Muslim League in Allahabad, where his fateful remarks have gone down in history as the genesis of the idea of Pakistan (Singh 89–90). As his biographer Iqbal Singh takes pains to point out, the term *Pakistan* was "scrupulously, and possibly deliberately, avoided" in the 1930 speech (91). According to the testimonies of close associates, Iqbal is supposed to have firmly repudiated the idea of sovereign statehood for Indian Muslims, desiring instead a cultural center with some measure of political autonomy. In fact, in his presidential address to the 1932 All India Muslim League conference in Lahore, he spoke in rather hopeful terms of Hindu-Muslim accord in the subcontinent:

> I do believe in the possibility of constructing a harmonious whole, whose unity cannot be disturbed by the rich diversity which it must carry within its bosom. The problem of ancient Indian thought was how the one became many without sacrificing its oneness. Today . . . we have to solve it in its inverse form, i.e. how the many can become One without sacrificing its plural character. (92)

The passage has notable resonance with the quote above from *Clear Light of Day*, where Bim reflects on her family home holding together "the separate histories" of all her siblings (182).

Even more striking is the overall thrust of Iqbal's philosophy, with its central emphasis on ***khudi***, the proper understanding of self. Separating himself from Sufi otherworldliness, Iqbal urges man's fulfillment of his human destiny through the perfection of the self, reaching out to his divine potential. But the ascension of the ego is not detached and self-absorbed. A conscious tension exists, as M. Irfan Iqbal points out, between the "self and other selves," between the individual and collective dimensions of the self (54). The tension provides the dynamic energy that moves the ego toward perfection. But "one must not lose sight of the fact that the initial emphasis is on the individual ego. Only that individual ego which has attained a degree of self-realization and self-understanding will be able to genuinely understand and constructively engage with other individual egos" (55). The self-aware self-surrender that Bim undertakes at the end then reflects the tension inherent in the concept of ***khudi***.

How much of Muhammad Iqbal's philosophy is consciously evoked by Desai at the novel's end is unclear. What is evident, however, is that the birth centenary of the great poet of Urdu was celebrated on both sides of the partition in 1977, around the time the novel was being written. Ironically, Iqbal is perhaps the least secular of the Urdu literati of his generation. Yet his name in the 1970s would still evoke the cultural world of Urdu that was secular in spirit, that was tolerant of differences, that embraced both Hindus and Muslims, and that survived the partition but declined slowly in the succeeding decades. In recalling that moment, the novel's end gestures toward a national culture systematically undermined by the sectarian ideologies of the nation-states. Of course, the cultural world of Urdu was never coextensive with the boundaries of the Indian nation, large areas of the country remaining unaffected by the spread of Urdu. Desai's novel does not in fact look beyond the culture of Old Delhi. Yet Urdu in the novel is a signifier of the plurality of subcontinental culture, "of how the many can become one." It reminds us of what was sacrificed in the formation of nation-states, of those that were silenced—among them the voices of women. The pedagogical value of Desai's novel lies both in its embodiment as an English-language text in 1980, heralding the dawn of an era of globalized Indian literature, as well as in its ironic enactment of linguistic dislocations in subcontinental politics.

Notes

1. Ironically, the opposite seems true today, as seen in the clamorous effort to claim as "Indian" writers from the diaspora, even second- and third-

generation members of that group, who have acquired fame and fortune in the global literary scene.

2. My intention here is not to limit us to an allegorical reading of the text. Certainly, Desai's characters are psychologically complex, especially so her protagonist Bim. But Desai is also interested in social and political questions, particularly the question of linguistic nationalism, which she further explores in the novel *In Custody*. *Clear Light of Day* offers a particularly rich and complex political subtext that I offer as one of many pedagogical possibilities for this novel.

3. In 1965 came the first of such organized challenges to national sovereignty, as the political party Dravida Munnetra Kazhagam (DMK) in Madras organized widespread protests against adopting Hindi as the national language of India. Clearly, the organization of linguistic states had not addressed deep-rooted discontent, which began to take the form of North versus South agitations. In the mountain region of the northeast, ethnic separatist movements, often believed to be fueled by China or Pakistan, gathered momentum through the 1960s (Frankl 342–43).

4. A certain Westernized upper class now lives comfortably in India, following a model of Westernization led by the United States, in an offshoot of global capitalism; however, this is not the group that Desai's novel focuses on.

5. In her essay on the novel, Arun Mukherjee points to the Radha-Krishna love story as a "ubiquitous theme in Hindu Indian culture," appearing in medieval devotional songs, temple idols, sculpture and painting, classical and folk dances, and especially contemporary Bollywood cinema.

Works Cited

Ahmad, Aijaz. *In the Mirror of Urdu: Recompositions of Nation and Community, 1947–65*. Indian Institute of Advanced Study, 1993.

Desai, Anita. *Clear Light of Day*. Penguin, 1980.

———. "The Indian Writer's Problem." *Explorations in Modern Indo-English Literature*, edited by R. K. Dhawan, Bahri, 1982.

———. "A Sense of Detail and a Sense of Order: Anita Desai." Interview by Lalita Pandit. *Literary India: Comparative Studies in Aesthetics, Colonialism, and Culture*, edited by Patrick Colm Hogan and Pandit, State U of New York P, 1995, pp. 153–75.

———. "Women Writers." *Quest*, Apr.–June 1970, pp. 39–43.

Frankl, Francine. *India's Political Economy, 1947–1977*. Princeton UP, 1978.

Gandhi, Leela. *Postcolonial Theory: A Critical Introduction*. Columbia UP, 1998.

Iqbal, M. Irfan. "Iqbal's Philosophy of Khudi." *The Qur'anic Horizons*, vol. 3, no. 2, Apr.–June 1998, pp. 47–56.

Mukherjee, Arun P. "Other Worlds, Other Texts: Teaching Anita Desai's *Clear Light of Day* to Canadian Students." *College Literature*, vol. 22, no. 1, Feb. 1995, pp. 192–201. *JSTOR*, www.jstor.org/stable/25112174.

Singh, Iqbal. *The Ardent Pilgrim: An Introduction to the Life and Work of Mohammed Iqbal*. 2nd ed., Oxford UP, 1997.

Aruni Mahapatra

Literature and Gender in Anita Desai's *In Custody*

In 1984 the Indian novelist Anita Desai published *In Custody*, an English novel about a poorly paid Hindi lecturer and his doomed love of Urdu poetry. Deven Sharma works at a government college in Mirpore, a fictional town in North India's famous "dust bowl." The novel begins when, after a typically uninspired Hindi lecture, Murad, Deven's friend from Delhi, asks him to interview Nur Shahjahanabadi, a renowned Urdu poet, for Murad's Urdu magazine *Awaz*. Deven embarks on this mission in the hope of restoring the fallen social status of Urdu, and his own lackluster career as a teacher, by interviewing the aging Urdu poet and recording his poems. However, instead of professional and personal success, Deven is continually humiliated in this quest. Deven perseveres by ascribing the harassment to his being a "custodian," not only of Urdu poetry but of Nur's "very soul and spirit," a responsibility and "great distinction" that he cannot "deny or abandon . . . under any pressure" (226). Such self-fashioning justifies the conceit in the novel's title, which ironically suggests that in addition to being a custodian of Nur's poetry, Deven is trapped, *in custody*, by his own ideas about the greatness of Urdu poetry. However, even as Deven gladly embraces his custodianship, he remains blind to the suffering of Nur's younger wife, Imtiaz, also a poet, who is forced, despite her best efforts, to remain in custody of her husband.

In this essay I contrast Desai's representation of Deven and Imtiaz to demonstrate how an anglophone South Asian woman novelist's artistic practice embodies the tension between artistic and societal custodianship. I suggest that instructors can engage fruitfully with these notions of custodianship and caution students that an impulse to mourn declining vernaculars in postcolonial India often naturalizes the exclusion of women's literary labor. Ultimately, Desai's novel empowers students to ask, What right do we have to mourn for a dying literary culture, if our ideas of the existence, production, and consumption of vernacular literature are so inherently patriarchal and fail to recognize that women who labor as wives and mothers can be poets too?

Deven's disillusionment begins with his first visit to Nur's house. The poet, now senile and infirm, is surrounded not by poets but by scheming sycophants and wives. The older wife, Safia Begum, extracts money from Deven in return for valuable interview time with Nur. The younger wife, Imtiaz Begum, also writes Urdu verse and aspires to be a poet like Nur. When she composes and recites verse, however, Nur's lackeys treat her merely as a courtesan or a dancing girl. Humiliated and frustrated, she directs her anger at Nur and Deven, the latest fan. Despite disappointments, Deven soldiers on, choosing to see himself not simply as a frail, poor Hindi lecturer but instead as the custodian of a literary tradition. This tradition, Urdu poetry, although centuries old, was severely marginalized in a newly independent India. By making her readers sympathize with Deven, Desai effectively reveals how much postcolonial India has changed for the worse: the rapidly globalizing nation had little patience for vernacular literature, and widespread Hindu nationalism aggressively pushed Urdu to the margins, calling it Islamic and foreign.

As an account of Indian life-worlds that exist beyond English, this anglophone novel seems tailor-made for students beginning a bachelor's course in English Honors at the University of Delhi, where I first taught it. Many such students choose to study English because a bachelor's degree in English will ensure a financially secure future in twenty-first-century India. Of those who are interested in literature, they are more likely to have heard of Arundhati Roy and Amitav Ghosh than, say, the vernacular language authors Phanishwar Nath "Renu" or Fakir Mohan Senapati. On one hand, Desai's account of Deven's willingness to suffer because of his admiration of Urdu literature invites students to understand the richness of vernacular Indian literature in relation to its economic and social precariousness in postcolonial India. On the other hand, by describing Deven's insensitivity to Imtiaz's private confinement and struggle, which is almost a consequence of Nur's success in the public literary culture of Urdu poetry, Desai arrests any simplistic impulse to mourn for the decline of Urdu literary culture. In addition to celebrating a man who gladly surrenders himself to the custody of a declining literary culture, Desai's novel also provokes students to question the gendered exclusions on which such a willing surrender is based. Deven may fashion himself a custodian of a literary tradition in danger of extinction, but Desai invites students to ask: does a tradition that excludes women truly deserve mourning?

Imtiaz's exclusion from the public culture of Urdu poetry, and Deven's insensitivity to such exclusion, culminates in a scene toward the end of the novel. Imtiaz asks Deven, via a letter, if he, who claims to love Urdu, has the "courage" to read verses written by a woman (196). Deven refuses to enter the "grotesque" world of "hysterics and viragos" and preserves his "merciful delusions" (197). Deven does not read, and Desai's novel does not reproduce, these poems, which are written in Urdu and enclosed with the letter. This moment, in which an anglophone woman novelist explains a male protagonist's misogynist dismissal of a woman poet as a "hysteric" and a "virago," as a necessary part of his "merciful delusions," represents the integration of two radically different forms of custodianship. For Desai, custodianship describes both how artists preserve traditions of artistic practice and how the present preserves the past. Desai states that "we are all born . . . into a state of custody—of our past, our history, as well as what we choose to be our 'calling'" ("Art" 30, 32). Deven's devotion to Urdu is Desai's fictional account of her anglophone novelistic practice as a custodian of South Asian vernacular literary traditions.

Compared to Deven's artistic custodianship, Imtiaz's confinement to the inner quarter of a Muslim home represents Indian society's custodianship of its women. Rajeswari Sunder Rajan has argued that the postcolonial Indian state has been able to grant the rights of citizenship to women only by imagining them as custodial subjects within patriarchal structures such as the family (*Scandal* 25–31). Imtiaz seeks to challenge such custodianship by writing Urdu poems, but such an attempt only elicits a violent reinforcement of her custodial status. From Deven's perspective, she remains at best the wife of a male poet and the mother of his children, and at worst a schemer, out to use her husband's fame to advance her own less deserving career. The English novel, itself in custody of an older literary tradition, cannot go further than describing Imtiaz's failure. In order to follow Desai's impulse, and give more voice to Imtiaz than the novel does, I suggest that instructors use the director Saba Dewan's documentary *The Other Song*, discussed in greater detail below.

"Vegetarian Monsters" and the "Language of the Courts"

The first half of *In Custody* culminates with Imtiaz challenging the misogyny inherent in Deven's ideas of the production, consumption, and value of literature. At the end of part 1, we see Nur doubled up in his own vomit. Deven blames the political rise of right-wing Hinduism for the sorry state of his beloved Urdu poet. Imtiaz, however, blames the poet and his sycophants. While discussing the interview over a meager vegetarian lunch that Deven can afford to buy, his friend Murad laments that Hindi, a "vegetarian monster" raised on "radishes and potatoes," enjoys a high status, while Urdu, the "language of the courts," languishes (15). Deven remains silent, perhaps because the "vegetarian monster" gives him his lecturer's salary. Later, when Deven visits Nur, the *mushaira* (a symposium of poets) quickly degenerates into a jeremiad. One poet says that sharing Urdu verse with Hindi readers is like feeding "red meat to cows," and another that in order to continue to write in Urdu one must go to Pakistan (53).[1] Nur has the last word and says that the matter is not one of "Hindustan and Pakistan, of Hindi and Urdu," but one of "time" (55). Over food, as some of the young men recite their compositions, Nur dismisses them as "cowards-babies" and their poems as "nursery rhymes [their] mothers had composed" (56). Instead of "rolling Urdu verses into little sugar pills for babies to suck," Nur says, "we need the roar of lions," to scare away the "Hindi-wallahs" (56).[2] Such machismo is short-lived; Deven finds Nur doubled over in a pool of his own vomit. The young lecturer rushes to help the aging poet and is forced to wipe the poet's vomit with pages on which he has written his latest poems (59–60). Deven sees a vivid illustration of Urdu's past greatness in its present decrepitude.

Scholars have questioned the ethics and the efficacy of a novel that mourns a dying literature and diagnoses the causes of such decline.[3] Urdu poetry has a long vintage, while the economic decline of elite North Indian Muslims postpartition is a recent phenomenon. Indeed, the fraught nature of the Hindi-Urdu conflict suggests that it is almost impossible to find a neutral position from which to give an account of the origin, development, and oppositional rise of these two languages.[4] In the eighteenth century there was one language called, variously, Hindi, Hindvi, Rekhta, Dihlavi, Gujri, Dakani, and Urdu. Today, any of these can be called the historical or original version of the language that is called "Hindi" and another language called "Urdu." Recently scholars have argued that vernacular languages cannot claim to be more authentic, pure, or indigenous than English, because both English and vernacular languages were constituted as literary forms through colonial power.[5] Doing away with a binary of the authentic vernacular versus the alien or elite English, however, does not do away with the paradox that a Hindi lecturer laments the decline of Urdu in English.[6] Alok Rai's work can help instructors situate this Hindi lecturer's admiration for Urdu in a complex context. For Rai, on one hand, Urdu is "the accumulated music of centuries of everyday language," an aesthetically refined sensibility for which many North Indians yearn. Both Hindi and Urdu as they stand today are stunted, communalized versions of what was a richer and more eloquent lingua franca of North India ("Longing" 280). On the other hand, there is a tendency to associate the Urdu language with the Urdu script, thereby marking its cultural and religious difference from Hindi. Examining Deven's personal admiration for Urdu in relation to the legacy of the Hindi-Urdu divide in North India may allow instructors and students to engage questions of authenticity, once they have learned how to "define saris, betis, or barsatis" (qtd. in Satpathy 63).[7]

Women, Poetry, and Exclusion

Imtiaz, Nur's youngest wife, takes a realistic look at the man lying prone on her bed. As Deven is about to help Nur, she asks, "Do you call that a poet, or even a man?" Imtiaz challenges a clueless Deven: "See what you've done to him? See what he's done to me?" (60). What Nur has "done," Deven learns in the rest of the novel, is deny Imtiaz the opportunity of being considered a poet.

On his next visit to Nur's house, Deven sees a "powdered and painted creature" singing Nur's verses to an audience of men who are thoroughly entertained, even though her voice "grate[s] on [Deven's] ear" (90). This creature—whom the narrator, assuming Deven's perspective, calls a "trained monkey"—is actually Imtiaz, which Deven eventually learns (91). A few months later, after Deven's attempt to record Nur's verse has ended in failure and humiliation, he receives a letter from Imtiaz. This letter explains that when Nur married Imtiaz, she was a young courtesan, and that he was attracted not to her body but to her literary skills, richly displayed in the poems she composed. However, after marriage, when she wanted to attend *mushairas* and share her work like other poets, the men, who were all Nur's fans, dismissed her as a dancing girl and dismissed her literary skills. Nur, for his part, did nothing to support Imtiaz. Now, she addresses Deven with both hope and skepticism. As a scholar, Deven can be less misogynist than Nur and his followers, but Imtiaz suspects that being a man he cannot really accept that a woman can rise to the standards established by men. She nevertheless throws him a challenge: "In this unfair world that you have created, what else could I have been, but what I am? Ask yourself that when you peruse my verses, if you have the courage . . ." (196).

Deven does not have the courage. The idea that a woman could write as well as his idol threatens to destroy him, in the way that "a moment of lucidity can destroy the merciful delusions of a mad man" (197). By calling Deven a "mad man" who places his delusions above a woman's ambition to become an Urdu poet, Desai emphasizes the tragic irony that Deven's desire to be a custodian of a literary tradition confines a woman to the custody of patriarchal definitions of women's roles: courtesan, wife, mother, but not poet. The lucidity that threatens Deven's sanity is the idea that a woman like Imtiaz can be a poet. Instead of accepting this lucid idea, Deven continues to mourn for the decline of Urdu, manifested in the troubles faced by two men, himself and Nur. In this way, by showing a young man's admiration of literature as inseparable from his notion that a woman's duty is to support her husband, Desai forces readers to question narratives of the decline of South Asian vernaculars that may be complicit in the nonrecognition of women's labor. Having hinted at Imtiaz's imprisonment, the novel ends by refocusing on Deven's Sisyphean cycle of admiring Urdu while making a living from Hindi. The intellectual labor of making a woman like Imtiaz speak in her own words seems too daunting for an English novel, even one as perceptive as this one.

This is the task that Saba Dewan undertakes in her 2009 documentary, *The Other Song*, in which she looks for a version of the 1935 *thumri* recorded by the legendary female vocalist Rasoolan Bai that, Dewan remembers, has the line "*Phool gendwa na maar, lagat jobanwa me chot*" ("Don't throw flowers at me / My breasts are getting wounded").[8] The original had not been preserved in governmental archives or played on All India Radio, the country's national broadcaster. Instead, a cleaner version of the same *thumri* became popular, which had the words "*Phool gendwa na maar, lagat karejwa me chot*" ("Dont throw flowers at me / My heart is getting wounded"). Through interviews and conversations, Dewan learns of a deliberate effort since the 1930s to sanitize Indian culture. A group of Hindu men who were appointed heads of institutions like All India Radio went about removing traces of famous courtesan poets like Bai from the government's public records of Hindustani music.[9] In Dewan's film this story emerges through interviews with women from various singing houses of North India. One of them, Saira Begum, describes a tragic irony in the fate of courtesans, for whom political decolonization produced a series of humiliations. Under British rule women like her were respected custodians of Urdu poetry and Hindustani music. They sustained and renewed traditions of classical music by performing the ghazels of renowned Urdu poets. After independence, they were seen as "immoral" and "obscene" dancing girls. Listening to these women speak on camera illuminates Desai's novel by situating the English novel in a history of colonialism, in which decolonization produced not freedom but greater restriction on women's artistic labor.

Situating English novels by South Asian women in the mutually implicated histories of South Asian vernaculars and women's artistic labor illustrates the possibilities and limitations of anglophone fiction about South Asia. Such fiction perceptively describes how English is one voice in a reverberating hullabaloo of languages in the subcontinent. Indeed, it is almost standard practice for English novelists like Salman Rushdie to use "chutneyfied" English to question the hegemonic status of English, even and especially as they benefit from such hegemony. Desai uses English to demonstrate how English is "in custody" of older traditions of writing in South Asia and questions the gendered biases inherent in the ethical impulse to assume their custodianship. Deven admires Urdu but refuses to read Urdu poems by a woman. Desai's English novel hints at these unread, unpublished verses, without translating or reproducing them, and thereby challenges readers to investigate the literary and cultural history of the subcontinent without forgetting the women whose labor created that culture.

Notes

1. Naim tells us that Nur's lackeys would have had very good reasons to speak of Pakistan as a haven for Urdu literature: the Indo-Pakistani war of 1965 had forced Urdu writers to explicitly declare their religious and national allegiance (277).

2. In late nineteenth-century colonial India, novelists, playwrights, and essayists turned Hindi into a national, Hindu language through caricatures of Urdu as an aristocratic, indolent Muslim woman termed *Urdu bibi*. This figure, often depicted as a courtesan, represented immorality and foreignness. See Rai, *Hindi Nationalism*; Dalmia.

3. Yaqin describes how and why the elegiac mood of Desai's novel may be ineffective. The novel subscribes too wholeheartedly to delusions of Urdu's aristocratic grandeur and thus fails to interrogate the historical forces that favor such communal identification of language and literature (130, 133). In Menozzi's reevaluation of *In Custody*'s elegiac tone, the novel is not history by other means. Instead, Desai's novel is better read as an experiment, an exploration of the different ways in which literature may be transmitted, among which the idea of custodianship is the most compelling (49–50). More recently Mufti has argued that the reflexive association of Urdu with a declining, semifeudal culture would be unthinkable in a Pakistani novel (169–70).

4. The literature on Hindi and Urdu is vast and can be overwhelming. Two excellent starting points, for which the author of this essay is indebted, are Faruqi; Mufti (esp. 119–45).

5. Anjaria argues that both English and *bhasha* languages were the site of consolidation of colonial power (6), and Mufti argues that the relation of English to vernaculars replicates the cultural logic of the colonial state in the mid-nineteenth century. For a genealogy of this debate in postcolonial theory and criticism, see Mukherjee; Chandra, "Arty Goddesses" and "Cult"; Sunder Rajan, "Dealing."

6. See Sadana for a historical exploration of the plausibility of "authentic" Indian characters speaking English in novels (136).

7. See Satpathy on the ironies of (not) teaching Indian novels for their real or imagined Indianness (63). In the period Satpathy discusses, *In Custody* was rejected from Delhi University's MA English syllabus but was valued for its Indianness in one course taught in an American university. The study guide Satpathy cites can be found online at www.auburn.edu/~mitrege/ENGL2210/study-guides/desai.html (accessed 12 July 2018).

8. Sinha defines *thumri* as "a semi-classical rendition of Hindustani classical music," with the songs mostly telling stories of romantic love for Krishna, a Hindi god (137). Translation taken from subtitles to the DVD of *The Other Song*.

9. See Sinha for the combined influence of men like the performer and teacher Vishnu Digambar Paluskar and the head of All India Radio B. V. Keskar in the selection and broadcast of vernacular music (138–40).

Works Cited

Anjaria, Ulka. *A History of the Indian Novel in English*. Cambridge UP, 2015.

Chandra, Vikram. "Arty Goddesses." *The Hindu*, 1 Apr. 2001, www.thehindu.com/todays-paper/tp-miscellaneous/tp-others/arty-goddesses/article27925488.ece. Accessed 30 Aug. 2017.

———. "The Cult of Authenticity." *Boston Review*, Feb. 2000, www.bostonreview.net/vikram-chandra-the-cult-of-authenticity. Accessed 30 Aug. 2017.

Dalmia, Vasudha. *The Nationalization of Hindu Traditions: Bhāratendu Hariśchandra and Nineteenth-Century Banaras*. Permanent Black, 2010.

Desai, Anita. "The Art of the Custodian." Interview by Filippo Menozzi. *Wasafiri*, vol. 30, no. 1, Jan. 2015, pp. 29–34. *Taylor and Francis Online*, doi:10.1080/02690055.2015.980998.

———. *In Custody*. Harper and Row, 1984.

Dewan, Saba, director. *The Other Song*. India Foundation of the Arts, 2009.

Faruqi, Shamsur Rahman. "A Long History of Urdu Literary Culture, Part 1: Naming and Placing a Literary Culture." *Literary Cultures in History: Reconstructions from South Asia*, edited by Sheldon Pollock, U of California P, 2003, pp. 805–63.

Menozzi, Filippo. *Postcolonial Custodianship: Cultural and Literary Inheritance*. Routledge, 2014.

Mufti, Aamir. *Forget English! Orientalisms and World Literatures*. Harvard UP, 2016.

Mukherjee, Meenakshi. "The Anxiety of Indianness: Our Novels in English." *Economic and Political Weekly*, vol. 28, no. 48, 27 Nov. 1993, pp. 2607–11. *JSTOR*, www.jstor.org/stable/4400456.

Naim, C. M. "The Consequences of Indo-Pakistani War for Urdu Language and Literature: A Parting of the Ways?" *The Journal of Asian Studies*, vol. 28, no. 2, Feb. 1969, pp. 269–83. *JSTOR*, doi:10.2307/2943002.

Rai, Alok. *Hindi Nationalism*. Orient Longman, 2007.

———. "Longing for Urdu." *India International Centre Quarterly*, vol. 35, no. 3/4, Winter 2008/Spring 2009, pp. 274–81. *JSTOR*, www.jstor.org/stable/23006266.

Sadana, Rashmi. "Writing in English." *The Cambridge Companion to Modern Indian Culture*, edited by Vasudha Dalmia and Rashmi Sadana, Cambridge UP, 2012, pp. 124–41.

Satpathy, Sumanyu. "Anita Desai and Sahitya Akademi." *Indian Literature*, vol. 52, no. 2, Mar.–Apr. 2008, pp. 57–64. *JSTOR*, www.jstor.org/stable/24159369.

Sinha, Madhumeeta. "Wayward Women, Wicked Singing." *Transcultural Negotiations of Gender: Studies in (Be)longing*, edited by Saugata Bhaduri and Indrani Mukherjee, Springer India, 2016, pp. 135–43.

Sunder Rajan, Rajeswari. "Dealing with Anxieties." *The Hindu*, 25 Feb. 2001, www.thehindu.com/todays-paper/tp-miscellaneous/tp-others/dealing-with-anxieties/article27918626.ece.

———. *The Scandal of the State: Women, Law, Citizenship in Postcolonial India*. Duke UP, 2003.

Yaqin, Amina. "The Communalization and Disintegration of Urdu in Anita Desai's In Custody." *The Annual of Urdu Studies*, vol. 19, 2004, pp. 120–41.

Henry Schwarz

Approaching the Unknowable: Teaching Mahasweta Devi in the United States

Prior to her death in 2016 at the age of ninety, Mahasweta Devi was a towering figure in modern Indian literature and a household name in her native state of West Bengal. Writing in Bengali, she has more than one hundred novels and more than twenty collections of short stories to her credit. Her complete works in Bengali stretch to twenty printed volumes, not counting writings published in small magazines or ephemeral publications, translations of Jim Corbett and Lu Xun into Bengali, or her voluminous correspondence with government officials and average citizens. She received the Indian state's highest honors, the Padma Shri and Padma Vibhushan, and the 1997 Magsaysay Award, often considered the Asian equivalent of the Nobel Peace Prize. Translated into every Indian language, her writing is synonymous with the struggle against oppression of India's groaning masses.

Teaching Devi's writing to students in the American university system demands not only an encounter with the reality of these struggles but also a reckoning with the element of mystery that is part of her message for the reader. In 1995 Gayatri Spivak published translations of three stories by the writer in *Imaginary Maps*, including an interview, preface, and afterword. The high-quality translations and editorial commentary are valuable for teaching purposes, because Spivak captures and promotes the mystery at the heart of the stories and the heightened sense of incommunicability or incommensurability between the thing said and the thing meant. This communication gap, referred to in deconstructionist code as a "secret" (xxv), operates on at least three levels. For the author, it signifies the sociocultural distinction between tribal (Adivasi) and mainstream Indian culture (*diku*); the yawning economic and educational gap between modern, educated, developed India and its primitive hinterlands; and the seemingly unbridgeable existential dilemma of truly understanding another human being of whatever cultural context, but especially those from distant social and linguistic environments. In Devi's words, the worlds of the Adivasi and the *diku* "have run parallel" (Spivak xii); there is no meeting point. Thus, every interaction between the two worlds is an exercise in translation, and it should come as no surprise that vast areas of incomprehension are revealed in the attempt, with much remaining unknown and perhaps unknowable.[1]

Spivak's translations foreground the importance of organized resistance alongside the difficulty of comprehending the other. In the process, Spivak claims to undo (or "deconstruct" [xxiv]) the binary opposition between theory and practice. As a Marxist, feminist, and deconstructionist, Spivak matches her theoretical Marxism to the actuality of tribal and peasant life in India. Her translations are literal, vibrant, and mysterious, as they render Devi's spare prose without embellishment. She leaves the English-language reader to sort out very foreign social contexts without explanation, making hers perhaps the most successful translations of the author's work and mission.

I have taught *Imaginary Maps* in many different classroom settings. Although undergraduate teaching requires me to translate the untranslatable into commonsense correlates for the sake of comprehension, most recently, in one of my most productive experiences, I have allowed the author to teach herself by minimizing commentary and allowing students' reading experiences, often marked by incomprehension, to register as a productive foundation for exploring abovementioned problems of translation. Beginning with the opening story "The Hunt," I assign two or three student facilitators to take responsibility but not to lead discussion. They must read the story at least twice, until they feel a certain ownership. I task them with simply making points about their reading experience, then to take a backseat to the rest of the class and allow the silences to speak. This restraint is difficult, but I believe it is important to highlight the mystery before introducing contexts and explanations. I explore students' first impressions. What does it feel like to read this for the first time? What needs explanation? If the discussion proceeds in a page-by-page sort of way, there will be many moments of incomprehension for both cultural contexts and the sheer difficulty of the writing. Devi does not use quotation marks, only indented tabs for dialogue, as did James Joyce in *Dubliners*. Students will necessarily get lost in following the speakers, as each carries a distinct identity of caste, class, gender, or region that will seem foreign and as each speaks past the other in multivalent "language cultures that float around the dialogues," as Samik Bandyopadhyay puts it. These moments of incomprehension are wonderful opportunities to comment on the richness of the hybrid and heteroglot populations of the regions under observation.

If, however, students choose to jump to the blockbuster ending of "The Hunt" for discussion, as they did in a recent postgraduate class, there is both much to say and much to miss. The events of the story revolve around Mary Oraon, a half-tribal girl who works for an estate owner, Mr. Prasad, and hacks to death her would-be rapist, Tehsildar Singh, a contractor come to the village to extract precious wood from the surrounding Sal forest. American students are surprised by Mary's spectacular resistance to sexual aggression, questioning their stereotype of Indian female passivity, and may attribute her fortitude to her mixed parentage, the vigor imparted by her white Australian missionary father. They will most likely know little of gender politics among tribals, which is far more equitable, by and large, than among caste Hindus. They may notice the pervasive images of redness that saturate "The Hunt," images that resonate with symbolic overtones of blood, spring rebirth, and tribal ritual, as symbolized by the bloom of a flamboyant tree. But they will most likely not grasp the cultural and political context of the Naxalite rebellion so integral to Devi's work and to this region, nor its symbolic resonance with the tribal charivari of the eponymous hunt ritual. I explain that the Naxalite movement takes its name from a peasant-tribal rebellion in Naxalbari, West Bengal, in 1967. It has become synonymous with a Maoist-style, communist revolutionary movement that currently controls approximately thirty percent of the Indian subcontinent. It figured very prominently in the middle-class cultural politics of Calcutta in the 1970s, when large numbers of college students joined its ranks (see Chakravarti; Roy).

Comparison with another story, also translated by Spivak but not in *Imaginary Maps*, is instructive for introducing contextual information.

Published by Spivak twelve years earlier, and by now a canonical work in the American postcolonial literature curriculum, Devi's "Draupadi" is situated explicitly in a Naxalite battlefield at the same chronological time and in the same geographical region. The heroine of "Draupadi" is a tactical commander of a guerrilla cell operating in Mary's region, but these strategic movements are nowhere acknowledged in "The Hunt," even as the endings of both stories celebrate the world turned upside down demanded of by utopian programs. The Naxalite revolution maps onto the mythical tribal version of charivari celebrated in the hunt ritual, but of course it is not identical to the political overturning promised by the cadres of "Draupadi." Mary, like Draupadi, may be considered an organic intellectual, but she shows no awareness of her counterpart.

This disjuncture points to the necessity of unreading our preconceived notions of space and time in considering these characters as somehow sympathetic or complementary, for they are not. As I explain, they are both displaced Adivasi females in ambiguous relation to revolutionary movements happening in their midst, yet they occupy different universes. While Draupadi is *in* the struggle, Mary is *of* it, however unknowingly. Her killing of Tehsildar Singh during the ritual hunt is a statement of female and lower-caste agency, as is Draupadi's resistance to the gang rape sponsored by Senanayak, but these acts are not politically equivalent; Mary kills her rapist and opportunistically steals his money to elope with her lover, while Draupadi enacts a suicidal guerrilla operation that ultimately serves the larger cause by destroying the confidence of the enemy. Each lives in separate ideological universes while inhabiting similar material conditions. In this way Devi illustrates at once the fragmentary and episodic nature of tribal resistance but also its larger, unifying logic with three hundred years of European imperialist oppression and three thousand years of Aryan oppression.

Biology is similarly differentiated. Draupadi is not a "half-breed" by blood—"crow would eat crow's flesh before Santal would betray Santal" (193)—but she is hybridized by her indoctrination through city learning, strategies that come from the urban "gentlemen" (*bhadralok*) who guide revolutionary tactics. This cultural fertilization is beneficial to the cause. The force of ethnic purity is informed by her betrayal by Budhna and Shomai, actual Santali mixed-bloods fathered by soldiers of the American occupation during World War II, who eventually give her up to the army. Mary Oraon, by contrast, is a product of actual racial miscegenation who learns to profit from both her halves. Her light skin and strong work ethic make her formidable in the market, while her Oraon tribal blood binds her to ancient ritual and the ancestral power of the hunt. One character is pure and the other is mixed by blood, but both are hybridized in quite different ways, with quite different ramifications, in each story.

Students are tempted to turn to the sensational endings first in discussion, resulting in conversations rich in complication and contradiction. But if they focus on the stereotype of female passivity, how many students will notice the landscape, an extremely potent character (or actant) in each story? In "The Hunt," the jungle ravine seems to become an actual speaking presence that provokes an authorial interruption. Mary drinks liquor and becomes sexually aroused; she begins to see things: "Stars are strobing in her head. Ah, the stuff is putting spangles in front of her eyes. Behind them is Tehsildar's face." A mysterious voice arises from within the text, which becomes dialogic during this moment of intoxicated arousal: "The bottle rolls off. Into the depths of the ravine. Not even a sound. How deep is the ravine? Yes, the face is beginning to look like the hunted animal's" (16). Who or what says "yes"? In response to what question? "How deep is the ravine?" is not a question that literally motivates its answer, yet the connection between the unmeasured depth of the ravine and the mystical transformation of human into animal are clearly related. We hear it again:

> Mary is watching, watching, the face changes and changes into? Now? Yes, becomes an animal.
>
> —Now take me?
>
> Mary laughed and held him, laid him on the ground. Tehsildar is laughing, Mary lifts the machete, lowers it, lifts, lowers.
>
> A few million moons pass. Mary stands up. Blood? On her clothes? She'll wash in the cut. (16)

Mary seems to expect that the face of the man will change into that of an animal. But why is it a question? Has it happened before? It is the festival of the hunt, Jani Parab, when once in twelve years the women perform the ritual of the hunt. Mary is eighteen. During the last women's festival Mary would not have set out "to hunt the big beast" (16). This time, "Against the background of the spring songs Mary thought he was an animal. A-ni-mal. The syllables beat on her mind" (13). Like the mysterious ravine, the ancient ritual provides her with an interlocutor that puts "syllables" into her head. This primordial language or voice is explained very precisely as something unknowable. Similar to the unknown depth of the ravine ("no one knows how deep the ravine is. No one has gone all the way down" [16]), the ritual itself is properly unknowable in ordinary language or, rather, knowable only in tribal language: "They don't know why they hunt. The men know. They have been playing the hunt for a thousand million moons on this day" (12). The peculiar narrative voice that emerges to answer these questions in the affirmative, I would suggest, is the distant voice of archaic tradition (however inadequate that term), an echo perhaps of a time before language, perhaps before the arbitrariness that we have learned constitutes the sign, at least within historical time.

The sheer thorniness of the language takes time to grasp. Students frequently complain they cannot differentiate the characters in dialogue and get lost when multiple characters speak. This is useful to delineate the distinct identity markers that structure such conversations and to note the ties that bind (and distance) speakers from one another. It is crucial, for example, to distinguish the voices of the "gentlemen" in "Draupadi" from those of other upper-caste Hindus who use similar diction and phraseology but who inhabit the other side of revolutionary ideology. Senanayak, who orders Draupadi's rape, could be the father of the gentlemen; they have almost identical backgrounds of caste, class, and education. Similarly, Tehsildar Singh manipulates his "caste brothers" to afford him entry into the timber market, yet swindles them in the eventual deal as an opportunistic capitalist.

In the story "Douloti the Bountiful," it can pay to interject literary critical terminology about character, psychological depth (or lack of it), social types, and formal elements such as linear narrative chronicle versus horizontal moments of deep time. The story is psychologically flat in comparison to the other two mentioned, with a surface appearance of unremarkableness that can lull the inattentive reader. This is quite representative of the author's larger output, such as in the epic novels *Chotti Munda* and *Aranyer Adhikar* (*Rights over the Forest*), in which the predominant mode is chronicle, and stories unfold slowly, over long periods of time, as opposed to the condensed, lyrically sensational epiphanies of "Draupadi" and "The Hunt." Stories like "Douloti" do not move on the plane of individual psychology but rather on that of event. This chronicle-like narrative is sometimes called *kahini* (fable) or *itikotha* (tale) in Bengali; it is a characteristic feature of the folk tradition and a substantial part of the writer's oeuvre, although not represented proportionally in her English translated work. Long time frames provide the reader with a sense of history unfolding and thus of cumulative or evolutionary scales rather than revolutionary moments.

"Douloti" begins with the story of her father, Ganori, or "Crook" Nagesia, whose body is broken pulling an ox cart. The first twenty-five pages of the seventy-five-page story are devoted to him, intermingled with other tales that provide local color and introduce significant characters and social relations. Locale is enormously important here and is expanded in great detail, as this is the rural canvas against which Draupadi's insurgency becomes not only justified but required. Caste oppression is boundless; it is enforced by indebtedness or bond slavery, which is basically interminable. Human trafficking is a norm, whether for manual labor in industry or sexual prostitution. Douloti's sale into prostitution forms the kernel of the story, but hers is only an instance, a type, of a vastly repeated enterprise. Thus, her individual psychology in this story is much less important than her representation as an example of something within an ensemble of similar types. The folksy means of presentation, through narrative storytelling, places her in a milieu of similar stories that makes her individual experience, however harrowing, typical rather than exemplary. Most other characters here similarly appear as types.

The one significant exception is Bono Nagesia, who eventually emerges as a revolutionary figure, an organic intellectual who joins a unique coalition of village actors that includes a schoolteacher and a Christian missionary at the time of the 1975 Emergency. This cultural context may be very perplexing to students, who learn to distrust the "bespectacled gentry" from early in the story (Devi, "Douloti" 20). As they should. But as Indian independence unfolds and evolves over the thirty-year span of the story, these gentlemen begin to exercise a greater role in the life of the nation, and eventually their enlightened influence begins to penetrate what Devi elsewhere calls the "Neanderthal darkness" of some of the villages (Devi, "Draupadi" 187). At first they are ridiculed for conducting a census and then elections. It eventually emerges they are trying to do some good in combatting bond slavery and trafficking. By the end of the story, unfolding over Douloti's lifetime, they have formed a movement that flickers into political power.

This alliance of the tribal, Dalit, and schoolteacher resounds with the political theorist Jayprakash Narayan's program for "total revolution" in Bihar at this time. Emphasizing public education, eliminating corruption, instituting a people's democracy, and eradicating social evils such as dowry, untouchability, and bond slavery, the program required teachers as much as subaltern organic intellectuals.[2] Bono and Prasad, in league with the schoolteacher, are cadres in a rural alliance largely responsible for Prime

Minister Indira Gandhi's declaration of Emergency in 1975, the year Douloti perishes on the school playground, on a map of India drawn to celebrate Independence Day.

Spivak elaborates on the poignancy of Douloti's reaction to this movement in her preface to great effect. As Bono and the cadres take their justice program to the prostitutes, Douloti speaks silently: "Don't grieve, Uncle Bono. Why don't you rather tell me those things silently just as I am speaking to you in silence? Let the gentlemen twitter this way. Those words of yours will be much more precious" (87). Spivak comments, "Here women's separation from organic intellectuality is a complicity with gendering that cannot not be perceived by many as sweetness, virtue, innocence, simplicity. . . . Internalized gendering perceived as ethical choice is the hardest roadblock for women the world over" (xxvii–xxviii). Poor, sweet Douloti, feverish with gonorrhea, who has raised more than forty thousand rupees from the labor of her flesh, unties the knot of her sari and offers Bono one rupee to buy a snack. "Bono wept out loud in lament" (88). The story is named for her, after all. What I take Spivak to mean is that Douloti's feminine innocence allows her to excuse her exploitation and to evade Bono's politics in the name of sweetness and intimacy. When she falls dead on the map of India, it is difficult to resist the notion that this might be a national allegory writ large.

In the collection's final story, "Pterodactyl, Puran Sahay, and Pirtha," I have found it very useful to dwell on the enormous communication gap between the tribal boy Bikhia and the journalist Puran in their efforts to understand the import of the pterodactyl's appearance as a vision. There is a wonderful summary of the main plotline and some significant exegesis two-thirds of the way to the end (158–59). Devi provides several such summaries in a variety of voices. Like most of the author's stories, the actual narrative is very simple, but the excitement of the reading experience lies in navigating the jagged contours of the prose. By now, after three or four classes and a week of reading, students have learned to internally soar on the currents of the dialogues. The thematics of unknowability are repeated stridently in "Pterodactyl," in which the mysterious creature, which cannot possibly exist in the modern world by scientific standards, nonetheless appears. This Gothic conundrum, by which the reader must accept an impossible occurrence as fact, is similar to a ghost story, except that for the main protagonists of the story, the abject tribals of Pirtha, the ghost is absolutely real and even more significant than their everyday reality. They must believe in the resurrection of the ancestral spirit in the modern world even as the Oraons of "The Hunt" must reenact the primordial ritual in a forest now devoid of wildlife. Within these themes of paradox, once again the landscape speaks, and the reader must wonder who (if anyone) hears it. As in "Draupadi" and "The Hunt," autochthonous nature has a speaking voice. Students usually miss this, so I point to this passage:

> Bikhia and Puran wait. Yes, a dark cavern in front. Perhaps it goes down to the hill base. As if the dark waits with its skirts forever spread. Give me, give me what you must keep secret. I will guard it with care. Now I have no mysterious secret of my own. . . .
>
> Bikhia drops a little stone.
>
> The sound of the fall reaches them in a few seconds. Bikhia, this is good. No one will know.
>
> Bikhia lowers his head. (176)

Divided by wanting to know, unknowing, and wishing to share a "secret," these stories haunt us with seemingly limitless teaching possibilities, shedding unusual light on the politics and poetics of translation in the classroom.

Notes

1. I have explained this extensively elsewhere: see Schwarz.

2. Jayprakash Narayan ("JP") was an influential leader in rural politics in the 1970s, primarily in Bihar. He is figured many times in Devi's fiction. His movement was characterized by its coalition of lower-class peasants, including Adivasis and untouchables (Dalits), and lower-middle-class intellectuals (primarily schoolteachers) to fight corruption and caste discrimination.

Works Cited

Bandyopadhyay, Samik. Unpublished video interview with Henry Schwarz. 1988.

Chakravarti, Sudeep. *Red Sun: Travels in Naxalite Country*. Penguin, 2008.

Devi, Mahasweta. "Douloti the Bountiful." Devi, *Imaginary Maps*, pp. 19–94.

———. "Draupadi." Translated by Gayatri Chakravorty Spivak. *In Other Worlds: Essays in Cultural Politics*, by Spivak, Methuen, 1987, pp. 179–96.

———. "The Hunt." Devi, *Imaginary Maps*, pp. 1–17.

———. *Imaginary Maps: Three Stories*. Translated by Gayatri Chakravorty Spivak, Routledge, 1995.

———. "Pterodactyl, Puran Sahay, and Pirtha." Devi, *Imaginary Maps*, pp. 95–196.

Roy, Arundhati. *Walking with the Comrades*. Penguin, 2011.

Schwarz, Henry. "Postcolonial Performance: Texts and Contexts of Mahasweta Devi." *Mahasweta Devi: Critical Perspectives*, edited by Nandini Sen, Pencraft International, 2011, pp. 175–89.

Spivak, Gayatri Chakravorty. Translator's preface. Devi, *Imaginary Maps*, pp. xxii–xxix.

Ambreen Hai

Mira Nair's Independence of Vision: Film Adaptations of *The Namesake* and *The Reluctant Fundamentalist*

This essay describes strategies for teaching anglophone South Asian women's fiction and film in conjunction and discusses the pedagogical benefits and challenges of teaching written and audiovisual texts together for the mutual illumination they provide. It addresses the importance to students of learning to read and analyze the politics and aesthetics of different media in a comparative framework, of acquiring the methodological skills of both close reading (of fiction) and close viewing (of film). I begin with two founding premises: one, that we see film adaptations of fiction as not secondary or derivative, lesser work but as active forms of engagement, elaboration, interpretation, transformation, or critique; two, that we extend our understanding of South Asian women's writing beyond the individual or solitary enterprise of literary writing (in the established genres of fiction, poetry, or drama) to include collective, collaborative teamwork such as filmmaking (screenwriting, adapting, directing, and editing).

I draw upon the work of poststructuralist theorists like Robert Stam and Linda Hutcheon in the growing hybrid field of film adaptation studies, which begins by challenging the notion of fidelity (how faithful a film is to its source).[1] Instead of privileging the literary precursor text (as literary critics tend to do) or relegating film adaptation to the margins (as film studies has done, to distance itself from the cultural dominance and prestige of literature over film), such scholars take an interdisciplinary approach to urge that we read literature and film as intertexts, as equal but different artistic and cultural forms, engaging medium specificity to identify what each can do that the other cannot. Reading comparatively enables us to see aspects of both forms that we might otherwise not see. Film adaptation critics adopt different metaphors to counter assumptions of essence and core, to argue for "intertextual dialogism," the back-and-forth dialectic between texts, and a recognition that all texts are intertexts, that even source texts have their own sources (Stam 66). Instead of assuming a hierarchy of source text over its adaptation, Hutcheon reads the adaptation as "a derivation that is not derivative—a work that is second without being secondary. It is its own palimpsestic thing." The adaptation could even be an adjustment or improvement that responds to a different environment where, as in evolution, "the fittest do more than survive; they flourish" (32). In his early, foundational work, George Bluestone wrote, "In the fullest sense of the word, the filmist becomes not a translator for an established author, but a new author in his own right" (62). As a critical practice, reading a text and its adaptation together can inculcate in students "an essential and persistent double-mindedness," requiring them to "hold at least two texts in their minds at once, and that can be very productive indeed" (Cutchins 88). Film adaptation scholars have tended to focus on mainstream American cinema or the British heritage industry of classic fiction and Shakespearian drama to the exclusion of global, transnational, or postcolonial work. However, drawing on theories of adaptation to read South Asian diasporic films can be mutually beneficial: it can augment the scope of the theory, attend to the specificities of different politics and cultural imperatives, and enable a theoretically informed understanding of the film adaptation.

Important recent pairings of South Asian women's fiction and film adaptations include Jhumpa Lahiri's *The Namesake*, adapted by the director Mira Nair, who cowrote the screenplay with her writing partner Sooni Taraporevala; Bapsi Sidhwa's *Cracking India*, adapted by Deepa Mehta as *Earth 1947*, who cowrote the screenplay with Sidhwa; Meera Syal's semi-autobiographical novel *Anita and Me*, adapted by Syal, who wrote the screenplay herself; and Monica Ali's *Brick Lane*, adapted by Sarah Gavron, with the screenplay written in consultation with Ali. These films emerged at the turn of the new millennium, as these diasporic South Asian women writers and directors from the United States, Canada, and Britain started breaking into the previously inaccessible, commercially more challenging, and traditionally male-dominated world of cinema.

I would also urge, in addition to pairings of novel-to-film adaptations, the inclusion of individual films (often written and directed by a team of South Asian women) not based on novels, such as Gurinder Chadha's *Bend It Like Beckham* and *Bhaji on the Beach*, Nair's *Mississippi Masala* and *Monsoon Wedding*, and Mehta's *Water* and *Fire*,[2] as well as women filmmakers' adaptations of novels by male writers, such as Nair's film adaptation of Mohsin Hamid's novel *The Reluctant Fundamentalist*, the screen story cowritten with Ami Boghani and William Wheeler. Teaching many of these texts together (as I have done in a seminar entitled South Asians in Britain and America) creates a comparative framework for the study of diasporic South Asian women's cultural production from various locations. Furthermore, studying a particular filmmaker's early and late work can allow students to consider her development over the course of her career. Reading different filmmakers' work with fiction enables students to think about the variety of contemporary forms of writing and the ways that South Asian women's filmmaking and screenwriting are also creative and politically interventionist forms of cultural work.

I also recommend teaching individual South Asian women writers and filmmakers in a broad variety of courses, especially those not explicitly concerned with otherness. This can have multiple intellectual and educational benefits: as a way to diversify the curriculum and the readings within a particular course, to draw students into fields that they might not otherwise explore, and to enhance students' understanding of a given topic or issue by expanding the contexts within which they think about it toward the more global and comparative. For instance, in a first-year seminar titled Love Stories in which I examine normative notions of marriage and sexuality and how cultural production can reaffirm, police, or disrupt those normative constructions, I teach, after Shakespeare's *Romeo and Juliet* and Jane Austen's *Persuasion*, Chimamanda Ngozi Adichie's *Americanah*, Nair's *Mississippi Masala*, and Shyam Selvadurai's *Funny Boy*. In an advanced seminar, Domestic Servants in Literature and Film, I teach, after Samuel Richardson's *Pamela* and Wilkie Collins's *The Moonstone*, Aravind Adiga's *The White Tiger* and Sidhwa's *Cracking India* with *Monsoon Wedding* and *Earth 1947*. Often students introduced to postcolonial texts in such a way follow up by taking a course explicitly focused on postcolonial or South Asian literature.

Since teaching is highly dependent on understanding the needs at particular times of particular students, and the specific social and historical conditions in which they are situated, I should clarify my institutional contexts. I teach anglophone postcolonial literatures in the English department at Smith College, the largest women's liberal arts college in the United States. Given the historically and still predominantly white composition of the student body, most students are not automatically attracted to courses and materials that do not have the cultural capital or legibility of canonical British or even American ethnic literatures. For much of my time here, my postcolonial courses have counted toward the English literature major but did not fulfill major requirements (as did courses in early British authors). This created a two-tier system, directing students into white canonical literatures and not into noncanonical ones.[3] Hence I have also designed courses under a variety of different rubrics (or ruses) to draw students interested in a particular topic as a way to introduce them to postcolonial literary or film texts. Often, given students' visual orientation and more visceral responses to the moving image and subliminal cues of music and sound, films become a powerful tool to make the fiction more vivid, more imaginable and real, occasioning more engaged and attentive reading of the source text. It can also be an important breakthrough for students, hegemonized by mainstream Western cinema, to see nonnormative faces and bodies on screen, whom they are called upon to empathize and identify with or care for, or places that make more material the non-American locations that they could not otherwise visualize.

Given space constraints, I propose here to look closely at some examples of Nair's film adaptations. Nair earned a name for herself with socially engaged documentary films like *India Cabaret* and moved to feature films with *Salaam Bombay*, leading to international hits like *Monsoon Wedding*.[4] More recently, she has turned to film adaptations that add to and, I would argue, intensify the political stakes of their source novels. A comparison of her adaptations of Lahiri's *The Namesake* and Hamid's *The Reluctant Fundamentalist* reveals an independence of vision and interventionist politics with regard to immigrant generational dynamics and post-9/11 Islamophobia, respectively, as well as the intersections of gender, nationality, and imperialism.

In studying pairings, I discuss the source novel first over two to three class sessions, interwoven with selected clips that I show to compare particular scenes. I start with the opening to compare how the film (versus the novel) sets up its key questions and concerns. I select scenes notable for their cinematography, intensity, thematic significance, or addition to the source, and I end with the closing scenes. To introduce students new to film terminology and techniques, I assign some basic readings on reading and writing about film and film adaptations (Muller and Williams 77–105; McFarlane; Corrigan). I reserve at least one full day for discussion of the film adaptation (students prepare by viewing the film outside of class, based on directed questions I give out ahead of time). I ask students to list omissions and additions and to discuss what they signify. In class, we start with first impressions—what they noticed. Students frequently report being startled by details or aspects that the film drew their attention to that they had overlooked (in such moments the film helps reflect or enhance something about the novel). But inventive adaptation can also create more radical or transformative effects; students also report dissatisfaction or (less frequently) appreciation for something being added, dropped, or changed. My work then is to move the class toward recognition of positive contributions that alterations may make, as well as of compromises that result from the commercial necessities of cinema and the need for greater accessibility for a wider audience. We explore the implications of each change as well as its political consequences. To prepare for class discussions, I also ask students to do "low-stakes" writing (required but ungraded one to two pages) on a close analysis of one scene, observing details of the key elements (mise-en-scène, lighting, sound, music, dialogue, camera movement, camera angles, shot sequences, editing, etc.) and discussing how the scene enhances, changes, or interprets something in the novel. In a seminar, we go around the room, so that students can make informal oral presentations, reporting their findings on a particular scene and learning from one another about different scenes or different readings of the same scene.

We begin our discussion of Lahiri's *Namesake* with the opening scene of heavily pregnant Ashima concocting from Rice Krispies and Planters peanuts (American brand-name foods) an approximation of the Calcutta street snack she craves. Gogol, in his mother's womb, is thus sustained, from the start, by both the hybrid food that his mother creates and the strength of (self-)reinvention, adaptation, and hybridity that immigrant Ashima exemplifies. By contrast, the film, disregarding the novel's achronological flashback to how Ashima met Ashoke, opens with Ashoke on the train that crashes and occasions his journey to America and Ashima taking classical music lessons and then winding her way through Calcutta—

thus locating the story of their arranged marriage in India as the real moment of beginning. I ask students how these different openings reveal key concerns and shifts of narrative emphasis. We discuss how the film starts with gorgeous shots of vibrant, bustling Calcutta as a former British colonial city and bridges the distance to America (the emblematic Howrah Bridge visually both links and contrasts with bridges in New York City), how it tracks the lives of Gogol's parents as the first generation that crossed multiple borders and concludes with Ashima's partial return to Calcutta thirty-odd years later. Unlike Lahiri's novel, which disappointingly drops the perspectives of the engaging couple it opens with and focuses somewhat flatly on Gogol, their son, and his struggles as a second-generation Indian American and his belated coming of age in the moment of his connection to his father's transnational legacy (reading the book by his Russian namesake), Nair's film maintains a more dynamic and rich multiplicity of perspectives and experiences and explores more powerfully the family's multigenerational differences, comparative life trajectories, and emotional intensities.

We look closely at various scenes from the film, but two work particularly well for different purposes. One is the scene where newly married Ashima mistakenly shrinks Ashoke's sweaters in a commercial dryer. Lahiri's single sentence, tucked away in a paragraph about how young Ashima "comes to know" her new husband—"He is fastidious about his clothing; their first argument had been about a sweater she'd shrunk in the washing machine" (10)—is transformed by Nair into a powerful sequence that opens a window into the alternating points of view and gendered dynamics of an immigrant South Asian arranged marriage. In the film, to the accompaniment of melancholic Indian music that evokes her sense of displacement and longing for home, Ashima valiantly trudges through unaccustomed snow, carrying her husband's clothes to the Laundromat, wrapped in a thin cotton sari and vibrant red shawl that contrasts with the bleakness of a gray landscape, intensified by bleached bypass photography. Close-ups of Ashima's face evoke both her alienation and her desire to adjust to her new environment. The next shot cuts to Ashoke's point of view as he holds up his shrunken sweaters and asks in bewilderment, "Who asked you to wash my clothes?" (15:47) even as the camera directs us to see him then seeing the mortification on her face. Used to doing his own laundry, he is befuddled by her attempt to play the traditional wifely role and upset by its result, as he reminds her that replacing his shrunken clothes will constitute some dent in their modest finances. The mood is soft, even as Ashima flees to weep in the bathroom, and the camera cuts to Ashoke's face, alarmed at this consequence of his rebuke. I ask students here with whom the film asks us to sympathize. We observe how the scene gives us both perspectives, inviting understanding of both, as the director moves from crosscutting to using a split screen to present both protagonists at once. Viewing closely this unexpectedly moving scene, students see how the film here does more than the novel, as it explores how this young couple moves from a difficult moment in their early married lives to greater intimacy in reconciliation, when Ashoke, acknowledging his relative power and gender privilege, apologizes: "Your intention was good, it was my mistake not to tell you" (16:36). As he repeats "My Ashima, open the door" with a new tenderness and claim of belonging, and gently teases her to win a smile, the marvelous acting, framing, and slow-paced shot highlight how Ashoke maintains a hesitant, respectful distance, then literally reaches across the divide before they move closer together (16:38–17:23). Nair thus delicately upends Western stereotypes of domination and oppression in an arranged marriage, acknowledging the difficulties and yet suggesting the possibility that both may turn toward and get to know each other better in their isolation and adjust, cognizant of their differently advantaged and gendered positions.

Brian McFarlane argues that "what [fiction and film] share is 'narrative'; what seems likely to keep them at arm's length is 'narration,'" where he defines *narrative* as "a series of events . . . connected by their involving a continuing set of characters" and *narration* as the "means by which the narrative has been put before reader or viewer" (19). Hence even when a filmmaker retains the same elements of plot or narrative, as Nair does in adapting Lahiri, her narration is different; the different means, such as her use of visual images, camera techniques, editing, sound, actors' performance, and spoken dialogue, produce very different emotional effects and signification. We discuss how Nair's added dialogue and cinematic cues in a later scene in the film enhance a brief scene in the novel. After Ashoke's death, Maxine arrives to visit Gogol at his parents' house to attend a religious ceremony. The novel, focalizing Gogol's perspective, describes how Gogol, caught up in grief and guilt about his father, starts to disconnect from Maxine. Instead of worrying about what she might think of the signs of Indianness in his home (by which he was previously embarrassed) or about publicly acknowledging his relationship with her before his parents' community, now "he doesn't care how the house, the pile of guests' shoes heaped by the doorway, might appear to her eyes. . . . [H]e doesn't bother to translate what people are saying, to introduce her to everyone, to stay close by her side." When Maxine finds him alone in his room and tries to persuade him to leave for a ski trip "away from all this," he resists: "I don't want to get away" (182). The film reinforces this narrative, but its narration adds more. The camera eschews a single perspective, starting with a high-angle shot that slowly descends to eye-level and directs us to see alternately from Maxine's perspective (her sense of estrangement as she walks into a room crowded with Indian family friends and is not welcomed by Gogol), his perspective (his observation of her obliviousness), and a neutral perspective, showing what she does not see: the inappropriateness of her attire (she is the only one wearing black in a gathering of people wearing white, the South Asian color of mourning, and the only one sleeveless, arms uncovered, her body revealingly outlined by a tight black tank top) in contrast to the women who glance at her and pull their saris more snugly around their shoulders. Failing to pick up cultural and interpersonal cues, Maxine reaches over to touch Gogol's face, and he backs off, looking visibly displeased at this inappropriate gesture in this environment. Maxine thus visually stands out, not because she is white, but because she is too wrapped up in her own dominant mode of being, unable to cross cultural bridges, in contrast with another blonde woman (Ashima's friend) who is dressed in a white *shalwar kamiz*. To the sound of the priest's Sanskrit incantation, the camera zooms in to reveal Maxine's alienated expression as she looks at Gogol, now distant from her in every way.

Nair's scene enables us to discuss intersectionality, the intersection of gender with other different dimensions of identity, and the crisscrossing of racial and gender privilege that becomes apparent in this interaction. As an upper-class white woman, Maxine has a relative class and racial advantage as a member of the dominant culture to which Gogol aspires and to which his Indian immigrant community does not have access. However, as a middle-class brown man privileged within a patriarchal culture, Gogol has a relative gender advantage. This scene allows for more of an intersectional understanding of what goes wrong with their relationship as we see the collision of her racial advantage with his gendered one, as each fails the other. Whenever I have taught this scene, white women students cringe at Maxine's behavior and talk about her cultural insensitivity and self-absorption. That is indeed the point in both the novel and film, though the film brings this home more clearly, especially for white or Western viewers. However, as some students also point out, in both, Gogol also fails in his responsibility to provide her with key cultural information.

(Others emphasize her failure to understand how he is unmoored by grief and guilt.) The film intensifies these perceptions, adding new dialogue to highlight Maxine's ethnocentrism and failure of empathy and nonverbal cues that suggest her hyperfeminine attempts to distract him. In Gogol's room, when Maxine deploys sex appeal, cozying up to Gogol and fluttering her eyelashes, he has the gendered power to refuse and to suggest, through his withdrawn body language, that his new role and responsibilities as the bereaved son supersede his obligations to her. But their dynamic changes as he sees (when she suggests that she should go with him to India to scatter Ashoke's ashes) her sense of entitlement, her demand that she attend to him, her inability to understand his shock and grief. Gogol's startled repudiation, "it's a family thing," bespeaks his understanding that her desire to go to India is more about exotic tourism than participation in his family's loss or religious rites (1:25:38). When he tries to open up to her—"I have so many regrets, Max" (1:25:54)—she does not listen, suggesting instead that they get away "from all this" for a ski trip (1:26:13). His response and her subsequent tears precipitate a crisis ("Max, this is not about you," he says in disgust [1:26:42]) that makes clearer how his father's death and Gogol's return to the cultural affiliations he had tried to disclaim also sound the beginning of the end of his relationship with Maxine. "Does race trump gender here?" I ask my students again at this point. They usually think it does. Gogol is repelled by Maxine's greater entitlement and inability to bring herself to care about less privileged others and enabled by his gender position in his family to buttress himself to reject her.

This highlighting of simultaneous privilege and disprivilege (as they come in conflict between a romantically entangled brown man and white woman) emerges even more intensely when I teach Nair's film adaptation *The Reluctant Fundamentalist.* When teaching Hamid's novel, I emphasize how it challenges clichés of religious (Islamic) fundamentalism as it critiques American economic fundamentalism, imperialist interventionism, and post-9/11 Islamophobia and explores the pernicious effects of the ensuing global climate of mutual suspicion.[5] We discuss the male narrator-protagonist Changez's gradual awareness of his complicity with American capitalist imperialism and its financial brutality and militarism, his realization that he has been a "janissary" fighting against his own people, his rejection of the economic logic of downsizing that demands profits at reckless human cost, and his eventual shift not to Islamic militancy but to an ex-janissary's anti-imperialist stance against American covert espionage and interference in Pakistan, as he argues for Pakistan's political, economic, and military independence from the United States (151–52, 179). Unfortunately, Hamid's postcolonial politics go amiss (especially for my white women students) when they collide, as they do, with his problematic gender and sexual politics.[6] To begin with, Changez's mode of describing Princeton as "rais[ing] her skirt for the corporate recruiters" to show "a perfect breast" (4–5), his inability to understand Erica's mental illness, and his eventual forcing of himself sexually, if somewhat ambiguously, upon her unresponding body all produce intense unease. "She did not respond; she did not resist; she merely acceded as I undressed her. . . . Mainly she was silent and unmoving, but such was my desire that I overlooked the growing wound this inflicted on my pride and continued," he reports (89). He notes at their next meeting that Erica, who is still mourning her dead boyfriend, has, after their last encounter, become "a pale nervous creature . . . too brittle to be touched" (102–03), but he tells her, "Pretend I am him," at which she becomes "wet and dilated" but also "oddly rigid . . . giving our sex a violent undertone" (105–06). Soon after this encounter Erica goes into decline and is institutionalized.

It is possible to argue here that we must distinguish between Hamid (the author) and Changez (the narrator-protagonist of a dramatic monologue), that Hamid presents Changez as a flawed character. But what is the purpose of this flaw? Is the author even aware that it is a flaw? How is that awareness indicated? What if the character's flaw undermines the author's very purpose? I would argue that not only is it important to avoid conflating author and narrator, it is important to differentiate the two precisely in order to hold each responsible for different things. We cannot use the distinction between author and narrator to exempt the author from critique or to shield him from the implications of his chosen structures of representation. Much as Chinua Achebe argued in his now classic critique of Joseph Conrad's modes of representation in *Heart of Darkness* as racist, when he distinguished between Conrad's authorial choices and Marlowe's ways of seeing, I would argue here that Hamid likewise fails to provide any signals that indicate how problematic Changez's approaches to women and sexuality are, to offer any calls for a critical distance from Changez or any suggestion that these are limited ways of being and seeing. Moreover, if Hamid's purpose is to push back against pernicious, dominant Western frameworks that vilify and stereotype nonwhite others, and in particular Pakistanis and Muslims after 9/11, how does it serve that purpose to portray his already precariously positioned protagonist in such a negative light? This is not to say that a character like Changez must be portrayed as perfect or above the human, but to present him as effectively a sexual opportunist—liable to deception, taking advantage of a white woman's vulnerability, driven only by his own desire, ignoring her evident sexual and emotional needs—is to reaffirm timeworn Western stereotypes of Muslims as potential rapists, as hypersexual threats to (white) women. All the problems in the novel cannot simply be assigned to Changez as a flawed character. It is, after all, Hamid who chooses to cast Erica as an allegory for America (both succumb to "nostalgia" after 9/11: Erica for Chris, America for a past putatively linked with white Christianity [113, 115]). Such an allegory implies that a brown Muslim man can gain entrance to the United States only by giving up his identity; it becomes even more problematic (to say nothing of crude and crass) when it asks readers to envision the United States as a woman who must open her legs to the (putatively only male) immigrant nonwhite other. Such modes of representation produce a concurrence, not a dissonance, between author and narrator, where both share in a toxic, masculinist cultural mind-set that allegorizes the nation and the university as sexualized and gendered as female in order to criticize and degrade them.

Nair's film notably takes a decisively different tack. With remarkable restraint, Nair writes in her book about the film, "I couldn't film a female character I didn't want to be with. I wasn't arrested by the novel's Erica" (57). The film's Erica is more assertive, joyous, and open and has a more reciprocal relationship with Changez. He does not pursue her obsessively: they meet by accident twice before they start seeing each other. Though she explains that her boyfriend has recently died, she initiates physical contact and intimacy with Changez. The film makes clear her desire for Changez. There is no nonconsensual sex, as in the novel; when Changez pauses and asks, "Should we stop?" her response indicates that he continue (36:20). Though Changez in the film does say, "Pretend I'm him," this becomes a turning point that, instead of leading to Erica's decline, enables her to move into a more steady relationship with Changez (37:00). All this results in a more positive and sympathetic representation of Changez, as more vulnerable and not "creepy" (as my students put it), than in the novel. This is not to say that Changez is a flawless paragon of virtue in Nair's film, but his character no longer unwittingly reaffirms orientalist stereotypes of Muslim men as sexual predators, as it does in Hamid's novel. Technically, Nair also avoids the limiting framework of the single perspective that monopolizes Hamid's novel and casts doubt on Changez; instead, she uses the multiple perspectives afforded by film to offer alternative viewpoints of events, often to create independent verification of Changez's story and hence to build audience's trust in him.

Nair's film also hints at Erica's self-absorption and exploitativeness from their very first meeting, when Erica asks Changez to submit (again) to a minor ordeal so that she can photograph his alarmed expression. After 9/11, they break up when Erica betrays him, not by disappearing (as in the novel) but by more clearly and horrifyingly exoticizing and exploiting him and their relationship for her photographic art installation. She misquotes his words, out of context, distorting their meaning and literally superimposing her distorted view of him over him, visually denying him agency. He arrives at Erica's exhibit to find his past words slapped over a collage of images of him: "Pretend I'm him," "I had a Pakistani once," "Throw on a burqa" (1:22:8–12). What he had said teasingly, ironically, as a way to upend her misconceptions and stereotypes about Pakistanis or Muslims is transformed now, in her work, into straight, unironic assertion, reaffirming those stereotypes, a form of symbolic violence perpetrated upon him by her. Nair adds affectively powerful, graphic episodes to make very clear how, after 9/11, Changez is repeatedly subjected to orientalist and Islamophobic racial profiling, injustice, and suspicion—from airport officials, the police, and the public at large to his colleagues at work. "You're the one goddam person I trusted in this city," he tells her bitterly (1:22:48). Hence this betrayal on Erica's part compounds his betrayal by America and is clearly aligned with the broader climate of American prejudice and ethical failure. It is significant that Nair's film casts Erica as a photographer, not an aspiring novelist (as in the novel), evoking appropriately, through its visual medium, the imperialist history of orientalist visual representation and instrumentalization of Muslim subjects as spectacles for Western self-titillation. In showing and exposing how Changez is subjected to orientalism by his own lover, the film thus both counters and critiques that (neo)orientalism.

Yet another problem with the novel is its abrupt and ambiguous ending, which leaves unclear whether Changez is in fact a terrorist and liar, involved in a plot to ambush the unnamed American, or whether the American is a CIA agent, sent to kill innocent Changez based on wrongful suspicion. My students debate the merits, demerits, and incompleteness of the ending of the novel, which leaves readers to imagine what happens next, opening up a range of possibilities of degrees of guilt and innocence. Some see pathos in the novel ending where it does, because the storyteller is killed (by the American) and hence silenced (he cannot describe his own death, so what we have are literally his last words). Changez thus becomes a failed Scheherazade figure, unable to escape the tightening net of American surveillance and violence that he can defer only so far. Others wonder if the American is ambushed by the "unusually attentive" waiter, by Changez, or by both (170). I suggest that we read the openness of the ending as a deliberate strategy on Hamid's part, designed to mirror to readers their own predispositions, to show them how they can rely on alternate sets of clues to see preferentially what they already presume. In this way, the novel could work as a way for readers to see and become aware of their preconceptions, to observe what they do and do not prioritize, to educate themselves out of their prejudices, once they become aware of them. The problem, however, is that if readers are not already self-conscious or willing to become self-aware, especially if unprompted by postcolonial class discussions about the politics of reading, the novel runs the very high risk of simply reaffirming those preexisting prejudices. Notably, often in my classes, American students of color and international students from Third World countries, especially South Asia, tend to see Changez as innocent, while many (though not all) white American students do not. The readings of the novel even in my classroom (as a microcosm of a broader global readership) thus rather depressingly confirm my concern that the novel's ambiguity enables readers not to challenge but to reconfirm their previously held suspicions and presuppositions based on their experientially conditioned subject positions, to duplicate, not dispel, the climate of mutual distrust.[7]

Nair's film, by contrast, unequivocally forges ahead to dispel the novel's confusion. "I knew this was to be a very complex adaptation," she reflects; "this . . . ambiguity would not work . . . in a film" (11). The film adds new background to explain why Changez is telling his story, where Rainier, an American professor who does turn out to be a CIA agent, is kidnapped by Pakistani extremists, and Changez agrees to meet with Bobby, an American journalist who has agreed to help the CIA, to enable Rainier's recovery. It also makes very clear Changez's noninvolvement with violence or militancy, even as it complicates Bobby, who understands and is sympathetic to Changez's position against American imperialism and Pakistan's economic and political dependence, yet still holds Changez in suspicion. With some heavy-handedness, the film ends with Bobby regretting how his zealous, mistaken suspicion of Changez led him to shoot Sameer, Changez's innocent student, and with Changez exhorting mourners at Sameer's funeral not to seek revenge.

Most reviews condescend to the film. Noting the ambiguities of the novel but failing to recognize the problems those ambiguities create, Mendes and Bennett describe Nair's film as having "less subtlety" than Hamid's novel (114). Insisting on seeing films as a priori lesser than fiction, they write, "while in Hamid's dramatic monologue the reader hears only the Pakistani side, Nair's film sets up a dialogue about the tragic events by showing both perspectives" (116). It is unclear why the reviewers claim that monologue as a form is more subtle than dialogue or why dialogue is "conciliatory" (117). And the assumption that there are only two sides, American and Pakistani, is simplistic. Mendez and Bennett question Nair's motives without asking the same questions of Hamid: "The (perhaps financially motivated) desire to produce a mainstream film will certainly have dictated the director's decision to recast the story as a political thriller and to abandon all nuance in favor of a sexier and more clear-cut tale . . . to use obvious injustice to generate sympathy for the Princeton-graduate-turned-terrorist" (118). Much about this statement is bizarre. First, there is no evidence in the novel or film that Changez is a terrorist. Second, if the film is necessarily a commercial enterprise, couldn't one say the same for Hamid's novel, which also has to sell copies to fulfill its publisher's expectations? As literary critics, Mendes and Bennet miss nuances in the adaptation, almost willfully elevating the literary text above the film adaptation and neither reading the film on its own terms nor fully addressing the audiovisual techniques or political contexts of the film.

In comparing Nair's film with Hamid's novel, many students initially repeat such Western reviewers' judgment that the loss of the novel's ambiguity compromises the film. Others commend the clarity and cultural-political work of the film, which they recognize as attempting to reach and educate a wider global audience without becoming merely didactic. They often note that where Nair eliminates the uncertainty of the novel, she adds dramatic intensity and verbal punch, giving Changez great lines, such as when Erica asks him why these "lunatics" would fly planes into buildings, and he replies pointedly, "What makes you think I know?" (55:21), or when he tells Bobby, "You picked a side. It was picked for me" (51:29). I point out that if we let go of fidelity as a criterion for evaluating film adaptations, we can appreciate how Nair's film wisely avoids attempting a faithful rendition of the novel with all its problems and, especially in the context of the virulent post-9/11 Islamophobia that has shaped American domestic and foreign policies, articulates a more independent, socially and politically responsible vision and politics. In this current global moment, which I think of as a continued aftermath to 9/11 (especially the European backlash to ISIS, the Syrian refugee crisis, and the 2016 US presidential election campaign and result), Nair's choices to contest Islamophobic readings with clarity seem even more necessary and germane.

We also discuss the powerful use of South Asian music in the film that underscores its affective and thematic effects. In addition to the fantastic opening sequence of the *qawwali* that is intercut with the kidnapping scenes (which suggests how everyday life in Pakistan includes not only terror but also pleasure, community, and cultural engagement), we focus on the sequence where Faiz Ahmed Faiz's famous poem "Mori Araj Suno," sung heartbreakingly by Atif Aslam, accompanies the turning point when Changez quits Underwood Samson, becomes an ex-janissary, and, as Nair writes, "sails down the Bosphorus in Istanbul" (158).[8] Emphasizing the heartache and longing for respect that Changez experiences, this music creates a powerful sound bridge that connects and enhances the scenes that show how Changez is denied that respect both by his lover (Erica) and the nation (America) for which he still maintains love.

In her adaptations of *The Namesake* and *The Reluctant Fundamentalist*, Nair makes bold interventions that change and intensify the political stakes of the source, demonstrating an independence of vision and achievement that make her work not secondary but different, not lesser but, at minimum, equal. Studying the fiction and film texts together as intertexts enables students to shift from a unidirectional approach to film as second to the novel to reading dialogically, from seeing film as merely entertainment or compromise (as if literature were more "pure") to a greater understanding of each text (as well as of both media) as doing equally meritorious, serious cultural work, engaging different techniques, conventions, and aesthetic and formal languages. Such a pedagogical approach also expands students' understanding of what counts as cultural production, enabling them to see the collaborative, inventive work of South Asian women's filmmaking as a significant and alternative mode of creativity and contemporary political work.

Notes

1. See in particular Stam.

2. In an interesting reversal of the usual direction of adaptation, Sidhwa wrote her novel *Water* based on Mehta's 2005 film.

3. Fortunately, these major requirements have recently changed.

4. For her biography, see Nair's entries in the online databases of *Encyclopaedia Britannica* and *IMDB*.

5. Given her film's focus on countering Islamophobia, and in support of Palestinians, Nair declined the invitation to attend the 2013 Haifa International Film Festival (meant to honor her) in protest against Israel's policies: "I will go to Israel when occupation is gone. I will go to Israel when the state does not privilege one religion over another. I will go to Israel when apartheid is over" (Sherwood).

6. South Asian women students in my classes are often both annoyed at their white peers, who focus on the white woman in the narrative at the expense of postcolonial questions, and embarrassed to discover that they had themselves overlooked the sexism in the novel.

7. It is often argued, usually by Western critics, that Hamid's ambiguity is better than Nair's clarity in unequivocally establishing Changez's innocence, because the ambiguity allows readers to understand the mutual stereotyping and especially allows different readers to come away with different understandings. But such readings fail to recognize the critical inequalities and imbalance of power—between Global North and South, between the West and Muslims—and the hegemony of Western frameworks of suspicion that cast greater suspicion on Muslims. "Mutual stereotyping" is not equivalent (just as "reverse racism" is not equal), nor is it equally unfounded. Pakistanis suspect Americans in Pakistan of being connected to the CIA because such suspicions have turned out to be true, as in the infamous case of Raymond Allen Davis, the CIA contractor who shot and killed two Pakistani men in 2011, though the American government denied his connection with the CIA until *The Guardian* broke the news (MacAskill and Walsh). Simply validating ambiguity by assuming equality in an unequal world is dangerous (like color blindness) because it allows for the reaffirmation of prejudice against the more vulnerable.

8. In the poem, the speaker reproaches God ("Listen to my heart's plea, Oh Lord") for the lack of respect humans suffer in the world, despite God's promises of a kingdom of riches. For a full translation, see Nair, *Reluctant Fundamentalist: From Book to Film* 154.

Works Cited

Achebe, Chinua. "An Image of Africa: Racism in Conrad's 'Heart of Darkness.'" *Heart of Darkness: An Authoritative Text, Background and Sources Criticism*, edited by Robert Kimbrough, 3rd ed., W. W. Norton, 1988, pp. 251–61.

Bluestone, George. *Novels into Film: The Metamorphosis of Fiction into Cinema*. U of California P, 1957.

Corrigan, Timothy, editor. *Film and Literature: An Introduction and Reader*. 2nd ed., Routledge, 2012.

Cutchins, Dennis. "Why Adaptations Matter to Your Literature Students." *The Pedagogy of Adaptation*, edited by Dennis Cutchins et al., Scarecrow Press, 2010, pp. 87–96.

Hamid, Mohsin. *The Reluctant Fundamentalist.* Harcourt, 2007.

Hutcheon, Linda. *A Theory of Adaptation.* 2006. 2nd ed., Routledge, 2013.

Lahiri, Jhumpa. *The Namesake.* Houghton Mifflin, 2003.

MacAskill, Ewen, and Declan Walsh. "US Gives Fresh Details of CIA Agent Who Killed Two Men in Pakistan Shootout." *The Guardian*, 21 Feb. 2011, www.theguardian.com/world/2011/feb/21/raymond-davis-pakistan-cia-blackwater.

McFarlane, Brian. "Reading Film and Literature." *The Cambridge Companion to Literature on Screen*, edited by Deborah Cartmell and Imelda Whelehan, Cambridge UP, 2007, pp. 15–28.

Mendes, Cristina Ana, and Karen Bennett. "Refracting Fundamentalism in Mira Nair's *The Reluctant Fundamentalist.*" *American Cinema in the Shadow of 9/11*, edited by Terence McSweeney, Edinburgh UP, 2017, pp. 109–124.

Muller, Gilbert H., and John A. Williams. *Ways In: Approaches to Reading and Writing about Literature and Film.* 2nd ed., McGraw-Hill, 2003.

Nair, Mira, director. *The Namesake.* Mirabai Films and Cine Mosaic, 2007.

———, director. *The Reluctant Fundamentalist.* Mirabai Films and Cine Mosaic, 2013.

———. *The Reluctant Fundamentalist: From Book to Film.* Penguin Studio, 2013.

Sherwood, Harriet. "Mira Nair Boycotts Haifa Film Festival." *The Guardian*, 20 July 2013, www.theguardian.com/world/2013/jul/21/director-mira-nair-boycotts-haifa-festival.

Stam, Robert. "Beyond Fidelity: The Dialogics of Adaptation." *Film Adaptation*, edited by James Naremore, Rutgers UP, 2000, pp. 54–76.

Sushmita Chatterjee

Graphic Novels in the Classroom: A Postcolonial, Queer Methodology

This essay engages with the dilemmas that characterize the politics of teaching graphic novels by South Asian women writers. A central question frames my pedagogy: how do we read and teach democratically? In *Feminism without Borders*, Chandra Talpade Mohanty argues, "If these varied stories are to be taught such that students learn to democratize rather than colonize the experiences of different spatially and temporally located communities of women, neither a Eurocentric nor a cultural pluralist curricular practice will do" (244). As underlined by Mohanty, neither a Eurocentric model nor superficial pluralism suffices since both colonize the differences among women. In this essay I grapple with the challenges of democratic pedagogy using two graphic novels: *Tina's Mouth*, by Keshni Kashyap, and *Kari*, by Amruta Patil. I have taught the two graphic novels in an undergraduate course on global women's issues along with other texts. This essay situates the unique work that graphic novels can do in the classroom, the politics of teaching images, and some useful tensions that permeate the process of teaching graphic novels by South Asian women writers through a methodology combining postcolonialism, feminism, visual studies, and queer studies.

In the first section of this essay, I outline why graphic novels can democratize teaching and learning practices. In the second, I briefly outline my methodology using critical sources that accompany these novels in my classroom. My goal is to present a postcolonial feminist and queer method of teaching the graphic novels. In the third, I provide further pedagogical reflections helpful to the reader interested in using these texts in the classroom, tackling the following questions: What pedagogical methods ensure that our students do not capture certain frames as *the* truth? How do we move toward a complex understanding of space and time that can complicate the notion of South Asia as a homogenous, static space?

Graphic novels constitute a unique medium with their combination of image and text. The term *graphic novel* is often used interchangeably with *comics*, though many maintain irreducible differences between the two forms. For instance, Daniel Stein and Jan-Noël Thon argue that there are significant differences between the two forms in style, format, and spatial location. They consider "graphic narrative" a broader and more inclusive category, distinct from the comic with its Anglo-American origins (5).

There is no consensus about the format for image-text combinations in graphic novels. Which comes first, image or text? Can we separate image and text? Questions such as these have occupied the attention of graphic novel scholars, since many graphic novels pose challenges to a simplistic categorization of image and text. Pamela J. Rader, in her study of Marjane Satrapi's *Persepolis*, draws our attention to how "Satrapi rebels against the conventions of serialized and sequential comics, the autobiography, and Islamic art" (123). For Rader, Satrapi's images and text work together instead of separating elements in a composition (124). Graphic novels such as *Persepolis* offer important insights into visual forms of representation in postcolonial studies. For instance, when showcasing veiled women, the images draw out specificities like hairstyle and facial features and frame an imagination different from the view of a homogenizing Islam associated with passive subjectivity for women (Rader 134).

Deciphering the politics of representation remains a central endeavor for postcolonial studies, understood broadly as an engagement with colonialisms and its varied strategies. Binita Mehta and Pia Mukherji, in their volume *Postcolonial Comics*, provide a lucid account of the importance of comics in postcolonial cultures. They write, "[T]he postcolonial comic thus becomes a particularly appropriate venue that offers radical and progressive alternatives to the notion of obsolete authenticities" (3). The unusual format of comics offers a graphic breakdown of reality through a play with heterogeneous images and text, which challenges and deconstructs any static and passive representation of the other, reducible to "authentic" characteristics. For this reason, deciphering the multiple functions and strategies of image-making remains a matter of central concern; graphic novels can help to instill alternative structures of attitude and reference in postcolonial literature and gender studies courses.

Teaching with graphic novels offers numerous advantages and perspectives. Graphic novels can, through their stylistic format, encourage empathy and capture attention, because the prevailing and predominant communication modes in contemporary global societies are predisposed to the use of images. As Suzanne Keen has noted, graphic novelists tend to adopt visual-textual combinations to elicit a "strategic narrative empathy," which "indicates their manipulation of potential target audiences through deliberate representational choices designed to sway the feelings of their reader" (135). However, adding to the intended empathy channeled by graphic novels, I find graphic modes of depiction an invaluable aid to critical discussions on the problems of representing bodies and identities. Teaching students to question emotional responses and adopt a more critical stance are key to politicizing pedagogy. Teaching graphic novels allows for a discussion of what Nicholas Mirzoeff calls the "commodification of vision" proper to the regimes of visuality of colonial modernity.

Graphic novels can accomplish a number of goals in the classroom such as aid alternative imaginations, promote discussion about the complexities of identity, and build empathy through a visualization of context. Democratically, graphic novels enable us to think between boxes and thus move beyond the consumption of the other based on presumed categorizations. However, it is naive to assume a simplistic correlation between democratic teaching and graphic novels simply because images have the proclivity to frame a particular version of truth. For instance, Sarah Graham-Brown draws our attention to photography of women in the Middle East at the turn of the nineteenth century where many photographs constructed harem scenes based on the colonizer's sexualized and exotic imagination of the Orient. As Graham-Brown writes, "The role of photography in creating and reinforcing this mythology was a singular one, and very influential in shaping popular conceptions" (505). The photographer's setting of the stage and composition of images arguably reinforced power hierarchies and prevailing modes of orientalizing the other. Images, and images and text in the case of graphic novels, are obviously susceptible to manipulation and can be used antidemocratically as simplified pictures to be consumed uncritically as otherworldly stories. This issue gets further complicated when teaching about South Asia and teaching graphic novels by South Asian women writers.

Informed by postcolonial critiques of Western feminist and queer theory, and the concomitant feminist critique of the absence of women in postcolonial discourse, I work to assemble a postcolonial, feminist, and queer teaching methodology attentive to multiple dimensions of representation and analysis. This methodology attempts to decolonize knowledge biases in a persistent effort to reread and challenge passive constructions of space and identity associated with femininity, sexuality, South Asia, and women writers. Postcolonial studies, queer theory, and feminism are often juxtaposed as different theoretical systems with dissimilar histories and politics, notwithstanding moments of convergence (see Chatterjee). I see useful tensions among the three schools without overemphasizing their differences. Building on these tensions, I teach and read images and texts as frames that can uncover the complicated politics of identities.

Jack Halberstam refers to "queer methodology" as a "scavenger methodology that uses different methods to collect and produce information on subjects who have been deliberately or accidentally excluded from traditional studies of human behavior." To Halberstam, a queer method would not resist the combination of "methods that are often cast as being at odds with each other" (13). In Halberstam's writing, queer methodology becomes a creative space to recover and forge new alliances and inclusions. Mohanty's work adds immensely to our repertoire of methods with her emphasis on "antiglobalization pedagogies" (238) and a "feminist solidarity model," which draws attention toward a complex understanding of relations between women that emphasizes "mutuality and coimplication" and "suggests attentiveness to the interweaving of the histories of these communities" (242). Despite the very different contexts of Halberstam's and Mohanty's theoretical formulations, I have found it useful to deploy both methodologies simultaneously in the classroom.

Students also read Judith Butler's *Frames of War* before we move on to an analysis of specific graphic novels. Butler's explanation of framing provides invaluable guidance for students as we attempt to understand the politics of images. As Butler points out, "'to be framed' is a complex phrase in English: a picture is framed, but so too is a criminal (by the police), or an innocent person (by someone nefarious, often the police), so that to be framed is to be set up" (8). Understanding framing enables an understanding of the intricacies of power where only certain images are seen and recognized and others are not. Combining different methodological trajectories enables a deeper understanding of inclusions and exclusions where the queer, feminist, and postcolonial can be framed as social and political constructions. *Tina's Mouth* and *Kari* offer interesting insights that students explore in relation to the critical questions opened through a queer-feminist-postcolonial perspective.

Kashyap's *Tina's Mouth* and Patil's *Kari* are distinctive in style and narrative trajectories. *Tina's Mouth* recounts the story of Tina, a fifteen-year-old living in Southern California with her Indian parents. Situated in India, *Kari* is a queer narrative about life, death, and different processes of coming out into the world. *Tina's Mouth* uses many interesting stylistic devices like the use of frames within frames (12, 13, 15) and also images of bodies not totally encased in frames. For instance, we read and see how Tina is frequently asked, "What are you Really?" (17). Tina retorts, "I'm an Alien" (18). These images are showcased as breaking through frames. The author uses images with sophistication to explain how difficult it is for Tina's classmates to completely understand or place Tina within a category because she lives in California, goes to a private school, and has parents who migrated from India.

Kashyap's graphic novel addresses Tina's negotiation of her public and private life through her relationships with her friends at school and within her family. We see and read about how her parents traveled to America after an arranged marriage in India and the varied dynamics of their life in California (13). Tina's sister and brother hold very different interests. While her sister is an artist, her brother is a surgeon in the making. Kashyap writes, "He's what you might call a square"; this opinion is followed by an image of Tina's brother encased within a square (15). The emphasis on the everyday rather than the spectacular is an important teaching moment, as it helps construct moments of relationality or mutuality, which offer us a starting point for questioning the mechanisms of identification at work in this novel. By focusing on the everyday, we move beyond a static conception of subjectivity and an othering of the text and instead participate in glimpses of specific challenges and trials in unspectacular moments of living.

Tina's mouth, as the name of the graphic novel suggests, has many roles in defining the meaning of the narrative. It stands for Tina's sexuality, her relationship to Neil, her unwanted kiss with Ted, her articulate expressions of life and existential philosophy, as well as the symbolism associated with the Hindu god Krishna as having "the entire universe" and "many more universes" inside his mouth (84). Tina's mouth almost stands as an actor in the novel without reduction to only one meaning. Her mouth is also a source of agony. After her first kiss with Neil ("What is nirvana, mon philosophe?"), Tina expects a buildup to their relationship (131). Her romantic illusions are soon shattered, and when she confronts Neil about why he had given her the wrong impression, Neil responds, "You're like my kooky Buddhist biking buddy" (206). Tina responds that she is not a Buddhist. Through this breakup scene, Kashyap illustrates the agony of both being rejected and being stereotyped. Neil does not consider Tina as a subject or agent of romance. Rather, her subjectivity is framed by a common stereotype. In its depiction of desire and disappointment, the novel presents a common and shared dimension of teenage life—experiences shared across differences—while allowing the reader to grapple with Neil's casual conflation of Buddhist and Hindu identity. Rooted in a somewhat mundane and ordinary experience of romantic disappointment, the incident resists generalization to all people in a certain identity group while nonetheless disclosing the peculiar pain of misrepresentation for groups marginal to the mainstream.

Tina's Mouth offers an intriguing assortment of images and text, which work in tandem to question static constructions of identity and inspire a postcolonial, queer methodology in the classroom. Vivid and graphic, the novel juxtaposes many framing styles, some with clearly outlined borders and others without borders, in various shapes and sizes. The textual narrative creeps through the panels to open up and undo a singular reading of image. For instance, when describing the wealth accrued by her uncle Mahesh, Tina describes "The chip," a computer chip that has been wealth generative (51). The readers see a potato chip followed by an intricate drawing of "The House," grandiose and ostentatious (51–52). Thus we see how image and text unravel each other and open up multiple narratives. Often the images elaborate on the textual explanation; at other times, they provide a humorous counterimage to the text that inspires us to think of the multiplicity of references, as in the word *chip*. With a light touch, Kashyap tucks into the novel's innocuous strings of images the larger problems of arrested representation and the recourse to easy or stereotypical representations that do not engage sufficiently with the complexities of minority identities.

Kari also offers an intriguing analysis of identity, though there are considerable differences between the two graphic novels. Using a scavenger methodology, as termed by Halberstam, how do we represent Kari's queer subjectivity in a social milieu where the language of LGBT politics derived from the West does not adequately represent varied cultures? Patil's *Kari* opens with the attempted double suicide of a pair of lovers from the top of a building. While her girlfriend, Ruth, is saved by a safety net and escapes to another country, the lesbian heroine Kari falls into and is "saved by a sewer" (8). A story about relationships and friendships, *Kari* showcases Kari rowing through her life, trying to survive heartbreak and the pressure of living in a heterosexual culture, and ultimately deciding not to throw herself off buildings anymore. Pia Mukherji draws out the complex configuration of identity work in *Kari* through an emphasis on alterity and loss (164). Mukherji's succinct analysis highlights the importance of fairy tales, retelling stories, movements back and forth, and other stylistic devices that enable us to reckon with the excluded and the absent when understanding constructions of identity. This analysis draws out the complexity of representation and its meaning-making through image and text, "the painterly, iconic, and magical intertexts" (158).

Kari's darkly sketched images with the occasional splash of vibrant colors is not a narrative of affirming an identity or of coming out. The graphic novel uses images and text to weave in the seepage between frames. Patil gives us a detailed architectural plan of Kari's apartment, which she shares with her two roommates and their respective boyfriends. Ironically, the tiny apartment is called "Crystal Palace." Patil juxtaposes a vividly colored frame of princesses, flowers, and pink stones with the stark floor plan of the apartment. Kari says, "The bookshelf is the dam that keeps our tempers from running amok. I try and imagine different worlds on the other side of the bookshelf" (17). Patil uses a number of frames like the bookshelf, the grid of the room, and a brightly colored panel to illustrate the juxtaposition of dream and reality, the imagined and material, even as her protagonist struggles with alternatives to rigid norms of femininity in the culture of her host city. In one panel we see Kari looking at herself in the mirror. She wonders at her reflection, "These things can be troubling. The girls are outside the door telling me to wear Kohl, and here I am wondering why I amn't looking like Sean Penn today" (60). Kari's naked profile jostles with words; image and text interplay to draw out complexities in representational politics. A postcolonial, queer methodology, following Butler, questions, Who is being framed? Who is doing the framing? And is it possible to escape framing?

Juxtaposing these graphic novels that share a focus on intersectional identity provides an inspiring venue to interrogate and democratize our conception of the other. The Indian and Indian American protagonists of the two novels situate their journeys and anxieties in two very different landscapes in which they both share the experience of alienation. Not at home at home and alienated abroad, neither is immune from the anxieties that beset those who do not fit into the mainstream order, whether because of reasons of racial difference or that of sexual orientation. A postcolonial, queer methodology developed through their juxtaposed examination can allow teachers to do justice to the complex dynamics of identification, empathy, and representation at work. It can give students a sense of the discrepancies and overlaps connecting images and texts and a way of exploring the complex subjectivities represented through the visual and the written. Most important, it avoids turning the teaching of South Asian graphic novels into another frame by which non-European works are pigeonholed into monolithic categories.

Practices of teaching and reading are of immense importance when deciphering the politics of framing and representation. Mohanty reminds us that "the existence of Third World women's narratives in itself is not evidence of decentering hegemonic histories and subjectivities. It is the way in which they are read, understood, and located institutionally that is of paramount importance" (77–78). The graphic novel demands an examination of how we read by obliging us to engage with visual registers of information that recall for us dominant regimes of looking, information provided by the visual scan of different bodies, associations that are summoned up with a mere look, and a tradition of imaging in orientalist as well as heteronormative discourses that frames others in an unflattering light. The unique confluence of images and text in graphic novels is particularly useful for examining issues of framing, the imaging of others into arrested fixity, even as they demand that we contend with the information that overflows all frames and asks for the paratext, subtext, and context of representation. Moreover, as a populist form, the graphic novel is received eagerly by students and can serve as a hospitable venue for studying identity, visual politics, textuality, and representation to reconnect gender, culture, and politics in nuanced ways that resist binary formulations.

Works Cited

Butler, Judith. *Frames of War: When Is Life Grievable?* Verso, 2009.

Chatterjee, Sushmita. "What Does It Mean to Be a Postcolonial Feminist? The Artwork of Mithu Sen." *Hypatia*, vol. 31, no. 1, Winter 2016, pp. 22–40.

Graham-Brown, Sarah. "The Seen, the Unseen and the Imagined: Private and Public Lives." *Feminist Postcolonial Theory: A Reader*, edited by Reina Lewis and Sara Mills, Routledge, 2003, pp. 502–19.

Halberstam, Jack. *Female Masculinity*. Duke UP, 1998.

Kashyap, Keshni. *Tina's Mouth: An Existential Comic Diary*. Illustrated by Mari Araki, Houghton Mifflin Harcourt, 2011.

Keen, Suzanne. "Fast Tracks to Narrative Empathy: Anthropomorphism and Dehumanization in Graphic Narratives." *SubStance*, vol. 40, no. 1, 2011, pp. 135–55.

Mehta, Binita, and Pia Mukherji. Introduction. *Postcolonial Comics: Texts, Events, Identities*, edited by Binita Mehta and Pia Mukherji, Routledge, 2015.

Mirzoeff, Nicholas. "On Visuality." *Journal of Visual Culture*, vol. 5, no. 1, 2006, pp. 53–79.

Mohanty, Chandra Talpade. *Feminism without Borders: Decolonizing Theory, Practicing Solidarity*. Duke UP, 2006.

Mukherji, Pia. "Graphic *Écriture*: Gender and Magic Iconography in *Kari*." *Postcolonial Comics: Texts, Events, Identities*, edited by Binita Mehta and Pia Mukherji, Routledge, 2015, pp. 157–67.

Patil, Amruta. *Kari*. HarperCollins, 2008.

Rader, Pamela J. "Iconoclastic Readings and Self-Reflexive Rebellions in Marjane Satrapi's *Persepolis* and *Persepolis 2*." *Crossing Boundaries in Graphic Narrative: Essays on Forms, Series, and Genres*, edited by Jake Jakaitis and James F. Wurtz, McFarland, 2012, pp. 123–37.

Stein, Daniel, and Jan-Noël Thon. Introduction. *From Comic Strips to Graphic Novels: Contributions to the Theory and History of Graphic Narrative*, edited by Daniel Stein and Jan-Noël Thon, De Gruyter, 2013.

Padmini Mongia

Contemporary Chick Lit in Indian English

In the first two decades of the twenty-first century, new genres of the novel in English appeared in India—chick lit, graphic novels, and fantasy fictions—which signaled significant changes in the field of Indian writing in English. Not since the early 1980s had there been as major a shift as with the new "pulp" fiction, written entirely for consumption in the domestic market of the third-largest producer of books in English in the world. Whereas English used to be and still is a marker of the elite in India, its contemporary usage—as the language of globally acclaimed literature but also of commerce, education, the service industry, and myriad other contexts—has changed its place. Its position is a much more complex one than that of an elite language in tension with the many other languages of India.

The anglophone Indian writer Raja Rao famously said of Indians using English for creative expression: one has to "convey in a language that is not one's own the spirit that is one's own" (5). Now, book production in English in India has changed to such an extent that popular novels resonate both linguistically and situationally with their broad general readership. No longer does the postcolonial framework, which helped institutionalize Indian writing in English on the world stage, offer a compelling or sufficient vocabulary for the place of English literary production in India. Many critics have pointed out that Indian writing in English produced a literature by and for the elite, replete with a focus on identity, migration, and transnationalism that spoke of and to a particular class of people. The new, popular literature, written to be mass-marketed, cannot be chastised for such class-based limitations.

Postcolonial studies articulated itself with an emphasis on nation and narration in the last decades of the twentieth century. Although the histories of the postcolonial novel and the novel in English in India are relatively young ones, fifty years of disciplinary formation now define these categories. Attention to and inclusion of popular novels in courses on the postcolonial novel, the Indian novel in English, and Indian or South Asian women's writing allow a fruitful engagement with the limitations that mark even new literary and theoretical categories such as the postcolonial. What follows is a brief history of the emergence of popular fiction in English in India with particular attention to chick lit. Discussion of some of the thematic concerns in this fiction and attention to a few of its practitioners suggest ways chick lit may intervene in a variety of courses to challenge the terms that define academic, canonical formulations.

The Emergence of Chick Lit in India

According to Suman Gupta, "Indian commercial fiction in English . . . is consumed primarily within India, seen to display a kind of 'Indianness' that Indians appreciate, and is not meant to be taken 'seriously' or regarded as 'literary'" (46). The novel in English, from Salman Rushdie's *Midnight's Children* through its grandchildren, was largely produced by what has been described by Harish Trivedi, for instance, as the St. Stephen's school of fiction ("St. Stephen's Factor"), but the new popular fictions are often avowedly and proudly antiliterary. Contemporary popular fiction seems to carry none of the colonial burden we associate with the literary production of the last fifty years of Indian writing in English. Instead, in an American idiom, this fiction examines the concerns of young people who may live in India but whose lives bear a startling resemblance to those of their counterparts elsewhere. The English in which these writers share their fictional worlds is theirs—incorrect, sometimes awkward, and wholly *desi*.

Unconcerned with the desire or capacity to write well, these writers are driven by publication figures. Ravinder Singh, the bestselling author of *I Too Had a Love Story*, proudly admits, "I am not an avid reader. I must have read one or two books before I started writing" (qtd. in Dutta). Now heading his own imprint, Black Ink, for Penguin India, Singh promises to mentor young writers and make their dreams of writerly success come true. The average bestseller in India needs to sell about three thousand copies to be called one, whereas a newly released Chetan Bhagat novel sells more than one hundred thousand copies in the first month. One of the most popular of the new writers and the one credited with ushering in the commercial fiction market, Bhagat altered the publishing scene in India with his *Five Point Someone* in 2004. Approaching books as commodities to be sold rather than as high-culture artifacts with a long shelf life, he priced his books at a modest ninety-five rupees, the cost of a Coke and a slice of pizza, making books as easily consumable and thrown away as the aforementioned snacks.

Along with successful writers such as Bhagat, the early 2000s brought *ladki lit* (chick lit) to India with significant aplomb. The success of the humorous travails of Bridget Jones as she floundered her way through a series of foolish job and relationship choices paved the way for the chick lit phenomenon on the world scene. From India to Brazil, chick lit found readers, writers, and publishers with a remarkable alacrity. The loves and lives of single twentysomethings in urban India as they search for settled jobs and relationships are a large part of the novels' concerns, as is the struggle for demarcating an individual identity within societal and familial norms that shape the protagonists.

The chick lit phenomenon of the 2000s shared common terrain with the work of Shobhaa De, whose novels were published by Penguin India in the mid 1980s. De's novels were liberally sprinkled with the slightly naughty escapades of young women who came to Bombay from smaller cities. As these women negotiated their relationships and careers, they also indulged in breaking various sexual taboos. De's slightly off-color, overly ambitious young women both succeeded splendidly and failed dramatically as their success produced predictable problems. Although De's novels were generally regarded without the respect accorded the works of other new, young authors writing in English at the time (authors like Anjana Appachana, Indrani Aikath-Gyaltsen, and Gita Hariharan), they sold in higher numbers than those of her literary peers. The space created by De in the 1980s remained essentially hers for the two decades that followed, although many old and new women's voices were also heard during that time. Nevertheless, De had created a new voice for women through her novels, and in the early 2000s, after the success of *Bridget Jones's Diary* and *Sex and the City* as well as genre fiction more generally, newer writers began to fill that space.

Swati Kaushal's *Piece of Cake*, published in 2004, became an immediate success and is widely accepted as the first chick lit novel in India. Meenakshi Reddy Madhavan began writing her popular blog in the early 2000s, and it became the basis for her first novel, *You Are Here*, which appeared in 2008. Also in 2008 Anuja Chauhan's *The Zoya Factor* was a runaway success, and the previous year, Advaita Kala published her immensely popular *Almost Single*. Of these three writers, Madhavan straddles the virtual and the novelistic. In addition to her blog and her fiction (she is now the author of six novels), her columns appear in *The Week* and *Youth Ki Awaaz*, a popular online publication. Much as De offered advice to the young and up and coming in urban centers in modern India, so does Madhavan, using her own life as the subject of her analysis as do many other chick lit novels.

In the 1990s De popularized Hinglish, both in her novels and in her witty column in *Stardust* magazine, and her true heir in this regard is Chauhan. With a remarkable effortlessness, Chauhan's prose captures the vitality and sauciness of the languages used by young, urban Indians. Her novels belong in a category quite different from the works of other chick lit writers; she is able to inhabit both the literary and the popular worlds and is easily the queen of the genre. Chauhan's novels are, however, too specific situationally and linguistically to appeal to the reader outside India. As Harish Trivedi writes, "The 'addressivity' of these newer novels (to use Bakhtin's succinct term) does not encompass the Western reader" ("Indian English Writing"). While Rushdie had "chutnified" English as early as 1980, the Hinglish, or masala quality, of Chauhan's prose is different, since it makes no effort to explain itself to the Western reader. Ulka Anjaria notes the Punjabi inflection to Chauhan's rom-com novels and also points out that in works such as hers "the intended audience is not the cosmopolitan elite but precisely those Indian readers who might potentially read in English *and* one of the *bhashas*" (12). Chauhan's novels are peopled by characters grounded in parts of Delhi or India more generally in very particular ways. In *The House that BJ Built*, the protagonist, Boni, may be unexpectedly independent, but she is physically and psychically the product of Hailey Road, a distinct section of Delhi. Zoya, of *The Zoya Factor*, is from Karol Bagh and carries on her shoulder a chip that comes along with that belonging. Encoded into this emphasis on specific locations is an implicit critique of the children of privilege who peopled earlier novels in English, cosmopolitans who belonged nowhere and everywhere.

Although Chauhan's protagonists also carry with them their desire for cosmopolitan belonging, their languages and situations place them quite firmly within specific contexts that impact their choices. Her novels suggest that these modes of belonging are central to the health and well-being of her characters. Zoya, for instance, is chaperoned on her cricket tour by her aunt and an older, married friend. While Zoya may be pursuing her love affair with the captain of the cricket team, she never behaves disrespectfully toward her aunt. Zoya accepts and even welcomes being chaperoned, and the tension between generations we might expect is dissipated. Dawson Varughese, reading postmillennial Indian chick lit, sees it as the site "for the articulation and contestation of modernity in India" (324). Often, though, as in novels such as Kala's *Almost Single*, "'contemporary' women can be both 'traditional' and 'modern' at the same time" (332). The expected tension between an arranged marriage and choosing one's own partner is made moot by the combination of both being possible.

A Bad Character, by Deepti Kapoor, pushes the boundaries of the genre much further than the other novels mentioned so far. Kapoor's first and only novel has her twentysomething protagonist explore her lack of belonging and her sexuality with a bad character who is already dead in the first line of the book. Offering a seamy examination of the young and the restless in a hot, airless Delhi, Kapoor's novel is as much an ode to a dying city as it is an assertion of a young woman's right to her body and her life outside of the gentle push toward marriage that *ladki lit* usually offers. The protagonist, Idha, is not opposed to arranged marriage per se. She may be testing the limits of acceptable behavior for a young woman in her twenties, but she is also open to meeting prospective suitors to see if one of them takes her fancy. Although contemporary chick lit in India and elsewhere generally exhibits the agency of its protagonists, Idha exhibits a kind of agency rarely seen in the genre. An orphan, Idha carves her own destiny, perhaps even sending her ugly lover (the bad character) toward his untimely end.

Idha has her own car and drives all over the city during times when other young women presumably would be safely at home. She chooses to be with her bad character, and she chooses when to leave him. Strangely reminiscent of the inappropriate wanderings of the traditional gothic heroine locked up in her castle, Idha and other women like her are challenging the roles, behaviors, expectations, and capacities made socially and culturally available to them. In a slightly tongue-in-cheek article for *Scroll .in*, the successful novelist Devapriya Roy suggests that the popularity of chick lit in India recalls an earlier moment of literary production: the eighteenth century in Britain, when women wrote novels about women to be read by other women. This early British novel found one of its successful articulations in the gothic, a genre to which the contemporary novel continues to owe much. Those "silly novels by lady novelists," as George Eliot dismissively called them in an essay published anonymously (461), did important work in offering female protagonists a range and capacity for explorations of selfhood. Although Catherine Morland in *Northanger Abbey* has to learn to read correctly, her earliest lessons in human behavior are those offered by these silly novels, so she becomes a fine judge of human character, well schooled by her novel reading.

Roy's emphasis on the novel as the form to which women have turned offers a nice segue into our consideration of chick lit in India at this time. Bringing together these very different historical moments offers a compelling way of considering the production of popular novels in English in India today. What work is chick lit doing for our young readers? Indeed, what work is chick lit doing for our young writers? Ira Trivedi, in her book *India in Love*, points out that "[l]ove matches have risen from just 5 per cent of Indian marriages to 30 per cent in the past decade" (8), a pace of social and cultural alteration that would inevitably bring unprecedented levels of behavioral change. That young India is in love, wants to be in love, or is encouraged to be in love is amply demonstrated by the collections of love stories issued by major publishing houses. Ravinder Singh edited a selection of the "stories that touched [his] heart the most" from a nationwide competition, published as *Love Stories That Touched My Heart.*[1] As a self-styled guru of love (by his second novel he had found true love again), Singh's popularity in the genre of lad lit is uncontested. Singh's collection of short stories was quickly followed by one edited by Anuja Chauhan, *An Atlas of Love*, likewise a compilation of the best stories culled from a nationwide competition. Both collections encourage individual voices, support the idea of love, and underscore the certainty that a special someone awaits everyone.

Chauhan's introduction to *Atlas of Love* approves of the publisher's initiative in launching the contest and hopes it will continue "to seek and find beautiful love stories—with the same single-minded, optimistic, never-say-die focus with which we should go through life, seeking love itself" (ix). In his editor's note, Singh says, "This anthology is my way of using my power and moving a step towards accomplishing my responsibility to create a platform for many of the upcoming debutante authors" (ix). Between 2008, when Singh was himself a struggling writer, and 2012, when he was the "highest selling romance writer of today,"[2] Singh had achieved the sort of success associated with Chetan Bhagat and Amish Tripathi. In their different ways, these popular writers take their successful positions seriously, suggesting that with their success comes a responsibility.

In her reading of Bhagat's novels, Priya Joshi suggests we consider his appeal in terms reminiscent of the place occupied by Charles Dickens a century ago. Bhagat's "popularity recalls a moment and a place when figures like him and the work they did—intrusively, insistently, and popularly—inserted themselves into a culture in which they *made* themselves matter" (324). While Bhagat commands audiences that Singh or Chauhan could only dream of, a common concern of so many of these writers is their sense of social responsibility, their sense that their success brings with it other demands. These books may be written by the unliterary (albeit with goals of great success in mind), but that does not diminish their seriousness. Whether they are educating their readers or offering them models for how to imagine and live satisfying lives, these writers have placed a responsibility upon themselves. Even in the ostensibly frothy world of chick lit novels, with their focus on shopping and self-indulgence within urban environments, the responsibility carried by chick lit writers is worth noting. There is work to be done in young India, and the popular novelists I've been discussing are conscious of the mantle both placed on them and which they choose to don.

The Classroom

So how and why might one accommodate books such as these into undergraduate or graduate courses on Indian writing in English in the United States? Let me share my experience teaching *The Zoya Factor* in New Delhi and in Lancaster, Pennsylvania. When I taught at Jawaharlal Nehru University between 2008 and 2010, years that coincided with the burst of new genres in the world of books in English, spending a couple of weeks on the new popular fictions toward the end of the semester was a natural place to take the course. By that time in the semester, graduate students were doing their oral presentations and far preferred reading and presenting on the new genres. The books spoke to them with an immediacy that other works, even contemporary ones, we had read did not. Students presented on consumption in chick lit novels, on the new mythological fictions of Amish Tripathi, on the consumer-driven Hindu India subtly and not so subtly offered by these books. For a course on Indian fiction in English, *not* to attend to the new genres would have meant a deliberate decision to ignore a very vivid, engaging moment of literary production.

However, what the specificity of that location and moment required did not translate so well when I returned to teach at my liberal arts college in Pennsylvania, where I taught *The Zoya Factor* at the end of the semester in my Indian Novel in English course in the fall of 2011. While my students and I had thoroughly enjoyed, in India, the shift to the popular novel via Zoya's escapades, my students in Pennsylvania did not. They found little to which they could relate in Zoya's life and language. The Punjabi idioms of Zoya's speech were lost on them; her slow road to new love was too slow and therefore annoying rather than charming. That very Hinglish that made Chauhan's novel so enjoyable to me made her distant from my American students. Zoya's travails did not translate well into an American context, and I should have anticipated that.

Nevertheless, I was reluctant not to offer my students exposure to works that brought them face-to-face with contemporary literary production in India. Having learned from this first failure, I approached the popular novel differently the next time. I chose not to teach a single novel, selecting instead excerpts from different kinds of novels of which chick lit was one. I chose from Madhavan, Bhagat, and Sarnath Banerjee. Offering a selection of authors and genres worked much better: students were energized by their contemporaneity and variety. Since the early part of the semester had established the burden felt by Indian writers using English and the subsequent alleviation of this burden in the post-Rushdie years, the English idioms in the works of the writers offered welcome instances of the altered place of English in India.

Students enjoy Bhagat and usually want to read all of *One Night at the Call Center*. I choose this novel since its setup is an easy one for my students to enter. Rather than continuing to use *The Zoya Factor* or a selection from one of Chauhan's novels, I have found the simplicity and immediacy of a segment from Madhavan's *You Are Here* to work much better for my American students. An excerpt from Banerjee's graphic novel *Corridor* allows a refreshing glimpse into urban Indian life via the popular form of the graphic novel.

The class period where we read these writers is followed by the last one of the semester, in which we read Ismat Chughtai's "The Quilt" and

Saadat Hasan Manto's "Toba Tek Singh." The inclusion of these Urdu short stories in a course devoted to Indian writing in English makes real the vitality of literary production in languages other than English. As the penultimate class period offers students a taste of the popular and contemporary, this last class challenges students' association of the modern with the use of English and tradition with other Indian languages. Together, my selection of readings in these last two class periods allows me to underscore that canons and literary history are made, and they are made always serving different interests. The course we have just completed, students see, is one such instance. The inclusion of the popular and nonliterary thus reveals the constructedness of the canon and the critical apparatus that buttresses it, allowing a productive critique of the Indian novel in English, especially the postcolonial one canonized in the last fifty years.

Notes

1. This phrase is from the blurb on the back of the book jacket.

2. This quotation is taken from the cover of Singh's *Love Stories That Touched My Heart.*

Works Cited

Anjaria, Ulka. Introduction. Anjaria, *Cambridge History*, pp. 1–30.

———, editor. *The Cambridge History of the Indian Novel in English.* Cambridge UP, 2015.

Chauhan, Anuja. Introduction. *Atlas of Love*, edited by Anuja Chauhan, Rupa Publications India, 2014, pp. vii–ix.

Dawson Varughese, E. "'New India/n Woman': Agency and Identity in Post-Millennial Chick Lit." Anjaria, *Cambridge History*, pp. 324–36.

Dutta, Amrita. "'A' Literature for Rs. 100." *The Indian Express*, 26 June 2010, www.indianexpress.com/news/a-literature-for-rs-100/638802/.

[Eliot, George]. "Silly Novels by Lady Novelists." *The Westminster Review*, Oct. 1856, pp. 442–61.

Gupta, Suman. "Indian 'Commercial Fiction' in English, the Publishing Industry, and Youth Culture." *Economic and Political Weekly*, vol. 47, no. 5, 4 Feb. 2012, pp. 46–53.

Joshi, Priya. "Chetan Bhagat: Remaking the Novel in India." Anjaria, *Cambridge History*, pp. 310–23.

Rao, Raja. *Kanthapura.* 1938. Orient Paperbacks, 1970.

Roy, Devapriya. "Eleven Books You Must Read If You Wish to Write Chick-Lit." *Scroll.in*, 25 Jan. 2015, scroll.in/article/702225/11-books-you-must-read-if-you-wish-to-write-chick-lit.

Singh, Ravinder, editor. *Love Stories That Touched My Heart.* Penguin Metro Reads, 2012.

Trivedi, Harish. "Indian English Writing." *Muse India*, no. 59, Jan.-Feb. 2015, www.museindia.com/Home/ViewContentData?arttype=focus&issid=59&menuid=5415.

———. "The St. Stephen's Factor." *Indian Literature*, vol. 34, no. 5 (no. 145), Sept.-Oct. 1991, pp. 183–87.

Trivedi, Ira. *India in Love: Marriage and Sexuality in the Twenty-First Century.* Aleph, 2014.

Part III

Feminism, Gender, and Sexuality

Cara Cilano

Place and Gender in Pakistani Women's Writing

Sara Suleri closes the first chapter of her 1989 memoir, *Meatless Days*, with a contradictory and confounding claim: "[T]here are no women in the third world" (20). Even before she makes this assertion, Suleri indicates her awareness of the contradiction she's offering. The whole of her first chapter is, after all, a catalog of the important women—grandmother, mother, sisters, and more—who populated her early life in Pakistan. Indeed, Suleri acknowledges that her statement stands "[a]gainst all [her] own odds" (20). To some degree, then, Suleri also sets out to confound, to ensnare her readers in a quandary that pits the actual existence of women in Pakistan against questions about what "women" and "third world" might signify, if anything at all, when found in such close syntactic proximity. While less explicit about questions of gender, Kamila Shamsie's 2002 novel, *Kartography*, asserts its preoccupation with place in its very title, which, with its substitution of a *k* for a *c*, invites readers to confront location as both specific and unstable. The *k* in the novel's title insists upon the specificity of Karachi in the 1980s and 1990s, a specificity that resists the overlap between map, territory, and the exercise of knowing a place and its people.

Together, these two texts by luminaries of the first and second generations of Pakistani English-language literature link gender and geography. In doing so, they present twin challenges: their place-centeredness evokes questions about relating to Third World writing in the Western academy, while their gender concerns invoke a range of scripts derived from colonial and neocolonial representations of brown women. In this essay, I will explore an adaptable pedagogical approach to Suleri's and Shamsie's texts that addresses these challenges. I focus on each text's specific textual strategies—Suleri's opening contradiction and Shamsie's incorporation of maps—to highlight how stories are shaped by their location and how places are defined by collections of stories intertwined with their histories.

Teaching Gender and Place: Locating Pedagogy

The following pedagogical approach encourages students to analyze the relations among place, gender, and plot. Plots locate characters in places and histories. As Hayden White states, "The [historical] events are *made* into a story by the suppression or subordination of certain of them and the highlighting of others, by characterization, motific repetition, variation of tone and point of view, alternative descriptive strategies, and the like . . ." (84). Place and history impact how the characters' stories unfold. Plots, thus, can suggest a character's interiority, normalizing a subjectivity through representation. Moreover, plots also frame how characters function when emplaced, or mapped into the arc of the story. This positioning, in turn, shapes how characters connect—or don't—to location. Thus, a focus on plots invites considerations of how we frame subjectivity and our relations to our own and others' places.

Discussions of postcolonial pedagogies frequently circle around the importance of place, particularly whether and how the pedagogical location contributes to what Deepika Bahri calls "managed encounters with otherness" (278). Bahri describes this politics as a condition of postcolonial literatures' inclusion in Western universities: "If [the empire] did not write back, if the colonial 'address' were absent or unintelligible, the postcolonial subject and text could not arrive at their destination" (285). In effect, by maintaining a center-periphery structure, the institutionalization of postcolonial literatures mandates recognition in specific terms.

As many teacher-scholars in the field can attest, the larger disciplinary and institutional framing of postcolonial studies is shifting, so that now departments seek specialists in world, transnational, and anglophone or global literatures. While the stakes of this shift merit attention in their own right, my concern here is to highlight shared challenges in teaching such literatures.[1] What Reed Way Dasenbrock calls "intelligibility" aligns with legibility, or the politics of recognition, in that all three terms speak to the reader's experience with an other text. In his analysis of recent revisions to the world literature anthologies most frequently used in the classrooms of Western universities, James Hodapp identifies a "dialogic approach" as a pedagogical dominant. This approach encourages comparison between Western and non-Western texts by pairing them in terms of "common themes and forms . . . [so as to] elucidat[e] formal, thematic, temporal contexts for texts from significantly different times and places." "Accessibility for American students" is, thus, central to this approach (72). This dialogic approach encourages students to recognize similarities between texts. Swaralipi Nandi asserts that such a comparative pedagogical model casts the "'world' in World Literature [as an] inferior version of the 'home' with no uncertainty of encountering difference" (89). Nandi also asserts that a similarities approach positions the author as a native informant with privileged access to "insider's knowledge" (92). Such presumptions are, in Nandi's view, "not only fallacious but also [a way to reinforce] the same hegemonic norms of appropriating otherness" (92). Clearly, the ways in which pedagogies manage encounters with otherness, to echo Bahri's phrase again, matter a great deal when teacher-scholars bring postcolonial, Third World, South Asian, and even more specified non-Western literatures into Western classrooms.

When she teaches about Third World women, Piya Chatterjee "name[s] the 'problem,'" which is "that the complexity of the historical and cultural material is often overshadowed by the stereotypes about the victimization and passivity of women in other parts of the world" (88). By recognizing the pervasiveness and power of such stereotypes, teacher-scholars can help students take the first step toward understanding how geography shapes knowledge. Edward Casey's formulation of being in place is useful here. Casey asserts the necessity of idiolocality, which "invokes the subject who incorporates and expresses a particular place, more especially its *idios*, what is 'peculiar' in both senses of this last word" (689). The term *idiolocality*, therefore, indicates a close relation among language, self, and place, emphasizing how a specific quality of the experience of place is mirrored in the unfolding of the story. The body and its lived experience factor heavily in Casey's understanding of the term (683). Idiolocality can be a powerful concept for drawing students into a productive engagement with otherness that, if analyzed carefully, can avoid recentering students' locations and preconceived notions, while creating the potential for an appreciation of the nuance and specificity so crucial to grasping—but not reducing or appropriating or managing—difference.

Teaching Shamsie and Suleri: Beyond Managed Otherness

I encourage students to examine how they narrate their own personal experience of space or the ways they actually move about and inhabit the places of their everyday lives. An example: a high school pep rally, hosted in the school gym, celebrating the football team's homecoming. The place itself sanctions a set of gender roles wherein the female students' formal participation is primarily as cheerleaders, while the male students are the vaunted athletes. Issues of race and class also emerge in our discussions, regardless of whether this school is public or private. Authority is present in the form of the principal, the coaches, and the teachers, but transgression is also possible. Moreover, regional specificity matters; a homecoming pep rally in Texas will be a different event altogether than one in, say, Rhode Island. This exercise encourages students to recognize how the places they move into and out of shape stories, while allowing for occasional resistance, even transgression. This recognition helps students develop a new kind of awareness stemming from the very act of narrating their familiar experience of bodies in specific places.

To connect this exercise to the teaching of Shamsie's and Suleri's texts, the teacher-scholar needs to establish for students the histories and idiolocalities of both texts. Both *Kartography* and *Meatless Days* focus explicitly on significant events in Pakistani history. In the former, the 1971 Bangladesh Liberation War looms large, as does the violence that racked Karachi through the 1980s and 1990s. The latter refers to that war, as well as to numerous other moments, such as Prime Minister Benazir Bhutto's rise to power and General Muhammad Zia-ul-Haq's dictatorship. As foreign and far away as these events may seem to students, they are central to apprehending the textual strategies both authors use. For decades, official Pakistani history, especially as taught in schools, has been obfuscatory. In her review of Pakistan studies textbooks, Ayesha Jalal sees the use of "bigoted narrative styles" (86). Similarly, K. K. Aziz views history textbooks' representation of the 1971 war as "repetitive, false, spurious and monotonous" (154). These assessments of Pakistani historiography begin to sketch the idiolocalities within which Shamsie and Suleri compose their stories.

Couple these broader national dynamics with specifically gendered ones and students can also develop a more enhanced understanding of how place and gender are interlinked. For example, Malala Yousafzai's story may resonate well with students, owing to her fame, their shared age, and its triumphalist arc. As Wendy Hesford contends, "Malala's claim to empowerment rights . . . enabled elite international media to project onto her the moral conscience of the globalized world" (408). This conscience is keenly attuned to gender equality and women's rights in Pakistan, a predilection that helps propel and maintain Yousafzai's high profile. Moreover, this story challenges colonial scripts of the white savior, such that Muslim women, in Miriam Cooke's terms, "are to be rescued not because they *are* more 'ours' than 'theirs,' but rather because they will have *become* more 'ours' through the rescue mission" (228). Specified via gender and geography, the relevant idiolocalities interlock globally while being located deeply in local circumstances.

For example, one of the central characters in Shamsie's novel is a Bengali living in West Pakistan (now Pakistan) in 1971, after Bangladesh (formerly East Pakistan), her homeland by ethnicity, has split into an independent nation. In the newly redrawn political map of Pakistan, with East Pakistan written out of the national story, her Bengali identity makes her a target of discrimination and recrimination. Years later, her son, Karim, struggles with how his Bengali heritage complicates his persistent need to claim belonging in Karachi. The violence in that city throughout the 1980s and 1990s in turn connects to the rewriting of maps and boundaries in the 1947 partition of India and Pakistan. The creation of the Pakistani nation transformed Karachi's demographics as the Hindu majority left and waves of Urdu-speaking refugees arrived from India. The latter's linguistic difference from native Sindhi speakers and their status as migrants marked them as other, not least because of the economic threat they presented as educated, highly skilled additions to the city's population. *Kartography* includes many references to their presence in the city and literally grounds this tension in scenes that unfold at the farm of a family friend. In the decades after partition, more migrants arrived in the city because of changing geopolitical circumstances, including the United States' proxy war against the Soviet Union in Afghanistan: more languages, more differences, more othering. This era also saw the most explicit Islamizing efforts under Zia's dictatorship, a development Shamsie's novel gestures toward in its depiction of newly emergent piety in one of the female characters. Shamsie's novel illustrates connections among places, histories, and identity, showing how the once familiar is othered, and identities morph in dialogue with changing circumstances. If places are made up of stories, they also *form* characters and their stories, with winds of change, political or interpersonal, creating a dense plot thickened by history.

Shamsie's inclusion of both a hand-drawn and a printed street map in the novel points to these instabilities in making sense of places and their signification. Highly individualized, Karim's hand-drawn map attempts to convey lived experience, to enmesh subjectivity in place and reframe the accompanying plot, conveying a range of Karachi's idiolocalisms in a variety of languages (300). Raheen, the novel's narrator, mentions the philosophical dispute between Eratosthenes and Strabo about the status of maps as sources of knowledge: "Eratosthenes, the grandfather of cartography, was the first man to make a distinction between scientific and literary mapping. Prior to Eratosthenes, no one ever said that cartography should concern itself with science and facts rather than stories . . ." (164). According to the novel, Strabo, another cartographer, strenuously objected to Eratosthenes's view, seeing maps as valid ways to tell stories. This elaborates on Raheen's reference to Eratosthenes forty pages earlier, with both discussions encouraging students to examine the idea of a place (Pakistan or the Third World) as a set of stories rather than as a fixed, objective space.

Meatless Days also works to destabilize narratives of place and self. Many of the vignettes in the book occur during particularly tumultuous times in Pakistan, historical moments that test the narrative's ability to represent the significance of these times for Suleri's family and, by extension, the nation. Stories are interrupted by history and its thick complexities such that the telling of one person's story necessarily involves references to the unfolding plot of history. For instance, many of the stories about the narrator's sister Ifat include references to the 1971 war, in which Ifat's husband fought. Her father's imprisonment, caused by his sharp critiques of various Pakistani governments, also illustrates how the memoir intertwines history with life. Through the text's metafictional impulses, Suleri offers a way of understanding why she is calling attention to these explicit connections. In recounting an angry interaction with her sister Tillat, for instance, Suleri recognizes that her family "began to lose that sense of the differentiated identities of history and ourselves and became guiltily aware that we had known it all along, our part in the construction of unreality" (14). Suleri conveys her view that a sense of unreality pervades much of what has occurred in Pakistani history, suggesting in turn a narratorial discomfort, dis-ease, and mistrust of the methods readily available to represent a Pakistani life in any linear, uninterrupted manner. Readers cannot follow any one person's story without its historical backdrop.

Further, the memoir's many metafictional moments create distance, self-consciously calling attention to Suleri's acts of writing and her struggle with conventional narrative structure. For example, speaking of her mother, father, and grandmother, Suleri wonders, "How can I bring them together in a room? My plot feels most dangerous to me when I think of bringing them together" (157). The claim that closes her first chapter, then—"there are no women in the third world"—specifies this anxiety in gendered terms. In effect, that chapter's closing points to the insufficiencies of the available representational forms—they perpetuate an unreality—while nonetheless insisting on the existence of a story of women in the Third World. As such, Suleri's text extends the ways in which Chatterjee "names the 'problem'" of teaching about Third World women. *Meatless Days* exhibits less concern over the stereotypes that accumulate around this group, as if it were a homogenous whole, and more interest in Pakistan's idiolocalities, for, as a specific location, it "increasingly complicated the question of context" (Suleri 8). These specificities include the circumstances of Suleri's parents' marriage—her father's second, after he divorces a cousin in order to wed Suleri's Welsh mother; the political volatility of the Pakistan to which the family returns after years in London; and the uniqueness of Suleri's *dadi*, whose presence in the memoir signifies a past to which Suleri is not wholly connected and, at the same time, a strong feminine narrative line that nonetheless connects generations, including Suleri's mother, a literature professor. Even while engaged in the act of representing her family, Suleri remains hesitant and circumspect, suggesting that lived specificities caught up in a politically charged history that is unfolding demand a befitting, idiosyncratic plot.

Suleri dismantles a single, cohesive approach to understanding place and gender—as if "all Pakistani women are . . ."—at the beginning of her memoir and, instead, marks and then shifts the relation between places and gender as her vignettes span time and geography. Such a claim accords with Suleri's comments that "Bhutto's hanging had the effect of making Pakistan feel unreliable, particularly to itself" (18). Suleri's identification of unreliability is not about a narrator's trustworthiness. Rather, the memoir's reference to Pakistan's unreality and unreliability is an attempt to grapple with the specifics of a nation that has become unintelligible and unfamiliar to itself, even as it might function as unfamiliar and strange to students in Western classrooms. Suleri's memoir not only challenges stereotypical or exoticized representations of otherness; it capitalizes on strangeness and unreality as the stuff of experience and lived reality. The many Pakistans that emerge as history evolves and the memoir's repeated references to the Pakistan that the Suleris find upon their return destabilize fixities of place even as they dissolve stable notions of the women populating them. Histories shape locations; gendered identities take form within the context of geography and history. The mutual imbrication of place and self points to the role of plotting in the representation of characters, rather than the discovery or transparent knowledge of women in the Third World.

The approach outlined above can engage students in an analysis of the interactions between places and identities that does not automatically recenter their readerly locations, be they ideological or geographical. Suleri's contradictions and Shamsie's maps confound and multiply the possibilities and processes of meaning making, thereby encouraging a recognition of the other as unmanageable. Otherness remains in both texts; neither resolves the unfamiliar nor domesticates the uncertainty that characterizes the places and histories that inform identities. Instead of taking the unintelligible and unmanageable as an obstacle to teaching, exploring how the recourse to the unmanaged informs Pakistani writing can help reopen questions of gender and locality in the classroom.

Note

1. See Hodapp for a helpful overview of the stakes of this shift.

Works Cited

Aziz, K. K. *The Murder of History: A Critique of History Textbooks Used in Pakistan*. Vanguard, 1993.

Bahri, Deepika. "Marginally Off-Center: Postcolonialism in the Teaching Machine." *College English*, vol. 59, no. 3, Mar. 1997, pp. 277–98.

Casey, Edward S. "Between Geography and Philosophy: What Does It Mean to Be in the Place-World?" *Annals of the Association of American Geographers*, vol. 91, no. 4, Dec. 2001, pp. 683–93.

Chatterjee, Piya. "Encountering 'Third World Women': Rac(e)ing the Global in a U.S. Classroom." *Pedagogy*, vol. 2, no. 1, Winter 2002, pp. 79–108.

Cooke, Miriam. "Islamic Feminism before and after September 11th." *Duke Journal of Gender Law and Policy*, vol. 9, no. 2, Summer 2002, pp. 227–35.

Dasenbrock, Reed Way. "Intelligibility and Meaningfulness in Multicultural Literature in English." *PMLA*, vol. 102, no. 1, Jan. 1987, pp. 10–19.

Hesford, Wendy S. "Introduction: Facing Malala Yousafzai, Facing Ourselves." *JAC*, vol. 33, nos. 3–4, 2013, pp. 407–23.

Hodapp, James. "The Problematic and Pragmatic Pedagogy of World Literature." *ARIEL*, vol. 46, nos. 1–2, 2015, pp. 69–88.
Jalal, Ayesha. "Conjuring Pakistan: History as Official Imagining." *International Journal of Middle East Studies*, vol. 27, no. 1, Feb. 1995, pp. 73–89.
Nandi, Swaralipi. "Reading the 'Other' in World Literature: Toward a Discourse of Unfamiliarity." *Critical Pedagogy and Global Literature: Worldly Teaching*, edited by Masood Ashraf Raja et al., Palgrave Macmillan, 2013, pp. 75–96.
Shamsie, Kamila. *Kartography*. Harcourt, 2002.
Suleri, Sara. *Meatless Days*. U of Chicago P, 1989.
White, Hayden. *Tropics of Discourse: Essays in Cultural Criticism*. Johns Hopkins UP, 1978.

Nalini Iyer

Dalit Feminism: Teaching Bama's *Karukku* to American Undergraduates

Very few universities in the United States offer courses exclusively focused on South Asian women writers. Often such writers are included in courses on women's literatures, postcolonial literatures, or South Asian literatures. Because of factors such as the publishing marketplace, the global flow of literary texts, the emphasis on global engagement at American universities that has resulted in innumerable study abroad programs, and the growth of the South Asian diaspora in the United States, certain women writers and texts tend to be frequently taught. An undergraduate is less likely to encounter a poem or novel by a Dalit[1] writer than a work by Arundhati Roy, Kiran Desai, or Jhumpa Lahiri. These writers produce works in English and have been recognized by major literary awards such as the Pulitzer and Booker Prizes, and, as a consequence, there is plenty of literary criticism on their works. Much of Dalit writing is produced in Indian languages, and although Dalit writing is increasingly available in translation through major presses such as Oxford University Press India, Orient Blackswan, and Navayana, among others, Dalit women writers are not often taught in courses on South Asian women writers.

The purpose of this essay is to make a case for teaching Dalit women's writing in classes devoted to South Asian or postcolonial literatures for the following reasons: first, to complicate students' understanding of India by foregrounding literary works that challenge the anglophone postcolonial canon (dominated by Salman Rushdie and others) by underscoring the caste and class privileges of these writers; and second, to nuance students' understanding of feminist literatures, particularly Indian feminist literatures, by teaching Dalit women's writing within an intersectional framework.

Dalit women's writing complicates intersectionality as a concept for students. Whereas intersectionality entered American feminist scholarly discourse through the works of the Combahee River Collective and, more famously, Kimberlé Crenshaw, it has also gained currency in other national contexts.[2] As Nivedita Menon has pointed out, intersectionality is problematic within the context of Indian feminism because it is a label borrowed uncritically from the West. She notes that "Indian woman" is not a monolithic category because anticolonial movements already recognized that the identity of woman is layered and located "within Nation and within communities of sorts." Therefore, it is important that students understand that within the history of Indian feminism, Dalit identities have been understood to be complicated by the vectors of caste, gender, language, region, and religion. Intersectionality as a method was practiced in Indian feminism although the label was applied later and emerged from the West. However, the vectors of identity for a Dalit woman are different from that of women of color in the United States, and close textual analysis of a Dalit feminist literary work helps elucidate that. Caste in India and race in the United States may function similarly, but they are not identical in their histories. The caste-race analogy runs the risk of conflating the two categories, although Dalit activists have themselves made that connection as part of their strategy of resistance.[3] Furthermore, in South Asian diasporic communities in the United States and elsewhere, caste is often elided into race, complicating the caste-race analogy that an unproblematic use of intersectionality might call forth.[4]

Dalit writing has gained prominence in the last couple of decades, and K. W. Christopher finds that within India there has been an institutionalization of Dalit studies. But Christopher also cautions, "Although Dalit literature has gained visibility in recent years, it continues to be suppressed, appropriated, and contained by hegemonic discourses." Furthermore, as Christopher notes, caste is a significant factor not just in Indian society but also in the Indian diaspora, and he argues, "Cumulatively, there appears to be an evasion of caste as a postcolonial problematic among India's academic diasporic and postcolonial thinkers in Western academia" (8). Thus, choosing what texts by South Asian women writers get taught in a university in the United States requires careful consideration of the institutional context of the course. It also requires the teacher to problematize his or her positionality in relation to the texts chosen, a point addressed later in this essay. Thus, while Dalit women writers challenge both postcolonial and feminist literature's claims to resistance, it is necessary for the teacher's intersectional framework to be attentive to cultural and historical nuances in the teaching of Dalit feminist texts. I teach at a Jesuit Catholic university and include South Asian women writers within the context of a couple of courses offered by the English department for undergraduates. The course readings always include Dalit writers, in particular Dalit women's writing. One of my frequently used texts is Bama's *Karukku*, published originally in Tamil and translated into English by Lakshmi Holmström.

Why Bama and Why *Karukku*?

Bama's autobiographical work *Karukku* is the first piece of Dalit life writing in Tamil, although this genre has been popular in other languages such as Marathi. As Ravikumar writes in the introduction to *The Oxford Anthology of Tamil Dalit Writing*, this genre never gained much popularity among Tamil Dalit writers as many turned toward poetry and fiction as their primary modes of expression. In *Karukku* Bama tells her life story not as a chronological narrative but as one clustered around themes such as village life, education, and religious beliefs and practices, and the narrative arc explores Bama's quest to integrate her Dalit and Christian identities. Holmström, the translator of the text, notes, "It is [Bama's] driving quest for integrity as a Dalit and Christian that shapes the book and gives it its polemic" (viii). The title of the narrative is a Tamil word that refers to the palmyra leaf. As Holmström points out, the title speaks to the double-edged nature of the palmyra leaf. It cuts your hands but is also necessary to build roofs and provide shelter. It contains within it the word *karu* or "embryo," which symbolically speaks to the emergence of a new self, a new identity. A *karu* knows no caste or class and can be male or female. Bama's original Tamil narrative uses Dalit Tamil instead of standard, upper-caste, literary Tamil, and while this distinction is lost in the English translation, it is an important aspect of this autobiographical work and how Dalit feminist identity is forged in it.

Although the Dalit liberation movement is a national one, *Karukku* does not overtly acknowledge the national context but locates itself very strongly in the regional and in everyday aspects of Dalit life in the *parayar* community. Holmström's introduction addresses the terminology of referring to Dalits as Dalits, and the evolution of naming in the Indian context is helpful for students. It is also useful to point out that Bama's caste identity as *paraya* is the root word for the English word *pariah* and that this caste identity has become synonymous with *outcaste* in the English language.

Debates on *Karukku*

In structuring discussion on any literary text, I frame the class around critical debates on the text. With *Karukku*, the discussion emphasizes three major issues: genre, language and translation, and Dalit feminism. *Karukku* offers the opportunity to consider genre, particularly the autobiography. Unlike traditional autobiography, as several critics have noted, Bama's work does not have a singular named central protagonist whose evolution and growth we can trace. Instead there is a communal sense of "we," and the work is an amalgam of community manifesto, testimonio, and life writing.[5] The narrative places Dalit community life at its center and the narrator remains unnamed. The reader learns about village life and social organization from the descriptions of how different castes inhabit different streets. As the narrator grows up, the reader learns about family, work, education, and religious beliefs and practices in the unnamed village in Tamil Nadu. The narrative also bears witness to the abuse suffered by Dalits from upper-caste villagers. Even as *Karukku* outlines in great detail how the police collude with the upper-caste villagers and beat Dalit men, who are forced to run and hide, it also describes the ingenuity of the women, who trick the police, hide the men, and facilitate a father's secret attendance at his son's funeral. The reader sees the narrator's increasing awareness of caste oppression and her desire for social change. The narrative arc draws from the genre elements of autobiography, testimonio, and community manifesto. Thus, class discussions can be productively engaged in delineating genre elements and the reasons the author might be pushing genre boundaries. Discussions can also pursue what it means to have a unitary self at the center of a narrative of female development (like Jane in *Jane Eyre*) and what makes the unitary self an impossibility in this Dalit work. A useful secondary source for the context of this discussion is Raj

Kumar's *Dalit Personal Narratives: Reading Caste, Nation and Identity* (esp. 115–56). Raj Kumar argues that the very act of writing an autobiography (or *atmakatha*, "life story") is one of resistance to different forms of oppression. Kumar also provides students an understanding of caste politics within a historical framework, thus mitigating a popular understanding of caste that students might bring into the discussion, where they view caste as an ancient Hindu practice stemming from religious texts and thus somehow immutable.

Karukku also raises some important questions about literary language and translation. Holmström's introduction to the text addresses Bama's decision to use the Dalit vernacular and to overturn upper-caste linguistic and aesthetic assumptions. For American students who do not know Tamil and who access the text through a translation, such an understanding of different class, caste, and regional variations on a language are not obvious. Holmström also discusses Bama's use of Sanskritized Tamil words such as *mantiram* or *poosai* to capture Tamil Dalit Catholicism.[6] Holmström notes that Bama's language is that of everyday Catholicism and not that of theologians. It is helpful for students to recognize the syncretic use of language (Hindu words adapted in a Catholic context) that demonstrates how religious practices coexist and are appropriated within the Dalit Catholic experience.

Even as Bama describes Catholic celebrations—Easter, Christmas, and New Year—she also draws upon local goddess legends like that of Nallathangal to tell her story. Anushiya Sivanarayanan notes that the story of Nallathangal is followed by the narrative of a caste war, as witnessed by an eleven-year-old child. Sivanarayanan argues that in the Standard English translation produced by Holmström these chapters seem disconnected, but in the Tamil version both narratives survive in an oral tradition and Bama uses them seamlessly (148). Similarly, Sivanarayanan observes that the many passages that speak like a Greek chorus, such as the bewailing of one's Dalit birth, come across as stock rhetoric in English but in the vernacular, spoken Tamil betray a deep vulnerability and anguish (146–47). For non-Tamil-speaking students in an American classroom, the differences in language between the Tamil and English versions of the narrative are accessible only through literary criticism by scholars like Sivanarayanan, whose work exhibits a deep understanding of both languages and the nuanced sensibility of a translator who is aware of the inability of English to carry forward the class and caste distinctions of Tamil.

However, the discussion about differences between the English and Tamil versions allow for a deep engagement with the practice and theory of translation as well as a consideration of how and why texts circulate globally. Students need to become aware that translation is not simply a one-to-one substitution of words but that each language carries a cultural history and matrix of which both translator and reader need to be aware. It is helpful for students to understand what S. Shankar notes about translation: "To my mind, translation is best regarded as a species of interpretation. Approaching translation as interpretation allows us, I believe, to have a more supple and enabling view of it" (155). Recognizing that Holmström's role is more than mechanical in the production of the English version of *Karukku* allows non-Tamil readers to read it as a text in its own right instead of finding themselves skeptical about translated works. Translation also necessitates recognizing that readers must do their best to unpack the context of words and phrases. I often use the example of *kuuzh* and *kanji*, two words used to describe foods that Bama's community consumes, and her repeated references to rice as a luxury food. While *kuuzh* can be described as porridge and *kanji* as gruel, to get an approximate understanding of the two foods, the class and caste elements need to be understood as well. Eating rice and having access to rice is a privileged position; increased consumption of rice carries with it a story of urban development and green revolution. *Kanji* is mostly starchy water, and *kuuzh*, while nutritious and made with locally grown millets, marks the poverty and rural culture of the community in this narrative. Thus, Bama's social mobility in the narrative can be traced based on the food references at various points in the narrative.

An important debate regarding *Karukku* is that of Dalit feminism. American undergraduates often approach the women writers in the course from a very basic feminist perspective of "voicing" female writers and recovering lost histories. They transpose a Eurocentric, feminist literary theoretical approach (drawn from Virginia Woolf, Elaine Showalter, and Sandra Gilbert and Susan Gubar) onto a South Asian context. A few students will draw upon theories of intersectionality, particularly race, class, and gender intersections, from their readings of American women of color feminists. *Karukku* helps trouble their notions of feminist theory. Students need a robust introduction to intersectional feminism, its history, and its recent resurgence in popular discourse. It is not enough to recognize that women of color experience multifaceted discrimination but to understand how race, class, and gender reinforce one another and how a singular lens is limiting. As mentioned earlier in this essay, in reading South Asian women writers, we cannot simply import the notion of intersectionality from an American women of color context and apply it like a cookie cutter; we must be cognizant of how and why ideas travel across geographic and national boundaries. Menon correctly notes that the issue is not that ideas travel but that Western ideas are viewed as having the possibility of universalization, while those of the Global South are never assured such easy passage. Menon also notes that the term *intersectionality* is easily used by NGOs working in India and the popularization of intersectionality in that context is linked to the flow of aid dollars.

Teachers must also recognize their own social positions as readers of Dalit literature, and I use myself as an example. As a Tamil Brahmin woman who grew up in metropolitan India and migrated to the United States as a student and is now a feminist academic teaching a Dalit text, it is necessary for me to acknowledge that my caste has been the oppressor of Dalits for centuries. The upper castes described in Bama's texts include people like me who had unfettered access to education, jobs, food, and places of worship and that the privileges of my community were derived from the very social inequities that Bama critiques. It is this caste privilege that allows me my place in American academia even if within that context I am a minority and person of color. My experiences with Brahminical patriarchy create empathy with Bama's story, but I cannot simply read us as sisters in a struggle against an undifferentiated patriarchy. My reading of Bama needs to be vigilant about cultural appropriation and caste privilege while recognizing structures that differentiate between us as women. I thus caution my students that they should not vest in me some uncritical authority about Indian texts because I am a woman of Indian national heritage.

As noted earlier, historical and cultural contexts are important, and discussions should also unpack the genealogy of the term *Indian woman* and its roots in nationalist and anticolonial movements and its progressive and regressive uses. By examining portrayals of Indian women in the many texts studied in the course, one can demonstrate that there is no singular notion of Indian womanhood and that to discuss intersectionality in the Indian context one must account for religion, region, caste, class, and sexuality. Anupama Rao's introduction to *Gender and Caste* is particularly useful for grasping the history of the Indian feminist movement and the place of Dalit women within the feminist and Dalit liberation movements.

In the entire narrative of *Karukku*, nowhere does Bama explicitly identify as a feminist. Can *Karukku* then be called a feminist text when Bama's preoccupation is with caste discrimination in the Tamil context and the oppressive role of the Catholic Church in perpetuating caste discrimination? While some critics see Bama less focused here on Dalit women than in her later works like *Sangati*, Bama's narrative has a liberational dimension and she does recognize that Dalit women are both oppressed within the caste and by upper castes. She also presents women's ingenuity and grit in resisting some of these oppressions within the community. It is here that an intersectional reading is useful; we cannot read *Karukku* as simply about caste or religion. For Bama, oppression and liberation have to address all aspects of her being, from caste and class to language and religion. Thus, the narrative is about social structures and inequities that can be transformed, and this narrative, by bearing witness to that transformation, is inherently feminist. Bama's philosophical and theological perspectives emerge from experiences and observations of her people and her community rather than from an extensive study of theology. Bama does reject being a nun and walks away from the hierarchical church, but she returns to her community to continue her ministry among the people and to enable social change.

While the above discussion demonstrates how one might teach *Karukku* to engage students in deep discussions about Dalit experiences, Dalit feminism, and intersectionality, this approach can be taken with other Dalit women's texts as well. All Dalit texts call for a rigorous intersectional reading such that we engage the vectors of gender, caste, class, religion, and language in our analyses. Dalit texts challenge both canonical postcolonial anglophone texts as well as canonical literature in the vernacular traditions. Any discussion of Dalit literature requires rigorous considerations of the politics of literary canons and the ethics of reading, and Dalit feminist texts compel us to examine what constitutes feminist critical analysis.

Notes

1. The term *Dalit* means "broken" or "oppressed" and is the name chosen by the nearly two hundred million Indians (per the 2011 census) who are considered "untouchable" or "outcaste." Mohandas K. Gandhi used the term *Harijan* to refer to Dalits. While the system of untouchability and caste (*varna*) has its roots in Hinduism, caste discrimination affects other religions in India including Sikhism, Christianity, and Islam. For further reading on the term *Dalit* and the history of caste in India, see Omvedt; Rao.

2. The history of the term *intersectionality* is complex and controversial, and Collins and Bilge outline this history in their work *Intersectionality* (63–87).

3. For example, the Dalit Panthers party deliberately models itself on the Black Panther Party in the United States. Similarly, the United Nations' World Conference against Racism, Racial Discrimination, Xenophobia, and Related Intolerance in 2001 helped forge alliances between Dalit activists and antiracist activists when caste discrimination and racial discrimination were understood as human rights issues.

4. Paik argues for what she calls a "margin-to-margin" framework, which allows an inclusive approach to investigate caste and race discrimination as experienced by Dalit and African American women, respectively. She argues that "centering on historical experiences, specific contexts, contradictions, and connections between the marginalized 'Dalit of the Dalits'—Dalit and African American women—allows for the most inclusive and productive politics, developing new feminist frameworks, and critical decoding of systemic power structures" (74). Paik's argument helps frame intersectionality in the Indian context without conflating caste and race.

5. Raj Kumar reads this work as a community manifesto. On testimonio, see Nayar's reading of the narrative.

6. Such substitution of Tamil words for Christian liturgical terms and use of syncretic equivalences between Hindu and Catholic practices can be traced back to Roberto de Nobili, an early Jesuit in Tamil Nadu, who learned Sanskrit, Tamil, and Telugu and worked to make Catholicism familiar to local Indian populations in his missionary work.

Works Cited

Bama. *Karukku.* Translated by Lakshmi Holmström, Macmillan India, 2000.

Christopher, K. W. "Between Two Worlds: The Predicament of Dalit Christians in Bama's Works." *The Journal of Commonwealth Literature*, vol. 47, no. 1, Mar. 2012, pp. 7–25.

Collins, Patricia Hill, and Sirma Bilge. *Intersectionality.* Polity Press, 2016.

Holmström, Lakshmi. Introduction. *Karukku*, by Bama, Macmillan India, 2000, pp. vii–xii.

Iyer, Nalini, and Bonnie Zare, editors. *Other Tongues: Rethinking the Language Debates in India.* Rodopi, 2009.

Kumar, Raj. *Dalit Personal Narratives: Reading Caste, Nation and Identity.* Orient Blackswan, 2011.

Menon, Nivedita. "Is Feminism about 'Women'? A Critical View of Intersectionality from India." *International Viewpoint*, 18 May 2015, www.internationalviewpoint.org/spip.php?article4038. Accessed 20 April 2016.

Nayar, Pramod K. "The Poetics of Postcolonial Atrocity: Dalit Life Writing, Testimonio, and Human Rights." *ARIEL*, vol. 42, nos. 3–4, 2012, pp. 237–64.

Omvedt, Gail. *Understanding Caste: From Buddha to Ambedkar and Beyond.* Orient Blackswan, 2011.

Paik, Shailaja. "Building Bridges: Articulating Dalit and African American Women's Solidarity." *Women's Studies Quarterly*, vol. 42, nos. 3–4, Fall-Winter 2014, pp. 74–96.
Rao, Anupama, editor. *Gender and Caste*. Zed Books, 2005.
Ravikumar. Introduction. *The Oxford Anthology of Tamil Dalit Writing*, edited by Ravikumar and R. Azhagarasan, Oxford UP, 2012, pp. xv–xxxiii.
Shankar, S. "Translation and the Vernacular: The Tamil Krishna Devotional 'Alaippayuthey.'" Iyer and Zare, pp. 155–62.
Sivanarayanan, Anushiya. "Translation and Globalization: Tamil Dalit Literature and Bama's *Karukku*." Iyer and Zare, pp. 135–54.

Pushpa Parekh

Intersections with Feminist Disability Theory in South Asian Women's Writing

Research on South Asian women writers, still a burgeoning category in literary fields, uncovers a critical gap in inclusion of disability as a category of analysis, critical lens, theoretical framework, or pedagogy and methodology. Focusing on my interlinked project of teaching and scholarship on anglophone South Asian women writers at Spelman College (an undergraduate, historically black women's liberal arts college in Atlanta, Georgia), I take a multipronged approach in this essay. My articulations of feminist disability theory and pedagogy make visible the value and contextual relevance of teaching and researching literary courses from interdisciplinary, intersectional, and cross-cultural perspectives.

When entering this topography of often embattled and unresolved struggles in academia, professors like myself, who straddle South Asia and its diaspora in the United States and who align their lived experiences with their research and teaching specialties, must contend with the scope and limits of their specialized "insider" and representational status. As Gayatri Spivak reminds us, we are often the elites who could "re-present" the subaltern to silence them, a form of "epistemic violence," or, alternatively, craft a new relational ethos and space to exercise "ethical responsibility" and "unlearn . . . privilege" (*Spivak Reader* 269–70; "Can the

Subaltern Speak" 295). To me, this responsibility is the pedagogical ground for active, engaged, and responsible learning, one that validates learning from below. It also means creating a pedagogical practice that intentionally engages in fine-tuning critical inquiry, intellectual rigor, as well as the ethics of "reeducating the emotions" of students for "social praxis" (Bracher 464).

Situating Pedagogy

At Spelman, I currently teach both general core and English major courses, including Images of Women in Non-Western Literature, Postcolonial Women Writers, Immigrant Women's Literature, and a recently developed course, Contemporary India: Literature and the Political. Many of these courses are gender informed and are cross-listed with comparative women's studies and international studies majors and Asian studies minor. In all these courses, I integrate South Asian writers and include modules on literary representations of disability as an intersectional category of analysis in the Global South and the South Asian diaspora. Underlying my analytical and pedagogical choices are the material circumstances that shape the politics of my identity and location, as well as constructions of new collaborative and transactional spaces. These include identifying social categories and specific ways in which not only the writers but also my students and I are positioned as well as the choices we make. In my earlier works, I have addressed my personal and political life living with polio in postindependent India and subsequently in the United States ("Technology," "Exploring," and *Intersecting*). These articulations of self are always in context of my pedagogical and ideological deconstructions of essential identities and master narratives and discourses. I also bring to the classroom the research implications for countering dominant theories and biased representations of South Asians, women, and identity categories. For example, I make clear that there is a growing body of research that aligns histories of subalterns transnationally—for example, Dalits in India and African Americans in the United States—based on comparative as well as transnational models (Pandey, "Can There Be"; Prasad; M. Roy). These studies counter the orientalist and model-minority representations of Indians within the category of South Asians (Prasad 168).

Contemporary women writers (anglophone and vernacular) in India focus on the sociopolitical and cultural tensions, emerging ethos of corporate mentality, and solidarities and politics of everyday resistance.

The feminist disability intersectional framework that I utilize is attentive to the literary representations and imaginings of South Asian women in cultural, geopolitical, and socioeconomic contexts. I foreground intersectional approaches, with particular care to include disability, a neglected category, with other markers of identity and in cross-cultural contexts. We are, after all, itinerants in the "crossings" of all kinds of borders, as M. Jacqui Alexander posits, and her "pedagogy of crossing" illuminates as well as dismantles "the multiple operations of power," from neocolonial to neoimperial state formations, including "the confluence of different geographies of feminism," the "unequal diffusion of globalized power," "machineries of war," "knowledge frameworks," and "modernity's practices of violence" (4–5).

In my courses, I link theoretical frameworks and literary texts through the pedagogy of connected learning. This approach involves making visible connections between course content, methods, and pedagogies and my students' identities and interests as heterogeneous and complex black women. I draw from African American and African diaspora women's intellectual traditions and social justice practices, such as intersectionality (Crenshaw), crossings (Alexander), and migratory subjects (Boyce Davies), to inform the linkages and divergences with theories and pedagogies I use for teaching anglophone South Asian women writers. Further, I integrate multiple configurations of disability in Global South and North, academia, activism, and everyday experiential accounts to determine textual selections and critical pedagogies for inclusion in course syllabi.

In my syllabi, I include literary anthologies and theory collections, as well as individual texts that represent, analyze, and frame identity in its plural and differing valences, in region-specific and transnational contexts. My students contend with concepts, phenomena, literary representations and geopolitics of South Asia, national agendas, migration, the global turn, and the politics of identity within transnational feminism, critical race theory, and intersectional analysis.

Teaching Disability

South Asian women's histories, experiences, and identities connect gender, class, caste, embodied vulnerability, and safety and security to considerations of disability. Disability operates in tandem with other identity categories, systemic oppressions, and activist movements in the context of South Asia, with specific implications for women. Disability pride, a concept embraced by disability movements in the West, is often complicated by modes of disablement—systems, structures, and practices that make women vulnerable in South Asia. Women are often "disabled" (not just symbolically) through continuations of old systems of patriarchy, son preference, wars, rapes, domestic violence (including forced and arranged marriages), dowry demands, and bride burning. In many South Asian cultures where marriages are arranged through viewings of the potential bride, the concept of the "marriage-able" is an ableist definer of embodiment where normativity is prized. Further, the practice reinscribes the social valorization of prescriptive standards of femininity, aesthetics, and health, including the expectations of women's childbearing functions, as grounds for rejecting the disabled body and enforcing heteronormativity (Nancoo; Grewal and Kaplan). Recent manifestations of these practices are disfigurement of women through acid attacks as revenge or punishment for rejecting male advances or dominance (Kalantry and Kestenbaum). Poor, rural women are vulnerable to multinational corporate displacements of women's distinct economic value in traditional farming practices and to exposure to ecological hazards, such as pesticides, pollution, and lack of clean water. Urban women's safety and security is predicated on the "widening gap between the rich and poor" and the ensuing "psychotic rage," according to Arundhati Roy, of young men displaced by globalization and modern ideologies and systems of workplace gender inclusion, as exemplified in the infamous 2012 Delhi gang rape (qtd. in Alston 132). The educated, middle-class women have limited and conditional access to public spaces, and their presence in these spaces has to be justified by a logic of respectability and valid purpose (Phadke 1511–12).

The methodology of pairing literary and theoretical texts enables students to understand the complexities of the text, define their critical lens, identify conceptual tools, and explore identities, languages, and discourses as contextual, constructed, as well as formative. Among theory readings on embodied difference and disability, I include DisCrit (Connor et al.) to unpack images, identity constructions, systemic oppressions, and inequities as well as discourses of and activism for rights (whether of citizenship or human rights). In my Postcolonial Women Writers and Contemporary India courses, texts such as Bapsi Sidhwa's *Cracking India* and Anita Desai's *Clear Light of Day* are read in conversation with postcolonial feminist and critical race approaches that foreground intersectional identities (Spivak, "Can the Subaltern"; Mohanty; Crenshaw; Alexander). In these courses, I have included interdisciplinary readings on physical disability and invisible psychological or mental disabilities. Further readings on class and caste politics, Adivasi displacements and marginalization, and local women's movements provide material and critical frameworks for analyzing literary texts such as Arundhati Roy's *God of Small Things* and Mahasweta Devi's *Imaginary Maps*. To unravel the generative forms of self and situated knowledge that the disability experience enables, I locate disability as socially constructed in interstitial matrices of oppression and experientially and ethically constituted to have potency for feminist self-making and resistance.

In the anthology *AIDS Sutra: Untold Stories from India*, edited by Negar Akhavi (taught in my Contemporary India course), disability is associated with multiple systemic and institutional forms of isolating, labeling, medicalizing, and treating or mistreating disease. The stories in the collection examine disease, disability, and the health care industry with careful scrutiny of local realities and systemic failures, AIDS activism, and women's rights movements. In "Mister X versus Hospital Y," Nikita Lalwani uncovers the biopolitics and institutional forms of discrimination that render economic, psychological, and social penalties on the HIV positive through the story of the Nagaland native and doctor Toku. Upon becoming HIV positive, he lives in exile because of systemic forms of discrimination. Lalwani's journalist narrator describes Toku's emergence as a survivor and his fight against the imposed stigma and invisibility in terms of being "thrust into . . . a fugitive skin" (25). In this context, the embodied experience of HIV/AIDS is articulated as the paradox of both living in and fleeing from one's own skin. The bio-narrative unfolds the transformation of Toku from disease survivor to well-respected human rights activist.

In another narrative from *AIDS Sutra*, "Night Claims the Godavari," Kiran Desai recounts her narrator's journey to the Peddapuram village in the delta region of the Godavari River in Andhra Pradesh. Assembling statistics, historiography, ethnography, as well as individual stories, Desai gives us the living histories of the Kalavanthulu *devadasi* women (hereditary courtesans who belonged to dancers' guilds), now reduced to sex workers for long-distance truckers who traverse the rapidly globalized spaces of "this Incredible India" (49). Desai marks the gap between feminists in the West waving banners for equal pay and girls in the developing world who are "sold for less than the cost of a bottle of beer" (52). Through the enumeration of statistical data, Desai charts the intersections of territorial challenges, vulnerable bodies, sexual trafficking, systemic failures, economic penalties, and official denial of the epidemic. Pairing Desai's narrative text with Kamala Kempadoo's theoretical essay "Women of Color and the Global Sex Trade: Transnational Feminist Perspectives," illuminates the local and global iterations of sex trafficking and vulnerability to diseases. Integrating quantitative data with qualitative documentation, Desai gauges the human crisis dimension of the AIDS epidemic through personal and particular stories. Despite the sadness and defeat of the sex workers, Desai portrays their lives as "lived with the intensity of art" (55).

Many of the stories in *AIDS Sutra* can be analyzed within the framework of the materialist theory of vulnerability, inclusive of embodied, cultural, and socioeconomic vulnerability in the Global South. In "Globalization, Political Economy, and HIV/AIDS," Dennis Altman notes the link between disease and globalization: "AIDS is a remarkably useful case study through which to understand the diverse meanings of 'globalization'" (560). In "At Stake, the Body," C. S. Lakshmi begins by noting the vulnerability of a girl's body in India:

> The body is not talked about. Hidden in its crevices are untold dangers for a woman. The body has to be trampled upon, and conquered as if it is a demon to be slain. The idea is to live with the body as if the body does not really exist; it is never discussed, nor openly mentioned. It is with such conflicts that a girl bears her body and grows with it, in most middle-class homes in India. (101)

"[B]ears her body" articulates the body as a burden, and the girl's body in Indian middle-class spaces is subjected to various modes of policing, curtailment, and punishment. If the girl's body bears the stigma of disease, poverty, caste, or religious ostracism, its burden becomes unbearable. Lakshmi recounts the stories of sex workers whose bodies, carrying the burden of AIDS, circulate as commodities in an exploitative system of exchange (101). While their bodies' availability enhances national GDP and meets the demands of sexual surplus in a postindustrialized, Internet-based, globally connected erotics entertainment industry, their bodies are emptied of value and physically marked: "The girls carry scars on their bodies—cigarette burns, knife marks, marks of other abuse—and there are times when their bodies feel like a festering wound" (104). Lakshmi, however, subverts their victim status by accessing the spaces that the sex workers reclaim and mediate.

> They may have all taken a decision to make their body their capital, but it is not a body to be ashamed of. It is a body that needs to be

> defended against infections, and when infected, the body needs to be medicated and cared for. It is also a body that needs to be defended against violence and misuse. It is this knowledge of the rights of their body that has given these women the confidence to speak out openly, to acknowledge facts about their life. (105)

Framing literary analysis with a rich and complex understanding of the disability experience in South Asia underscores the interplay of key topics: identity construction, language politics, historical processes, and cultural representations of disability in glocal contexts (Rao and Kalyanpur; Ghai). Among critical issues specific to contemporary India is the intersection of stigmatized identities and social devaluation and deficit of the othered through gender divisive, racist, ableist, and caste deterministic regimes of normativity, social shaming, and biomedical discourses of corporeality and body politics. Inclusive of oppressed social categories that have not been generally included as linked to or within the purview of disability are bodies defined by fatism or colorism; constructed as vulnerable to rape, infertility, or femicide; or marked by transgender identities and indigeneity. Harpreet Singh's short story "Fat Like Me" uncovers the discursive biomedical and sociocultural constructions of fatness as disease, the obesity epidemic, and the pathologized and stigmatized identity. Narrated through the naive yet knowing voice of a preadolescent immigrant Sikh girl, the story uncovers the multiple ways in which fat embodiment circulates as the pathologized currency for disease, disability, and a global rhetoric of obesity epidemic complicated by racism, religious bigotry, and hostility toward immigrants. Anne Mollow's theory of fatness as a feminist response to pop culture, articulated in "Sized Up: Why Fat Is a Queer and Feminist Issue," reveals how "obesity parallels and intersects with homosexuality, both terms serving as proxies for American anxieties about death, disability, and disease." In "Fat Like Me," the young girl's alienation, confusion, and self-loathing trace the real consequences of fat oppression, promoted by experts through the "slow death" formulation of global healthism (Berlant).

The pedagogical implications of studying the literary treatment, representation, and subject position of anglophone South Asian women writers, inclusive of disability, suggest transformative and culturally responsive strategies for intercultural education and an inclusive approach to the teaching of literary texts. Ultimately, they might encourage social justice paradigms in countering societal problems (Bracher). Besides classroom application of diverse disability theories in textual study of South Asian women's writing, the integration of the study of disability actualizes active learning, as well as attitudinal shifts to avoid simplifying or universalizing complex experiences of disability.

Works Cited

Akhavi, Negar, editor. *AIDS Sutra: Untold Stories from India*. Anchor, 2008.

Alexander, M. Jacqui. *Pedagogies of Crossing: Meditations on Feminism, Sexual Politics, Memory, and the Sacred*. Duke UP, 2005.

Alston, Margaret. *Women, Political Struggles and Gender Equality in South Asia*. Palgrave Macmillan, 2014.

Altman, Dennis. "Globalization, Political Economy, and HIV/AIDS." *Theory and Society*, vol. 28, no. 4, Aug. 1999, pp. 559–84.

Berlant, Lauren. "Slow Death (Sovereignty, Obesity, Lateral Agency)." *Critical Inquiry*, vol. 33, no. 4, Summer 2007, pp. 754–80.

Boyce Davies, Carole. *Black Women, Writing and Identity: Migrations of the Subject*. Routledge, 1994.

Bracher, Mark. "Teaching for Social Justice: Reeducating the Emotions through Literary Study." *JAC*, vol. 26, no. 3/4, 2006, pp. 463–512. *JSTOR*, www.jstor.org/stable/20866751.

Connor, David J., et al. *DisCrit: Disability Studies and Critical Race Theory in Education*. Teachers College P, 2016.

Crenshaw, Kimberlé Williams. "Mapping the Margins: Intersectionality, Identity Politics, and Violence against Women of Color." *Stanford Law Review*, vol. 43, no. 6, July 1991, pp. 1241–99.

Desai, Anita. *Clear Light of Day*. Penguin, 1980.

Desai, Kiran. "Night Claims the Godavari." Akhavi, pp. 39–55.

Devi, Mahasweta. *Imaginary Maps*. Translated by Gayatri Chakravorty Spivak, Routledge, 1995.

Ghai, Anita. "Disability in the Indian Context: Post-colonial Perspectives." *Disability/Postmodernity: Embodying Disability Theory*, edited by Mairian Corker and Tom Shakespeare, Continuum, 2002, pp. 88–100.

Grewal, Inderpal, and Caren Kaplan. "Global Identities: Theorizing Transnational Studies of Sexuality" *GLQ: A Journal of Lesbian and Gay Studies*, vol. 7, no. 4, 2001, pp. 663–79.

Kalantry, Sital, and Jocelyn Getgen Kestenbaum. "Combating Acid Violence in Bangladesh, India, and Cambodia." Avon Global Center for Women and Justice at Cornell Law School and the New York City Bar Association, 2011. *Scholarship@Cornell Law*, scholarship.law.cornell.edu/avon_clarke/1.

Kempadoo, Kamala. "Women of Color and the Global Sex Trade: Transnational Feminist Perspectives." *Meridians*, vol. 1, no. 2, Spring 2001, pp. 28–51.

Lakshmi, C. S. "At Stake, the Body." Akhavi, pp. 101–08.

Lalwani, Nikita. "Mister X versus Hospital Y." Akhavi, pp. 19–35.

Mohanty, Chandra Talpade. "Under Western Eyes: Feminist Scholarship and Colonial Discourses." *Boundary 2*, vol. 12, no. 3, Spring-Autumn, 1984, pp. 333–358.

Mollow, Anna. "Sized Up: Why Fat Is a Queer and Feminist Issue." *Bitch*, Summer 2013, www.bitchmedia.org/article/sized-up-fat-feminist-queer-disability.

Nancoo, Lynda. "Marriage-able? Cultural Perspectives of Women with Disabilities of South Asian Origin." *Canadian Woman Studies*, vol. 13, no. 4, 1992, pp. 49–51.

Pandey, Gyanendra. "Can There Be a Subaltern Middle Class? Notes on African American and Dalit History." *Public Culture*, vol. 21, no. 2, Spring 2009, pp. 321–42.

Parekh, Pushpa. "Exploring Intersecting Identities in Postcolonial Contexts." Women of Color Caucus workshop, Thirty-First Annual Conference of Association of Women in Psychology, Ypsilanti, MI, March 2006.

———, editor. *Intersecting Gender and Disability Perspectives in Rethinking Postcolonial Identities*. Xlibris, 2008. Special issue of *Wagadu*, vol. 4, 2007.

———. "Technology of Flexibility: Multi-Modal Dimensions of Disability." Disability and Access: Enabling the People, Technologies, and Spaces of Composition workshop, Conference on College Composition and Communication, San Francisco, CA, March 2005.

Phadke, Shilpa. "Dangerous Liaisons: Women and Men: Risk and Reputation in Mumbai." *Economic and Political Weekly*, vol. 42, no. 17, 28 Apr.–4 May 2007, pp. 1510–18.

Prasad, Vijay. *The Karma of Brown Folk*. U of Minnesota P, 2000.

Rao, Shridevi, and Maya Kalyanpur, editors. *South Asia and Disability Studies: Redefining Boundaries and Extending Horizons*. Peter Lang, 2015.

Roy, Arundhati. *The God of Small Things*. Random House, 1997.

Roy, Mantra. *"Speaking" Subalterns: A Comparative Study of African American and Dalit/Indian Literatures*. 2010. U of South Florida, PhD dissertation, digital.lib.usf.edu/content/SF/S0/02/77/06/00001/E14-SFE0003391.pdf.

Sidhwa, Bapsi. *Cracking India*. Milkweed, 1991.

Singh, Harpreet. "Fat Like Me." *Her Mother's Ashes: Stories by South Asian Women in Canada and the United States*, edited by Nurjehan Aziz, vol. 3, TSAR, 2009, pp. 22–27.

Spivak, Gayatri. "Can the Subaltern Speak?" *Marxism and the Interpretation of Culture*, edited by Cary Nelson and Lawrence Grossberg, Macmillan Education, 1988, pp. 271–313.

———. *The Spivak Reader: Selected Works of Gayatri Chakravorty Spivak*. Edited by Donna Landry and Gerald MacLean, Routledge, 1996.

Susmita Roye

Rokeya Sakhawat Hossain's *Sultana's Dream*

In the field of Indian women's writings in English, one is familiar with names like Anita Desai, Shashi Deshpande, Arundhati Roy, and Shobhaa De. In contrast, Rokeya Sakhawat Hossain will be unfamiliar to most students in North America. She is less visible on the literary landscape of anglophone South Asian women's writing. For that reason, one may wonder why and how one should teach Hossain's work.

Such considerations are important not merely because of Hossain's role as one of the earliest Muslim feminist writers from South Asia. They are very timely because of the Islamophobia that pervades and distorts any discourse on feminism, cultural differences, identity politics, and gender equality in relation to Islam in North American and European classrooms. Understandably, an instructor has to tread a tightrope in managing any semblance of meaningful, multipronged, balanced classroom discussions on such sensitive topics. I usually find it helpful to focus on Hossain's representation of womanhood, the impact of purdah (the social custom of women's seclusion)[1] on women's lives, the prejudice against female education, and the role of Islam (or the misinterpretation of it) in keeping women from reaching their full potential; in fact, more often than not, such discussions are eye-opening, making students realize the similarities of women's plight and the need for their empowerment and the abuses of institutionalized religion and social customs across national, cultural, religious, and temporal boundaries. Consequently, although Hossain has been neglected for so long in the teaching of South Asian women writers, it is time that we, as teachers, retrieve her from that amnesia to use her thought-provoking oeuvre to deliberate upon its relevance to wider sociopolitical questions of our times. This essay, therefore, addresses the significance of teaching Hossain and how to propose her work to students.

Why Teach Hossain's *Sultana's Dream*

Hossain is the pioneering feminist figure from Muslim Bengal in British India and is credited with paving a path for (Indian) Muslim women's voices to be heard. One of her earliest daringly feminist works that attracted widespread attention was her novella *Sultana's Dream*, written in English and published in 1905. It is the first work of science fiction, not only among Bengali Muslim women but also among early Indian women writers in general. Additionally, it presents perhaps the earliest portrayal of a feminist utopia in South Asian women's writing in English and, in fact, predates those created by her Western counterparts (like Charlotte Perkins Gilman's *Herland*). It is, therefore, important that this groundbreaking work reclaims its formative prominence in the study and teaching of anglophone South Asian women's writing.

Hossain was born into a respectable Muslim family of East Bengal in colonial India. She was placed in strict purdah at the tender age of five but she, keenly feeling the injustice of deprivation, yearned for the freedom and opportunities that the male members of her family enjoyed. She tried to educate herself and was also secretly taught Bengali and English by her eldest brother, who was in favor of female education. Her first biographer, Shamsun Nahar Mahmud, describes how they had to wait for the dead of night to be able to conduct their clandestine lessons since the family objected to such untraditional learning for girls (23). Later, her husband, Syed Sakhawat Hossain, actively fostered her education and encouraged her to write. Thus, in spite of never having been to school, Rokeya Hossain grew up into an exceptionally knowledgeable woman. But her struggle to achieve that feat unambiguously establishes the strong social prejudice against female education. Moreover, when she later decided to open a school for girls with the money left to her by her dead husband, she faced immense opposition from her in-laws. In fact, they defeated her plan to establish a school in Bhagalpur (the town where her in-laws lived) and drove her away to Calcutta, where the strong-willed young reformer reopened her school. She had to overcome innumerable obstacles to educate the few girls who came to her school. Besides educating girls, Hossain wrote about and relentlessly campaigned against the custom of purdah. However, even if she did not like it, she had to continue observing purdah to retain people's faith in her integrity and her allegiance to her culture, because without the support of her few sympathizers, her radical reformist activities stood little chance of succeeding.

Sultana's Dream, her debut literary piece, was first published in the *Indian Ladies' Magazine* in Madras. It narrates the dream of a purdahnashin woman, Sultana. The eponymous protagonist accompanies a friend for a stroll in the backyard supposedly during dusk but becomes painfully shy when she sees that it is broad daylight outside. Soon her anxieties are put to rest when she realizes that not a single man is to be seen anywhere, and instead, women are walking, talking, and working all around her. Then she is told that this place is called Ladyland. Years ago, after the men of this land fled from a battlefield, women went out of their seclusion to defeat the foe, and ever since, women have come to rule the land under the guidance of their wise queen. A strong feminism colors both the activities of women leaders of this fictional land as well as the grand vision of the writer herself.

How to Teach Hossain's *Sultana's Dream*

The setting of this novella can be unfamiliar to many students. Therefore, we need to first set the background for them to better understand the context and appreciate the text. It may be wise to focus initially on two things: the concept of purdah and the history of women in British India. First, they need to know the kind of purdah Muslim women (like Sultana in this story) practiced in colonial India. Purdah is a custom mainly to ensure gender segregation. In Hossain's times, purdah consisted of leading a life of seclusion where women were not permitted to meet people outside their immediate family circle, go out without an escort, or leave their house premises without being entirely covered. They lived in the *zenana* (women's quarters), which were usually at the rear of the housing compound and consisted of less accessible, often windowless rooms. In short, the kind of purdah that they had to observe was not merely restricted to covering themselves with a burqa; more often than not it meant living in what Hossain calls *abarodh* (a Bengali word that means "confinement").[2] It is very important that students understand this extremely strict form of purdah to realize why Sultana's dream of walking out in the open daylight is radical for her times. In fact, it explains why the happenings in the story constitute a dream, and Sultana wakes up at the end to discover that she is still in the darkness of her *abarodh*.

Second, it is equally important to provide students with a brief history of Indian women's conditions. Geraldine Forbes brings to our notice that Hossain was not the first Muslim woman to set up a school for Muslim girls, but "her systematic and undaunted devotion to this project has earned her the title of pioneer" (55). Several decades before Hossain established the Sakhawat Memorial School in Calcutta in 1911, Faizunnessa Chaudhurani opened a free madrassa and later an English-language school for girls in Comilla in 1873 (Amin 115). By the turn of the twentieth century, we have numerous well-known, educated Muslim women, but they presented an anomaly, not the norm. In light of her times when female education was a taboo (so much so that Hossain had to educate herself secretly), students should realize the enormity of her achievement in writing this novella.

Feminist Vision

This tale reveals Hossain's strong feminism because Sultana's dream throws into sharp relief Hossain's reality. In the world Sultana dreams of, women are happily liberated and know no hindrance. Not a single woman is mentioned to be wearing a veil. This is clearly light-years away from what Hossain (and, in fact, Sultana herself) lived through. The irony is that despite condemning purdah in her polemics, Hossain had to wear a burqa when she went out into public. Whereas men in Ladyland are thrust into enclosed spaces wittily called "murdanas" (a masculine version of the word *zenana*), women around Hossain were confined in *zenanas*. The idea of purdah arose from a concern for becoming feminine modesty, but this was stretched too far by the jealousy of domineering males when it gradually took the shape of total incarceration. Sonia Nishat Amin points out how many Muslim *bhadramahilas* (gentlewomen) of modern Bengal around this time had begun distinguishing between *purdah* and *abarodh*. *Purdah* was seen as "modesty in dress and behaviour," whereas *abarodh* was a "patriarchal distortion of purdah which makes women invisible behind the *andarmahal* [inner quarters for women]" (Amin 139). In *Sultana's*

Dream, Hossain's subversive idea of protecting women's modesty by instead putting men into confinement is her powerfully acerbic critique of the system of *abarodh*.

Sultana's dream world is one where women run universities and are highly educated. That is possible only as a dream for Sultana and Hossain. Hossain lived in a world where she was permitted only a narrow, traditional, religious education at home, meant to limit the mental horizons of aspiring girls and to equip them solely for a confined life as a wife and mother. In fact, it merely entrenched in them a complacence with their confinement, and they were thus not quite able to realize the lamentable lowliness of their condition. Hossain meant *Sultana's Dream* to awaken her fellow women from such self-hurting complacence.

Language and History

While discussing this feminist text, the question that inevitably arises is why Hossain chose to write in English when she must have known that the majority of her fellow women, whose awareness she was attempting to arouse by creating an inverted gender order in this tale, were hardly educated enough to be able to read it in that foreign language. Given Hossain's struggle to become learned, students in my class wonder at her choice of language. Why choose to write in English at all? Who is her target audience, if not her fellow purdah women? Was writing in English merely a tool to show off the heights of achievement by this self-educated woman? Quite understandably, with English, Hossain could reach an international audience and get her radical message across to a larger readership. In fact, amid the multiplicity of languages spoken in the Indian subcontinent, English became the lingua franca that helped bridge linguistic gulfs. No wonder, then, that sitting and writing in Bengal in the north of the subcontinent, she was able to get *Sultana's Dream* published in a magazine in Madras, situated in the south of India. Therefore, choosing English was not necessarily an indicator of her anglophile attitude. It helped her gain a wider platform for her message, making it possible for her to arrest the attention of both her compatriots as well as an international English-speaking populace, thereby strengthening her crusade against female deprivation.

Since English was the master's tongue, using it inherently involves political baggage. Questions that students may ponder: Does it merely reflect Hossain's anglophile attitude or is something more involved here?

How does it become more problematic and politics-ridden in a colonial setup? Is there cultural translation at work here? Clearly, a colonized woman's dissenting voice can be traced. Ladyland is ruled over by a wise queen, who takes drastic measures to improve the conditions of her fellow women. There is surely a hint of censure at the prevailing poor conditions of women in India despite having been ruled by Queen Victoria for years. Is it an oblique comment on the half-hearted measures taken by the British government to ameliorate their plight and improve their situation? Above all, the invasion of Ladyland by the neighboring king on the slightest of pretexts can easily be read as a covert critique of conquests of distant lands under the banner of imperialism, including that of India by the British. All the same, Sultana's "fall" from the air-car of her dream back to the reality of her dark bedroom is simultaneously a signifier of women's denigration, a measure of injustices committed by the native patriarchy, and an exposé of the failure of imperial rulers to fully honor their promises. Many critics and scholars like Roushan Jahan and Bharati Ray have perceived a strong anticolonial stance in this debut novella that defined Hossain's later feminist as well as nationalist work. In the classroom, it is essential that students learn to detect the intertwined layers of nationalism couched in feminism in this text not only to better understand the historical context of Hossain's subjecthood as a colonized woman in the British-controlled Indian subcontinent, but also to be able to appreciate the nuances of a tale that navigates the tricky waters of female identity and agency against the dual oppression of colonialism and patriarchy; without it, an instructor misses an opportunity for productive discussion of the text.

Utopianism and Science Fiction

This feminist vision creates a utopia. Ladyland is ruled by virtue and purity, embodied by the farsighted, wise queen. There is no want or sin or suffering here. Since men, who are corrupt and evil by nature, are safely confined, there arises no need for a police officer, magistrate, or military force in this land. Even when someone errs, the person is punished by being banished from the land forever, because the authorities do not believe in taking away a life that God has gifted. But, at the same time, mercy is shown to sincere penitents. Thus, justice seems to be delivered in the best possible manner. Similarly, agriculture and commerce are well looked after by these women, who plan to turn their land into a large, beautiful horticultural garden instead of just blocking the open air with innumerable ugly brick buildings. Their religion is based on truth and love, which prevents all kinds of communal fanaticism. There are no epidemics and early deaths. There is no time for petty jealousies and quarrels among these women because they are always busy with more fruitful occupations. There is also no dearth of water for their crops and daily needs. In the absence of railroads or paved paths, there arise no possibility of unfortunate life-taking accidents. Their time for transportation is considerably reduced by their aerial conveyances that take them from one place to another in a surprisingly short time. The author, in fact, sketches her utopia to the minutest details: not only is there no crime or want or crushing class system here but the fortunate denizens are also free from mud, dirt, and even mosquitoes. In every way, Ladyland is the perfect h(e)aven for women.

In other words, Ladyland is a feminist utopia. The very concept of utopianism is wrought with contradictions and complexities, particularly given the ambivalences inherent in the vision endorsed in seminal texts like Sir Thomas More's *Utopia*. Hence, when this concept is applied to the vision of perfection by a triply marginalized subject (woman, secluded, colonized), one has to tread the slippery path carefully. Each instructor may sketch her own plan for this tough discussion. I usually focus on the Greek roots of the term because, as Barnita Bagchi reminds us, "[utopia] is, most of all, about embodying a dream, a dream of an ideal place ('eu-topia') which is, at the same time, no place ('ou-topia'), for it does not exist until imagined into existence by those strongly inspired by the dream of an ideal life" (Introduction xviii); this feminist utopia is, after all, only a dream, and the author makes that clear in her title.

What is striking is that the existence of this feminist utopia relies not so much on women's physical prowess as on their ingenious scientific and technological innovations. Ladyland has become what it is because its women are great scientists. It is a fruitful activity for students to closely read the text to detect such examples and to place them in the context of scientific developments at that point in history. With contemporaneous science still struggling to achieve many of its wonders, like trapping renewable sources of energy or fulfilling man's desire to soar among clouds, Hossain's imagination is remarkably prescient.

Although not yet widely acknowledged, Hossain's story can be seen as the first feminist science fiction in English in the literary history of South Asian women's writings. It seems surprising that the earliest feminist science fiction should come from the pen of an Indian woman from a colonized corner of the earth, where voices like hers were easily crushed by centuries of native patriarchal traditions and additionally by male predominance in the imperialist machine. Moreover, teaching Hossain allows students to discuss the question of sci-fi in South Asia, especially given that she received no formal education that would have given her exposure to scientific studies. Most of her male contemporaries chose to write realist social novels or poetry. Far fewer in number, contemporary women writers tended to focus on household matters. How does Hossain's debut novella mark a huge departure from that well-trodden path? Delving into such queries can inform a pedagogical practice that is able to situate Hossain's work and to address her significance within the feminist tradition in South Asia.

Colonial fiction certainly favored realism, as evident in works from Krupabai Satthianadhan, Cornelia Sorabji, Mulk Raj Anand, Premchand, and R. K. Narayan. As Ulka Anjaria explains, "Reclaiming realism was in this context [of colonialism] an act of self-determination—a refutation of the colonial project" (2). So why did Hossain refuse and refute realism? Or, paradoxically, is her utopianism more realistic about the aggressive measures that need to be taken for real improvements in women's education to get tangible results? As many scholars like Bagchi ("Towards Ladyland"), Forbes, and Ray have noted, female education, despite decades of grand rhetoric by a so-called benevolent colonial master or enlightened Indian patriarchy, certainly did not progress by leaps and bounds. Maybe such a bold "dream" is what emphasizes the reality of the drastic measures required; hence, in eschewing the confinements of realism, Hossain both underpins a depressing reality of and envisages an enabling future for her fellow women.

This single text is a rich source that sheds light on historical, political, cultural, religious, linguistic, and many other issues associated with South Asian women's writing. This essay focused on mainly five strands of discussion: feminism, anglophilia, (post)colonialism, utopianism, and science fiction. Furthermore, as previously mentioned, this text not only sheds light on the history of (Muslim) women's conditions and fight for justice in the Indian subcontinent, but it is also a good place to jump-start discussions of numerous sociocultural-political issues of our own times across the globe.

Notes

1. Hossain wrote a book, *Abarodhbashini*, or "women living in confinement" (my translation), about the real-life experience of purdah women. See Ja-

han for alternative translations of the title as "inside seclusion" or "the secluded ones" (x).

2. For a detailed analysis of the contrast, see Roye.

Works Cited

Amin, Sonia Nishat. "The Early Muslim *Bhadramahila*: The Growth of Learning and Creativity, 1876 to 1939." *From the Seams of History: Essays on Indian Women*, edited by Bharati Ray, Oxford UP, 1995, pp. 107–48.

Anjaria, Ulka. *Realism in the Twentieth-Century Indian Novel: Colonial Difference and Literary Form*. Cambridge UP, 2012.

Bagchi, Barnita. Introduction. Sultana's Dream *and* Padmarag*: Two Feminist Utopias*, by Rokeya Sakhawat Hossain, Penguin, 2005, pp. vii–xxvi.

———. "Towards Ladyland: Rokeya Sakhawat Hossain and the Movement for Women's Education in Bengal, c. 1900–c. 1930." *Paedagogica Historica*, vol. 45, no. 6, 2009, pp. 743–55.

Forbes, Geraldine. *Women in Modern India*. Cambridge UP, 1999.

Hossain, Rokeya Sakhawat. "Sultana's Dream." *Women's Voices: Selections from Nineteenth and Early-Twentieth Century Indian Writing in English*, edited by Eunice de Souza and Lindsay Pereira, Oxford UP, 2002, pp. 163–72.

Jahan, Roushan, editor and translator. *"Sultana's Dream" and Selections from* The Secluded Ones. By Rokeya Sakhawat Hossain, Feminist Press, 1988, pp. 24–36.

Mahmud, Shamsun Nahar. *Rokeya Jiboni [The Life of Rokeya]*. 1937. Sahitya Parishad, 2009.

Ray, Bharati. *Early Feminists of Colonial India: Sarala Devi Chaudhurani and Rokeya Sakhawat Hossain*. Oxford UP, 2002.

Roye, Susmita. "*Sultana's Dream* vs. Rokeya's Reality: A Study of One of the 'Pioneering' Feminist Science Fictions." *Kunapipi*, vol. 31, no. 2, 2009, pp. 135–46.

Antonia Navarro-Tejero

South Asian Feminisms and the Politics of Representation

Teaching feminism in an undergraduate course titled South Asian Writing in English in a southern Spanish university is challenging for many reasons. Because of a heavy course load and required reading from lists of canonical texts, the majority of our English majors do not take any women's studies or postcolonial literature courses. It is only when they opt to take my course in the first semester of their fourth year that they are exposed to feminist debates and South Asian women's writing for the first time. In my twenty-some years of experience, most of my undergraduate students are reluctant to discuss feminist issues, whether in the classroom or outside it. Broaching feminist concerns in class requires us to confront our inability to admit that we still live within a male-dominated, male-identified, and male-centered society. When students perceive misogyny in the literature, they are apt to treat it as exclusive to Indian culture, which they also perceive as monolithic. The overall objective of this course is to introduce literature by South Asian women writers in the English studies curriculum at my university and to dismantle students' stereotypes about Indian women, which are routinely reinforced by a persistently orientalist discourse in the mass media as well as paternalistic attitudes still present in contemporary European societies. This essay describes the theoretical scaffolding I have developed in order to introduce key concerns about the politics of representation from postcolonial and feminist theory, followed by a reading of Githa Hariharan's short story "The Remains of the Feast," featuring a traditional Brahmin widow, to demonstrate how even a text replete with representations some might consider near stereotypical affords us the opportunity to explore agency and transgression. Additionally, this essay includes suggestions for exploring the possibility of global feminist solidarity, as I demonstrate through my inclusion of material from the local Spanish press to highlight the ways in which feminist concerns transcend national borders.

The Politics of Representation

A class discussion on the concept of representation serves as an introduction to the course and as a key piece of my pedagogic toolkit. I offer a group of questions related to Edward Said's theory of orientalism. Said argues that the West creates and represents a homogenous and stereotyped Orient (47–49). He asserts that colonialist ideology uses the other to locate the self and define the normal. The binary separation of colonizer or colonized asserts the naturalness and primacy of the colonizing culture and worldview. After reading excerpts from Said's *Orientalism*, we discuss stereotypes of the East as exotic or demonic and reach the conclusion that the idea of the normal is a prejudicial construction. We then move on to consider a feminist response to Said. In *Colonial Fantasies*, Meyda Yegenoglu interrogates Western fascination with the veiled woman and notes,

> [T]he veiled woman is not simply an obstacle in the field of visibility and control but her veiled presence also seems to provide the Western subject with a condition which is the inverse of Bentham's omnipotent gaze. The loss of control does not imply a mere loss of sight, but a complete reversal of positions: her body completely invisible to the European observer except for her eyes, *the veiled woman can see without being seen.* (43)

The oriental woman does not yield herself to the Western gaze and challenges the customary relation between subject and object. Our discussions on orientalism in the classroom are designed to interrogate default assumptions about others, as well as to resist the power dynamic that treats the non-Western woman as an object to be unmasked in accordance with preset assumptions.

Next, we contend with Western-centric assumptions that are often reproduced within the tradition of Western feminism. Teaching in this way requires us to challenge what Chandra Mohanty describes as a discursive colonization of the "material and historical heterogeneities of the lives of women in the third world" (334) as well as the othering of non-Western women (see Kristeva). Several postcolonial theorists analyze how the image of the liberated Western woman is constructed against that of Third World women or women of color, who are stereotyped as oppressed (Mohanty; Ong; Minh-ha). According to Deepika Bahri, a postcolonial feminist perspective requires that one learn "to read literary representations of women with attention both to the subject and to the medium of representation" to promote "the capacity to read the world (specifically, in this context, gender relations) with a critical eye" (200). In my teaching practice, I ask students to question stereotypes about Indian women as if they were a monolithic entity. Mohanty points out that Third World women are frequently defined as "underdeveloped" by Western standards, considered religious (read "not progressive"), family-oriented ("traditional"), legal minors ("not conscious of their rights"), illiterate ("ignorant"), and domestic ("backward") (337). Finally, we read Gayatri Spivak's "Can the Subaltern Speak?" and engage in discussion about the subaltern racialized other and the assumptions made about her (292). As we read Spivak, we also explore a related question concerning the problem of authenticity and representation through Sara Suleri's "Feminism and the Postcolonial Condition," a response to Mohanty in which Suleri famously observes, "The claim to authenticity—only a black can speak for a black; only a postcolonial subcontinental feminist can adequately represent the lived experience of that culture—points to the great difficulty posited by the 'authenticity' of female racial voices" (251).

Each of these theoretical interventions adds a layer of complexity to the problems of representation, posing direct challenges both to the perception of women as monolithic as well as to assumptions of authenticity. Moreover, the range of readings introduces students to the inherent diversity and heterogeneity of feminist interventions in South Asia. To drive home this point, students read a pivotal volume edited by Ania Loomba and Ritty Lokuse, who adopt the plural term *South Asian feminisms* to refer to a rich and complex terrain of activism and expression. They advocate "a sustained focus on the dense histories, interconnections, and dynamic complexities of South Asia as a location of feminist theory and praxis" to resist both "the reductive ways in which Western feminist frameworks incorporate their others" and "the parochialism of South Asian feminisms that function within nationalist frameworks" (24). Through these readings and discussions, I guide students toward an investigation of who is represented and who represents, of what the silences are, of how to challenge the ways in which Western discourse can flatten the complexities of representation and distort perceptions of the non-West, and, finally, of the diversity of South Asian feminist responses, which attempt to shed light on a whole array of issues in response.

Since I believe that we need to bridge the classroom and real-world struggles, the personal and the political, theory and practice, I use the solidarity model proposed by Mohanty's feminist pedagogy in her influential article "Under Western Eyes" as we focus on the links and intersections among different groups. Mohanty argues that by focusing on solidarity across traditional divisions of class, nation, and race, we can grasp the interconnectedness of the human experience. Therefore, I bring to class articles and pieces of news that challenge prejudices against Indian women as monolithic objects of oppression. In order to offer a mirror to my students, we also read Fatema Mernissi's *Scheherazade Goes West: Different Cultures, Different Harems*, which exposes patriarchal domination as a globally shared condition. We discuss unhealthy standards of beauty in the West that foster an obsession with physical appearance, thinness, and dieting as an example of the ways in which popular media is used to control women's choices. Every topic we discuss in class is an opportunity to explore the misogyny and racism of our own institutions and society. For instance, although Spain is not represented as dangerous for women, many women are murdered as a result of domestic violence and struggle to succeed in their careers as they confront the glass ceiling. In doing so, we construct civic engagement learning activities; reflection on these interconnections opens the world to the students, their own as much as that of others', in all its complexities.

Teaching Feminism through Hariharan's "The Remains of the Feast"

In Hariharan's short story my students encounter a Brahmin woman, Rukmini—the narrator's "ignorant village-bred" great-grandmother (9)—widowed young and living the prescribed life of austerity, till the age of ninety, when, dying of cancer, she begins to cross prohibited borders and transforms herself into an abject body whose desires challenge

Brahminical laws. In the flourish of death, a new life bursts forth for Rukmini in a hitherto controlled appetite that declares its scandalous self. Her demands are defined as "unexpected, inappropriate" (13). Rukmini tests all taboos, desires everything that has been forbidden: cakes with eggs in them from the Christian shop with a Muslim cook, Coca-Cola laced with the delicious delight that it might be alcoholic, *bhel-puri* from the fly-infested bazaar possibly touched by untouchable hands, chickens and goats (15). This most traditional of figures from the register of stereotypes about Hindu women, a staple of colonial orientalist discourse, bursts through the pages as a transgressive, inappropriate widow intent on fulfilling her appetites through the consumption of foods forbidden to her by religious decree and generations of social practice. As South Asian women's cultural expression evolves in the twenty-first century, a new range of texts has become available that presents confident, openly resistant female protagonists in films such as *Queen*, directed by Vikas Bahl, and popular novels such as *The Private Life of Mrs. Sharma*, by Ratika Kapur. Arguably, these representations of contemporary Indian women present more readily legible texts of agency and resistance. My choice of Hariharan's story, however, is intended to draw attention to the question of *how* we read rather than *what* we read to meet the challenges of confronting the politics of representation and the possibility of global solidarity.

In order to practice the lessons learned from the theoretical texts explored as an introduction to the course, students analyze how Hariharan responds to the traditional representation of the Hindu widow by depicting a female character who is ambivalent and transgressive in the final moments of her life. Traditionally, the representation of the widow corresponds to ascetic widowhood and *sati*, the two prescribed options for her in some interpretations of religious texts. Ania Loomba remarks in her important essay "Dead Women Tell No Tales" that the practice of *sati* is a form of patriarchal violence that "casts the burning widow as a sign of normative femininity: in a diverse body of work, she becomes the privileged signifier of either the devoted and chaste, or the oppressed and victimized Indian (or sometimes even 'third world') woman." Loomba exposes the role of colonial discourse in consolidating this view in the essay, which is committed to "reconceptualising the burning widow as neither an archetypal victim nor a free agent, and to analysing the interconnections between colonialism and its aftermath" (242). Following

Mohanty, we resist learned tendencies to "appropriate and 'colonize' the fundamental complexities and conflicts which characterise the lives of women of different classes, religions, cultures, races and castes in these countries" (335).

Like many other writings by South Asian women writers, this story discloses the cultural and political complexities of India; the quest for a flagrantly transgressive self at an old age becomes a quest for a nation, with rules to be revised and myths to be retold. Hindu nationalist discourse has produced a complex politics of corporeality by which, ideologically, the female imaginary has served to articulate the abstract concept of the nation. Ashis Nandy argues that since the late nineteenth century, Hindu nationalists have imagined India as the "Great Mother" (92). Although the short story reinforces a view of Indian women as constructed, controlled, and disciplined by agents of power, by demanding and committing pleasurable, prohibited acts, Rukmini subverts the norms and regulations of her society. Her daughter-in-law is apt to dismiss this behavior as part of senile delirium—"She's losing her mind, she is going to be a lot of trouble" (14)—but this end-of-life experience is depicted as liberation; what is traditionally considered a polluted body is reconsidered from a feminist stance. Rukmini's last-minute unconventional desires reconfigure traditional views of the widow. The familiar shaven-headed figure of the victim-widow is replaced by a female body that rejects deprivation of pleasure in favor of the flesh reasserting its primal authority. As Susie Tharu says about Hariharan's short story, the figure of the widow as sufferer "has been replaced by a body whose robust appetite and Rabelaisian humour is a capable substitute for feminist struggle" (1312). Teaching this short text builds on Tharu's thought-provoking analysis and leads to productive discussions on the intersectional dimensions of gender, class, and caste. As Tharu remarks, "[T]he feminist salience of the story is based on the fact that its protagonist is not just a Hindu widow but a *brahmin* widow" (1312), a character challenging the system that has restricted not only her freedom of movement but also every dimension of her daily life, down to what she may or may not eat.

Since feminist pedagogy is concerned with notions of power and authority, I encourage students to examine literary characters as both disciplined and subversive. Since we have adopted a solidarity model, comparative readings become possible in the classroom. For every oppressed and neglected woman we find in the text, students bring up clear and current examples of gender violence in our community. I remind them of Mernissi's comments on the ways in which fashion can be read as the Western Ayatollah or a neo-Brahminical code of restrictions, as Western women fast twelve months a year to fit into the standards of beauty promoted by the popular media. The politics of food and women's bodies emerges in instructively comparable scenes of binge eating, fasting, and self-denial in both cultures.

Yet, as Tharu argues, the story runs the risk of rendering "historical and present-day struggles redundant." Significantly, the widow challenges the system by consuming proscribed foods rather than denouncing discrimination and struggle. Moreover, as Tharu notes, "the late-capitalist, fund-bank widow *consumes* her way to freedom" (1312). Tharu's observations draw attention to a societal context of late capitalism in which consumption might read not as transgressive but rather as a normative and widespread response to the machinations of the marketplace that manufactures these desires. How does the binding of Rukmini's desires with developments in the capitalist marketplace complicate the question of feminist agency? Who gets to define agency and which acts are acceptably feminist and which are inadmissible by a discourse that continues to be dominated by the standards and staples of Western theory? In the course of discussing these issues, the students and I examine the idea of agency through a prism of questions prompted by our earlier exploration of orientalist discourses and blind spots about the other in Western feminist theories. Moreover, in considering the context of "historical and present-day struggles" together, we are compelled to pay attention to the new challenges posed by the examination of feminism in a late-capitalist world. Tharu's reading compels teachers to question the kind of cultural politics enacted in fictional texts and to examine the ways in which literary representations can simultaneously reiterate, partially obscure, and reframe feminist concerns.

The reading of this short story is but one example of how I use theory to shape the reading practices of students so that we learn to analyze literary texts in solidarity, honor their contexts and complexities, and question monolithic representations of South Asian women. We come to understand that ethnic and caste differences are related to power systems, that gender differences are part of structures of patriarchy as well as class, and unequal relations emerge as products of global and local power structures that go beyond cultural or religious boundaries. It is my mission to encourage students to avoid reproducing the boundaries between us (represented as civilized independent citizens) and them (traditionally represented as disempowered subjects) through the analysis of literary texts. Thanks to a postcolonial feminist methodology, students are trained to read texts with a view to dismantling stereotyped dichotomies while examining their own world more thoughtfully.

Note

The author wishes to acknowledge the funding provided for the writing of this essay by the Junta de Andalucía Ministry of Economy and Knowledge (research project Embodiments, Genders, and Difference: Cultural Practices of Violence and Discrimination, ref. 1252965) and by the European Regional Development Fund. Her most sincere gratitude goes to the editors of this volume for their helpful and constructive comments.

Works Cited

Bahri, Deepika. "Feminism in/and Postcolonialism." *The Cambridge Companion to Postcolonial Literary Studies*, edited by Neil Lazarus, Cambridge UP, 2004, pp. 199–220.

Hariharan, Githa. "The Remains of the Feast." *The Art of Dying*, Penguin, 1993, pp. 9–16.

Kristeva, Julia. *About Chinese Women*. Translated by Anita Barrows, Boyars, 1991.

Loomba, Ania. "Dead Women Tell No Tales: Issues of Female Subjectivity, Subaltern Agency and Tradition in Colonial and Post-colonial Writings on Widow Immolation in India." *Feminist Postcolonial Theory: A Reader*, edited by Reina Lewis and Sara Mills, Routledge, 2013, pp. 241–62.

Loomba, Ania, and Ritty A. Lukose, editors. *South Asian Feminisms*. Duke UP, 2012.

Mernissi, Fatema. *Scheherazade Goes West: Different Cultures, Different Harems*. Washington Square Press, 2002.

Minh-ha, Trinh T. *Woman, Native, Other: Writing Postcoloniality and Feminism*. Indiana UP, 1989.

Mohanty, Chandra Talpade. "Under Western Eyes: Feminist Scholarship and Colonial Discourses." *Third World Women and the Politics of Feminism*, edited by Mohanty et al., Indiana UP, 1991, pp. 333–56.

Nandy, Ashis. *The Intimate Enemy: Loss and Recovery of Self under Colonialism*. Oxford UP, 1998.

Ong, Aihwa. "Colonialism and Modernity: Feminist Re-presentations of Women in Non-Western Societies." *Feminism and Race*, edited by Kum-Kum Bhavnani, Oxford UP, 2001, pp. 108–18.

Said, Edward. *Orientalism*. Penguin, 1978.

Spivak, Gayatri Chakravorty. "Can the Subaltern Speak?" *Marxism and the Interpretation of Culture*, edited by C. Nelson and L. Grossberg, Macmillan Education, 1988, pp. 271–313.
Suleri, Sara. "Woman Skin Deep: Feminism and the Postcolonial Condition." *Critical Inquiry*, vol. 18, no. 4, Summer 1992, pp. 756–69.
Tharu, Susie. "The Impossible Subject: Caste and the Gendered Body." *Economic and Political Weekly*, vol. 31, no. 22, 1 June 1996, pp. 1311–15.
Yegenoglu, Meyda. *Colonial Fantasies: Towards a Feminist Reading of Orientalism*. Cambridge UP, 1998.

Lisa Lau

No Longer Just Victims: New Fiction and New Gender Roles

Indian women's fiction in English as a substantial literary subgenre was pioneered around the 1960s and 1970s by a handful of writers such as Anita Desai, Ruth Prawer Jhabvala, Kamala Markandaya, Attia Hosain, Nayantara Sahgal, and Shashi Deshpande. In the 1980s, with Salman Rushdie's *Midnight's Children* throwing open the floodgates of Indian writing in English, more and more Indian women writers came to the fore and some (like Arundhati Roy, Kiran Desai, and Jhumpa Lahiri) became prominent prizewinners and household names.[1]

The Trope of Victimhood

At the start, Indian women's writing in English focused primarily on issues of home, domesticity, marriage, and family—concerns that were infrequently set within wider political contexts. Moreover, the focus was on the individual, usually a female protagonist, and her social standing, constraints, struggles, and relationships with family. In this kind of realist fiction, Indian women's writing in English outlined the double colonization women underwent, of nationality and race and of gender. The focus was so strongly on the unequal and unjust treatment of Indian women that the trope of the victim quite naturally came to the fore in this emergent body of literature. As Yasmin Hussain points out, women characters "are often projected in Indian women's fiction as trapped in the categories of wife, mother and daughter. These women are usually depicted as victims of social and political injustice, cruelty and exploitation" (55). In fact, Indian women's literature in English became all but characterized by women protagonists being victims of patriarchy, culture, and tradition.

Both literary and nonliterary studies note the subservient position typical for many Indian women, from childhood right through the stages of a woman's life. As Nabar observes, "[T]here is no gainsaying the fact that the typical Indian girl-child . . . has to learn quite early on that she is a second-class citizen even in her mother's home. . . . Her breaking-in is all the more rigorous if she happens to belong to an economically deprived class . . ." (60). Rajeswari Sunder Rajan baldly states that the Indian family

> is the major, if not primary site of women's oppression. For it is within the family that girl-children . . . may be required to perform hard domestic labour, denied the freedom to come and go, married off, frequently without their consent and on payment of dowry, and then subjected to the vicissitudes of married life, which would include harassment by in-laws, marital discord, unwanted pregnancies, domestic drudgery, and the continuing cycle of the burden of girl-children of their own. ("Heroine's Progress" 80)

In a 2003 publication, studying *What the Body Remembers* by Shauna Singh Baldwin, I identified the novel as an example of writing focused on recurrent themes of submission, sacrifice, and suffering, consistently depicted with culturally ingrained and societally constructed fears, keeping women obedient and self-sacrificing. I argued that whether submissive or rebellious, women characters inevitably seem to end up as victims for a variety of reasons: apart from the fears of dispossession, challenging authority through hard-earned seniority may be a threat to their precarious toehold on power in the domestic sphere; some may prefer known evils to unknown ones; others may subscribe to the idea of being keepers of their culture and would be resistant to or suspicious of change; still others may not wish to bring dishonor to their natal families; or it may simply be that through the ages, women have internalized the orthodox rhetoric of praise for the obedient daughter and self-effacing wife. I concluded that not only does Indian women's writing in English posit female protagonists as victims in their societies, but they all but "equate the very position of women with that of victimhood" ("Equating Womanhood" 369).

Post-2000 literature may still depict the victimhood of women, but in fiction about urban, middle-class India, there has been a significant change that supplements this singular depiction. With the rise of the middle classes, particularly in urban India, social norms began to change. As a demographic, women of this group are increasingly better educated, permitted to take up paid employment outside the home, and given greater freedoms than a generation or so before. However, although the professional middle class educates its young women typically to degree level and even above, career advancement for women is still regarded as lower priority than family needs and concerns (most women's jobs are deemed "time-pass" while awaiting marriage), as are individual fulfillment and autonomy. Moreover, women of "good families" are constrained in terms of choices of employment to some extent, because it would be unthinkable for them to go into anything other than professional jobs (Caplan), though this range of middle-class jobs has been augmented by multinational corporations, banks, offices, services, and information technology (Fernandes).

Social changes and social attitudes have paralleled, to some extent, the rapid urbanization and economic changes taking place in a fast-developing India. Smitha Radhakrishnan's research on knowledge professionals notes that "[o]nly recently has it become common for middle-class women in urban India to work full-time; consequently, these women are at the helm of key ideological transitions within the Indian middle class" (144). For Indian women, the struggles used to be along domestic and gendered lines, but the rise of the single, young workingwoman, particularly in metropolises, has fueled a quiet cultural revolution in the sense that this cohort is making respectable what was once suspect: a young, unmarried woman, living on her own sans family, with almost complete autonomy, financially as well as in other ways. It is not that her struggles have decreased; rather, her intersectionalities (age, caste, religion, etc.) are beginning to be brought forefront alongside her gendered identity.

The position of the New Indian Woman has changed faster and more drastically than ever before; rebellion and breaking with tradition are not as uncommon as they used to be or even as harshly penalized. India is no longer depicted as timeless or static, particularly where gender norms are concerned. Consequently, Indian women's writing in English reflects "a period when new machineries of control were established, and new ways of being Indian shaped and circulated" (Chowdhury 308). I will now turn to some of these new themes and textures of Indian women's writing in English, particularly in realist fiction, which have taken this young literary subculture in radically new directions.

It is important to note that Indian women's writing in English has moved on considerably from the early days of depicting the struggles of Indian women who were twice colonized. In the teaching of these writings, it would perhaps be a fairer representation of current India to include a selection of texts in which Indian women are increasingly breaking with convention, no longer mere upholders of traditional culture or representatives and clichés of their race, nation, or linguistic group. In the classroom, going beyond the image of the victim can raise debates on the question of agency and the ways and spaces in which contemporary women in the subcontinent have redefined sites of empowerment. These novels can be used to forge a contemporary pedagogical approach linking literary representation to questions about modernity and the vernacular, as well as challenging stereotypes and prejudices in the reading of South Asian novels. The following section outlines a few texts that are particularly useful in depicting what would have previously been considered unusual, but which are increasingly becoming mainstream, Indian women.

For instance, post-2000 Indian women's literature features many women earning their own living, even if residual constraints on their autonomy persist: Nagaratna in K. R. Usha's *The Chosen*, Akhilandeswari of Anita Nair's *Ladies Coupé*, Moyna in Anita Desai's "The Rooftop Dweller," even Nisha of Manju Kapur's *Home*, just to name a few. However, most of these women's families nevertheless oppose their being careerwomen (except for Nagaratna, whose income is an absolute necessity), and in cases where the woman's income is not a necessity, the families are often unsupportive and disrespectful of their careers and work, making clear their preference that their daughters and sisters not work. "Nisha must understand that women's [salaried, outside] work was allowable only in unconventional situations (no children), and that respectability demand it be avoided as much as possible" (Kapur, *Home* 212). It seems that "the greatest obstacle to change in the direction of equality is the value system by which women abide" (Chitins 10). "She [Nisha] was the sole occupant of the tower her family was laying siege to. With promises, threats, presents, kindness, reminders of obligations, with tenderness, love, and blackmail" (Kapur, *Home* 213). Meenakshi Thapan refers to this emotional and mental siege situation as "the all-encompassing nature of the Indian family life that somehow keeps young girls trapped within its complacent world of warmth and contentment" (366–67).

The selection of texts below illustrates the radical changes in Indian women's writing in English; these are all texts by renowned Indian women writers of literary fiction who have achieved not only national but international recognition. Their texts have been chosen precisely because they are among the movers and shakers who create cultural understanding of Indian women and influence ideology through their representations.

New Directions of Indian Women's Writing in English

Indian women's writing in English is susceptible to varying degrees of re-orientalism; Indian cultural representations are usually in the hands of an elite, Western-educated, middle- or upper-class minority who still refer to the West as the center and to some extent cannot help looking through Western lenses (even if only partially) and working within the paradigms of Western-constructed knowledge systems. Re-orientalism is the process of self-othering, along orientalist lines, such that non-Europeans are seen to be inadvertently (or otherwise) perpetrating orientalisms (Lau, "Re-Orientalism"). Indian women writing in English represent—or are regarded as representing—their race, culture, linguistic group, and, most of all, gender through text and literature. Writing within the arena of global literature in English makes it difficult to entirely escape the hegemony of Western metanarratives, reference points, knowledges, and lenses.

One of the most remarkable challenges to tradition in twenty-first-century Indian women's writing in English is the redefinition of gender roles and societal values. From time immemorial, Indian womanhood had been transfixed on an essentialist notion of "purity" that defined Indianness (Sarkar). Indian women have long represented national cultural identity and been upholders of sacred values and ordered society, and thus it was on women that the stability of family life rested, which in turn cemented the stability of the nation (Puri; Caplan). Good daughters would defer to the authority of patriarchal family (Mankekar). Furthermore, a good woman was characterized by being self-effacing, virtuous, and modest (one who understands shame). Once, wives, girls, and women were expected to be dutiful, docile, nurturing, chaste, and, above all, faithful. Indian women's literature in English had always contained depictions of sexually transgressive women, painted as either villainous or fallen; adultery was always punished "if not by death, then at least by disillusionment and despair" (Kalpana 67). Recent work has challenged this worldview as well as the long-standing notion of the "good girl." In my study of eight novels,[2] I found examples of good girls and women who transgress and of transgressors who are neither evil nor become fallen, thus blurring binary definitions of good and bad girls ("No Longer Good Girls"). They are neither angels nor monsters, neither victims nor temptresses. Rather, women who transgress in these novels are also "classy, elegant, sincere, family-oriented and highly conventional" (291). These contemporary works of Indian women's writing in English depict solid citizens, pillars of society, and respectable middle-class wives and mothers having pre- and extramarital affairs, committing adultery, divorcing, and fighting for child custody and doing so with neither bad consciences nor severe (if any) social consequences.

Another radical departure from tradition in Indian women's writing in English is the increased focus on the woman as individual, not relationally defined. Previously, the Indian woman was seldom depicted in isolation, always depicted within a network, her sense of identity dependent on and drawn from her family and society. Anuradha Roy's second novel, *The Folded Earth*, departs from this convention, refusing to focus on issues of family and kinship ties, depicting an autonomous young widow relocating far from family on her own, whimsical and independent, wholly unafraid of other people's opinion and not looking for protection or approval.[3] Moreover, this novel moves away from a plot-driven narrative to focus on form, tone, and style; Roy uses these techniques to weave her atmosphere, rather than relying on clichés, convenient stereotypes, and exotica, needing none of "[t]he exotic representations used to market South Asian texts, particularly those written by women" (Rajan and Phukan 4). Roy has taken a bold new step in refusing to trade on cultural cachet and in avoiding gender clichés and roles. Avoiding discussion of domestic details of foods, textiles, weddings, and cultural festivities and celebrations and breaking away from the urban, middle-class, career-oriented, commodity-consuming "New Indian Woman" (Lau, "Literary Representations"), Roy has written an un-Indian Indian woman. Her representations of female characters can be used in the classroom to discuss how Roy eludes and challenges the orientalist assumptions and expectations of readership in Europe and North America. Instead of reproducing the postcolonial exotic, novels such as *The Folded Earth* can suggest nuanced ways of reading and teaching Indian women's writing in English beyond Eurocentrism and orientalism.

Moreover, Indian women writers are increasingly broadening their scope from the private and domestic to the public sphere. Kavery Nambisan's *The Story That Must Not Be Told* addresses the representation of poverty in a lyrical and political way, depicting the face of India from which the middle and upper classes in India routinely avert attention.[4] She writes of a slum called Sitara; there is nothing domestic, delicate, or "feminine" about the very raw depictions of the dire conditions in the slums. Nor does her scathing commentary spare the societal arrogance and hypocrisy that enforces such conditions. Nambisan's writing is boldly confrontational, spelling out the degradation of poverty, joining a political discussion often dominated by men.

Yet another break is found in the diasporic literature. The first wave of diasporic Indian literature focused on issues of homesickness and nostalgia, problems with assimilation and acceptance from the host country, generational conflicts of tradition versus modernity, and the clash of Eastern and Western values and practices. Meera Syal's *The House of Hidden Mothers* moves the discussion of British Asians beyond these well-rehearsed tropes, depicting diasporic Indians who are now quite comfortable in their own skins, in their hybridity and duality of identities.[5] The interesting new focus in such literature is on the relationship between diasporic Indians and resident Indians, including the power and financial disparities that give rise to practices like British Asians utilizing India's provision of surrogate mothers, with its complicated class, power, and exploitation issues.

It can be useful to remind students that at a time when Hindutva is on the rise and hard-line Hindu values are being touted and extolled, Deshpande, Nair, Kapur, and a host of other women writers are depicting women blithely departing from tradition. Part of this is due to the rise of the New Indian Woman, who, largely emerging from the ranks of the urban middle classes, has been tracked, reflected on, and developed extensively in this body of writing (see Lau, "Literary Representations"). Newer writing is invaluable for understanding the anxious, experimental construction of fledging new roles for and definitions of Indian women. While apt to re-orientalize characters, this writing is increasingly boldly experimental and challenges stereotypes of submissive Indian womanhood.

In classroom analyses of Indian women's writing in English, it is important to debate and discuss issues pertinent to twenty-first-century Indian women, but at the same time, it is useful to have a good understanding of their provenances, not only so that old tropes need not be rehearsed unproductively in a reinvention of the wheel but, perhaps more important, to provide context, because current topical debates do not exist in cultural vacuums but extend from and build on a foundation of previous battles and struggles fought (and to some extent won). Identifying changing, subtle, and fluid gender negotiations within the framework of shifting Indian social norms can therefore be a productive way of teaching Indian women's writing in English, allowing us to displace tired tropes about Indian women in the classroom, to reconsider questions of agency and gender, and to connect literary texts to pressing social issues in India, in particular women's responses to gender inequality and the rise of new forms of nationalism and rapid changes in the economy.

Notes

1. Women writers resident in India, such as Arundhati Roy, Kavery Nambisan, Anita Nair, and Manju Kapur, are less likely to be known outside India.

2. Shashi Deshpande's *In the Country of Deceit*; Manju Kapur's *Difficult Daughters*, *A Married Woman*, *The Immigrant*, and *Custody*; and Anita Nair's *Ladies Coupé*, *Mistress*, and *Lessons in Forgetting*.

3. Maya, the protagonist, becomes a young widow when her husband dies in a climbing accident. She moves to Ranikhet, a small village in the foothills of the Himalayas, near where her husband died. Maya takes up a post as a schoolteacher, and her life soon encompasses several intriguing, eccentric individuals who become almost family to her. This story depicts Maya moving from mourning to reengaging with community and the wider world, albeit firmly on her own terms.

4. Nambisan's stories of Sitara's residents are uncompromisingly bleak for the most part. There is much violence against women, including girls sold into prostitution by their parents or sexually abused by familiar adults and even against foreign women working in Sitara. Her depiction of poverty can be contrasted with other important representations of the marginalized by canonical, politically engaged authors who do not adopt English as literary medium, in particular Mahasweta Devi, who has represented empowered, resisting female characters in her short fiction since the 1970s.

5. This novel addresses the contentious topic of commercial surrogacy in India. A British Indian woman commissions a surrogate from India to carry her fetus and unexpectedly brings the surrogate mother to Britain. Syal's narrative device enables her to draw further East-West comparisons.

Works Cited

Caplan, Patricia. *Class and Gender in India: Women and Their Organizations in a South Indian City*. Tavistock, 1985.

Chitnis, S. "Feminism: Indian Ethos and Indian Convictions." *Women in Indian Society: A Reader*, edited by Rehana Ghadially, Sage, 1988, pp. 81–95.

Chowdhury, Indira. "Mothering in the Time of Motherlessness: A Reading of Ashapurna Debi's *Pratham Pratisruti.*" *Paragraph*, vol. 21, no. 3, Nov. 1998, pp. 308–29.
Desai, Anita. "The Rooftop Dweller." *"Diamond Dust" and Other Stories*, Chatto and Windus, 2000, pp. 158–207.
Deshpande, Shashi. *In the Country of Deceit.* Penguin, 2008.
Fernandes, Leela. "Restructuring the New Middle Class in Liberalizing India." *Comparative Studies of South Asia, Africa and the Middle East*, vol. 20, nos. 1–2, 2000, pp. 88–104.
Hussain, Yasmin. *Writing Diaspora: South Asian Women, Culture and Ethnicity.* Ashgate, 2005.
Kalpana, R. J. *Feminist Issues in Indian Literature.* Prestige, 2005.
Kapur, Manju. *Custody.* Faber and Faber, 2011.
———. *Difficult Daughters.* Faber and Faber, 1998.
———. *Home.* Faber and Faber, 2006.
———. *The Immigrant.* Faber and Faber, 2009.
———. *A Married Woman.* Faber and Faber, 2003.
Lau, Lisa. "Equating Womanhood with Victimhood: The Positionality of Women Protagonists in the Contemporary Writings of South Asian Women." *Women's Studies International Forum*, vol. 26, no. 4, July–Aug. 2003, pp. 369–78.
———. "Literary Representations of the 'New Indian Woman': The Single, Working, Urban, Middle-Class Indian Woman Seeking Personal Autonomy." *Journal of South Asian Development*, vol. 5, no. 2, 2010, pp. 271–92.
———. "No Longer Good Girls: Sexual Transgressions in Indian Women's Writings." *Gender, Place and Culture*, vol. 21, no. 3, 2014, pp. 279–96.
———. "Re-Orientalism: The Perpetration and Development of Orientalism by Orientals." *Modern Asian Studies*, vol. 43, no. 2, Mar. 2009, pp. 571–90.
Mankekar, Purnima. *Screening Culture, Viewing Politics: An Ethnography of Television, Womanhood, and Nation in Postcolonial India.* Duke UP, 1999.
Nabar, Vrinda. *Caste as Woman.* Penguin, 1995.
Nair, Anita. *Ladies Coupé.* Vintage, 2003.
———. *Lessons in Forgetting.* HarperCollins, 2010.
———. *Mistress.* St. Martin's Griffin, 2006.
Nambisan, Kavery. *The Story That Must Not Be Told.* Penguin / Viking, 2010.
Puri, Jyoti. *Women, Body, Desire in Post-colonial India: Narratives of Gender and Sexuality.* Routledge, 1999.
Radhakrishnan, Smitha. "Rethinking Knowledge for Development: Transnational Knowledge Professionals and the 'New' India." *Theory and Society*, vol. 36, no. 2, Apr. 2007, pp. 141–59.
Rajan, V. G. Julie, and Atreyee Phukan, editors. *South Asia and Its Others: Reading the "Exotic."* Cambridge Scholars, 2009.
Roy, Anuradha. *The Folded Earth.* MacLehose Press, 2012.
Sarkar, Tanika. "Nationalist Iconography: Image of Women in Nineteenth-Century Bengali Literature." *Economic and Political Weekly*, vol. 22, no. 47, 21 Nov. 1987, pp. 2011–15.

Sunder Rajan, Rajeswari. "The Heroine's Progress: Feminism and the Family in the Fiction of Shashi Deshpande, Githa Hariharan and Manjula Padmanabhan." *Desert in Bloom: Contemporary Indian Women's Fiction in English*, edited by Meenakshi Bharat, Pencraft International, 2004, pp. 80–96.

Syal, Meera. *The House of Hidden Mothers.* Doubleday, 2015.

Thapan, Meenakshi. "Adolescence, Embodiment and Gender Identity in Contemporary India: Elite Women in a Changing Society." *Women's Studies International Forum*, vol. 24, nos. 3–4, May–Aug. 2001, pp. 359–71.

Usha, K. R. *The Chosen.* Penguin, 2003.

Roger McNamara

South Asian Muslim Women's Writing

I have been teaching South Asian literature for nearly fifteen years, first as a graduate student at Loyola University, Chicago, and now as an assistant professor at Texas Tech University. As a teacher, my primary objective is to introduce students to diverse literatures and cultures within South Asia and, by doing so, for them to gain insights as to how these texts and cultures differ from and are similar to their own. However, at both institutions one major obstacle to achieving this goal has been the conventional attitude of many well-meaning undergraduate students who tend to stereotype South Asian societies, especially Islamic communities, as oppressive or unchanging. It does not help that many of the authors that we read are critical of their communities and are committed to transforming them. Then there is the reverse problem: some students either exoticize or refuse to criticize practices of different cultures for fear of being politically incorrect.

So how does one overcome this conundrum over respecting different cultures while practicing critique? One method that I use to achieve this balance is to situate literature within the social, political, and economic contexts it is produced. In addition, I also examine how it reflects and responds to the debates over aesthetics in that historical moment. This methodology serves a second purpose. It also creates a vocabulary that students can deploy to engage these writers. Once they have these tools (context and vocabulary), students bring less of their cultural baggage when they engage texts and ideas that are different from their own. As a teacher, I do not want my students to simply observe and then judge a culture based on their own criteria; instead, I want them to be participants, perhaps a little late to the conversation, but nonetheless wholly committed to an intellectual discussion in that cultural context. Obviously, this is highly idealized, but I think even nudging my students in this direction produces a more enriched conversation.[1]

To further enrich this methodology, I compare how two or three authors respond to the same social, political, and economic issues. This produces multiple perspectives that complicate my students' understanding of the same social phenomena. A case in point is when I examine how two female Muslim authors, Ismat Chughtai and Attia Hosain, writing in early to mid-twentieth-century colonial North India, explore the tension between a Muslim zamindari culture (a feudal system where the landlords wield economic as well as political and social power over their tenants) and a modern education that promotes individual rights and autonomy. Chughtai's short story "Scent of the Body" focuses specifically on how men of the zamindari household, with the complicity of their wives, sexually exploit working-class women and how this culture is threatened when a modern-educated young man falls in love and marries his female servant. By contrast, Hosain's novel *Sunlight on a Broken Column* is a bildungsroman about a girl called Laila who belongs to a zamindari family. Written from Laila's perspective, the novel explores the dilemma of the modern Muslim woman who must navigate between the traditional Islamic and zamindari cultures she has grown up in and the modern education she has received that allows her to move out of the domestic sphere and participate in the public sphere as a citizen. The modern Muslim woman is inextricably linked to what Rajeswari Sunder Rajan has described as the *new woman*, who is simultaneously modern and Indian.[2] While the novel explores how Laila negotiates this tension between tradition and modernity, it also records India's transformation from a colonial state that protected elite zamindari interests into two independent nation-states (India and Pakistan) that are controlled by modern, educated, middle-class Hindus and Muslims, who, in the name of the people, consolidate their own power and wealth.

Situating South Asian Muslim Women's Writing

Though a course exclusively on South Asian writing (as opposed to a course on world or global literature) appears to sacrifice diversity as it focuses on depth instead of breadth, by narrowing my lens I am able to reveal that even within the same culture (in this case, North Indian Muslim communities), Islamic traditions and practices are not singular but diverse. I divide this course on South Asian writing into three sections. In the first section I lecture on British colonial rule, the response of the colonized (especially Hindus and Muslims), and the caste system.[3] I then explore fiction by male writers—Rabindranath Tagore's *The Home and the World* and Premchand's short stories in *Temple and the Mosque*—that engages these issues. Thus, when I begin the second section, "The Modern Muslim Woman," students already have a broad overview of the social and historical relationships in South Asia. This section begins with a similar structure. Students read extracts from a social history that examines the construction of the modern Indian woman, with an emphasis on the Muslim woman; a political history that deals with how different political groups (the Indian National Congress, the Muslim League, and the princely states) responded to the British and one another; and a literary history that focuses on the creation of the Progressive Writers Association (PWA), which propagated a new literary aesthetic and social reform. After I discuss these extracts in class, I then provide a brief overview of Chughtai and Hosain, both Muslim women writers who received a modern education, were contemporaries, and were part of the PWA. However, whereas Chughtai came from a middle-class family, Hosain belonged to the aristocratic *taluqdars* (zamindars).

To cover this background, I require students to read excerpts from Barbara D. Metcalf and Thomas R. Metcalf's *A Concise History of India*, Susie Tharu and K. Lalita's *Women Writing in India*, and Ali Husain Mir and Raza Mir's *Anthems of Resistance: A Celebration of Progressive Urdu Poetry*. The excerpts from *A Concise History of India* explore the construction of the modern woman, a subject who came into being from the tension between colonialism and emerging religious, ethnic, and caste identities and who came to embody the "essence" of the respective community (167–230). The excerpt from *Anthems of Resistance* provides an overview of the PWA and its literary influences (European writers, Premchand, and the *Angaaray* collection), cultural background, and major objectives—to use realism to criticize British colonialism and those indigenous practices that suppressed people, especially women, minorities, and untouchables (1–7). *Women Writing in India* complements the history by emphasizing how this identity of the modern woman both facilitated and restricted women's freedom. Furthermore, it contextualizes the contributions made by the PWA, Chughtai, and Hosain within the larger corpus of women's writing between 1930 and 1960 (43–116).

While students read the above selections, I also go over this information in two lectures so that they gain a clear understanding of this historical period. Furthermore, as I review this material, I am also developing the vocabulary that students can use to analyze the literary texts. This vocabulary includes sociopolitical structures and events like the zamindari system, the Indian National Congress and the Muslim League (the two major political parties during the colonial period that represented the Hindu majority and Muslim minority, respectively), and the Government of India Acts (through which Indians were given more representation within the colonial government before complete independence in 1947); certain customs like purdah (a practice in which middle- and upper-middle-class women maintained their respectability by separating themselves, whether by living in a different part of a house or wearing a veil, from men who were not part of the family), the joint family (in contrast to the modern nuclear family, the joint family was an extended household that included a patriarch and matriarch, their sons, the sons' wives, their grandchildren, their unmarried or single children, and poorer relations), and *tawaif* (courtesans); and difficult concepts like *patriarchy*, *realism*, *modern*, and *tradition*. When discussing these concepts, I ask students to write down what they think these concepts mean and then to summarize how the secondary reading defines them. The objective is to help students realize that concepts like *modern* and *progressive* are complex and fluid, having different connotations in different contexts. Creating this vocabulary and reviewing it in the classroom encourages students to move away from their early twenty-first-century American frameworks and to pay attention to how these concepts are evoked in literary texts we are reading.

After the lectures, students read Chughtai's short stories, which help them map family relationships and contextual elements that will also recur in Hosain's *Sunlight on a Broken Column*. Furthermore, the edition of Chughtai's stories that I use has a list of kinship titles and a glossary that explains the meaning of words like *mehr* (the bride price) and *nikah* (the ceremony where the marriage contract is made and the *mehr* agreed upon). I spend a week and a half teaching six or seven stories, but here I will restrict my comments to three: "The Rock," "Sacred Duty," and "Scent of the Body." After analyzing Chughtai's short stories, the class reads *Sunlight* over two and a half weeks. While the short stories examine different aspects of the domestic sphere, *Sunlight* creates a cohesive picture of Islamic culture as it explores the domestic and the public spheres. It focuses on the nation in transition from being a British colony to being divided into India and Pakistan and the tense relations between the British, the *taluqdars*, the Indian National Congress, and the Muslim League. Against this political backdrop, Hosain explores the position of the modern Muslim woman and, more broadly, the different manifestations of the modern Indian woman.

Reading Chughtai and Hosain

The remainder of this essay briefly sketches the strategies I use to help students see the nuances in the way zamindari culture and the modern Muslim woman are represented. "Scent of the Body" underscores the modernity-tradition binary as the conflict takes place between the young, educated zamindar Chhamman and other members of his traditional family, who are furious when he marries his maidservant, Haleema. In its historical context, the story is a searing indictment of zamindari traditions; yet read in contemporary America, it reinforces stereotypes that Islam is patriarchal, backward, and feudal. To challenge this binary, I invite my students to interrogate the correlation between being modern and being ethical. For instance, Chhamman's half brothers and cousins also have a modern education, but they sexually exploit their maids. The question that I pose to the class is whether Chhamman's criticism of zamindari culture stems from his modern education or from something else. There is no consensus as to the origins of his ethics, and this dialogical reading of the text poses problems about finding definitive answers about the influences upon one's conscience.

Unlike "Scent of the Body," *Sunlight* provides a broader picture of the zamindars. While the narrator-protagonist Laila mentions that one of the family friends, a ruler of a princely state, has numerous concubines (63), within her own zamindar family there is no culture of working-class women being used to fulfill the sexual needs of the men. This provides the perfect foil to "Scent of the Body," which could leave one with the impression that all zamindari cultures sexually exploit working-class women. The novel also explores the tension between the traditional and the modern.

When Laila's grandfather, a traditional patriarch, dies, his son (Laila's uncle), who is estranged from his father because of his modern lifestyle, takes control of the property. I provide students with selected passages, divide them into groups, and ask them to come up with a list of characteristics of the grandfather's traditional values and the uncle's modern ones, as well as how the narrator represents both. Students recognize that the grandfather is traditional because he speaks only Urdu, he is proud of his heritage, and the women in his household keep purdah (32–34), while the uncle is modern because he insists on speaking English, he dresses in European attire, and his wife enters the public sphere (86–87). Yet Laila dislikes her uncle and aunt, because even though they educate her, they do so because it is fashionable, not out of familial love (86). Laila also notices that while both patriarchs have friends belonging to different religious and racial backgrounds, her uncle uses his friends to promote his political ambitions, while her grandfather developed intimate friendships for their own sake (201–02). Just as I asked students to consider if Chhamman's ethical behavior in "Scent of the Body" is a result of his modern education, I ask students to debate whether the uncle's shallowness is a result of his modern lifestyle or his personal character. I ask the same question about the grandfather's character and whether tradition is responsible for his depth.

The second topic I discuss is the position of the modern woman, with a specific focus on the Muslim woman. Using Sunder Rajan's "Real and Imagined Women: Politics and/of Representation" and an excerpt from *A Concise History of India* (144–150), I explain how the modern woman came into being as a response to the pressures of colonial rule. Based on the Victorian model, she was educated, was a companion for her husband, and participated in social reform. However, this came at the cost of undermining traditional all-female spaces, for in the name of respectability, the modern woman stopped interacting with the working-class woman. More significantly, the modern woman was to safeguard the culture of her respective community and became the "[upholder] of their sacred religious traditions" (Metcalf and Metcalf 146).

Taken together, Chughtai's and Hosain's texts explore variations of the modern woman. Chughtai's stories "Sacred Duty" and "The Rock" and Hosain's protagonist Laila reveal the consequences when modern women threaten the status quo by marrying for love, instead of accepting an arranged marriage. Chughtai's stories are more radical because her female characters marry Christians and Hindus. The class compares the strategies patriarchal structures use to control these women's choices, as well as the means deployed to guarantee that younger daughters will not follow their elder sisters' "bad" examples of marrying men from other religious communities. Furthermore, I ask my students if these liberated women upend patriarchy or succumb to it. Students also compare and contrast the more typical modern women—Laila's aunt (her uncle's wife) and Laila's cousin Zahra—with a more traditional woman, Abida (Laila's aunt). Which of these two groups of women is empowered? On the one hand, Laila's aunt and Zahra accompany their husbands in the public sphere, socialize in a community of sophisticated people, and are involved in social reform (87, 140), while Abida keeps purdah and maintains a traditional lifestyle (38). On the other hand, Laila describes her aunt and cousin as appendages of their husbands (87, 147–48), but Abida momentarily wields power over the estate when the grandfather is ailing, and she is emotionally and intellectually independent of her husband (60–62, 250–52).

To complicate the status of the modern woman further, I ask the class to explore Laila's female college friends who are more concerned with politics than with romance. Whereas Laila espouses secular nationalism, her Anglo-Indian, Hindu, and Muslim friends support colonial rule, Indian (Hindu) nationalism, and Islamic nationalism, respectively (124–28). I invite students to examine whether these women are truly liberated. While they reject their gendered status as "upholders of sacred religious traditions," are they autonomous individuals if they simply identify with their community? Students explore in more detail the rhetorical strategies the girls use to endorse their positions and to describe their conflicted commitments to their communities and the rights of others, as well as their friendships despite their differences. For instance, when examining Laila's Anglo-Indian friend Joan, I ask my students to explore how she can simultaneously support colonial rule and identify with the British but refuse to be called "white" and consider India to be her home. At the same time, she is also the most "radical" or "progressive" because she plans to become a doctor and remain economically independent (126–27).

At the end of this section, students write a five- to six-page essay on how Chughtai or Hosain explore zamindari culture or the modern Muslim woman. Over these five weeks, we have examined the historical and social contexts and familiarized ourselves with a vocabulary that we have applied in discussions of the literary texts. My methodology echoes Edward Said's assertion that critique must not only be based on a close scrutiny of the context in which a text is produced but also pay close attention to the rhetoric and language (and, by implication, concepts) of that historical moment in order to elucidate "the way in which certain structures of attitude, feeling, and rhetoric get entangled with . . . some historical and some social formulations of their context" (61). Using this pedagogical framework in the classroom allows my American students to desist from holding on to their own social context to make sense of a different culture. Thus, when they analyze these literary texts, they are sensitive to cultural differences by engaging these texts on their own terms—within the political, social, and cultural debates in which they are immersed.

Notes

1. To a large extent, I am influenced by Qadri Ismail's argument that the reader cannot simply be an objective observer who passes judgment but must be a participant who has a stake in the argument. See his *Abiding by Sri Lanka*, xi–xivi.

2. Sunder Rajan explores the evolution of the new woman in South Asia and how she negotiates modernity and tradition. See also Metcalf and Metcalf 144–50.

3. For the historical background I use Metcalf and Metcalf 123–66. For an overview of caste I use Nehru 84–87, 250–57.

Works Cited

Chughtai, Ismat. *"The Quilt" and Other Stories*. Translated by Tahri Naqvi and Syeda S. Hameed, Sheep Meadow Press, 1994.

———. "The Rock." Chughtai, *Quilt*, pp. 47–57.

———. "Sacred Duty." Chughtai, *Quilt*, pp. 13–24.

———. "Scent of the Body." Chughtai, *Quilt*, pp. 127–50.

Hosain, Attia. *Sunlight on a Broken Column*. Penguin, 1992.

Ismail, Qadri. *Abiding by Sri Lanka: On Peace, Place, and Postcoloniality*. U of Minnesota P, 2005.

Metcalf, Barbara D., and Thomas R. Metcalf. *A Concise History of India*. Cambridge UP, 2006.

Mir, Ali Husain, and Raza Mir. *Anthems of Resistance: A Celebration of Progressive Urdu Poetry*. India Ink, 2006.

Nehru, Jawaharlal. *The Discovery of India*. Penguin, 2008.

Premchand. *Temple and the Mosque*. Translated by Rakshanda Jalil, HarperCollins, 2011.

Said, Edward. "The Return to Philology." *Humanism and Democratic Criticism*, Columbia UP, 2004, pp. 57–84.

Sunder Rajan, Rajeswari. "Real and Imagined Women: Politics and/of Representation." *Real and Imagined Women: Gender, Culture, and Postcolonialism*, Routledge, 1993, pp. 129–46.

Tagore, Rabindranath. *The Home and the World*. Penguin, 2005.

Tharu, Susie, and K. Lalita. "The Twentieth Century: Women Writing the Nation." *Women Writing in India: 600 B.C. to the Present*, edited by Tharu and Lalita, vol. 2, Feminist Press, 1993, pp. 43–116.

Krupa Shandilya

A Patchwork of Desire: Queering Translations of Ismat Chughtai's "The Quilt"

Ismat Chughtai (1915–91), one of the foremost Urdu writers of her generation, wrote boldly of women's lives and their problems in her fiction, essays, and letters. In the years leading up to independence from British rule, a time of great social and political upheaval in South Asia when her contemporaries were preoccupied with questions of nationalism, she unabashedly criticized the patriarchal structure of Indian society. Chughtai forged her own unique brand of feminism, and this is most clearly evident in her short story "The Quilt," which simultaneously reveals and obscures the secret life of women.

Chughtai's publication of "The Quilt" in 1942 created a furor in South Asian society because of its taboo subject: the homoerotic relationship between two women. In 1944 the enraged reading public waged a court case (*Chughtai v. the Crown*) charging Chughtai with obscenity and immorality. Chughtai won the court case because the court was unable to find words or sentences that were explicitly "indecent."[1] The story is narrated from the perspective of Begum Jaan's naive young niece who is spending time at her aunt's house while her mother is away. She tells us that on account of being neglected by her husband, Begum Jaan suffers from an unknown illness, a persistent all-body itch that the doctors have been unable to cure through the traditional course of medicines. Rabbu, a masseuse, comes to the rescue, and through her constant massaging Begum Jaan's itch is cured.

When the narrator arrives at Begum Jaan's house she witnesses her being massaged for hours at end by a tireless Rabbu and wonders at their relationship. One night the narrator hears sounds in the bedroom and thinks there is a thief in the room, but Begum Jaan reassures her that it is only Rabbu and the narrator instantly falls back asleep. The narrator thinks no more of it until she is once again awoken in the middle of the night by slurping sounds that seem to come from Begum Jaan's bed. She also sees a large elephant-like figure heaving on the bed below a blanket. The curious narrator tiptoes to the bed and lifts the blanket, and the story ends here; we do not see or know what the narrator discovers.

The story's refusal to narrate this scene of desire can be explained in part by the political context in which it was written, where lesbianism was not recognized as such.[2] How do we read the story's politics of (in)visibility in today's political context? I suggest that the story's narration of same-sex desire and its queer and feminist politics are rooted in its social and cultural milieu, but that it is difficult to parse its politics in English translation. This problem is further compounded by the narrative voice, which fluctuates almost seamlessly between the child and the adult narrator, making it difficult to distinguish between the child narrator's naïveté and the adult narrator's knowingness about female sexuality.

On Teaching and Translating "The Quilt"

When teaching this story in English translation in the American classroom, one confronts a host of problems. First, the story's inconclusive ending confuses students. They are told that "The Quilt" is a queer, feminist story and are expecting to see explicit evidence of this in it. Second, Chughtai's exploration of homoeroticism does not conform to students' imagination of Third World women's sexuality, as they are prone to see Third World women as objects of violence rather than subjects of pleasure.[3] Further, students often read translations without a critical understanding of the text in its context, because they often assume that Third World literatures are "waiting to be recovered, interpreted, and curricularized in English/French/German/Dutch translation; delivering the emergence of a 'South' that provides proof of transnational cultural exchange" (Spivak 114). Gayatri Spivak suggests that translations often obscure the otherness of

Third World literatures, flattening differences embedded in language and idiolect.

How then do we teach Chughtai's story in the American classroom, where we battle the problem of translating the Urdu world, the particularities of idiom, the nuances of language, and the entirely different worldview, while also challenge the assumptions that American students bring to the reading of a Third World text? In this essay, I articulate a postcolonial, queer pedagogical practice of close reading that focuses on queering the act of translation. I suggest that through the act of close reading we learn to recognize the otherness of translation; that is, we learn to see the untranslatability of the textures of the original language by thinking through the nuances of multiple translations of the host language. In my pedagogy, I focus on differences in language and nuance between translations and also emphasize a close study of idiolect and metaphor as a means of breathing under the skin of the translation, as it were. This pedagogical practice enables what Spivak terms a "worlding" of the Third World text, foregrounding a deep knowledge of the literariness of the short story as essential to understanding its meaning (114).

This pedagogy also reveals the ways in which desire is structured through implication in the short story and, in doing so, challenges the assumptions of a First World feminist practice while making explicit the sexual politics of a Third World queer and feminist practice that is premised on (in)visibility. As I argue elsewhere, this scopic politics of (in)visibility challenges the "state's visibility politics, its insistence that the rights of minority subjects be made contingent on their visible abjectness, and illuminates new visual, semantic and political possibilities for thinking queerness in the postcolonial state" (Shandilya 5).

Thus, pedagogically, the short story serves as an opportunity to teach students about the complex intersectionality of Muslim, queer female sexual desire and also introduces them to a postcolonial feminist politics of reading desire through difference. The title of this essay, "A Patchwork of Desire," is a metaphor for the pedagogical practice of close reading by piecing together translations of the text with critical theory to create an understanding of Third World queer desire; it is also an acknowledgment of the "Quilt" in Chughtai's title as both a metaphor and a structuring trope for reading the politics of queer desire.

To begin, I ask students to study the two most widely used English translations of Chughtai's short story, namely the translation by M. Asaduddin and another more feminist translation by Tahira Naqvi. I ask students to do a close reading of both translations, underlining passages where they find the starkest differences in the use of language and metaphor. I ask them to focus specifically on the short story's narration of the homoerotic relationship because it is here that the translations most struggle with rendering the Urdu text's complexities.

The first aspect of the short story that I ask students to focus on is the child narrator's relationship to Begum Jaan, because the homoerotic desires of the adult women are filtered through this perspective. Conversely, the sensuality of the adult relationship also mediates the child's relationship to Begum Jaan. Our first clue to this is the child narrator's fascination with the massaging process: "Those puffy hands were as quick as lightning, now at her waist, now her lips, now kneading her thighs and dashing towards her ankles. Whenever I sat down with Begum Jaan, my eyes were riveted to those roving hands" (Chughtai "Quilt" 8). On the brink of puberty herself, the child narrator is fascinated by the eroticism of this massage. The text leaves ambiguous whether the child narrator's desire for proximity to Begum Jaan (her initial desire to massage her) stems from a newly ripening sexual consciousness or a more childlike desire for proximity to a beloved adult, and the text suggests that it is both.

Allowing for this ambiguity and uncertainty is crucial to understanding the narrator's rendering of the Begum Jaan–Rabbu relationship. Since students are usually unfamiliar with the social and cultural milieu of the short story, they often mistake this narrative anxiety as the text's latent homophobia. I approach this problem by leading the close reading of these passages with a series of questions: Does the child narrator fully understand what is happening around her? What instances in the text suggest that she is confused? What differences do we note between the two translations in the ways in which they render the child's reactions to what is happening around her? I then point the students to a particular instance in the text to illustrate the translations' anxieties:

> Aur meri khaak samajh main na aaya ke faisla kya hua. Rabbu hichkichiya lekar royi, phir billi ki tarah sapad-sapad rakabi chatney jaisi awaaz aaney lagi, uh! Main tou ghabrakar so gayi. (Chughtai, "Lihaaf" 86)
>
> And I understood nothing of what decision had been made. Rabbu began to whimper, then there was a sound like a cat licking a plate, oh! I became afraid and went to sleep. (my trans.)
>
> I could not hear what they were saying and what was the upshot of the tiff but I heard Rabbu crying. Then came the slurping sound of a cat

> licking a plate . . . I was scared and got back to sleep. (Chughtai, "Short Story" 38)
>
> I could not make out what conclusion was reached, but I heard Rabbo [sic] sobbing. Then there were sounds of a cat slobbering in the saucer. To hell with it, I thought and went off to sleep! (Chughtai, "Quilt" 9)

The child narrator is witness to a scene of desire that she scarcely understands. In Asaduddin's translation, her confusion is rendered as fear, because Asaduddin translates the child's lack of understanding into a literal failure to hear—"I could not hear what they were saying"—when the more accurate translation rendered by Naqvi is "I could not make out what conclusion was reached." Further, the child narrator's frustration with her inability to comprehend what is going on around her is rendered by an exclamation, "unh!" which Asaduddin ignores entirely in his translation and instead marks by ellipsis. This ellipsis suggests that the child understands but is unable to speak of what she understands because it either disgusts her or makes her fearful. Naqvi's translation marks the child narrator's frustration with the phrase "To hell with it!" which more accurately depicts the narrator's feelings but misses the fear that accompanies this frustration by omitting translation of the word *ghabrakar*, or "afraid," that follows the frustration.

In teaching this text, I make clear that the child's inability to understand what is going on both frustrates her and makes her afraid, but this is not a fear of sexual desire but rather a fear of the unknown. To foreground this point I gesture to an earlier moment in the text when the child narrator hears shuffling sounds and whispering and is afraid because she believes that a thief has stolen into the room. Once she is reassured by Begum Jaan and Rabbu that there is no thief she falls asleep, not in the least perturbed by Rabbu's presence in the room. I also refer to the child narrator's earlier fascination with the massage, which suggests her ease with sensuality.

Drawing attention to these details enables students to see that the scene of desire is marked by its rendering. And thus, although they are unable to access the Urdu text, this method of double close reading of its translations enables them to understand that the text's idiolects and its particularities cannot be easily collapsed into English. The translation only partially captures the complexities of the original. In addition, the focus on the multiplicity of translations enables students to appreciate the story's literary registers and to understand that these multiplicities are a means to understanding the very particular cultural and social context of the story—what Spivak calls its "worlding." They are thus able to appreciate the story's otherness without collapsing it into preexisting frameworks for reading Third World texts.

Queering Context

In addition to translating idiom and language in the American classroom, we need to also translate the context of the short story—that is, the Indo-Muslim worldview that permeates the text. This is an essential component of the "worlding" of the text within the "axioms of imperialism" that continue to structure readings of Third World texts (Spivak 114). In the context of "The Quilt" the abrupt conclusion that falls short of revealing cunnilingus and testifying to the sexual relationship between Begum Jaan and Rabbu becomes prey to the "axioms of imperialism" as it is often read as a failure to name lesbian desire and thus the failure to articulate a suitably feminist and queer consciousness. Such a reading is premised on a First World feminist practice that locates sexual agency only when it is marked by visibility. In order to deconstruct this perspective, I assign two essays that argue that First World feminist understandings of agency are premised on liberal ideas of visibility and voice. These essays are Mahua Sarkar's "Looking for Feminism" and Gayatri Gopinath's "Local Sites / Global Contexts: The Transnational Trajectories of *Fire* and 'The Quilt,'" from her book *Impossible Desires* (123–52).

Sarkar's essay argues that although the veil and the *zenana* (women's quarters) have had shifting significations in the history of Indo-Muslim society, they "are recuperated (or made visible) within the enlightened folds of feminist accounts only as exceptions—as instances of feminist consciousness out of time/place" (327). I ask students to consider Sarkar's statement in the context of the short story and pose the following leading questions: What are the many ways in which the short story narrates the space of the *zenana*? How might we read these as sites of feminist agency? I follow this with a brief discussion of Gopinath's argument that in order to read queer desire in "The Quilt" we need to deconstruct First World feminist epistemologies that conceive of agency largely through a scopic politics of visibility and use alternative strategies to counter "modern epistemologies of visibility, revelation, and sexual subjectivity" (12).

In the short story, the politics of (in)visibility are best exemplified through the veil and the quilt, which serve both a literal and a metaphorical function in obscuring our view of queer sexual desire. To illustrate this idea, I point to the opening sentence of the story, which defies our seeking gaze:

> Jab main jadho main lihaaf udhti hoon tou paas ke devaar par uski parchayi haathi ki tarah jhoomti hui maloom hoti hai. Aur ekdum se mera dimagh beeti hui duniya ke pardon main daudhne bhagne lagta hai. (Chughtai, "Lihaaf" 81)

> In winter when I pull the blanket over me, its shadow on the wall seems to sway like an elephant. And then all of a sudden my mind races to lift the curtain of the past. (my trans.)

The word *purdah* (curtain or veil) is obscured in both Naqvi's and Asaduddin's translations. In their work it is translated as "dark crevasses" (Chughtai, "Quilt" 5) and "labyrinths" (Chughtai, "Short Story" 36), which suggest that the narrator is uncovering memories buried in the "dark crevasses" of her subconscious. My translation foregrounds the centrality of the veil to understanding the particular scopic politics of the short story, for the metaphor of the veil offers the reader a "moment of bafflement that discloses not only limits but also possibilities to a new politics of reading" (Spivak 98). I read the memories as enclosed behind the curtain or veil of the women's quarters, a female space that exists both spatially and temporally in the narrator's past. The story that follows is an attempt to narrativize this space, but as the conclusion suggests, the narrator cannot and will not make this space visible.[4]

I suggest that the short story's inconclusive ending can be read as privileging the discourse of (in)visibility. Just as the quilt obscures the sexual acts between the women, so too does the veil or curtain that separates the women's quarters obscure our vision of what happens within. In making invisible women's desires, I suggest that the story reconfigures the space of the *zenana* as a site of agency by refusing to make knowable that which is unknowable. In other words, the veil and the quilt refuse to be co-opted by the male, heterosexual gaze with its desire to uncover and "know" queer female sexuality. The title of the short story can thus be read as a metonym for the story's queer and feminist politics of desire as remaining under cover.

The postcolonial feminist pedagogy of queering translation outlined in this essay honors the complexity of the Third World text for the reader and student unfamiliar with its context. *Queering translation* implies the refusal to make transparent the otherness of the text in favor of multiple close readings to emphasize its difference. This strategy enables us to understand the literariness of the text and foregrounds the ideological and political differences embedded in these specific literary registers. In addition, by situating the short story in the context of postcolonial critiques of feminist theory, we are able to arrive at a postcolonial, queer, feminist theory of sexual agency that arises from within the text—that is, the short story itself becomes the site for an alternative theorization of sexual desire. This essay advocates a postcolonial queer and feminist pedagogy that insists on using multiple translations of a text to foreground its radical difference—both literary and political—to enable an understanding of Third World women's sexuality and agency.

Notes

1. As Chughtai mischievously narrates in her autobiography *Kaghazi hai Pairahan* (*Clothes of Paper*), "No word capable of inviting condemnation could be found. After a great deal of searching a gentleman said, 'The sentence "she was collecting *ashiqs*" (lovers) is obscene'" ("Excerpt" 441).

2. Chughtai declared in an interview with a literary magazine, "You know, when I first wrote *Lahaf* [sic] this thing [lesbianism] was not discussed openly. We girls used to talk about it and we knew there was something like it, but we didn't know the whole truth" ("*Mahfil*" 2).

3. As Kapur argues, the Third World subject is "constructed almost exclusively through the lens of violence, victimization, impoverishment and cultural barbarism" (382).

4. The feminist critic Geeta Patel suggests, "*Parda* (veil, curtain), and LiHaaf, the two covers that open the sentence, can be read in different directions. . . . *Parda* is also the word for curtain, which is drawn aside to reveal the theatre of the zenana and its activities, its sexuality" (180).

Works Cited

Chughtai, Ismat. "An Excerpt from *Kaghazi Hai Pairahan* (The 'Lihaf' Trial)." Translated by Tahira Naqvi and Muhammad Umar Memon. *The Annual of Urdu Studies*, vol. 15, 2000, pp. 429–43.

———. "Lihaaf." *Ismat Chughtai: Pratnidhi Kahaniyan*. Rajkamal Prakashan, 1988, pp. 81–91.

———. "*Mahfil* Interviews Ismat Chughtai." *Mahfil*, vol. 8, no. 2/3, Summer–Fall 1972, pp. 169–88.

———. "The Quilt." Translated by Tahira Naqvi. *"The Quilt" and Other Stories*. Translated by Naqvi and Syeda S. Hameed, Sheep Meadow Press, 1994, pp. 7–19.

———. "Short Story: Lihaaf [The Quilt]." Translated by M. Asaduddin. *Manushi*, vol. 110, Jan.–Feb. 1999, pp. 36–41.

Gopinath, Gayatri. *Impossible Desires: Queer Diasporas and South Asian Public Cultures*, Duke UP, 2005.
Kapur, Ratna. "Out of the Colonial Closet, but Still Thinking 'Inside the Box': Regulating 'Perversion' and the Role of Tolerance in De-Radicalising the Rights Claims of Sexual Subalterns." *NUJS Law Review*, vol. 2, no. 3, 2009, pp. 381–96.
Patel, Geeta. "Marking the Quilt: Veil, Harem/Home, and the Subversion of Colonial Civility." *Colby Quarterly*, vol. 37, no. 2, June 2001, pp. 174–88.
Sarkar, Mahua. "Looking for Feminism." *Gender and History*, vol. 16, no. 2, Aug. 2004, pp. 318–33.
Shandilya, Krupa. "(In)visibilities: Homosexuality and Muslim Identity in India after Section 377." *Signs: Journal of Women in Culture and Society*, vol. 42, no. 2, Winter 2017, pp. 459–84.
Spivak, Gayatri Chakravorty. *A Critique of Postcolonial Reason: Toward a History of the Vanishing Present*. Harvard UP, 1999.

Ruth Vanita

Teaching Suniti Namjoshi in Montana

The contemporary Indian writer Suniti Namjoshi is a pioneer who has as good a claim as Salman Rushdie does to having reinvented magical realism, but she receives much less critical attention than he does and even less attention than her female contemporaries, such as Bharati Mukherjee. Namjoshi's books are hard to find in the United States, although they have come back into print in India, where she has a substantial following.

This relative neglect of Namjoshi is largely because she wrote as a lesbian and on lesbian themes from the 1980s onward, at a time when such openness was a career killer. In 1985 she published *The Conversations of Cow*, a playful portrait of the artist as a young Indian lesbian, and in 1989, *The Mothers of Maya Diip*, a dystopian novel on lesbian feminist separatism set in India. At that time, Namjoshi was practically the only Indian writer openly writing about gay and lesbian lives in English.

This was before the Indian women's movement had come to terms with same-sex sexuality and at a time when it was generally assumed in the West as well as in India that homosexuality had always been represented much more in Western than in Indian literatures and cultures. I teach *The Conversations of Cow* (henceforth *Conversations*), which I consider a tour de force, in several classes at the University of Montana. I first wrote about this text in my book *Gandhi's Tiger and Sita's Smile* (Vanita, "'I'm an Excellent Animal'"), but this is my first set of reflections on the experience of teaching it.

Conversations is hard to categorize. Is it a 112-page novelette, an extended fable, a philosophical dialogue, or a magical realist memoir? Its malleability allows it to fit into different courses in different ways. I have taught parts or the whole of it in lower-division courses like Introduction to India and Introduction to Women's Studies, and I also regularly teach it in upper-division courses such as Gender and Sexuality in Twentieth-Century English Fiction and Same-Sex Unions: International Histories and Debates.

Conversations opens up the field of English-language writing into the global in an unpretentious yet self-reflexive way, drawing as it does on European, British, and Indian literary traditions. It shatters stereotypes about India and Indian women even while it reinvigorates some old associations, such as that of India with cows. Because of the way it explores ideas of love and of the divine, drawing on both Hinduism and Christianity, I find it a good preparation for students who wish to take other courses of mine, such as Talking to God: The Bhagavad-Gita or Love in Bombay Cinema.

What Is *Conversations of Cow* About?

When students first encounter *Conversations*, it puzzles them. This is partly because they are expecting it to tell a story about an Indian woman struggling against sexist and racist oppression and it does not quite do this. Its narrator, Suniti, does struggle but in surprising and amusing ways, and not with parents, a husband, or in-laws. Likewise, in terms of form, it does not fit any of the categories they recognize. It draws on the Aesopian fable, the *künstlerroman*, the bildungsroman, the Indian animal narrative (such as the *Panchatantra* and the *Hitopadesa*), Upanishadic and Platonic dialogues, Ovid's *Metamorphoses*, the quest narrative, and satirical or allegorical fantasies of the *Gulliver's Travels* or *Alice's Adventures in Wonderland* type. The book also presents traits of autobiographical writing and of magical realism, preventing any stable classification in terms of genre.

The book is built around a series of encounters between Suniti, a young Indian lesbian living in Canada, and other characters, primarily a being variously known as Bhadravati, B, Baddy, Bad, and Bud, who changes her form without notice, manifesting usually as a Brahmini cow but also as an Indian lesbian, as two different white men, and as a Goddess. Suniti is unnerved to find that she herself changes into or emerges as a heterosexual woman, a lover, an incurable romantic, a person with a split identity, a poodle, and a Goddess.

I have not had any Indian-origin students in the classes that have read this book. Most of my students are from Montana and neighboring states; several are Native American or of mixed heritage. Many are first-generation college-goers, and almost all work their way through college. In contrast to students I taught at Delhi University, a significant minority of Montana students are married, some have children, and several are out as LGBT. They know little about India and even less about Hinduism. Students in Montana tend to be confused by the book's deceptive simplicity, lack of a linear plot, rapid narrative switchbacks, and character transformations reminiscent of Virginia Woolf's *Orlando*, but above all, by the dizzying way the book draws on multiple literary traditions from ancient Greek and Indian philosophy to folk stories and science fiction. However, the book's playful style allows students to engage with the text and to find analogues in their own experiences to Suniti's questions about the nature of the self and the world.

Why Cow?

I ask students to think about the title and how its meaning might change if it were slightly tweaked to read, say, "Conversations with a Cow" and also to think about the choice of Cow as the central figure instead of, say, Dog or Elephant. The cow is perfectly suited to get to the heart of cultural differences between India and North America.

When asked to think of English-language idioms that relate to cows, students notice how contemptuous almost all of these are in their assumption that cows are unintelligent and exist to be eaten and that, consequently, any other view of them is itself unintelligent; examples include "holy cow," "sacred cow," "stupid cow," and "she's a cow" and book titles like *Sacred Cows Make the Best Burgers.* All of this contrasts with the cult of dogs, since numerous popular books in America explore a person's relationship with a particular dog or with dogs in general. I point out how Bhadravati's feisty personality undermines these negative Western views but also conventional Indian views of a cowlike woman (*gau jaisi aurat*) as praiseworthy for being meek and domesticated.

We discuss what attitudes to femaleness and to animals are overtly present in such usages and what attitudes to Hinduism lie hidden in them. At talks I have given in the United States on cows in Indian literature, students from farming backgrounds have pointed out that cows are intelligent, recognize one another and the humans they know, respond to their names, and also engage in affectionate same-sex behaviors.

Cows are among the very few species for which the word for the female designates the species, instead of the female being a diminutive of the male (as in *lioness*) or the species term being assumed to be male (as in *mankind* or *monkey*). The cow is thus suited to bring femaleness to the center of discourse. Not attaching an article to the noun *Cow* in the title makes us confront speciesism, the arbitrary prejudice in favor of our own species, which allows us to torture and destroy members of other species and also allows us to use *Man* ("Of Man's first disobedience") or *Human* (*Of Human Bondage*) without an article while not referring in this way to any other species. Likewise, sexism, the arbitrary prejudice in favor of men, has historically prevented us from using *Woman* to encompass the species in the way *Man* has been used.

I then inform students of some Hindu literary images of and philosophical ideas about cows. In the Rig Veda, rivers and Goddesses repeatedly appear as agile cows of various colors. Many later texts, such as the epic Mahabharata, narrate stories about a wish-fulfilling cow (*kamadhenu*) who represents the Goddess earth, named Prithvi or Surbhi, the source of all wealth. From these texts develops the idea of the cow as mother, since one drinks her milk, and as Goddess, since Goddesses are mothers and mothers, Goddesses. I show visuals, including miniature paintings and folk art, of the cow and calf, a symbol found in sculpture from the first millennium CE and still often painted on Indian trucks and other vehicles. I tell them about Mohandas K. Gandhi's interpretation of the cow as a "poem of pity," a symbol of all animals and of nature, and his view of cow protection as a reminder to treat nonhuman beings with respect and gratitude.

Since *Conversations* plays with names, I also tell my students how virtually every Hindu name is one of the thousands of names of different Gods or Goddesses or an attribute of a God or Goddess, and how surnames were rarely used in Indian or in European literature before the nineteenth century. Namjoshi's use of just one name for each character, such as Suniti and Bhadravati, echoes such names as Sita, Mary, and Penelope in canonical texts and also reflects current usage among many rural and lower-income people in India.

We then discuss ideas of Goddesses in relation to ideas of nonhuman animals. I ask the students to think of texts in which Goddesses and animals appear as characters. They find that both are present in English poetry but largely absent from English prose fiction. English texts that feature animals as speaking characters tend to be classified as children's literature, but this is not the case with premodern Indian literature.

I ask them to think about whether it matters that God is generally referred to with male pronouns in English, even though theologically most religions would agree that God is genderless. We also talk about the bias implicit in capitalizing the God of Judeo-Christian tradition but not the Gods and Goddesses worshipped by millions of Hindus. We read aloud some Goddess hymns from the Rig Veda. We talk about the presence of Goddesses and Goddess-like figures in modern Western culture (from Mary and the female saints to figures like Justice in American courtrooms and Goddesses of varied provenance in the landscape of Washington, DC, as well as the Statue of Liberty).

When I teach *Conversations* in my course on same-sex love in literature, we talk in more detail about animals in the writings of lesbian and gay authors, such as J. R. Ackerley's *My Dog Tulip*, Woolf's *Flush*, and Gertrude Stein's "As a Wife Has a Cow: A Love Story," which playfully reverses the meaning of the idiom "having a cow" so that the cow comes to stand for female orgasm. We discuss how an interspecies relationship can function as a trope for a same-sex relationship, both having been considered "impossible," abnormal, unnatural, and unspeakable. We talk about Goddesses in the writings of lesbian and bisexual poets such as Hilda Doolittle (H.D.) and Elsa Gidlow ("For the Goddess Too Well-Known"). Through these discussions, the idea of the cow as Goddess, which would earlier have seemed to them impossibly alien if not repugnant, starts to become comprehensible, even familiar.

A Is Also B

Conversations breaks down simple oppositions and demonstrates likeness among apparently unlike or even opposed things and categories, using strategies both similar to and different from those of Hindu, Buddhist, and Jain logicians. Thus, the simple assumption of cows' femaleness is complicated early in the text by the Canadian cow Cowslip's discussion of gender and of passing:

> The world, as you know, is neatly divided into Class A humans and Class B humans. The rest don't count. . . . Class A people don't wear lipstick, Class B people do. Class A people spread themselves out. Class B people apologize for so much as occupying space. Class A people stand like blocks. Class B people look unbalanced. Class A people never smile. Class B people smile placatingly twice in a minute and seldom require any provocation. Now, it's quite obvious that cows have all the characteristics of Class A people. Our very size and shape take care of that. Your best bet is to let them assume you are one. (24)

I show students *YouTube* videos of cows standing or sitting implacably on busy urban streets in India, to suggest one context from which Namjoshi may have derived this idea that is both amusing and serious.

From the book's dismantling of gender, race, and nationality categories, we proceed to the much less considered question of the construction of species categories. This leads into discussion of ideas of transformation, including the idea of transmigration. I give them an extract from Ovid's *Metamorphoses* that sums up the theories of Pythagoras with regard to transmigration and vegetarianism, both issues raised in *Conversations*. Before the Enlightenment, animals appeared in European literature as capable of thought and emotion (Patroclus's horses and Odysseus's dog come to mind). This allows the students to posit different historical and civilizational worldviews against one another and to consider how a text reads differently when readings are based on different assumptions or worldviews.

Confronted with the humanness of Cow, Suniti is impelled to reconsider not only who Cow is but also who she herself is and what she wants. Like protagonists of many anglophone Indian novels over the last few decades, Suniti is a migrant to the West and struggles with issues of identity as a woman, a lesbian, and an Indian immigrant. What distinguishes this struggle, though, is the humor with which it is represented, a humor directed as much at the self as at the world. While Suniti takes herself very seriously, Bhadravati and her cow friends gently poke fun at her, and the narrative moves from amusing everyday annoyances to manic upheavals. For example, letting an Indian name be modified into an American-sounding one might seem like a capitulation to American prejudices, but it turns out to be somewhat more complicated. Bhadravati allows her friends to call her Baddy, saying, "[Y]ou have to adjust" (18), but when her Canadian cow friends cannot pronounce Suniti's name and say they will call her "Sue for short" (18), she forbids them to do so. They then try to say her name but end up saying "Snooty," and it also turns out that one of them, Sybilla, is called Sybbie for short.

Later, Suniti's anxieties are calmed by a dream in which Bhadravati is an Indian woman and Suniti is a happy poodle who feels "very clean and alive and healthy" (47). The next day, it turns out that Bhadravati has actually turned into a woman and has had the same dream. Suniti asks her what the poodle's name was, and she replies, "Let me think now. Su—, Suzanne! That's right. Her name was Suzy. She was so loving, so intelligent" (52). Offended, Suniti thinks, "My mind is made up. Whatever I become, I'm not going to be a poodle. If necessary, I shall be churlish" (52). The play here on being or existing as a particular type of creature (a poodle, a woman, an Indian) and being or behaving in a certain way (snooty, churlish, cheerful) is one that recurs throughout the book. The humor in this particular episode arises both from variations on Suniti's name that link it to plant and animal worlds (*Suzanne* derives from the Hebrew for "lily," of which *Sue*, which she had rejected earlier, is a diminutive) and from Suniti's preference for being a churlish human rather than a loving, intelligent, and happy poodle merely because she arbitrarily associates inferiority with dogs. All of this facilitates discussion among students about identity categories and their limitations, especially those categories that we take most for granted, such as species.

The Fragmented Self

Conversations is written in deceptively simple, idiomatic English. There are almost no Indian-language words, no references to Indian objects or practices that might require italicization or explanation, and no Indian-English usages. Early on, the protagonist reveals that she is "from India" (14), but nothing in the language or events reveals that the author is of Indian origin.

Indianness in the text inheres in certain narrative devices and also in the philosophy that gradually emerges. The text is anchored by a series of pronouncements simultaneously simple and profound, which function like mantras for everyday living; for example, reflections on the question of being and becoming: "since one must be something, one might as well be cheerful" (60), "All I ever wanted . . . was to be an ordinary animal" (32), and "I am an excellent animal" (47).

The book allows me to introduce students to some Indian philosophical debates around epistemology, metaphysics, and ethics; for instance, how are all things and beings connected? Are they real manifestations of one unified reality, or are they merely somewhat unreal reflections of that reality, or is each individual thing an isolated existent made up of similar components, or is there indeed no ultimate reality, only perceived illusion? Halfway through the book, Bhadravati recounts the fable of Spindleshanks, a cow who suffered from "an incessant craving" (80) and tried to assuage it by devouring everything. Having consumed the world, she found herself alone with Nothing and was terrified, so she proceeded to scream until she burst and the world spilled out, permeated by Spindleshanks. This cautionary fable is realized later when Suniti, frustrated by B's ever-changing forms and especially by her male incarnations, says she wants to be by herself.

The limitations of the postmodern notion of embracing the fragmented self then emerge as Suniti wakes up the next day to find that she is with a clone of herself called S2. The self-absorbed ego's loneliness and terror surface in a nightmare: "Bit by bit the world is stripped away, the blue carpet, the walls. It peels off like so much paint. At last there is nothing left, except a small and transparent something. It is shapeless and composed of terror. It cannot penetrate the blackness around it. It cannot make any sound. But it's shrieking with the intensity of its own terror" (120).

The last section of the book, entitled "Conjuring Cow," circles back to the start. The book begins with Suniti waiting for the Goddess to manifest herself, which she does in the form of the Cow of a Thousand Wishes. It concludes with Suniti and S2 calling upon Cow to return and invoking her (as in numerous Hindu texts that invoke a God or Goddess with 1,008 names) by a thousand names, including the names of almost all the characters that appear in the book, including minor ones, thus calling her, for instance, Surabhi and Sybilla and also Peter and S2.

Suniti calls Cow a Goddess, and Cow, amused, replies, "So are you, Suniti" (124), an exchange reminiscent of William Blake's response to the question "Do you believe that Jesus is the son of God?": "Yes, and so am I, and so are you." Antinomian and mystical strands in other religions correspond to the dominant tendency of Hindu thought, wherein self-realization consists of recognizing, embracing, and making real the divinity of all things including the self. Suniti, feeling "so very, so extraordinarily happy" (124), tells Cow that she finds her "wholly engaging" (125) in all her manifestations, even as B or Baddy or Bud all were (the last two were white males whom Suniti resented when they first appeared).

Woolf concludes *A Room of One's Own* with the reflection that the woman writer of the future will address the fact that "our relation is to the world of reality and not only to the world of men and women" (108). Women writers' gaze has too often been focused on the sphere of interpersonal relationships that has been considered women's sphere. Namjoshi's Cow, like the cow with which E. M. Forster opens *The Longest Journey*, stands for existence that persists as an idea as well as a reality: "The cow is there. . . . She is there, the cow. There, now" (7).

Conversations opens up ways for students to consider how ideas circulate between cultures and how different cultures have approached the same questions about the nature of existence, perception, communication, and consciousness. It also allows teachers to address a variety of contemporary debates, including those around gender- and sexuality-based identity categories, the necessity and limitations of identity, nationality, and animal studies.

Works Cited

Forster, E. M. *The Longest Journey*. 1907. Penguin, 1960.

Namjoshi, Suniti. *The Conversations of Cow*. Women's Press, 1985.

Vanita, Ruth. "'I'm an Excellent Animal': Cows at Play in the Writings of Bahinabai, Rukun Advani, Suniti Namjoshi and Others." *Gandhi's Tiger and Sita's Smile: Essays on Gender, Sexuality, and Culture*, Yoda Press, 2005, pp. 290–310.

Woolf, Virginia. *A Room of One's Own*. 1929. Grafton Books, 1977.

Part IV

Situated Pedagogy: The Text and the World

Reshmi Hebbar

Bharati Mukherjee's *Jasmine*: Unsettling Nation and Narration

This essay engages with the challenge of teaching Bharati Mukherjee's 1989 novel *Jasmine*, a novel revolving around the vicissitudes of a South Asian woman who migrates to America. It argues that the novel should be read as a literary representation of social tensions and antagonisms that, at the same time, unsettle the closure of narrative form and of national identity. To explore this argument, I propose a multidimensional teaching and reading practice able to connect the transnational experience of migration at the heart of the novel to pressing domestic issues in twenty-first-century America. In particular, the essay considers how Mukherjee's rewriting of the bildungsroman genre can stimulate classroom debates over domestic labor, illegal migration, and national ideology. Teaching these themes in the novel can show the continuing relevance of *Jasmine* as a rich and suggestive literary text, speaking to contemporary realities marked by the rise of the so-called alt-right (a white nationalist, populist movement) as well as chauvinistic myths about American identity. The novel's complexities and contradictions as an unsettled and unsettling literary piece mirror unresolved political tensions linking the late 1980s to the early twenty-first century. The essay is organized in two parts: while the first section focuses on some key themes and passages stressing how the novel disrupts the closure of nation and narration, the second section offers some reflections on the pedagogical challenges of teaching *Jasmine*, a novel from the 1980s, in the twenty-first century.

Jasmine as Bildungsroman: Unsettling Nation and Narration

Students in my undergraduate course "The Master's House": Postcolonialism and Writing Back read *Jasmine* after covering Charlotte Brontë's *Jane Eyre* and other similar pairings, including Charles Dickens's *David Copperfield* with Salman Rushdie's *Midnight's Children*. Such combinations aim to locate Mukherjee's novel within a broader tradition of novelistic writing, especially the tradition of the novel of formation, or bildungsroman. Indeed, *Jasmine* reimagines the marginalized British heroine of nineteenth-century literature as a transnational laborer and migrant in America. Like Brontë's famous heroine, Jasmine begins her story as "Jyoti," a young girl in Punjab with no prospects. Mukherjee refashions the trope of the orphan heroine's restless search for belonging into Jasmine's narrative of continuous migration for survival. Jyoti marries Prakash, an educated would-be American immigrant who renames Jyoti as "Jasmine," but she becomes a young widow after Prakash is killed in an act of terrorism committed by Sikh separatists. Seeing no future in India, Jasmine immigrates illegally to the United States via a smuggler (Half-Face) who rapes her upon her arrival in America. She murders Half-Face in self-defense and travels up the East Coast, eventually becoming an au pair for a wealthy New York couple. After falling in love with her male employer (Taylor), she suddenly leaves this family and heads to the Midwest upon learning that the Sikh terrorist Sukhwinder, who killed her husband, is now in New York. Jasmine reflects on these past events, told in flashbacks, while deciding whether she will stay with her current lover (Bud Ripplemeyer), an older man whose baby she is carrying and with whom she has adopted a Vietnamese-refugee son (Du Thien). The novel ends as Taylor arrives with his daughter to take Jasmine away from stagnation and presumably toward greater fulfillment and a new life in California.

Including *Jasmine* in my university course allows students to address some broad social questions represented in the text, highlighting the intersections between transnational and domestic political issues in America: the dependency upon domestic labor performed by, as Barbara Ehrenreich and Anne Russell Hochschild discuss in their 2003 *Global*

Woman, "the striving woman from a crumbling Third World . . . economy" (11); increasingly acrimonious domestic debates about undocumented immigrants; and the link between feelings of white male disenfranchisement and extremist (and violent) alt-right nationalist ideology. The presence of these themes in the novel should, in the era of Donald Trump's presidency and its aftermath, provide justification for focusing less on the ramifications of Jasmine's seemingly successful assimilation into American culture and more on what students might learn from the novel's remake of the bildungsroman as a tale of economic exploitation, social antagonism, and geographical displacement. Indeed, *Jasmine* complicates the bildungsroman story line by interspersing the conclusion of Jasmine's journey with impressionistic allusions to "the smell of singed flesh," stowaways, "immigration cops," and untilled "dead corn stalks" (237–40). These fragmentary references to the grittier realities of twentieth-century America, and the complications of Jasmine's conclusive romance with Taylor, underpin Mukherjee's attempts to stifle the conventions of the bildungsroman by unsettling the happy ending and romance. Noting that by the novel's end Jasmine is not a legal American citizen, Deepika Bahri maintains that Jasmine's continual maneuverings underscore the ways in which America itself "is presented as a geographic and temporal state/space that is always in the process of becoming a new nation" (143). Such a reading invites us to take note of the problematic and dynamic notions of America that Jasmine evokes—ones that trouble the myth of American exceptionalism and foresee America's increasingly unsettled role as a global superpower. *Jasmine* often deemphasizes the mythical image of America and its promises by connecting, for example, the economic volatility of poverty and underemployment in rural India (62–64) to similar hardships in the rural American Midwest (190–93), as Mukherjee uncovers links between feelings of disenfranchisement and political volatility on both continents. Taylor's joke that Jasmine is in a "free country" and can therefore do whatever she wants is undercut by Jasmine's mourning over "all the lives" and "dead" she must carry with her (239–40), while "never wholly [being able to] deny, forget, or escape the previous ones" (Hoppe 138). Among these lives is the specter of her trafficker and rapist, Half-Face, a Vietnam War veteran and self-professed "Bubba" involved in the "nigger-shipping bizness" (Mukherjee 111). These disparate characterizations inscribe multiple Americas: the refugee's versus the privileged professor's, the bankers' versus the farmers', and so forth, introducing cultural divides that are still evident when teaching the novel in the early twenty-first century.

Jasmine's American lover, Bud, is shot by "a disturbed and violent farmer who saw himself betrayed by his bank" (191–92), and Darrel, her poor farmer neighbor, considers leaving his farm and blames the "Eastern bankers" for his struggles (217). When Darrel later embraces the propaganda of the Aryan Nation Brotherhood, an extremist group that anticipates the alt-right movement of twenty-first-century America, Jasmine conceals her "terror" and leaves her neighbor's home, "worried that the frontier of madness is closer" (218). Darrel's struggles as a midwestern farmer who, despite his best efforts, cannot keep pace with his debts predispose him to a fundamentalist political ideology; this characterization thus offers insights into the historical development of the notion of white men as being left behind, which is today an increasing force of political discourse and mobilization in the era of Trumpism. Mukherjee's reappropriation of the word *frontier*, a typically American idea that she rearticulates with the politically charged term *terror*, might suggest that Darrel's delirium is meant to be analogous to Sukhwinder's, whose terrorist acts in India Mukherjee parallels here. In this narrative vision, the closure of the American context is blasted open by representing a national space traversed by antagonism, violence, and extremist ideologies that embed American domestic issues within global political dynamics. Jasmine illuminates the ways in which America is also a site of chaos and violence, where refugees and native-born alike undertake journeys within "the global condition of culture, economics, and politics as a site of 'migrancy' and 'travel,'" which "seriously problematises the subject position of the 'native'" (Brah 181).

Jasmine's fictionalized scenarios uncannily foresee Trump-era sociopolitical debates, perhaps most obviously in Jasmine's decision to flee to California with a member of the supposed cultural elite and leave behind "the anguished face of a man who is losing his world" in a conservative American Midwest that, during the Reagan-era 1980s, contrary to more nostalgic recollections, is already in conspicuous decline (239). Half-Face's resentment of any implication that people in Asia are technologically advanced ("I been to Asia and it's the armpit of the universe" [112]) is similar to Darrel's; these characters anticipate the fear and insecurity of white American males who feel historically displaced in advanced-stage capitalism. There is something "deplorable," to use a word from the 2016 presidential campaign, about Half-Face's sociopolitical speechifying and then rape of Jasmine on the night of her arrival in America; that his murder is not seen as a loss by the reader may take on new weight given the understanding of a post-2016 United States as at an increasingly violent crossroads, both physically (a surge in the numbers of hate crimes, an anti-alt-right protester's murder in the fall of 2017 in Charlottesville, Virginia) and psychically (the American media's continual references to the cultural resentment "on both sides"). The trafficked and raped Jasmine perhaps now more than ever clearly symbolizes the exploitive conditions upon which the American dream thrives, and her experiences more forcefully expose the darker side of the American promise. Of course, acknowledging Jasmine's status as an undocumented migrant also elicits questions about security and membership within the America her story is said to so unequivocally champion. We might ask students where she would be in the hands of today's Immigration and Customs Enforcement. Mukherjee's characterization of the immigrant advocate Lillian Gordon's arrest for "harboring undocumenteds" and the vague promise of a new life in California (a state that was embroiled in legal battles about its status as a "sanctuary state" during the Trump administration) throw into relief ongoing debates about the ethics of mainstream acceptance of dividing "illegal" from "legal" labor, the realities of racialized low-wage labor, as well as the idea of America as a refuge (136).

Teaching *Jasmine* in the Twenty-First Century

Jasmine's efforts at tackling mythological constructs of America in 1989 matter even more today given the rise of populist sentiments to "make America great again." Mukherjee's stated beliefs in American cultural opportunity have often provided support for the charge that *Jasmine*'s narrative is assimilationist or antithetical to the critical project of postcolonial literature. But students should note the efforts of an immigrant writer who has also admitted to wanting to counter "how unconsciously racist or ethnicist [she] may have been in relation to marginalized persons in earlier periods of [her] life" and who strives to highlight how "there is no one unified story about the immigrant experience or the immigrant passage" (Mukherjee, "Remembering"). Students may be more inclined to believe, for example, that rather than immigration to America, a village girl today might instead find greater fulfillment by migrating to one of India's urban centers. Such an observation might, in turn, promote a more complex reading of *Jasmine* in relation to the key question of national identity and assimilationist ideology. For example, though Mukherjee arguably plots Jasmine's Indian husband Prakash's death so that she might be brought to America in a more sympathetic position to twentieth-century American readers, her decision to set Jasmine's childhood in rural Punjab (and not the author's native urban Bengal) elicits comparisons of impoverishment in agrarian contexts in both India and the American Midwest. Though Jasmine appears to be able to settle comfortably within America by the end of the novel, she does so while at the same time unsettling American readers' notions of the opportunity and security their country purportedly offers. The increasing mainstream advocacy for refugees, victims of human trafficking, and persons of color within the United States should inspire more attention now to the realities of the other marginalized laborers to whom Mukherjee attempts to give voice (the Kanjobal women working under the radar in Florida, the resettled Vietnamese refugees starting over on the West Coast), whose stories problematize the notion of belonging within such contexts.

Teaching *Jasmine* should do justice to the representational complexities of this novel: both Mukherjee's polyphonic combination of the voice of Jasmine with the discrepant experiences of characters representing multiple ways of being American, and the narrative's seemingly simplified representation of American identity in passages such as Jasmine's claim that "We're puritans, that's why" (237). Because of the force of Jasmine's propulsive narrative voice, "arising from nowhere and disappearing into a cloud" (241), which stakes a claim on the sundry lives of both "the dispossessed as well as the dispossessor" (Mukherjee, "Immigrant Writing"), the meaning of this phrase is not easy to interpret. Is the "we" of Jasmine's statement indicative of Bud's forefathers or all the Ripplemeyers together, including Jasmine? Can one be a "puritan," in this context a stand-in for American, and a refugee simultaneously? Should this potential merging of the puritan and refugee perspective—the novel's need to bridge the gap between America's privileged forefathers and America's newer migrant subjects—provoke readers to see *Jasmine* as an oversimplified promotion of American opportunities, or might readers instead note the value of Mukherjee not being able to resolve the narrative problem she creates for herself? Engaging with the novel means being able to explore, while not necessarily to settle or exhaust, the unresolved tensions, contradictions, and antagonistic political forces that this text reveals and symptomatically expresses.

Jasmine, I want my students to note, is not only a reconsideration of American national identity and the realities of social injustice, violence, and exploitation underlying the global flow of labor, but it is also an attempt to revise the conventions of the prototypical novel of development so that the heroine does not end up as a fixed, settled, and fully formed character but, rather, remains forever caught in contradictions mirroring antagonistic forces in societies, not being finally herself but rather "always becoming" (Bahri 154). Thus, for students exploring formal innovations within anglophone fiction, or for students studying immigration narratives, *Jasmine*'s conflicting projects—that of seeking to access the promise of America while also disrupting the myth of American security and opportunity—might more productively be read as a rich embodiment of and engagement with the contradictions of the myths that have been told about the promise of a better life on distant shores, as well as the narrative promise of a happy ending.

Works Cited

Bahri, Deepika. "Always Becoming: Narratives of Nation and Self in Bharati Mukherjee's *Jasmine*." *Women, America, and Movement: Narratives of Relocation*, edited by Susan L. Roberson, U of Missouri P, 1998, pp. 137–57.

Brah, Avtar. *Cartographies of Diaspora: Contesting Identities*. Routledge, 1996.

Ehrenreich, Barbara, and Arlie Russell Hochschild. Introduction. *Global Woman: Nannies, Maids, and Sex Workers in the New Economy*, edited by Barbara Ehrenreich and Arlie Russell Hochschild, Metropolitan Books, 2003, pp. 1–15.

Hoppe, John K. "The Technological Hybrid as Post-American: Cross-Cultural Genetics in *Jasmine*." *MELUS*, vol. 24, no. 4, Winter 1999, pp. 137–56.

Mukherjee, Bharati. "Immigrant Writing: Give Us Your Maximalists!" *The New York Times Book Review*, 28 Aug. 1988, www.nytimes.com/1988/08/28/books/immigrant-writing-give-us-your-maximalists.html.

———. *Jasmine*. Grove Press, 1989.

———. "Remembering Bharati Mukherjee, an Indian-Born American Writer." *Fresh Air*, 6 Feb. 2017, www.npr.org/2017/02/06/513711541/.remembering-bharati-mukherjee-an-indian-born-american-writer. Accessed 7 July 2018.

Pranav Jani

Anglophone South Asian Women's Fiction: A Marxist, Intersectional Approach

With the right pedagogical tools, anglophone South Asian women's fiction has the power to explode mythologies about gender, sexuality, race, class, nationality, and empire that dominate classrooms in the United States. These mythologies range from stereotypes about passive brown women in need of white saviors to narratives of Westernization and capitalist development as inevitable paths to progress. But South Asian women's fiction pushes readers beyond the critique of orientalism and racism, because it does not absolve South Asian patriarchies and nationalisms. The political and cultural legacies of the colonial conquest of South Asia and the problems of racism, poverty, and alienation for immigrant communities are combined with sharp critiques of women's oppression within South Asian families and traditions. Situated at the crossroads of gender, sexuality, race, class, and nationality, anglophone South Asian women's fiction forces students and readers to think about culture, society, imperialism, and the movement of peoples in global and holistic ways. In my experience, a Marxist and intersectional pedagogy helps to draw out these manifold aspects of South Asian women's fiction because it is attentive to the simultaneous interactions of socioeconomic, political, ideological, and cultural forces.

The critical power of anglophone South Asian women's fiction develops from its inherent drive toward *intersectionality*—a term originally coined by the black feminist scholar Kimberlé Crenshaw in the late 1980s to describe interlocking and mutually constitutive systems of oppression and exploitation. Two challenges confront us, however, when focusing this intersectional lens. The first is at the narrative level: the explosive, critical possibilities of the genre are not necessarily explicit, and the texts often might seem apolitical in cursory readings. The intersectional analysis produced within the genre, then, is revealed through our critical engagement with it. The second challenge is that today, the term *intersectionality* covers a confusingly wide range of meanings. Sometimes it is applied very narrowly as a way to center particular identities over others ("identity politics on steroids," as Crenshaw noted in a recent interview); sometimes it is so broad that it means everything to everyone. Questions abound. In what ways do various systems intersect? Or are they complex parts of the same overarching system? Have these intersecting categories changed over time? How do they look in different places with different histories?

Marxism's linking of women's oppression, the family, and capitalist society, on the one hand, and of imperialism, immigration, and nationalism, on the other, offers a more precise interpretive framework for analyzing the intersectional concerns of anglophone South Asian women's fiction. In each section below, I pair a core concept from classical and contemporary Marxism (class analysis, ideology, nationalism, social reproduction) with a passage from one of three works of fiction by South Asian women in the diaspora: Jhumpa Lahiri's short story collection *Interpreter of Maladies*, Monica Ali's *Brick Lane*, and Kiran Desai's *The Inheritance of Loss*. I argue that Marxism is relevant to anglophone South Asian women's fiction—but only when we understand it as a living tradition that develops and grows with the times. Indeed, debates among Marxists about these terms are ongoing and productive. While I'm persuaded by those who regard social reproduction theory, intersectionality, and Marxism as compatible (see Bohrer; Smith; Taylor), others have criticized intersectionality in their explanations of social reproduction theory (see Bhattacharya; McNally and Ferguson).

Class Analysis

Many have argued that anglophone South Asian women's fiction, especially Indian writing from the United States, is mainly interested in the lives of middle-class women and assimilation into mainstream white society. To the extent that this is true, the genre reflects the class and caste background of many Indian immigrants to the United States after the passage of the Immigration and Nationality Act of 1965, writers' acceptance of the model-minority myth, and the demands of a neoliberal marketplace that values stories of women in whom the so-called exotic, backward East clashes with the liberated, modern West. But there are important exceptions to this middle-class focus. The three texts selected here offer complex portrayals of poor and working-class South Asians, female and male, whose gender and sexual identities are integral to their experience of class. Ali's protagonist, Nazneen, lives in public housing in London and her sister in Dhaka moves from sweatshop work to sex work. Desai's *The Inheritance of Loss*, taking a transnational approach, centers the experiences of Gyan, a poor Gurkha student in India, and Biju, an undocumented restaurant worker in the United States. Figures like Bibi Haldar, Mr. Kapasi, and Boori Ma, moreover, disrupt the story-worlds of the graduate students, businessmen, and suburbanites who populate Lahiri's *The Interpreter of Maladies*.

Furthermore, class analysis can address topics like the alienation of middle-class women and men, the nostalgia of relatively well-settled immigrants, and the hybrid lives of cultural and financial elites—not just the struggles of workers. At its best, Marxism takes a holistic approach to the world, asking how the material conditions of life in a given place are related to every aspect of its culture, society, identities, and ideas. As I have argued in "A Home of One's Own," Marxist analysis of fiction by and about South Asian American women needs to understand struggles to define home—even within middle-class domestic spaces—as responses to anti-immigrant racism, neoliberalism, and imperialism.

Lahiri's "The Third and Final Continent" (*Interpreter* 173–98) might be read as the perfect example of a liberal, assimilationist politics—but it also contains a rich critique of cultural alienation, the by-product of securing the American dream. The middle-class, middle-aged narrator, looking back at his journey across continents, exudes a world-weariness that has not been satiated by his list of accomplishments: getting a job, owning a home, sending a kid to Harvard. The matter-of-fact narrative voice pushes against the rags-to-riches framework that the narrator puts forward and to which the implied and real author may also subscribe:

> Though we visit Calcutta every few years, and bring back more drawstring pajamas and Darjeeling tea, we have decided to grow old

> here. . . . We have a son who attends Harvard University. Mala no longer drapes the end of her sari over her head, or weeps at night for her parents, but occasionally she weeps for her son. So we drive to Cambridge to visit him, or bring him home for a weekend, so that he can eat rice with his hands, and speak in Bengali, things we sometimes worry he will no longer do after we die. (197)

This passage evokes a vision of intergenerational devastation, in which "home" is an empty, failed signifier. For the narrator and his wife, Calcutta is reduced to commodities—pajamas and tea—that will not fill the ontological void. The implied author is clearly aware of what the narrator only feels: that the parents' attempts to bring their son home from Cambridge in order to maintain food and language habits will be just as empty as their own trips to India. The narrator's bitter observation that his son will soon graduate and be "alone and unprotected" while carrying "the same ambition that hurled [him] across the world" (197) is hardly assuaged by the empty assertion that "there is no obstacle he cannot conquer" (198). The middle-class migrant meets all the criteria for success in the United States, but at the cost of everything that once composed his cultural identity. Class analysis is crucial in teaching South Asian fiction from the United States, in particular, because it allows students to question the model-minority stereotype that defines South Asian Americans and to recognize that for a racial minority, success in education may not translate into freedom from oppression and marginalization.

Ideology

South Asian women's fiction is not always explicitly feminist, but its focus on female protagonists, its goal of exposing women's constraints within the family, and its desire to create spaces for women's empowerment bend the genre in a feminist direction. Circulating in an anglophone marketplace that paradoxically values diverse voices while exoticizing South Asia, this fiction takes the opportunity to educate readers who may be uninformed about the lives of women from postcolonial and immigrant communities. Indeed, rather than preaching to an implicit white reader, this fiction often achieves its pedagogical tasks by having its protagonists reflect critically on their own ideas about gender and society over the course of the text. As I will explain, the classical Marxist understanding of ideology and consciousness speaks directly to what is implied in the genre—that despite the prevalence of oppressive ideologies in society, individuals are capable of change.

The following passage from Desai's *The Inheritance of Loss* offers an excellent portrayal of how ideologies of gender, class, ethnicity, and nation work. The sixteen-year-old Sai, granddaughter of a retired, anglicized Indian judge in the Himalayan town of Kalimpong, has discovered with a shock that Gyan, her seventeen-year-old math tutor and first romantic love, is from the Nepali-speaking Gurkha community—and very poor. After protests for Gurkha rights begin and Gyan stops coming to see her, Sai's developing feminism combined with her class arrogance lead her to defy curfew and cross into Gyan's neighborhood. But Sai then sees his house, "a small, slime-slicked cube. . . . Crows' nests of electrical wiring hung from the corners of the structure . . . an open drain that told immediately of a sluggish plumbing system" (279). Sai feels betrayed and shamed:

> The house didn't match Gyan's talk, his English, his looks, his clothes, or his schooling. . . . Every single thing his family had was going into him and it took them to live like this to produce a boy, combed, educated, their best bet in a big world. . . . And she felt distaste, then, for herself. How could she have been linked to this enterprise, without her knowledge or consent? (280)

Gyan, entering into the scene, catches "her expression of distaste before she had a chance to disguise it" (281) and responds with masculinist rage. The breakup that follows is class warfare on a micro level, in nasty, gendered language.

Flitting inside and outside Sai's consciousness, the novel expertly reveals Sai's ignorance while teaching readers about class realities. As readers experience the scene through Sai's perceptions (sight, smell) and eventual shame, they are also offered a commentary on poverty that necessarily comes from beyond Sai's cloistered world. Gyan's family, we learn, is one of those that "had struggled to the far edge of the middle class—just to the edge, only just, holding on desperately—but were at every moment being undone" (280). Desai's ability to allow the reader to view and understand this struggle from a distance even while entering into the consciousness of the flawed characters—displayed also in her treatment of the undocumented worker Biju—offers a complex portrayal of the unevenness of social consciousness.

In *The German Ideology*, Karl Marx offers an explanation of ideology that allows us to appreciate the novel's representation of Sai's experience.

On the one hand, Marx argues, "The ideas of the ruling class are in every epoch the ruling ideas, i.e. the class which is the ruling material force of society, is at the same time its ruling intellectual force" (1: part I, sec. B). Marx confirms the crucial role that the ruling classes of society have in shaping consciousness through their control of institutions that produce, standardize, and commodify knowledge, like schools and various media outlets. On the other hand, for Marx, the ruling ideas are not the only ideas, and oppositional, revolutionary consciousness can also develop. Sai's and Gyan's material circumstances push them toward mainstream ideas about class, gender, and ethnicity, and they fall back on these ideas when they are challenged (Sai's elitism, Gyan's shame and sexism). But the narrator, allowing us to stand above the scene and to register Sai's growing self-criticism, also offers a map for how consciousness might shift. South Asian women's fiction, at its most compelling, is compatible with such a dynamic theory of ideology because it seeks to shift consciousness and challenge systems of power, not only to describe them as they are.

Nationalism

Anglophone South Asian women's fiction in the diaspora represents a variety of positions on nationalism, ranging from a desire to identify with the new nation to a conviction that only the South Asian country of origin can truly count as home. These debates about national identity and belonging are sometimes explicitly political, but they are often proxies for concerns about cultural identity—less about histories and passports than about language, dress, food, sexuality, and gender. In fiction by women, the struggle against gender norms in the family immediately raises conflicts about both nation and culture. South Asian women's fiction thus offers a range of views, from a deep skepticism toward nationalism as the marker of patriarchal tradition to an acceptance of national culture as a defense against racism and alienation.

Unlike academic theories that reject all nationalism as reactionary, Marxist theories of nationalism distinguish between the nationalism of dominant and oppressor nations and the nationalisms of colonized and minority groups. This approach developed especially before and after World War I, when Vladimir Lenin and the Bolsheviks took a firm position against imperialism and, along with anticolonial and antiracist revolutionaries from around the world, discussed the emergence of radical, oppositional nationalisms. Such flexible and contextualized treatments of nationalism are much more attuned to the diverse forms of nationalism expressed in South Asian women's fiction and related genres. Consider, for instance, the following passage from "When Mr. Pirzada Came to Dine," in Lahiri's *The Interpreter of Maladies.* Mr. Pirzada is a Muslim from Dhaka and a visiting scholar at a northeastern American university at the time of the 1971 Bangladesh liberation movement. He frequently visits the home of the narrator, a ten-year-old girl at the time, whose parents—Indians and Bengali Hindus—are affiliated with the university. Mr. Pirzada soon becomes a fixture in the home, and the child narrator adds a plate for his dinner each night. But at one point the young narrator, who has a poor knowledge of India, gets a lesson in national identity. When she says she is getting "water for the Indian man," her father checks her and says that he is "no longer considered Indian" (25).

Why does the father say Mr. Pirzada is not Indian? The question consumes the Indian American narrator—and, as I have found, the mainstream American student. I then explore the possibilities with my class. Is the father merely asking his daughter to be precise about Mr. Pirzada's nationality, given the dominance of "Indian" as a label for South Asians? Is he educating his daughter on the history of partition in 1947 that made Dhaka a city in East Pakistan, not in India? Or on the 1971 war that would make him a Bangladeshi? Or is the father being parochial, harboring a sense of national and cultural difference despite his friendliness with Mr. Pirzada? The girl is confused: since her parents and Mr. Pirzada "spoke the same language, laughed at the same jokes, more or less looked the same," and followed the same eating habits, like eating "pickled mangoes with their meals . . . rice every night for their supper," they must all be Indian (25). The child, learning to be Indian herself, as it were, now questions her father's refusal to include Mr. Pirzada in this national and cultural category.

An internationalist approach shows us that the father is not being parochial but respecting Mr. Pirzada's nationality and educating his daughter to do the same. While the father's politics are not explicitly stated, his actions show the importance of defending a marginalized national identity from erasure. As an Indian defending Bangladeshi identity and the demand for national independence, the father poses a challenge to the assertion of Indianness or Hinduness as the de facto identity for South Asians. Indeed, a flexible perspective on nationalism is key to understanding texts from across the colonized and postcolonial world, in which varieties of national thinking jostle together. For example, such an understanding helps illuminate the character of Karim in *Brick Lane*, a young man who articulates a militant Muslim identity that is both antiracist and antifundamentalist. An internationalist lens allows a more open approach to South Asian women's writing that can allow students to distinguish between a narrow national chauvinism and rebellious assertions of national and cultural self-determination.

Social Reproduction

At the center of much anglophone South Asian women's fiction is the immigrant family, where the pressures of racism, cultural alienation, and job scarcity in the outside world intersect with prevailing gender and sexual norms in the home. Marxist-feminist work on social reproduction lays out a framework for linking capitalist exploitation with gender and social oppression that is very useful for interpreting feminist fiction by women of color. In brief, social reproduction is the idea that while surplus value is generated by capital's exploitation of workers' labor power in the workplace, that labor power itself is sustained and reproduced in various sites outside of the workplace, including the privatized space of the family. In addition to being the vehicle for passing down property, the family unit is essential to capitalism as a center for the reproduction and care of new generations of workers (childbirth and childcare), for the daily replenishment of labor power (when workers are at home), and for sustaining the disabled and the retired. Differences between families in terms of genders norms, class, race, sexuality, and nation, of course, change the role they play in social reproduction.

Brick Lane centers on the developing political consciousness of Nazneen, a working-class Bangladeshi Muslim woman who arrives in East London after a "proper" arranged marriage to Chanu. Though ensconced in the home and forbidden to work, Nazneen is hungry for new ideas; her consciousness shifts throughout the novel on questions of religious, gender, sexual, and national identity. Combining our discussions of class, ideology, and national identity with social reproduction, we can draw out the critical power of this novel, which always contextualizes Nazneen's actions and thoughts against the landscape of post-9/11 Islamophobia and the crisis of neoliberalism. Indeed, Nazneen's experience of oppression in the family is represented as a problem of the West itself: its poor and working-class ghettos are the product of structural racism, pushing Muslims and immigrants of varying ideological bents into the same box and exacerbating the pressures on the family. In *Brick Lane*, we are inside a house that is forever failing to be middle class, experiencing from within the slippery modernity that Sai of *The Inheritance of Loss* could only witness from without.

Ali's insistence on linking gender oppression to class and racial oppression creates a fissure in the story. On the one hand, readers cheer Nazneen's rebellion against her husband Chanu's authority. Secretly earning money through her sewing and sleeping with the young activist Karim—two rebellions that are linked together in the plot—Nazneen comes to recognize the overlapping nature of her financial and sexual dependence on Chanu. On the other hand, *Brick Lane* shows us that Chanu too is oppressed by the same factors that impact Nazneen's life; we are repeatedly made to feel sorry for him and come to realize that Chanu will never have the privilege of achieving the middle-class, middle-age angst of the narrator of "The Third and Final Continent." Even as we hate his treatment of Nazneen, we are made to see Chanu also as oppressed and exploited.

Ali's resolution of this tension is incredibly powerful, allowing empathy for both Nazneen and Chanu while emphasizing that Nazneen's freedom requires the end of that patriarchal household. Nazneen refuses to go along with Chanu's plan to move the family back to Bangladesh in order to escape poverty and racism in the United Kingdom—and the two realize that her path to freedom ("I can't go with you") is diametrically opposed to his ("I can't stay"). And yet this moment of parting is also a common recognition of the overwhelming pressure of migration and working-class life that impacts them in opposite ways: "they clung to each other inside a sadness that went beyond words and tears, beyond that place" (Ali 358). These homeless subjects have to keep moving to find peace—"hurled . . . across the world" as the narrator of Lahiri's "The Third and Final Continent" puts it (197)—and Nazneen and Chanu part with an understanding of their joint sadness, their intersecting oppressions. But this awareness can happen only when the patriarchal family is broken and Nazneen and Chanu can be, for the first time, something like equals.

Anglophone South Asian women's fiction and Marxist methodology might not seem very compatible, especially given the ideas prevalent in both activist and academic circles of Marxism as white, masculinist, Eurocentric, class reductionist, teleological, and uncritical of Enlightenment reason. I have attempted to show, rather, that Marxism's dynamic and dialectical understanding of class, ideology, nationalism, and society provides frameworks that can be useful in teaching about the intersectional life-worlds projected by South Asian women's writing in the diaspora. Capitalism—a multifaceted system of production relying on the factory as well as the family, exploitation as well as oppression, coercion as well as ideology, domestic hierarchy as well as imperialist conquest and immigrant labor—is a system that extends far beyond the economic. Resistance and rebellion, then, at every intersection of oppression and exploitation, are not only valid but also essential, and the prime condition of this is the conviction that people are capable of thinking new thoughts and challenging dominant ideologies. Anglophone South Asian women's fiction, implicitly and explicitly, challenges readers to think in such dynamic and intersectional ways, with the aid of Marxist concepts.

Works Cited

Ali, Monica. *Brick Lane.* Scribner, 2003.

Bhattacharya, Tithi, editor. *Social Reproduction Theory: Remapping Class, Recentring Oppression.* Pluto Press, 2017.

Bohrer, Ashley S. "Intersectionality and Marxism: A Critical Historiography." *Identity Politics*, special issue of *Historical Materialism*, vol. 26, no. 2, 2018, www.historicalmaterialism.org/articles/intersectionality-and-marxism. Accessed 24 Apr. 2019.

Crenshaw, Kimberlé. "No Single-Issues Politics, Only Intersectionality: An Interview with Kimberlé Crenshaw." Conducted by Laura Flanders. *Truthout*, 8 May 2017, www.truth-out.org/opinion/item/40498-no-single-issue-politics-only-intersectionality-an-interview-with-kimberle-crenshaw. Accessed 24 Sept. 2017.

Desai, Kiran. *The Inheritance of Loss.* Grove Press, 2006.

Jani, Pranav. "A Home of One's Own: Gender, Family, and Nation in Indian-American Literature and Film." *Tracing the New Indian Diaspora*, edited by Om Prakash Dwivedi, Rodopi, 2014, pp. 271–97.

Lahiri, Jhumpa. *Interpreter of Maladies.* Houghton Mifflin, 1999.

Marx, Karl. *The German Ideology.* 1845–46. *Marxists Internet Archive*, www.marxists.org/archive/marx/works/1845/german-ideology/. Accessed 25 Aug. 2017.

McNally, David, and Sue Ferguson. "Social Reproduction Beyond Intersectionality: An Interview." *Viewpoint Magazine*, 31 Oct. 2015, www.viewpointmag.com/2015/10/31/social-reproduction-beyond-intersectionality-an-interview-with-sue-ferguson-and-david-mcnally/. Accessed 26 Sept. 2017.

Smith, Sharon. *Women and Socialism: Class, Race, and Capital.* Revised ed., Haymarket Books, 2015.

Taylor, Keeanga-Yamahtta, editor. *How We Get Free: Black Feminism and the Combahee River Collective.* Haymarket Books, 2017.

Joel Kuortti

Teaching South Asian Women's Writing in Finland

My pedagogical aim as a teacher of English-language literatures in Finnish universities has been to enrich the syllabi by introducing texts by Indian women writers. This has been challenging, as the number of literature courses in the English curriculum today where this is possible remains regrettably limited. However, in a postcolonial, transcultural world, it is important to facilitate students' exposure to literary representations outside the mainstream in order to gain a better understanding of changing cultural landscapes. Furthermore, the persistent gender imbalance in syllabi prompted me to select women's writing to challenge the conventional curriculum. I see this move as a response to the prevailing cultural politics in the English-speaking context. Although not self-evident, Indian women's writing is a valuable resource that enables students to encounter issues such as feminism, migration, multiculturalism, transculturation, hybridity, and other sociopolitically relevant issues. The experiences transmitted through an engagement with literary material open up avenues for thinking critically about the world at large. Furthermore, the right-wing populist protests in Finland against immigration have made it even more important to enable students to develop their critical judgment through literature and other cultural products. The results of this can be seen in the choice of topics of students' papers and theses: there is notable interest in questions of gender, environment, social justice, and other ethically motivated issues. Contemporary literature and cinema from the Finnish context—such as Emmi Itäranta's novel *Memory of Water*, Hassan Blasim's short stories in *The Madman of Freedom Square*, and Aki Kaurismäki's films *Le Havre* and *The Other Side of Hope*—provide further material for comparative approaches, even though it is not common practice in the English departments in Finland to approach literature from a comparative perspective.

Literature Courses in English Studies in Finland

Traditionally, English departments in anglophone countries are essentially departments of English-language literature. Outside the English-speaking context, however, language skills, linguistics, translation studies, and sociocultural components dominate the curriculum at the expense of literature. Moreover, in the last decade or so, the pressure to create more working-life-oriented syllabi and general education courses makes it even more difficult to expand students' exposure to literature. This leaves less room for credits in the degree for courses vital to the development of an English major's expertise, such as literature in general and South Asian women's writing in particular.

Furthermore, in a country where English is not a native language, English-language literatures are not necessarily familiar even to students of English when they enter the university. Teachers of English literature in Finland find that there is no shared experience of the English literary canon among the students. Some may not have heard of *Winnie-the-Pooh*, while others are well versed in detective fiction or fantasy literature; some cannot recognize biblical references and allusions. Shakespeare is known by name, or perhaps through film adaptations, but the poems of Romanticism may not ring a bell. Therefore, there is pressure to focus on traditional mainstream literary history so that students can develop a basic knowledge of literatures is English.

With emphasis on British and American English, Indian English has not been considered as important in the English departments in Finland. Rather than prescriptivism, this choice reflects the vocational direction of English studies in order to enhance students' employment prospects as future secondary school English teachers with curricular requirements of a standard form of English—often British or American. However, with the expansion of global Englishes (see Ashcroft et al. 8), the situation is changing. Although the statistical figures are not certain, India is currently (still) the place where more people than anywhere else outside the United Kingdom and the United States use English.[1] In 2006 David Graddol estimated the number of English users in India to be five percent (*English Next* 94). Four years later Graddol provided new numbers: "No one really knows how many Indians speak English today—estimates vary between 55 million and 350 million—between 1% of the population and a third" (*English Next India* 68). All in all, Indian English keeps growing. English continues to be important in the context of India and Indian literature.[2] Teaching this literature gives us opportunities to examine the linguistic features of different Englishes, creoles, code-switching, multilingualism, and other phenomena. Finnish students of English have found Indian writing inspiring, and if they manage to hold on to their interest, often despite the lack of material in libraries, they make perceptive observations in their analyses, which is very rewarding for the teacher.

Since 1999 Finnish universities, following the overall restructuring of university teaching within the Bologna process to ensure compatibility with higher education in Europe, have attempted a standardization of the structures of BA and MA studies, with variable success. Standardization may have prevented literature (or any other specialty for that matter) from having a focal presence on the basic or intermediate level. This has meant that there are typically one to two courses of compulsory English literature studies in basic studies. In intermediate studies, students have more options as they begin to specialize. Here, literature may have a stronger presence or, in the case of some departments, be omitted completely. Because of the range of possible choices, in advanced studies it can be exceptional to include compulsory literature elements. In departments where literature is one of the foci, however, there are a good number of students who do pursue literary studies, which enables the development of literary studies and research within language departments. Against such a background, it is no wonder that introducing South Asian women's writing or other nonmainstream writing is challenging, to say the least. In the following, I discuss the hows and whys of my attempts at this arduous but rewarding task.

The Relevance of South Asian Women's Writing

My interest in Indian writing in English began with my research on Salman Rushdie. Since then, I have wanted to incorporate in the syllabus works and themes that are particularly pertinent in postcolonial and diasporic literatures. Alongside obligatory courses on other topics, I have been able to modify or create some courses to include such content. Sometimes this has meant simply one or two Indian or other short stories or poems were brought in alongside more mainstream texts. At times it has been possible to build whole courses on postcolonial topics. Regarding my specialization, there have obviously been courses on Rushdie but also on postcolonial women's writing, where it has been possible to introduce resident and diasporic Indian women writers such as Saumya Balsari, Rukmini Bhaya Nair, Anita Desai, Githa Hariharan, Jhumpa Lahiri, Bharati Mukherjee, Arundhati Roy, and Bulbul Sharma. However, the diversification of syllabus needs to be done carefully in order to avoid the tokenism embedded in the selection process and to avoid overt essentializations, misrepresentations, or exclusions. Furthermore, teaching particular writers such as these has required some foregrounding, as knowledge of Indian culture is still limited.

Just like with other postcolonial and non-European literatures, only a handful of South Asian—and exclusively Indian—women writers' works from the 1950s to 1980s were translated into Finnish: three of Kamala Markandaya's novels, Santha Rama Rau's travel book, and one of Ruth Prawer Jhabvala's novels.[3] The situation was almost the same with male writers: only some works of Rabindranath Tagore, Jim Corbett, Khushwant Singh, R. K. Narayan, Salman Rushdie, T. N. Murari, Amitav Ghosh, and Premchand had been translated by 1990, and of these Tagore and Rushdie are the only authors who have had more than one or two books translated into Finnish. In a non-English-speaking country where there is a large reading public for literature, translations are vital for cultural transfer, and thus the lack of translations is a sign of lack of interest.

With such dearth of materials and prior knowledge of South Asia, teaching texts from India and the diaspora can be complicated. Literature can function as an introduction to the contextual reality, but it cannot be read as a straightforward image of that reality. How then to convey the literary merit of a book that comes from a very different cultural background? This has meant introducing Indian culture, literary history, diasporic movements, and other elements relevant for understanding the texts under discussion (cf. Aerila and Kokkola 41, 48). In this way, students learn to construct a context for the material they are reading; the context is produced in actual interaction with the text and the reader.

While teaching Arundhati Roy's debut novel, *The God of Small Things*, for example, I find myself explicating social issues such as the status of

Dalits, communist politics in Kerala, and the position of the English language in India as not an official language but as a language used especially in higher education and business. I also try to connect this novel to local interests and issues. For Finns, Kerala has become a favorite tourist destination, and thus *The God of Small Things* provides material beyond that found in guidebooks. In Finland, the communist aspect is likewise of interest because of, among other things, the Finnish civil war (1918), the wars with the Soviet Union (1939–40, 1941–44), as well as the geographical proximity of Russia, which shares an 833-mile (1,340-kilometer) external border with the European Union. From the contemporary postcolonial perspective, the status of Dalits, central to the novel, resonates with the status of the Sámi, an indigenous minority community in Finland. Roy's more recent novel, *The Ministry of Utmost Happiness*, along with her critical essays, offers material for further consideration and could also be taught.

Literature and Literary Theory: The Poetry of Rukmini Bhaya Nair

The strong emphasis on political readings of literature, which has been a defining element of postcolonial studies, makes Indian literature relevant for Finnish students of English. Beyond its aesthetic function, writers often tackle transculturation, migration, multiculturalism, and other issues that are significant and under discussion in the contemporary world. This does not mean reducing literature into an unequivocal reflection of society but considering it as a forum where diverse voices can debate and explore ideas. Alongside postcolonial studies, another way to incorporate Indian writing in the syllabus has been through literary theory. Women's writing frequently features characters, situations, contexts, and themes that are fruitful from the perspective of critical theory. Thus, questions of gender, history, hybridity, place, ecology, or politics, for example, are productive in reading these writers.

Although the most popular genre of postcolonial literature is the novel and poetry is more marginal, poems are in fact practical for teaching purposes because the texts are mostly short and often focus on few topics, even if brevity does not mean less complexity or interpretative challenges. An example of Indian feminist writing I have used in teaching is Rukmini Bhaya Nair's poetry. Bhaya Nair is relevant in many ways, as she is a poet, a critic, and a professor of English at the Indian Institute of Technology,

New Delhi. Some critical books by Nair that offer an introduction to her work are *Poetry in a Time of Terror: Essays in the Postcolonial Preternatural* and *Lying on the Postcolonial Couch: The Idea of Indifference.* These books approach postcolonial theory from a different perspective from those of the most used critical works by such scholars as Homi Bhabha, Edward Said, and Gayatri Spivak. Furthermore, Bhaya Nair's treatment of gender is appealing to Finnish students, as feminist theory is popular with them.[4] Her poem "Genderole," from her collection *Yellow Hibiscus*, begins as follows: "Considerthefemalebodyyourmost / Basictextanddontforgetitsslokas." In the poem Bhaya Nair not only plays with the English and Sanskrit languages but also provides a feminist challenge to Adi Shankara's revered Sanskrit verse form, slokas. The ancient form—with Sanskrit run-on graphemics, punctuation, and stanza structure—is transposed into English and used to overwrite male hegemony (see Bhaya Nair, "'This Is for You'" 283). Bhaya Nair's text presents vital issues for critical intervention that has proved relevant to Finnish students, despite the context that initially seems unfamiliar.

In "A Politically Incorrect Ode to Whitman," Bhaya Nair openly and ironically challenges the male literary canon through critical references to influential authors from Walt Whitman ("dandelions") to Jacques Derrida (phallogocentrism):

> Forever thirty-seven
> And in perfect health chewing
> The heads off dandelions and theorists
>
> Which right-thinking critic
> Would not like to put to sleep
> This unconcerned ecologically hazardous
>
> Phallogocentric brute
> Once and for all in that
> Endlessly rocking cradle of his? (lines 16–24)

Again, the topic is relevant for Finnish students and provides a new perspective on issues that might be familiar from other literatures but which in the Indian context enable heuristic discoveries.

Bhaya Nair not only points her critical finger at canonical literature and literary theory but also examines Indian culture, practices, and interpretations that could be seen as narrowly sectarian. In the poem "Kali," she connects Indian mythology and epics to contemporary social critique:

A goddess chews on myth
As other women might on paan
Red juices stain her mouth.
. . . .
Where should such a goddess turn?
Kali, mistress of the temporal worlds
Wants bliss defined in human terms. (lines 1–3, 28–30)

The poem is acutely aware of the cultural intricacies—with Kali, Shiva, Durga, Parvati, Chandi, and Ganesha—while it is also highly critical of the norms set by a monocultural heritage. Similarly, in the poem "Love," the narrator thinks about her son, Viraj, who has just told her about love intricacies at school.

dear god, how we lie to our children
my son, named for procreation

amalgam of wild Aryan rituals
my son, the first Vedic man. . . . (lines 28–31)

The everyday intimate situations between mother and son, "not-quite-seven," and school subjects "Hindi, Maths, English / and something mysterious called E.V.S." (i.e., environmental studies) are amalgamated into age-old, shared Hindu religious traditions, as well as with American popular cultural icons Ali MacGraw and Ryan O'Neal, the star couple of the 1970 film *Love Story*. In the poem "Feasts (A Song for Spice Girls Everywhere)," an analogous cultural mixture is introduced. Indian recipe instructions—"this memory of spices" (line 18)—are connected with the global Spice Girls phenomenon. In "Gargi's Silence," the character of Gargi from the Upanishads speaks in a critical feminist tone: "Gargi whispers in Yagnavalkya's ticklish ear / Your metaphysics is shaky! We're not chained / To Brahman. He is a prisoner of our senses" (lines 22–24). The bridges that Bhaya Nair's poems build between popular and traditional cultures are convenient in the classroom, as students are likely to recognize the popular references; they provide material for cultural exchange and for expanding the dialogue.

More Collaboration

Despite the challenges, students benefit from the opportunity to develop an understanding of the literary world that is wider than mainstream British and American literature. Therefore, any attempt at widening the scope of literary studies is worthwhile. When practical constraints limit this attempt, one way to overcome the obstacles is through collaboration. If, for example, South Asian women's writing is considered from the theoretical, sociopolitical, and linguistic points of view discussed above, then it is possible to build content for joint courses with departments of other languages, comparative literature, history, or social sciences. The approaches could be thematic, geographic, or chronological, but they enable different contextualizations of literature. In sum, Indian women's writing can be seen from many perspectives as relevant not only to English studies but to all fields where culture, transnational relations, or social practices are important.

My experiences of teaching joint courses on multilingualism, multiculturality, popular culture, or hybridity have proven to be fascinating and worthwhile. Highlighting context rather than aesthetic form may be less than ideal, but it helps position teaching in settings that enrich reading and learning by the students. In Jhumpa Lahiri's story "This Blessed House," for instance, there is a reverse colonial setting when a young Indian couple, Sanjeev and Twinkle, settle in their new house in Connecticut. Twinkle is excited about the Christian paraphernalia they keep finding in the house, left behind by the previous owners. She explains the situation to their housewarming guests: "Every day is like a treasure hunt. It's too good. God only knows what else we'll find, no pun intended" (153). Lahiri's anecdote offers an interesting metaphor for rethinking university teaching as a constant process of cultural exchange and discovery. In a similar spirit, it would be ideal to be able to foster in students an interest in South Asian women's writing as an endless source of study and research, constantly rediscovered through a more inclusive and collaborative university curricula.

Notes

1. For comparison, the *Wikipedia* page "List of Countries by English-Speaking Population" gives the top seven countries of English speakers in the following order: United States, India, Nigeria, Pakistan, China, the Philippines, United Kingdom.

2. The Constitution of India declares Hindi as the official language of the union and lists twenty-two scheduled languages used in the states. English is given a special mention in article 343(2): "for a period of fifteen years from the commencement of this Constitution, the English language shall continue to be used for all the official purposes of the Union for which it was being used

immediately before such commencement" (Government of India). For practical reasons, English has overstayed its constitutional invitation and has a strong status in India.

3. For a bibliography of resident and diasporic Indian women writers until 2002, see Kuortti.

4. For gender studies in the English departments in Finnish universities, see Valovirta and Kuortti.

Works Cited

Aerila, Juli-Anna, and Lydia Kokkola. "Multicultural Literature and the Use of Literature in Multicultural Education in Finland." *Bookbird: A Journal of International Children's Literature*, vol. 51, no. 2, Apr. 2013, pp. 39–50.

Ashcroft, Bill, et al. *The Empire Writes Back: Theory and Practice in Post-colonial Literatures.* Routledge, 1989.

Bhaya Nair, Rukmini. *Lying on the Postcolonial Couch: The Idea of Indifference.* U of Minnesota P, 2002.

———. *Poetry in a Time of Terror: Essays in the Postcolonial Preternatural.* Oxford UP, 1999.

———. "'This Is for You': Emotions, Language and Postcolonialism, Rukmini Bhaya Nair Speaks with Dorota Filipczak." *Text Matters*, vol. 3, no. 3, 2013, pp. 271–84.

———. *Yellow Hibiscus: New and Selected Poems*, Penguin, 2004.

Government of India. *The Constitution of India.* 1950. *National Portal of India*, www.india.gov.in/my-government/constitution-india/constitution-india-full-text. Accessed 16 Feb. 2016.

Graddol, David. *English Next: Why Global English May Mean the End of "English as a Foreign Language."* British Council, 2006.

———. *English Next India: The Future of English in India.* British Council, 2010.

Kuortti, Joel. *Indian Women's Writing in English: A Bibliography.* Rawat, 2002.

Lahiri, Jhumpa. "This Blessed House." *Interpreter of Maladies*, HarperCollins, 1999, pp. 136–57.

"List of Countries by English-Speaking Population." *Wikipedia*, en.wikipedia.org/wiki/List_of_countries_by_English-speaking_population. Accessed 24 Apr. 2020.

Valovirta, Elina, and Joel Kuortti. "Moderate Finnish Feminism: From a Struggle for Equality in the Welfare State to Diverse and Established Gender Studies." *Rewriting Academia: The Development of the Anglicist Women's and Gender Studies of Continental Europe*, edited by Renate Haas, Peter Lang, 2015, pp. 247–76.

Cecile Sandten

Sujata Bhatt's Poetry in a Cross-Cultural German Context

This essay discusses the teaching of South Asian women's writing to students of English literature in Germany. In doing so, I will focus on my experience in teaching the Gujarati Indian poet Sujata Bhatt's works, specifically with regard to how issues of cultural identity, diaspora, and hybridity can be explored within the cross-cultural context of the anglophone German university classroom. As Bhatt has a transnational background (born in Ahmedabad, Gujarat; immigrated to the United States in 1968 and to Bremen, Germany, in 1988), the question of how she represents herself and her multiple selves and how she shapes and reflects her voice(s) in her poetry is central to my classroom discussions of her work. Moreover, the issue of language and translation is a crucial prelude to a sustained engagement with a selection of Bhatt's poems, some of which explicitly address the legacy of English and its creative possibilities.

Because of a steady stream of migration into Germany in recent decades, the topic of multiculturalism has increasingly been included in the syllabi of courses offered in the humanities and social sciences in German schools and universities. It may therefore be useful to begin by discussing the relevance of key terms such as *cultural identity*, *diaspora*, and *hybridity* before discussing how these notions, as well as what it means to write from a South Asian minority position, are explored in Bhatt's poetry in the German educational context. Bhatt employs a variety of personae (lyrical voices) that bridge continents, languages, and cultural identities. By examining a selection of her poems, I will demonstrate how the poet creatively explores and negotiates "imaginary homelands" (Rushdie) in her writing, while interweaving multiple historical, cultural, geographical, and linguistic contexts.

Cultural Identity, Diaspora, Hybridity, and Language in Bhatt's Poetry

Identity, as Kobena Mercer claims, "only becomes an issue when it is in crisis, when something assumed to be fixed, coherent and stable is displaced by the experience of doubt and uncertainty" (43). Similarly, Stuart Hall speaks, on the one hand, of diaspora populations as "scattered tribes whose identity can only be secured in relation to some sacred homeland to which they must at all costs return" and, on the other, of identities "which are constantly producing and reproducing themselves anew, through transformation and difference" (235); cultural identity in the latter instance is regarded more as a process (of "becoming") than a product (of "being") (225). In the face of multiple and continually shifting definitions of identity, the sociologist Zygmunt Bauman observes, "One thinks of identity whenever one is not sure of where one belongs" (19). This might factor into the lived realities of inhabitants of or from the former British Empire, many of whom have experienced dislocation, (forced) migration, and diaspora in the postcolonial period.

Calling for a shift toward transcultural and transdisciplinary methodologies and perspectives, the field of postcolonial studies has emphasized the significance of cross-cultural interactions in contact zones where, in the wake of postindependence migration, diasporic communities negotiate and rework notions of cultural identity, belonging, and citizenship. Diaspora, originally associated with the Jewish experience of dispersal, highlights issues of spatial, temporal, and cultural dislocation and relocation in contemporary discourse, as well as the negotiation of cultural identity and heritage among minority communities. Because South Asians are one of the smaller minority groups in Germany, the inclusion of Indian literature (whether in Indian languages or in German translation) is rare on course syllabi in German departments. Anglophone Indian literature is typically taught in English departments and programs in which there is an emphasis on postcolonial theory and literature and, peripherally, in Indology departments where the tendency is to focus on nonanglophone Hindi, Urdu, Bengali, and Punjabi literature. Although Bhatt has made English her chosen language for aesthetic explorations of particular emotions, moods, situations, and memories linked to her intercultural journeys, she reveals both her Indian upbringing and her transcultural way of life in an intercultural mode of writing. To highlight the notion of cultural difference and specificity, she at times inserts into her English texts words or phrases from other languages, such as Gujarati (her mother tongue), German, or Spanish, which are occasionally glossed or explained in a footnote. There currently exists one translation of her work into German, *Brunizem*, which comprises only sixteen poems. Therefore, students who study her poetry in my literature classes are asked to do their own translations, and by doing so, they create new linguistic structures of meaning and, thus, create greater affinity to what Bhatt expresses. This process of re-creating and redefining meanings and phrases helps them understand that language, functioning as a means of literary communication and agency, is constructed with reference to locations and their predominant ideologies. To further illustrate this point, I have taught Bhatt's poetry alongside the works of diasporic South Asian women poets such as Meena Alexander, Shanta Acharya, and Raman Mundair, as well as writers such as Meera Syal, Bharati Mukherjee, and Chitra Banerjee Divakaruni.

A discussion of the concepts of cultural identity, diaspora, hybridity, and language is central to the exercise of reading and teaching Bhatt's poetry in an English literatures classroom located in a German university. These issues are variously explored in Bhatt's poems, which enact a negotiation of cultural identity through an intercultural or cosmopolitan awareness and engage with the notion of home. Significantly, the poems suggest that diasporic cultural formations tend to comprise "[d]ecentered, lateral connections" rather than linear narratives "formed around a teleology of origin/return" (Clifford 306). As James Clifford has argued, "Whatever their ideologies of purity, diasporic cultural forms can never, in practice, be exclusively nationalist. They are deployed in transnational networks built from multiple attachments, and they encode practices of accommodation with, as well as resistance to, host countries and their norms" (307). Clifford's notions of "transnational networks" and "resistance" are, metaphorically speaking, employed in Bhatt's poetic texts via a unique choice of images, personae, and linguistic registers from the fields of science, history, arts, literature, and philosophy.

The following section outlines a number of teaching approaches that involve close readings and critical analyses of a selection of Bhatt's poems. I offer practical classroom techniques used to foster a critical awareness of issues of diaspora, hybridity, and transculturality. As a means of introducing Bhatt's work to students, specific aspects of her poetry addressed might include the use of English as her chosen language of poetic composition; her additional use of Indian languages such as Gujarati, Hindi, and Sanskrit as well as German, Low German, and Spanish in her poems; the inter- and transcultural contexts of the poems that demonstrate an intercultural mode of writing. When engaged in the close readings of a selection of poems, students are asked to clarify unknown words and create their own translations of the texts (into their mother tongue). But before we broach the poetry, we begin by discussing students' associations and impressions of India and Indian cultures with the help of images of India, including famous sites such as the Taj Mahal, places of religious worship, a map of India, Indian food, Indian people from different classes and castes, and so forth. We examine the notion of stereotypes and partial representation. As we read Bhatt's poems, we consider how to dismantle stereotypically exotic representations of India in the mainstream media. In the close readings of Bhatt's poems that follow, a variety of key issues are illuminated through vigorous discussion.

Journey, Home, and Diaspora in Bhatt's "The One Who Goes Away"

Bhatt's poem "The One Who Goes Away" broaches the main themes of journey, diaspora, and home or loss of home. The poem's setting and mood, as well as its refrain, "I am the one / who always goes away" (variously used in the poem), should be considered, in order to highlight the themes of collective and individual migration. The poem begins with an epigraph by Eleanor Wilner, an American poet and one of Bhatt's creative writing teachers, who initiates a discussion about the notions of home, journey, and diaspora: "There are always, in each of us, / these two: the one who stays, / the one who goes away." In Bhatt's "The One Who Goes Away," the starting point of the journey, the speaker's departure from India, epitomizes the beginning of a process of transforming home from a physical place to a mental and emotional entity, such that it "does not fit / with any geography," as the last two lines of the poem suggest. The notion of "hybridity" as a space of "in-betweenness" (Bhabha 20) is also explored in the poem by the speaker, who is shaped and influenced by multiple homes, cultures, and identities through constant journeying or displacement. Written in free verse, the poem is subdivided into sixteen longer and shorter sections that revolve around the theme of leaving, searching for, finding, or preserving home. In a flashback situation, the speaker of the poem reveals her first journey as an overwhelming event in her life. The intensity of emotions can be seen in the repetition and the speaker's silence and voicelessness:

> I did not speak,
> did not answer
> those who stood waving
> with the soft noise
> of saris flapping in the wind. (lines 6–10)

The mention of the saris indicates a South Asian context. The speaker's voice is a distinctive one that, during the course of the poem, changes from a sad tone to one that is mixed with irony, with the speaker questioning the use of lucky symbols and propitious rituals that also invoke specific locations in India. For instance, the speaker watches beggars recovering the coconuts that have been flung into the sea for good luck: "And in the end / who gets the true luck / from those sacrificed coconuts?" (lines 17–19). During the course of the poem, the speaker justifies herself with regard to the concerns of others; when asked why she is the one who must always go away, she seems self-assured but also expresses ideas that reveal confusion, mismatch, and chaos:

> Because I must—
> with my home intact
> but always changing
> so the windows don't match
> the doors anymore—the colours
> clash in the garden—
> And the ocean lives in the bedroom. (lines 58–64)

Eventually, the speaker expresses certainty as to where exactly her home is. Accordingly, it is in her "blood," outside "geography" (lines 69, 70).

The poem alternates at times between an individual experience put forward by the lyric persona and a collective experience, represented by the first-person plural, as in the lines: "We weren't allowed / to take much / but I managed to hide / my home behind my heart" (lines 38–41).

These lines show the speaker to be someone who is already different from the others, setting herself apart, and they represent the voice of someone who is childlike, because she is secretly doing something that is apparently not allowed.

At the end of the poem, the persona has seemingly freed herself of the desire to search for her home in the external environment, since home exists within her, herself, and, by extension, her memory—which does not imply that this experience is without pain, as the tone of voice of the poem suggests. Bhatt's poem demonstrates a profound engagement with the topics of home, journeying, and, by extension, an individual form of diaspora, which she describes as a home that exists without territorial attribution. Home has transformed into a mental landmark, which is re-created by childhood memories that are invoked by particular people, experiences, and events, including sensory memories, such as colors and noises. The idea of home being stored in the inner self seems quite intriguing and is an apt metaphor for what I would call an individual diasporic experience. This is in line with the notion that the inner self is difficult to define, since it is determined by subjective experiences that no one else is able to perceive. Students can be asked to reflect on whether they have ever experienced homesickness in order to explore what feelings are entailed. They could also consider how those feelings might be intensified if they were forced to leave their home(land).

Linguistic Variation and Cross-Cultural Spaces in Bhatt's "Brunizem" and "Muliebrity"

Many words, such as *Brunizem*, *brummagem*, *Mapplemus*, and *Augatora*, that Bhatt uses as titles or in the poems themselves are neologisms that, in the vein of "organic poetry" (Levertov 14–15), represent or reproduce the sound and feeling of a specific personal experience. In the poem "Muliebrity," language becomes a marker of cultural space (Ashcroft et al. 72). The term *muliebrity* is normally used in a literary context to refer to qualities of womanhood or womanliness. In the eighteen-line poem, an explicit lyrical persona contemplates a girl who gathers cow dung at the roadside in India close to the speaker's house as her particular example of womanliness. Thus, Bhatt plays with and subverts the reader's assumptions and traditional associations of literary femininity in Western canonical texts from Petrarchan and English sonnets to the Victorian novel, while at the same time addressing olfactory aspects. Moreover, the poem is characterized, as are many of Bhatt's poems in which the poet recalls her childhood in India, by words that invoke the Indian atmosphere—"Radhvallabh temple in Manigar" (line 4) or "canna lilies" (line 7)—in a flashback situation. The poet is trying to bridge the gaps between a specific past event, the speaker's own memory-induced starting point, and the moment in the present, here the metapoetic situation, at which the process of remembering is initiated: "I have thought so much / but have been unwilling to use her for a metaphor / for a nice image" (lines 12–14). At first glance, these flashbacks give the impression of a discontinuity with the present, but they are also introduced in order for the poet-speaker to make meaning of the past, which has to be imagined. When thinking about the girl who gathers cow dung, the persona remembers particular olfactory aspects of the scene (line 7). And although the speaker is unwilling to "explain to anyone the greatness" of the act performed by the girl (line 15), she nonetheless does exactly this: create an image. Yet this image contradicts and subverts caste and class issues, demonstrating the speaker's state of in-betweenness, caught between now and then, which is also produced at the level of language itself.

Similarly, in the autobiographical poem "Brunizem," a love poem written for her husband, Michael Augustin, when they first met at the University of Iowa Writers' Workshop, language becomes a marker of cultural identity and origin. The title word *Brunizem*—which is a neologism referring to brown soil that can be found in parts of Asia, Europe, and America, thus combining the three worlds that Bhatt has lived in—is repeated in the poem several times, as is the word *brummagem*, representing, again, sounds that Bhatt particularly uses to express certain feelings. The speaker, having dreamed that English is her middle name, cries and rejects this anglophone marker of her cultural identity, telling her mother:

> "I don't want English
> to be my middle name.
> Can't you change it to something else?"
> "Go read the dictionary," she said. (lines 18–21)

This stanza clearly shows the speaker as someone who finds herself in an in-between situation as the flashback in the form of a dream reveals. Having to struggle, as a child, with the imposition of the colonial language English, and thus being afraid of losing the mother tongue, in this case Gujarati, the speaker feels imprisoned in this linguistic confinement. Like the flashback, in order to make sense of the past, the dream too can be perceived as a territory that helps to explore present and past. When she meets Michael, who is German, the speaker eventually senses a mode of escape from this linguistic imposition: "I feel brunizem / when this man kisses me / I want to learn another language" (lines 25–27). At once a commentary on the colonial history of the English language throughout the British Empire (and the rejection of that history), as well as an acknowledgment of the debate surrounding the usage of English as a language of poetic creation over that of nonanglophone and indigenous Indian languages, Bhatt's "Brunizem" is a poem that reflects the complexity of processes of identity formation and identification within a cross- or intercultural framework, beyond strict South Asian traditional concepts (e.g., arranged marriage). Students can be made aware of, on the one hand, language issues related to colonialism and, on the other, India's cultural and linguistic diversity as well as of the question of linguistic and cultural identity. Bhatt's poems offer their readers an in-between position with regard to race, culture, gender, and South Asian stereotypes. They offer an opportunity to explore identity outside of the usual boxes of cultural, linguistic, or religious certainty by representing a voice that simultaneously belongs to and explores many cultures and that creatively negotiates these cultures.

In reflecting on the literary process of transcribing and translating her lived experiences in India, America, and Germany, Bhatt's personal, largely autobiographical poems lend themselves particularly well to an exploration of issues of cultural hybridity, diasporic identity, and linguistic variation in a late twentieth-century and early twenty-first-century context. In using her poems to discuss these issues with university students, educators are able to offer a different approach to strategies of inclusion, integration, and diversity in mainstream German sociopolitical discourse that often remains enmeshed in Western neoliberal ideologies. Despite the fact that Indian literature in English has become a popular academic subject in higher education, particularly because of the large number of publications in this field, the purpose of teaching about writers such as Bhatt in university courses is to raise awareness and make students familiar with a transcultural, anglophone German-resident Indian writer. In particular, students learn about a woman poet who creatively engages in hybrid multi-, inter-, and transcultural issues, thus helping them to challenge the image of a homogenous, predominantly white majority culture. As they foreground questions of diasporic identity, lessons on Bhatt's poems are rewarding in various ways, since the multicultural female poet provides a refreshing voice within the traditional, male-dominated English literary canon, thus helping students to discuss, revise, and even correct gender, caste, and class stereotypes, thereby revising their often Eurocentric perspectives. In addition, they also invite cross-cultural readings and thus a more comparative framework within which to approach South Asian literatures and cultures in a German university classroom.

Works Cited

Ashcroft, Bill, et al. *The Empire Writes Back: Theory and Practice in Post-colonial Literatures.* Routledge, 1989.

Bauman, Zygmunt. "From Pilgrim to Tourist; or, a Short History of Identity." *Questions of Cultural Identity*, edited by Stuart Hall and Paul du Gay, Sage, 1996, pp. 18–36.

Bhabha, Homi. *The Location of Culture.* 1994. Routledge, 2010.

Bhatt, Sujata. "Brunizem." Bhatt, *Brunizem*, p. 105.

———. *Brunizem.* Carcanet, 1988.

———. "Muliebrity." Bhatt, *Brunizem*, p. 26.

———. "The One Who Goes Away." Bhatt, *Stinking Rose*, pp. 3–4.

———. *The Stinking Rose.* Carcanet, 1995.

Clifford, James. "Diasporas." *Cultural Anthropology*, vol. 9, no. 3, Aug. 1994, pp. 302–38.

Hall, Stuart. "Cultural Identity and Diaspora." Rutherford, pp. 222–37.

Levertov, Denise. *The Poet in the World.* New Directions, 1973.

Mercer, Kobena. "Welcome to the Jungle: Identity and Diversity in Postmodern Politics." Rutherford, pp. 43–71.

Rushdie, Salman. *Imaginary Homelands: Essays and Criticism, 1981–1991.* Granta, 1991.

Rutherford, Jonathan, editor. *Identity: Community, Culture, Difference.* Lawrence and Wishart, 1990.

Ragini Tharoor Srinivasan

Teaching South Asian Women's Writing to South Asian Students

This essay is motivated by my experience, first as a college student in the opening decade of the twenty-first century and now as an assistant professor, in American universities. As a South Asian American woman student, I once took a class on anglophone South Asian women's literature. The class was taught by a scholar of literature and cultural studies who was neither South Asian nor a woman. The two of us students in the class who were South Asian women took this as a provocation: how exactly was this professor going to teach us to read "our" literature? Over the years, I have come to question my assumptions about this body of literature and about the complications of identifying as a South Asian woman student and teacher.

The class addressed fiction by women from the Indian diaspora, from the partition of India and Pakistan in 1947—thematized, for example, in Bapsi Sidhwa's *Cracking India*—to the struggles of diasporic women featured in texts by Monica Ali, Sunetra Gupta, Jhumpa Lahiri, Shani Mootoo, and Meera Syal: women writers who represented a range of voices, a spectrum of issues, and many literary genres and styles.

That was my first experience taking a literature course organized around an identitarian rubric with which I personally identified. A decade later, I have a hazy memory of a discussion of Dublin-born, Trinidad-raised Mootoo's *Cereus Blooms at Night*, with its wrenching depictions of child abuse and nonnormative gender identities. I have forgotten the details of the lectures on Sandhya Shukla's *India Abroad: Diasporic Cultures of Post-war America and England*, from which we derived our working definition of *diaspora* as an extra- or nonterritorial, rhizomatic map of communities dispersed across the world. I do remember, however, the fingernails pressed into my palm under the seminar table, a not-so-subtle expression of frustration at what I experienced as the course's disciplining effects.

What was my problem? In part, I was not sure what I—a South Asian American woman—was doing in the course. Was I the subject of knowledge or its object? Was I there to learn about myself or, to adapt Judith Butler's phrase, to "give an account of myself"? With each text we read, I felt assailed by notions of Indianness that flew against my ambivalent and evolving conceptions of it. I chafed against my classmates' exuberant reception of Jhumpa Lahiri's *The Namesake* and the professor's praise of its anthropological rendering of the second-generation Indian American immigrant experience. I both recognized Lahiri's descriptions of experiences, such as Indian parents allowing "American dinner once a week as a treat" (65), and worried about their being read as representing *me*.

Over the course of the semester, we studied Stuart Hall and Edward Said, and we developed a conception of identity as a differential quantity, as something taken up strategically, which has "to go through the eye of the needle of the other before it can construct itself" (Grossberg 13). And yet, we two South Asian women students were, in an immediate visual register, the embodied subjects of the course, and our identities appeared before the eyes of the others fully formed. We often felt called to testify as "native informants" among our peers, that is, as subjects with cultural authority and, in some cases, linguistic expertise, as if we were data for our class's ethnographic inquiry. At the same time, our experiential relations to the material felt wanting.

More than a decade later, I better appreciate the challenge that my professor faced in teaching anglophone South Asian literatures to students like me who felt implicated by the course texts. Now, I take that class experience as an opportunity to think about not only what should be taught in a course on anglophone South Asian women's writing but how it should be taught and to whom. What will constitute our archive, and what constitutes knowledge of it? Are South Asian women students the ideal readers of South Asian women's texts, and if so, why, or why not? What background knowledges enable (or, for that matter, disable) what forms of engagement with the course texts? How do we teach South Asian women's writing to South Asian women students?

My experience studying South Asian women's literature need not be representative of that of all South Asian students in South Asian fiction courses in order for it to begin to illustrate the ethical and epistemological challenges of organizing a pedagogic environment around an identitarian rubric. In this case, the rubric in question is South Asian women's writing (the possessive construction of which importantly suggests both writing by South Asian women and writing for South Asian women), but it could just as well be literatures of the Americas, global Chinese speculative fiction, or queer biography. While such courses typically aim to present a range of competing voices, genres, or themes, and in so doing to challenge monolithic or reified conceptions of Americanness, the Sinophone, or the queer subject (among other potential categories), they do not always extend that same critical invitation to students who understand themselves to be interpellated by the course material.

And yet, they should. This is particularly important when the students in question are undergraduates, who come to the humanities classroom with varying degrees of high school–level preparation for critical inquiry. Often, after primary and secondary education in canonical American and British literatures, they are encountering literatures by and of populations they resemble or recognize for the first time. As institutional histories of cultural studies, women's studies, and ethnic studies remind us, one inaugural aim of canon-busting knowledge formations was precisely to create "a space for historically silenced people to construct knowledge" predicated on an understanding that the "act of knowing [is] related to the power of self-definition," and in so doing to offer "a fundamental challenge to hegemonic knowledge and history" (Mohanty 147–54). This is the underpinning aspiration of the study of minority and multiethnic literature in the American university, including anglophone South Asian women's writing, and it requires pedagogical criticality and aliveness to the field of forces in which we as teachers present a set of literary texts as discourses of hitherto undervalued knowledges.

Moreover, the archive of anglophone South Asian women's writing is, in most cases, a postcolonial one. This means that many of the texts we might teach have already been problematically cast and received by publishers, distributors, critics, and anthologists as what Deepika Bahri calls species of "native intelligence," as "ethnographic and ideologically saturated text[s]" (5). As researchers, we may respond to Bahri's call to reanimate the aesthetic dimensions of postcolonial literatures in order to better understand their political content and efficacy as social critique. As teachers, however, we must be attuned precisely to those ethnographic and ideological claims that students will make on such texts and that we, in selecting these texts, are making on our students in turn.

Having now taught South Asian women's writing myself at the undergraduate and graduate levels, I believe there are three primary challenges in teaching students who hear themselves named by the course rubric, who are taking the course in part to learn about themselves or who seek to resist from an "insider" perspective the course's presentation of authors and texts. Approaching them as fundamental preconditions of the course inquiry (as opposed to problems to be overcome) will enable us as teachers to better negotiate the interpersonal dynamics of classroom identity politics, while foregrounding the critical potential of approaching identity as epistemology beyond the classroom and in the broader public sphere.

First is that some students will express familiarity with, if not firsthand knowledge of, themes like diasporic nostalgia and historical events like partition. How, when, and why will we make space for student contributions of relevant lived experiences, like a narrative of a grandparent's participation in anticolonial resistance? What weight might a student's description of her parents' love marriage have in the context of a conversation on Chitra Banerjee Divakaruni's *Arranged Marriage*? On the one hand, we don't want the class to simply traffic in the currency of intimacies, anecdotes, and uncritical evidence of experience. By that same token, however, we don't want to dismiss as essentialist that which may be essential to our students.

Second is the inevitable burden of representation borne by the South Asians in the class. How will we respond when students ask a Bengali peer to corroborate the picture of Calcutta in Gupta's *Memories of Rain* as a deluged city that is "one large sea of mud and dung, and floating waterlogged Ambassador cars" (5)? How will we respond when students turn to their legibly South Asian classmates for the pronunciation of what are to them unfamiliar names, like "Nazneen" in Ali's *Brick Lane*? South Asian students may very well be able to complicate the depictions of South Asian life-worlds on offer in the course texts, and in so doing advance the aim of "demystifying the act and process of representing by revealing how meanings are produced within relations of power that narrate identities through history, social forms, and modes of ethical address" (Giroux 47). By that same token, individual gestures of corroboration or complexification should themselves be scrutinized for their pretenses to universal validity.

Third, and most significant, is the necessity of offering a critique of literature's purchase on South Asian "truths," whether the text in question issues from the territorial bounds of South Asia or from the diaspora. How will we negotiate this thorny legacy of poststructuralist theory, namely the critical insight that while our embodied experiences condition what we know, it is nevertheless impossible to be fully knowing subjects of ourselves and our texts? As teachers of anglophone South Asian women's writing, we have the occasion to take up what Elleke Boehmer and Rosinka Chaudhuri have called "the invitation of the postcolonial text to think as other, to submit to the difference of the other's ideational world" (191). By that same token, we must be alive to the ways in which we as teachers and students are also, ultimately, others to ourselves.

Teaching anglophone South Asian women's writing after critiques of the subject means that we must be careful not to present the literature in question as the truth of the individual or collective South Asian woman self, even as we strive to make space for our students to appear and think as themselves in the classroom. We must warn against the valorization of liberal humanist conceptions of agency and autonomy, especially as we encounter texts like Bharati Mukherjee's *Jasmine*, which specifically "articulate[s] the trope of the Asian woman within the context of a liberal idea of America" (Grewal 62). We must encourage students not to attribute to all South Asian women subjects the same desires and aspirations, not to reduce operations of power to ready binaries, and not to theorize subjectivation without concern for forms of embodied attachment.

By that same token, we ought not to get carried away with the practices of "suspicious interpretation" and "critical reading," which Rita Felski has argued dominate the contemporary literature classroom. Felski notes that the overemphasis on suspicion and critique forecloses attention to the other modes of affiliation, attachment, and aesthetic response that characterize students' encounters with texts. In the South Asian women's literature classroom, the hermeneutics of suspicion is matched by the identity politics of native informancy, making doubly important the work of "delving into the mysteries of our many-sided attachments to texts" and of critically interpreting how textual signifiers "hook up to imaginative, ethical, cultural, and sociopolitical lifeworlds" (Felski 31–32).

Our question is: How can we teachers of anglophone South Asian women's writing encourage our South Asian women students in particular to embrace—while striving to work through and against—their positions as subjects "caught between knowing and being" (Radhakrishnan 2)? Can we teach the construction of meaning without evacuating that term of epistemological force? Can we engage moments of recognition not simply as instances of identitarian interpellation but rather as philosophical projects of "knowing again and knowing anew" (Felski 32)?

I want to turn here to Donna J. Haraway's canonical revision of standpoint feminism and her argument that "the only way to find a larger vision is to be somewhere in particular" (196). The goal of scholarly inquiry is not what is conventionally understood as objectivity—not knowing everything about the text definitively, what it says, how it works, and what it means—nor is it the relativistic perspective that all readings of the text are created equal. Rather, the goal of feminist, critical scholarship is a kind of knowledge predicated on "limited location" (188). This kind of inquiry demands that we recognize that we are all speaking, seeing, and reading from somewhere, from some body.

Haraway's argument for "situated knowledges" derives its urgency from her sense that feminist (and, equally, postcolonial) scholars and teachers have run too far afield with theories of social construction and the rhetoricity of all truth claims. "It is not enough," she writes, in words that anticipate Felski, "to show radical historical contingency and modes of construction for everything" (187). There is still a real world out there. For our purposes, there is a territorial South Asia. There are South Asian subjects whose very genetic profiles link them to South Asia and to one another. That means that South Asian women students may very well make truth claims about the texts in question that are neither capital *T* Truths nor simply species of bias. Following Haraway, our goal as teachers should be to foreground the radical historical contingency of such claims in addition to the radical historical contingency of our even appearing, being, and reading together in the same classroom space.

The philosophy of Jacques Rancière, specifically his contrast between stultifying and emancipatory pedagogy, also offers a critical vocabulary with which to approach the issue of such contingency. Rancière argues that the stultifying pedagogical relation functions according to a principle of "self-suppressing mediation" (133); it takes as its starting point a gap between knowledge and ignorance that must be suppressed by the pedagogue. Although the teacher purports to be reducing the space between her knowledge and the ignorance of the student, what results from the effort to transmit knowledge is the continual reinstatement of the gap between what it means to know and what it means not to know. It is "precisely the attempt at suppressing the distance that constitutes the distance itself" and "[endlessly verifies] inequality" (134–35). Rancière demonstrates the inevitable failure of the attempt to suppress the gap between intelligences, but he does not advocate doing away with the gap entirely. Rather, he argues for a conception of distance as "the normal condition of communication" (134). The radical equality of intelligences is, then, dependent on the very thing that was originally assumed to represent inequality: the gap, or distance, between subjects.

If Haraway helps us foreground location, then Rancière helps us to marshal distance as the second enabling condition of teaching anglophone South Asian women's writing to South Asian women students. This might, on first blush, appear a counterintuitive suggestion: distance, as opposed to recognition of the proximate intimacies with which our South Asian women students approach the texts? There are a number of distance-gaps involved in teaching: the gap between what we teachers know of the texts and what we wish our students to learn; the gap between the South Asian content of the literary archive and the South Asianness of South Asian readers; the gap between representation and reality; the gap between literature and the world to which it points, with varying degrees and formal strategies of referentiality. We must foreground the criticality of all these gaps in our teaching, for they will move us beyond the routinized critique of the autonomous, knowing subject, while easing the problems of overdetermined familiarity and the burden of representation in turn.

How do we teach South Asian women's writing to South Asian women students—and why? The above discussion makes clear that if our ultimate goal is a critical pedagogy that is hospitable to and challenging for all students, then it must be equally, perhaps even doubly, so for those who recognize themselves in the ethnic, racial, temporal, gendered, and sexualized formations that occasion the course inquiry.

At the time of this writing, educators in and beyond the Anglo-American university are grappling with the imperative of decolonizing the university, the histories of institutional racism, and the careers of a much-maligned identity politics that has become the favorite scapegoat of conservative advocates of "academic freedom." The project of teaching South Asian literatures to South Asian students must be situated within this broader critical landscape. It is not enough for statues of Cecil Rhodes to fall in Cape Town or for buildings in New Haven to drop the name of John C. Calhoun if our pedagogical practices remain tethered to colonial imaginaries of native informancy, on the one hand, and dismissive of the multifold attachments that drive students into our classrooms, on the other.

As teachers, as embodied subjects, we must recognize both the problems and the possibilities of teaching South Asian women's writing to South Asian women students in order for all students to fully engage our courses' aims. Under what conditions do students in the Anglo-American academy have the historically specific, radically contingent opportunity to take classes in anglophone South Asian women's writing in the first place? This, I want to stress in closing, is where the inquiry must begin.

Works Cited

Ali, Monica. *Brick Lane.* Scribner, 2003.

Bahri, Deepika. *Native Intelligence: Aesthetics, Politics, and Postcolonial Literature.* U of Minnesota P, 2003.

Boehmer, Elleke, and Rosinka Chaudhuri, editors. *The Indian Postcolonial: A Critical Reader.* Routledge, 2011.

Butler, Judith. *Giving an Account of Oneself.* Fordham UP, 2005.

Divakaruni, Chitra Banerjee. *Arranged Marriage: Stories.* Anchor, 1996.

Felski, Rita. "After Suspicion." *Profession*, 2009, pp. 28–35.

Giroux, Henry. "Living Dangerously: Identity Politics and the New Cultural Racism." Giroux and McLaren, pp. 29–55.

Giroux, Henry A., and Peter McLaren, editors. *Between Borders: Pedagogy and the Politics of Cultural Studies.* Routledge, 1994.

Grewal, Inderpal. *Transnational America: Feminisms, Diasporas, Neoliberalisms.* Duke UP, 2005.

Grossberg, Lawrence. "Introduction: Bringin' It All Back Home: Pedagogy and Cultural Studies." Giroux and McLaren, pp. 1–25.

Gupta, Sunetra. *Memories of Rain.* Grove Press, 1992.

Hall, Stuart. "Subjects in History: Making Diasporic Identities." *The House That Race Built*, edited by Wahneema Lubiano, Vintage Books, 1998, pp. 289–99.

Haraway, Donna J. *Simians, Cyborgs, and Women: The Reinvention of Nature.* Routledge, 1991.

Lahiri, Jhumpa. *The Namesake.* Houghton Mifflin, 2003.

Mohanty, Chandra Talpade. "On Race and Voice: Challenges for Liberal Education in the 1990s." Giroux and McLaren, pp. 145–66.

Mootoo, Shani. *Cereus Blooms at Night.* Press Gang, 1996.

Mukherjee, Bharati. *Jasmine*. Grove Press, 1989.
Radhakrishnan, R. *History, the Human, and the World Between*. Duke UP, 2008.
Rancière, Jacques. "The Emancipated Spectator." *Art Forum*, vol. 45, no. 7, Mar. 2007, www.artforum.com/print/200703/the-emancipated-spectator-12847.
Said, Edward. *"Reflections on Exile" and Other Essays*. Harvard UP, 2000.
Shukla, Sandhya. *India Abroad: Diasporic Cultures of Postwar America and England*. Princeton UP, 2003.
Sidhwa, Bapsi. *Cracking India*. Milkweed, 1991.

Shane A. McCoy

Counter-Narratives of Liberal Multiculturalism in Jhumpa Lahiri's *The Namesake*

Patriotic education (Sheth), or what Henry Giroux terms *patriotic correctness* (2), has been historically influential in producing students in the United States who can be uncritical of nationalist discourses of assimilation as well as the contradictions of liberal multiculturalism. I draw my understanding of liberal multiculturalism from Jenny Sharpe, who defines it as an intellectual and historical project that is "[c]onstituted around diversity and difference rather than racism and the unequal distribution of power." Liberal multiculturalism also eschews the "original goals of multicultural education, which were to redress the debilitating effects of racial (and sexual) discrimination" (115).[1] In this essay I focus on counter-narratives in Jhumpa Lahiri's first novel, *The Namesake*, that expose these problems through a focus on "little stories."[2] Specifically, I examine ways of reading the novel that challenge the rhetoric of liberal multiculturalism and cultural homogeneity, while exposing the pressures of assimilation.[3] I frame my analysis within theoretical debates in critical and antiracist pedagogy (Giroux; Leonardo) and contend that teaching *The Namesake* as a counter-narrative of little stories can challenge the reproduction of a "patriotic education" and "white ways of seeing" (Davis 149).[4]

In *Represent and Destroy*, Jodi Melamed examines how universities have historically used literary studies as a tool for producing "enlightened multicultural global citizens" (45). Teaching *The Namesake* within a critical pedagogical practice that opposes the habits and ideological assumptions of liberal multiculturalism draws attention to institutional imbalances of power. In institutional settings such as the family, medical facilities, and the school (Althusser 127–86), some characters, as I argue, function as metonyms for institutional insensitivity to culturally specific practices such as naming within an ostensibly liberal multicultural society (Ferguson 41–75, 147–79). My aim is to focus on the pedagogical function of teaching *The Namesake* through the perspective of what Patricia Hill Collins calls the "outsider within" as a "valid source of knowledge" for interrogating cultural hegemony (S30). Accordingly, I advocate for a critical pedagogical agenda that focuses on unequal relations of power within liberal multiculturalism and against a liberal multiculturalism that seeks to fetishize difference and diversity.

The Namesake and Disrupting Liberal Multiculturalism

Born in 1967 in England to West Bengali parents, Nilanjana Sudeshna "Jhumpa" Lahiri migrated with her family to the United States at the age of two and settled in the American Northeast. Lahiri's parents insisted that the author be made familiar with her Bengali heritage. As such, the Lahiris frequently visited Calcutta, and this aspect of Lahiri's life is reflected in *The Namesake* in her account of the Gangulis's experiences. In Lahiri's novel, the Gangulis navigate the uneven terrain of living in two cultures while also raising children born in the United States. In my classes, I begin with the author's biography alongside Inderpal Grewal's essay "Becoming American: The Novel and the Diaspora." Grewal focuses on how South Asian diasporic writers work through various models of assimilation, nationalism, and disidentification. Grewal shows the relevance of examining the American dream as a racialized discourse that complicates the image of the United States as a multicultural, inclusive, and hospitable society (35–79).

Pedagogically, *The Namesake* furnishes an occasion for discussing the history of the 1965 Immigration and Nationality Act and its sociopolitical implications.[5] Roderick Ferguson historicizes the year *The Namesake* begins—1968—and stages the institutional conflicts that the Gangulis experience with the naming of their son, Gogol, when he is born at the hospital and when he enters primary school (147–79). The passage of the 1965 Immigration and Nationality Act did not come without challenges to American national identity, especially in the wake of the civil rights movement. As newly arrived Indian immigrants to the United States, Ashoke and Ashima Ganguli venture into a sociocultural landscape that prides itself on being hospitable and accommodating to immigrants while proposing a rhetoric of national belonging and assimilation into the nation-state. The couple migrates from Calcutta to Cambridge, Massachusetts, where Ashoke, Ashima's husband, is a doctoral candidate at MIT. *The Namesake* opens with a pregnant Ashima standing in the kitchen of her home in Cambridge, assembling her favorite snack. Lahiri juxtaposes this image of the Gangulis against their landlords, Alan and Judy Montgomery, a tenured professor and a homemaker. The Montgomerys' Volkswagen—covered with political bumper stickers that read, "QUESTION AUTHORITY! GIVE A DAMN! BAN THE BRA! PEACE!"—profiles the quintessential liberal, upper-middle-class, suburban white family (30–31). The Montgomerys function as "enlightened multicultural global citizens" (Melamed 45), and MIT, the institution where Ashoke studies and teaches, represents how educational institutions accommodate cultural heterogeneity while, at the same time, acculturating immigrants into the educational system.[6] As Ferguson puts it, the international student (in this case Ashoke) "would be trained to export liberal capitalist ideologies to their communities abroad" (148).

To encourage engagement with these ideas, I develop open-ended questions that allow undergraduates to address secondary research while reading *The Namesake* closely. In this exercise, students need to find passages in the novel in order to compose a short response to each guided question. Questions include the following:

What is Ferguson's argument about medical and educational institutions as they relate to multiculturalism? What do you make of these episodes in the novel, and what purpose might they serve for Lahiri's text?

To what extent does Lahiri's portrayal of Ashima and Ashoke complicate normative narratives of immigration, national belonging, and multiculturalism?

These questions make explicit connections between the secondary critical source (Ferguson) and the primary text (*The Namesake*). Furthermore, the questions foster students' independent critical thinking skills, as they allow students to interrogate national belonging and liberal multiculturalism in literary representations through ideas they encounter in critical readings.

In teaching Lahiri's novel, I invite students to study the novel's treatment of the tradition of naming in Bengali families and how the Gangulis wait for Gogol's official name to arrive from India (25). However, the letter from Ashima's grandmother containing Gogol's "good name" never arrives, and in order to receive a birth certificate, Mr. Wilcox, a hospital administrator, informs the Gangulis that they must name their child: "For they learn in America, a baby cannot be released from the hospital without a birth certificate. And that a birth certificate needs a name" (27). Mr. Wilcox suggests that the Gangulis name the child "after yourself, or one of your ancestors," since naming a child after a parent or grandparent is "a fine tradition. The kings of France and England did it." "This sign of respect in America and Europe," the narrator comments, "would be ridiculed in India" (28).

Although some students can grasp the pernicious effects of Mr. Wilcox's lack of cultural awareness, others have a stronger reaction to Gogol's first day of kindergarten because of the significance of this event in their own lives. In this episode, Ashoke accompanies Gogol on his first day of school. Ashoke and Ashima wish for Gogol to be called Nikhil at school, the "good name" the Gangulis have chosen for their son. The principal Mrs. Lapidus asks Gogol his age. Young Gogol, however, remains silent, which provokes the principal to question Gogol's ability to speak English. Ashoke explains that "Nikhil" is "perfectly bilingual" (57). Unaware that Mrs. Lapidus is eavesdropping, Ashoke calls Gogol by his pet name rather than his good name when he demands that Gogol respond to Mrs. Lapidus. Overhearing this, the principal analyzes the registration forms and notices the discrepancy, despite already having two children in the school who are from Bengali families. Mrs. Lapidus explains to Ashoke that according to the birth certificate, "Gogol" is his son's legal name. Ashoke attempts to explain the difference between his son's good name and the name he and his wife use for the child at home. The principal misinterprets the name to be a nickname or middle name, but Ashoke corrects Mrs. Lapidus: "It is very common for a child to be confused at first. Please give it some time. I assure you he will grow accustomed [to his good name]," Ashoke pleads. Ashoke says goodbye to his son while Mrs. Lapidus quickly records Gogol's pet name on the registration forms. Later that day, the principal prepares a letter for Ashoke and Ashima, detailing for the Gangulis "that due to their son's preference he will be known as Gogol at school." In response to what is tantamount to a fait accompli, Ashima and Ashoke comply, "since neither of them feels comfortable pressing the issue" (60). Moreover, as I point out to students, in a telling exposition of the ways in which immigrants respond consciously and unwittingly to the pressure to assimilate, Ashoke's choice of Nikhil, the intended good name, is motivated at least in part by the fact that it will be "relatively easy to pronounce" (57).

In this episode, Lahiri portrays how an institution, such as Gogol's school, fails to comprehend cultural heterogeneity in general and Bengali culture in particular, but also how immigrants are conditioned into modes of assimilation that do not challenge institutional power. This episode also makes clear how Gogol's name causes the protagonist much anxiety. The conflict with his name is an extended metaphor for Gogol's feelings of alienation despite being American, but not being *of America*. Iffat Sharmin argues that the oscillation between Gogol and Nikhil represents the protagonist's inability to feel "at home." Gogol's ambivalence therefore signals that he "is firmly of America, but is not quite an American, in part because he is not recognized as such by others" (39). The quest for recognition is elaborated through multiple references to a process of learning that undergirds the nationalist agenda of assimilation.

Throughout the novel, I ask students to pay attention to the ways in which the Gangulis learn to live an American lifestyle: "They learn to roast turkeys" for Christmas and Thanksgiving and "color boiled eggs violet and pink at Easter." They learn to buy "ready-made" clothing items, while Ashoke "trades in fountain pens for ballpoints, Wilkinson blades and his boar-bristled shaving brush for Bic razors bought six to a pack" (65). The novel's emphasis on the processes of learning cultural habits continues well into Gogol's adulthood, as he "learns to love the food" his girlfriend, Maxine, and her parents, Lydia and Gerald, prepare for dinner: "He learns that one does not grate Parmesan cheese over pasta dishes containing seafood. He learns not to put wooden spoons in the dishwasher. . . . He learns to anticipate, every evening, the sound of a cork emerging from a fresh bottle of wine" (137). Gogol "does not question" his new social and cultural habits. Rather, he becomes socioculturally conditioned by Maxine and her parents to accept them without question. Although Gogol also learns "to read and write his ancestral alphabet" in a conscious nod to his heritage, we are told that he "hates" this alternative education, which keeps him from a drawing class he would prefer to attend (65–66).

Gogol's ambivalence toward his family's cultural ancestry is matched by that of a mainstream culture that remains uncertain of his claims to the identity he is learning and making habitual.[7] Gogol's twenty-seventh birthday exposes the limits of liberal multiculturalism and the duplicitous rhetoric of cultural pluralism. For the first time, Gogol decides to spend his birthday with his friends rather than with his family and "his mashis and meshos, his honorary aunts and uncles" (73). While at Lydia and Gerald's lake home in Maine, Gogol meets Pamela, a friend of the family who is also from Boston. Pamela, however, assumes that Gogol was not born in the United States and asks Gogol "at what age he moved to America from India" (157). Gogol replies that he is "from Boston"; Pamela moves on with the conversation and confesses that she knows nothing about India. After an awkward exchange, Maxine's mother points out that "Nick's American. . . . He was born here." Lydia, unsure of her own statement, turns to Gogol and asks, "Weren't you?" (157). Her uncertainty indicates how Gogol occupies the position of the "outsider within," despite being born in the United States.

Toward a Critical Multiculturalism

As a queer, white, non-binary-gendered instructor with United States citizenship, this means "unlearning" my privilege and "working critically through [my] history, prejudices, and learned, but now seemingly instinctual, responses" (Landry and MacLean 4).[8] My experience with unlearning my privilege motivates me to teach *The Namesake* using a critical pedagogy that shows students how to also unlearn their privilege, especially those that stem from race and citizenship. Lahiri's novel provides students with a culturally relevant narrative that many underrepresented students at the university find to be commensurate with their own experiences. Students who benefit from the unearned privileges of white male insiderism, however, might also gain from the cultural relevance of the novel. To promote reflection and reassessment, I incorporate an in-class essay that requires students to discuss *The Namesake* among other primary and secondary literary and critical texts, so they can summarize what they have learned about the concepts, themes, and ideas presented in the course and how they might apply this knowledge in future contexts. Peter McLaren reminds us that "[m]ulticulturalism without a transformative political agenda can be just another form of accommodation to the larger social order." A critical multiculturalism, which emphasizes "the role that language and representation play in the construction of meaning and identity" (53), is imperative for designing a curriculum that dismantles a depoliticized liberal multicultural agenda. The framework of critical multiculturalism coupled with teaching *The Namesake* through the lens of the "outsider within" begins that necessary and urgent pedagogical process.

Notes

1. Sharpe goes on to say that liberal multiculturalism aims to dismantle a radical political agenda that seeks to make transparent the workings of power within institutions (115).

2. My use of counter-narratives is developed from Michael Peters and Colin Lankshear, who claim that counter-narratives are stories that work against grand narratives so often found in Western literatures.

3. My understanding of cultural homogeneity is analogous to the ways in which Slavoj Žižek theorizes multiculturalism, or, as he puts it, the "cultural logic of multinational capitalism" (43). Žižek argues that "in order to be a 'good American,' one does not have to renounce one's ethnic roots" (44). Cultural homogeneity therefore depends upon the absorption of racial and ethnic particularities by the nation-state while also remaining ostensibly multicultural.

4. My close reading of this novel is largely drawn from my experience teaching it in general education courses at predominantly white institutions. While my intention is not to assume that the classroom is not impacted by differences of race, class, gender, sexuality, and national origin, most of the students I have encountered do, in fact, buy into the myth of liberal multiculturalism.

5. See Chin and Villazor.

6. According to Melamed, an archetype emerged in the late 1960s of the "enlightened multicultural global citizen" (45), which the Montgomery family embodies and thus portrays. Within the context of Althusser's essay "Ideology and Ideological State Apparatuses" (127–86), both the family and the university function as ideological extensions of "enlightened" liberal multiculturalism exercised by the state and state actors.

7. Gay argues that "culturally responsive pedagogy" aims to develop a curriculum that is culturally responsive and culturally relevant to the lives of multicultural students. Culturally responsive pedagogy and curriculum aim to make "instructional delivery more congruent with the cultural orientations of students from different ethnic, racial, social, and linguistic backgrounds" (xxix). Culturally responsive pedagogy and curriculum ultimately aim to affect students' sense of self-making and world-building in positive ways.

8. I develop my interpretation of this unconscious learning from Spivak's notion of "habit" (1–34). In *An Aesthetic Education in the Era of Globalization*, Spivak, borrowing from Gregory Bateson's *Steps to an Ecology of Mind*, suggests a habit "does not question" and often goes unexamined (6–8). As Bateson puts it, habits are "hard programmed": "We may say these [habits] are partly 'unconscious,' or—if you please—a habit of not examining them is developed" (qtd. in Spivak 6).

Works Cited

Althusser, Louis. *"Lenin and Philosophy" and Other Essays*. Translated by Ben Brewster, Monthly Review Press, 1972.

Chin, Gabriel J., and Rose Culson Villazor, editors. *The Immigration and Nationality Act of 1965: Legislating a New America*. Cambridge UP, 2015.

Davis, Kimberly Chabot. *Beyond the White Negro: Empathy and Anti-Racist Reading*. U of Illinois P, 2014.

Ferguson, Roderick. *The Reorder of Things: The University and Its Pedagogies of Minority Difference*. U of Minnesota P, 2012.

Gay, Geneva. *Culturally Responsive Teaching: Theory, Research, and Practice*. 2nd ed., Teachers College, 2010.

Giroux, Henry A. "Academic Freedom under Fire: The Case for Critical Pedagogy." *College Literature*, vol. 33, no. 4, Fall 2006, pp. 1–42.

Grewal, Inderpal. *Transnational America: Feminisms, Diasporas, Neoliberalisms*. Duke UP, 2005.

Hill Collins, Patricia. "Learning from the Outsider Within: The Sociological Significance of Black Feminist Thought." *Social Problems*, vol. 33, no. 6, Oct.–Dec. 1986, pp. S14–S32.

Lahiri, Jhumpa. *The Namesake*. Houghton Mifflin, 2003.

Landry, Donna, and Gerald MacLean. "Introduction: Reading Spivak." *The Spivak Reader: Selected Works of Gayatri Chakravorty Spivak*, edited by Donna Landry and Gerald MacLean, Routledge, 1996, pp. 1–14.

Leonardo, Zeus. "The Story of Schooling: Critical Race Theory and the Educational Racial Contract." *Discourse: Studies in the Cultural Politics of Education*, vol. 34, no. 4, 2013, pp. 599–610, https://doi.org/10.1080/01596306.2013.822624.

McLaren, Peter. "White Terror and Oppositional Agency: Towards a Critical Multiculturalism." *Multiculturalism: A Critical Reader*, edited by David Theo Goldberg, Blackwell, 1994, pp. 45–74.

Melamed, Jodi. *Represent and Destroy: Rationalizing Violence in the New Racial Capitalism*. U of Minnesota P, 2011.

Peters, Michael, and Colin Lankshear, editors. *Counternarratives: Cultural Studies and Critical Pedagogies in Postmodern Spaces*. Routledge, 1996.

Sharmin, Iffat. "Cultural Identity and Diaspora in Jhumpa Lahiri's *The Namesake*." *East West University Journal*, vol. 2, no. 2, 2011, pp. 35–44.

Sharpe, Jenny. "Postcolonial Studies in the House of US Multiculturalism." *A Companion to Postcolonial Studies*, edited by Henry Schwarz and Sangeeta Ray, Blackwell, 2000, pp. 112–25.

Sheth, Falguni A. "Why Our Best Students Are Totally Oblivious." *Salon*, 13 Sept. 2013, www.salon.com/2013/09/13/why_our_best_students_are_totally_oblivious/. Accessed 11 Apr. 2017.

Spivak, Gayatri Chakravorty. *An Aesthetic Education in the Era of Globalization*. Harvard UP, 2012.

Žižek, Slavoj. "Multiculturalism; or, The Cultural Logic of Multinational Capitalism." *New Left Review*, vol. 1, no. 225, Sept.–Oct. 1997, pp. 28–51.

Rajini Srikanth

Arundhati Roy's Nonfiction Writing

Arundhati Roy first came to the attention of literary scholars with her 1997 novel, *The God of Small Things*, which won the prestigious Booker Prize that same year. The novel went on to sell some six hundred thousand copies and amass nearly $6 million in sales.[1] It has been translated into forty languages (Annesley 146). For the next twenty years, Roy wrote no fiction, channeling her energies instead into hard-hitting essays critical of the government of India, particularly its neglect of rural populations, destruction of tribal peoples, pursuit of global capitalism, and jingoistic militarism, with occasional diatribes against the United States' new imperialism. In 2017 Roy returned to fiction, publishing *The Ministry of Utmost Happiness*, but as the critic Parul Sehgal notes, this novel essentially "acts as a companion piece to Roy's political writings." Roy's writing inspires a transformative pedagogy, whereby literature and politics cannot be easily disentangled, but her nonfiction writings introduce students overtly to an ethics of engagement and a call to participate in the struggle for a nonexploitative and just social and economic order. In the classroom, Roy's essays and speeches can help students gain knowledge of political issues affecting the disenfranchised in the Global South while illustrating the interconnections between local and international issues.

Teaching the conflicts and controversies that surround the nonfiction writing, moreover, can foster critical thinking about the role of reason and emotion in expository writing.

The point of teaching Roy's political writing is to examine how she challenges sanctioned ignorance and willful indifference among those comfortably situated or in power. Roy notes that "the most successful secession movement in India is the secession of the middle and upper classes to outer space. They have their own universe, . . . their own media, their own controversies, and they're disconnected from everything else" ("Un-Victim"). This criticism of middle- and upper-class Indians can be extended to American society, often trapped in its own exceptionalism and unable to see or to empathize with the plight of people in other parts of the world, especially the Middle East, in which the United States is nonetheless deeply involved, politically and economically.

Roy's essays function as jeremiad, lament, and manifesto, melding inquiry, exploration, critique, accusation, and exhortation. A superb wielder of words, Roy employs the linguistic and aesthetic toolkit to shock, seduce, and skewer. Writing in a vein that eludes the categories both of journalism and academic prose, she produces riotous combinations of manifestoes, reportage, and speeches that are marked by heteroglossia.[2] Though heteroglossia is typically associated with the genre of the novel, Tedra Osell's analysis of the early eighteenth-century "essay periodical" uncovers "structural patterns of heteroglossic dialogue and exchange" that "model and maintain the emerging idea of the public sphere as the arena in which individuals . . . could engage," contributing to "public debate on a variety of subjects" (284). Joseph Epstein's characterization of the personal essay as "a form of discovery" offers a useful context to probe Roy's work, for she uses the essay as personal exploration of her position "on complex issues, problems, questions, subjects," testing her "feelings, instincts, thoughts in the crucible of composition" (qtd. in Ryan 41). Yet she directs others to invest in similar examination. Emily Apter argues that Roy's articulations are "weaponized thought," loaded exhortations to the reader to join her in becoming informed and engaged (7). Roy translates the dull "technocratic report that camouflages violence" into impassioned prose (Nixon 76). By doing so, she tells a story ordinary people can understand so we can "snatch our future back from the world of experts": "Only the young or the very naïve believe that injustice will disappear just as soon as it has been pointed out. But sometimes it helps to outline the shape of the beast in order to bring it down" (Roy, *Shape* 151, ix).

Along with criticism of the Indian state, Roy exposes the global workings of militarism and industrial and commercial development. Appealing simultaneously to a local and an international audience, Roy resorts to the shared goal of "saving the environment" for maximum appeal: "The war for the Narmada valley is not just some exotic tribal war, or a remote rural war or even an exclusively Indian war. *It's a war for the rivers and the mountains and the forests of the world*" ("Greater Common Good" 65; emphasis added). To this war, against the state as well as ambitious industrial and commercial interests, she invites anyone ready to do battle: "All sorts of warriors from all over the world, anyone who wishes to enlist, will be honoured and welcomed. Every kind of soldier will be needed. Doctors, lawyers, teachers, judges, journalists, students, sportsmen, painters, actors, singers, lovers. . . . The borders are open, folks! Come on in" (65).

Roy's brand of "ecocentrism" (Vadde 534), however, is not just about the natural landscape but equally about the "human landscapes in which marginalized groups and the environment are coextensive" (Lobnik 126). While an ecocritical lens is pedagogically fruitful for studying Roy's writing—because it allows for an appreciation of her stunning and arresting imagery and her keen sensitivity to the value of every sentient being and small facet of nature—it is important to emphasize that in her essays she is not talking about saving pristine landscapes; rather her energy is directed to humanizing the vulnerable people and communities who are often rendered invisible and expendable by well-meaning naturalists and environmentalists who are passionate about preserving untouched nature. In Upamanyu Pablo Mukherjee's view, Roy underscores "the relationship between a state and its citizens" as "a matrix of contest (profoundly unequal) for land, river, forests, and fish" (23). The state's most marginalized citizens who live in intimate relationship with the "land, river, forests, and fish" often lose the battle as they are forcibly displaced or have no option but to move elsewhere for their livelihood. Roy's "The Greater Common Good," which thrust her forcefully into the thick of a national conversation on development, modernity, and big dams, brings together facts culled from government documents, World Bank studies, and testimonials from activists for a fulmination that is both a sharply crafted analysis and a tirade. Tabassum Ruhi Khan offers a compelling reading of it as irony, satire, and symbol and shows how Roy exposes the farcical reasoning of the state.[3]

Amid the big story, with facts and figures about the millions of hectares of inundated land and cubic meters of water, Roy inserts small, particular stories of the people she meets, effectively illustrating the conscious use of heteroglossia. She describes the big and the small simultaneously, juxtaposing an "aesthetic of largeness" with an "aesthetic of smallness" (Najmi). Woven through these articulations are lightning bolts of pronouncements that are clearly intended to shock: "India lives in its villages, we're told, in every other sanctimonious public speech. That's bullshit. . . . India doesn't live in her villages. India *dies* in her villages. India gets kicked around in her villages" ("Greater Common Good" 50). Paying attention to her expressive techniques as we study this and other essays prevents Roy from being turned into a sort of sociological introduction or case study and enables one to highlight the complex politics of representation and narration at work even in the most factual of her writings.

Teaching Roy's polemical essays is nonetheless fraught with challenges that must be discussed in the classroom. Roy's onslaughts against the government of India, for instance, are anchored in research that some consider meticulous and others sloppy. The issues she embraces are wide-ranging: the nuclearization of India, the construction of big dams that displace thousands of people from their homes, the opening up of tribal lands to mining companies so that they can extract commercially lucrative ore, the continued occupation by Indian military forces of Kashmir. Given the breadth of issues broached in her essays, researchers in particular subject areas often take issue with specifics, while nonspecialists may find that the author's knowledge across these areas is nothing short of impressive. Roy's range of interests can sometimes be construed as betraying a lack of focus—unlike, say, P. Sainath, the equally internationally renowned investigative journalist whose stories feature the plight of rural communities, specifically the Indian farmer, or Mahasweta Devi, the famous Bengali novelist and short story writer who has devoted herself to the cause of the tribal peoples.

The resistance to Roy's message seems to stem from the clamorous nature of her critique, the wide range of her targets, and the heteroglossic, literary quality of her nonfiction, displayed in her inclusion of diverse small stories and impassioned declarations. The noted historian of India Ramachandra Guha uses strong words to characterize Roy as "self-regarding and self-indulgent" ("Arun Shourie"). In "Perils of Extremism," Guha delivers this forceful assessment of Roy's intervention in debates on development and environmental activism: "The essays she writes are unredeemingly negative. . . . There are no alternatives and no solutions: only rage, and more rage." Guha is himself sympathetic to the Adivasi (tribal peoples) and the ravages to the land and to their lives that they have endured. However, he believes in the possibility of "a sensitively conceived and sincerely implemented plan to make adivasis true partners in the development process" ("Adivasis" 3311). By contrast, Roy has no faith in the judiciary, the media, and the state—all of whom, she declares, are handmaidens to corporate powers. If her objective is to express rage—because those whose lives are being devastated are not even permitted the "grace of rage" ("Greater Common Good" 81)—then she has succeeded.

Guha and other critics of Roy are harshly critical of what they perceive as her lack of nuance. Roy is part of a subset of Indian citizens who resist and reject the narrative of development and question the government's attachment to what they see as a destructive path. There are no modulations to her harsh denunciations, no willingness to consider how development and harnessing of natural resources could proceed alongside care and attention to people's lives and cultures. In her essay "Walking with the Comrades," Roy gives us portraits of the Maoists and their lives with details she gleans from spending three weeks with them in the forests (that the Maoists admitted Roy into their midst is clear evidence of the trust they have in her and her writings).[4] She has been harshly criticized for her romanticized portrait of the Maoists, which is vastly different from the Indian government's characterization of them as an "infestation" (*Walking* 45). At the end of a day of seemingly endless walking, she and the Maoists settle down outdoors for the night. She is enthusiastic about her sleeping quarters: "It's the most beautiful room I have slept in in a long time. My private suite in a thousand-star hotel" (57). Her description of the armed Maoists as smiling comrades who "sang sweetly, as though it was a folk song about a river or a forest blossom" (61), presents them, despite the omnipresence of weapons, as bucolically innocuous. One could reject this rose-tinted portrayal outright, or one could see it as an invitation to understand the Maoists' motivations and engage them as complex human beings.

Roy's combination of reasoned argument with emotionally charged statements offer examples of a form of rhetorical heteroglossia that can be problematic for her critics. In "The End of Imagination," Roy's outraged cry against India's testing of nuclear weapons in 1998, the author connects India's nuclear ambitions with a betrayal of the needs of the masses: "India's nuclear bomb is the final act of betrayal by a ruling class that has failed its people. However many garlands we heap on our scientists, however many medals we pin to their chests, the truth is that it is far easier to make a bomb than to educate four hundred million people" (27). Roy points out that the bomb would destroy not just Pakistan (India's archenemy) but also India, writing, "Though we are separate countries, we share skies, we share winds, we share water. . . . [B]omb Karachi, then Gujarat and Rajasthan, perhaps even Bombay, will burn" (17). Alongside this commonsense argument are passages entirely focused on emotional outburst. Consider this utterance: "If protesting against having a nuclear bomb implanted in my brain is anti-Hindu and anti-national, then I secede. I hereby declare myself an independent, mobile republic. . . . I have no flag. . . . My world has died. And I write to mourn its passing" (15–16).

Such passages have led to charges of not only self-indulgence but also antinationalism, which she anticipates in the passage above. On the international stage, Roy takes on the seemingly unstoppable adversarial forces of global capitalism and American militarism, posing a potential challenge for teachers using her essays in classrooms in the United States. In her 2001 essay "The Algebra of Infinite Justice," she fulminates against the government of George W. Bush for its decision to bomb Afghanistan in retaliation for the September 2001 attacks on the United States. She is fierce in her castigation of the United States' global interference:

> America's foreign policy: its gunboat diplomacy, its nuclear arsenal, its vulgarly stated policy of "full spectrum dominance," its chilling disregard for non-American lives, its barbarous military interventions, its support for despotic and dictatorial regimes, its merciless economic agenda that has munched through the economies of poor countries like a cloud of locusts. Its marauding multinationals who are taking over the air we breathe, the ground we stand on, the water we drink, the thoughts we think. (164–65)

Roy is not interested in nuance; in fact, she eschews nuance. For example, there were undoubtedly American soldiers who were sensitive to the Iraqi people and who displayed nuanced behavior, but Roy focuses on the fundamental ethical failure that led to the invasion and occupation of Iraq. Roy's refusal to allow nuance to soften her protest against injustice might lead to a perception of her writing as hyperbolic and hysterical, but one might also argue that nuances might tacitly buttress an oppressive status quo in the name of rhetorical fairness. Students should be invited to explore charges of the lack of nuance and antinationalism as well as the debates and controversy that stem from her heteroglossic use of reasoned and emotion-laden appeals.

In the two essays discussed above, Roy criticizes the blind nationalism of those who rally around nation and flag without sufficient analysis. The use of the first person in "The End of the Imagination" suggests that she does not presume to speak for all Indians, but she implicitly exhorts others to examine their own frameworks. Roy's antinationalistic stance even led to her being imprisoned, testifying to her commitment to freedom of speech and truth rather than national belonging. In the classroom, we can productively explore our own stance toward the sometimes conflicting demands of patriotism and a responsible critique of policies that might be unjust or even devastating for others. Roy's criticism of Indian governmental actions and policies can lead us to discussions of several important questions and issues: Is questioning the violence of "national security" discourse antinational? Is there room in North America (and Europe) to criticize one's country, as Roy is doing in her essay? What is the place of emotions, especially rage and outrage, in expository forms of writing?

Far from being restricted to the South Asian region, Roy's engagement has a global reach. Roy's essays and writings command a formidably large audience. In the United States and Europe, newspapers such as *The Guardian* and *The New York Times* review her work and interview her, as do magazines like *The Paris Review* and the *New Statesman*. She has also appeared on National Public Radio. In India, her essays are first published in the newsmagazine *Outlook* and then later gathered into collections. Roy continues to wage a constant war in the face of criticism as well as her opponents' efforts to silence her. Teaching her nonfiction requires the ability to translate her interventions into an American pedagogical context. The issues she raises are urgent and pressing and can connect the study of textual technique to wider political issues in India as well as the United States. Roy's nonfiction stimulates an eclectic border-crossing pedagogy able to locate her work within a complex social arena of a combative, engaged rhetoric. She will not cease the harangue, and she will not go gently into the good night.

Notes

1. According to 2012 figures on all Booker winners ("Booker Prize").

2. Bakhtin sees heteroglossia as a "decentralizing tendenc[y] in the life of language" (274). It is not surprising, therefore, that Roy, who seeks to unsettle and disrupt, should employ this type of rhetorical technique.

3. Among the many analyses that have been written about "The Greater Common Good," Khan's and Nixon's stand out for their textured and compelling engagement.

4. "Walking with the Comrades" first appeared in the Indian news magazine *Outlook* in 2010 and was reissued in book form in 2012. My quotations are taken from the book.

Works Cited

Annesley, James. *Fictions of Globalization*. Continuum, 2006.

Apter, Emily. "Weaponized Thought: Ethical Militance and the Group-Subject." *Grey Room*, no. 14, Winter 2004, pp. 6–25.

Bakhtin, Mikhail. "Discourse in the Novel." *The Dialogic Imagination: Four Essays by M. M. Bakhtin*, edited by Michael Holquist, translated by Holquist and Caryl Emerson, U of Texas P, 1981, pp. 269–422.

"Booker Prize 2012: Sales for All the Winners and the 2012 Shortlist, including Hilary Mantel." *The Guardian*, 10 Oct. 2012, www.theguardian.com/news/datablog/2012/oct/10/booker-prize-2012-winners-sales-data.

Guha, Ramachandra. "Adivasis, Naxalites and Indian Democracy." *Economic and Political Weekly*, vol. 42, no. 32, 11–17 Aug. 2007, pp. 3305–12.

———. "The Arun Shourie of the Left." *The Hindu*, 26 Nov. 2000, www.thehindu.com/2000/11/26/stories/13260411.htm. Accessed 21 May 2016.

———. "Perils of Extremism." *The Hindu*, 17 Dec. 2000, www.thehindu.com/2000/12/17/stories/1317061b.htm. Accessed 21 May 2016.

Khan, Tabassum Ruhi. "'Dam' the Irony for *The Greater Common Good*: A Critical Cultural Analysis of the Narmada Dam Debate." *International Journal of Communications*, vol. 6, 2012, pp. 194–213.

Lobnik, Mirja. "Sounding Ecologies in Arundhati Roy's *The God of Small Things*." *Modern Fiction Studies*, vol. 62, no. 1, Spring 2016, pp. 115–35.

Mukherjee, Upamanyu Pablo. "Arundhati Roy: Environment and Uneven Form." *Postcolonial Green: Environmental Politics and World Narratives*, edited by Bonnie Roos and Alex Hunt, U of Virginia P, 2010, pp. 17–31.

Najmi, Samina. "Naomi Shihab Nye's Aesthetics of Smallness and the Military Sublime." *MELUS*, vol. 35, no. 2, Summer 2010, pp. 151–71.

Nixon, Rob. "Unimagined Communities: Developmental Refugees, Megadams and Monumental Modernity." *New Formations*, vol. 69, no. 3, 2010, pp. 62–80.

Osell, Tedra. "Tatling Women in the Public Sphere: Rhetorical Femininity and the English Essay Periodical." *Eighteenth-Century Studies*, vol. 38, no. 2, Winter 2005, pp. 283–300.

Roy, Arundhati. *The Algebra of Infinite Justice*. Penguin, 2013.

———. "The Algebra of Infinite Justice." Roy, *Algebra*, pp. 151–67.

———. "The End of Imagination." Roy, *Algebra*, pp. 1–31.

———. "The Greater Common Good." Roy, *Algebra*, pp. 31–99.

———. *The Shape of the Beast: Conversations with Arundhati Roy*. Viking, 2008.

———. "The Un-Victim." Interview conducted by Amitava Kumar. *Guernica*, 15 Feb. 2011, www.guernicamag.com/interviews/roy_2_15_11/. Accessed 21 May 2016.

———. *Walking with the Comrades*. Penguin, 2012.

Ryan, Kathleen J. "Subjectivity Matters: Using Gerda Lerner's Writing and Rhetoric to Claim an Alternative Epistemology for the Feminist Writing Classroom." *Feminist Teacher*, vol. 17, no. 1, 2006, pp. 36–51.

Sehgal, Parul. "Arundhati Roy's Fascinating Mess." *The Atlantic*, July-Aug. 2017, www.theatlantic.com/magazine/archive/2017/07/arundhati-roys-fascinating-mess/528684/.

Vadde, Aarthi. "The Backwaters Sphere: Ecological Collectivity, Cosmopolitanism, and Arundhati Roy." *Modern Fiction Studies*, vol. 55, no. 3, Fall 2009, pp. 522–44.

Jill Didur

Landscape and the Environmental Picturesque in Kiran Desai's *The Inheritance of Loss*

Within environmental humanities, postcolonial studies has provided significant insight into how environmental change is interwoven with the narratives, landscapes, histories, and material practices of colonialism and globalization. Anglophone South Asian women writers have played a key role in foregrounding the relations between imperialism, patriarchy, and the exploitation of the environment in the name of human progress. This essay briefly traces how Kiran Desai and Anita Desai have explored these links through representations of the Himalayan environment, with particular attention to the Booker Prize–winning novel *The Inheritance of Loss*. Attention to the way the history of the environment bears on the settings of these writers' novels provides students with an essential interpretive tool in their study of South Asian women's writing. *Inheritance*'s account of everyday life in the picturesque hill station of Kalimpong, amid the rise of the Gorkha National Liberation Front (GNLF) in 1985–86, enables an exploration of how extractivist capitalism, social hierarchies, and the history of imperialism continue to shape and be shaped by the environment in postcolonial South Asia. Kiran Desai's "environmental picturesque," I argue, affords a useful vantage point from which to investigate the entanglement of nature, culture, gender, and empire in the postcolonial context.

Though outside the realm of creative writing, Vandana Shiva's *Staying Alive: Women, Ecology and Development* represents one of the earliest books in English to examine the link between ecological crisis, the oppression of women, and so-called development in South Asia. Shiva's book profiles the emergence of the Chipko movement in the 1970s and highlights how local women in the Garhwal Himalayas of Uttarakhand resisted the felling of trees in the Alaknanda Valley by a sporting goods company with permission from the state government. Soil erosion, landslides, and flooding have been linked to a long history of deforestation in the region despite so-called conservation policies established through the Indian Forest Act during colonial rule. Shiva's analysis of the Chipko movement underscores the gendered dynamic of this protest, where local women with long-established practices of living with the land were pitted against men with chain saws and a perception of the environment as a commodity to be extracted. What Shiva identifies as a form of ecofeminism, Chipko (which translates as "embrace" in English) involved women literally hugging the trees slated to be felled in order to prevent their removal. Through her analysis of the history of this movement, Shiva draws attention to the roots of postcolonial development practices in extractivist capitalism and colonialism and highlights how women's opposition to these practices questions the discourse of human ascendancy over nature and the environment.

Teaching the Environmental Humanities in South Asian Women's Writing

Predating Shiva's intervention into environmental debates in India, but sharing its focus on gendered responses to the environment, Kamala Markandaya's *Nectar in a Sieve* represents one of the first examples of an ecofeminist novel in anglophone South Asian women's writing. *Nectar in a Sieve*, as Dana Mount argues, "chronicles Rukmani's attempt to retrieve and recuperate those elements of her rural life that she feels most deeply about, namely her sense of community and connection with the land" (1). Foregrounding the novel's ecofeminist sensibility, Mount tracks how Markandaya's text complicates Romantic ideas of rural Indian women's connection to the land in ways that resonate with Shiva's analysis. Pointing out that ecofeminist scholars have sometimes "inappropriately borrowed from and appropriated the identities of non-Western women, . . . and especially Indian women" (5), Mount contends that *Nectar in a Sieve* deflects this tendency and instead portrays Rukmani as developing a close relation to the land through the embodied experience of labor, rather than coming to it innately. Rukmani's expression of connectedness to the land is also associated with a sexualized pleasure (thus resisting the patriarchal and colonial stereotype of passive Indian womanhood) (3) and questions capitalist ideas of land ownership, when she ultimately returns to the countryside to happily inhabit "land she had never owned to begin with" (15). *Nectar in a Sieve* also instantiates the kind of "environmental double consciousness" Rob Nixon has associated with postcolonial writing that invokes the landscape aesthetics of nature writing only to subvert them ("Environmentalism" 239). As Mount explains, Markandaya's novel "first offers, and then resists, the pastoral": on the one hand, the farm Rukmani labors on is described as an "unspoilt, fecund, provincial landscape," while on the other it is also the site of difficult labor, as well as death and violence following a storm (6). The "postcolonial pastoral," as Nixon describes it, "cannot be contained by the historical and spatial amnesia demanded by an all-English frame" ("Environmentalism" 240). As I demonstrate below, along with Markandaya, the work of anglophone South Asian women writers Anita Desai and Kiran Desai imagines alternative ways of representing the landscape and the environment in India's hill stations—what I call an environmental picturesque—while also foregrounding the history of patriarchal and colonial ways of knowing, looking, and dominating the nonhuman. Familiarizing students with picturesque aesthetics associated with Indian landscapes during the colonial era through drawing (Thomas and William Daniell), photography (Samuel Bourne), and travel writing (Fanny Parkes) allows the instructor to highlight how both Desais' novels mobilize and subvert this discourse in the postcolonial context.

Markandaya's subversion of British landscape aesthetics and Shiva's attention to the patriarchal underpinnings of extractivism resonate with Anita and Kiran Desai's challenge to the picturesque mode that has come to be associated with the Himalayan setting and Indian hill stations since their establishment in the early nineteenth century. "The aesthetics of the picturesque," argues Indira Ghose, "were enormously influential in moulding nineteenth-century travellers' perceptions of India" (38). "An attack on classical notions of beauty," the picturesque "advocated 'disorder' and 'irregularity' in landscape in both art and nature and suggested that even artificial rudeness was to be preferred to order and neatness" (Mitter 122). Ghose explains that while early modes of the picturesque focused on the English landscape and worked to unify this with representations of nature in the rest of the British Isles, the use of the picturesque in written and visual accounts of travel in India extended "the project of cultural and national self-definition" to colonial regions (39). Colonial travel narratives, as Jill Casid argues, "depended on the picturesque as a discourse of aesthetic and political control for the translation and forcible reshaping of the foreign and exotic into the familiar and tamed" (47). The exercise of representing India in picturesque terms gave the colonial artist the opportunity to define India as a place that could be known, controlled, and made familiar for settlement, despite the awe-inspiring Himalayan mountain range in the case of hill stations such as Shimla, Darjeeling, and Kalimpong. "To feel dwarfed and overawed by the untamed forces of nature," the historian Dane Kennedy argues, "may have been emotionally edifying for the passing traveler, but it was intensely disturbing to the invalid or other sojourner trying to find sanctuary from the plains. Such respite necessitated a landscape that had been tamed of its danger and reduced to human proportions, which is to say a landscape that had been made picturesque" (46).

This taming of the Himalayan landscape and its people involved a "selectivity of . . . vision" (Kennedy 40) in representations of these places in literature, photography, and visual art, as well as a physical remaking of the landscape surrounding hill stations. This included the construction of meandering hillside pathways, vistas encircled with guardrails, and European-style architecture that included Swiss cottages and Tudor houses reminiscent of "home"; the cultivation of plants and trees associated with the English gardens and countryside; and the stereotyping of indigenous groups. As Sarah Besky explains, the environment of the Darjeeling region in particular was also adapted for "an extractive landscape" made up of tea, "the *Camellia sinensis* variety, smuggled from China by British bioprospectors," as well as "the Japanese conifer *Cryptomeria japonica* . . . which made ideal packaging for exporting tea" (22). Within the hybrid botanical and cultural setting of the hill station, the aesthetic of the picturesque tamed the foreignness of the landscape, and its transplants imposed an uneasy harmony on far-flung biological and ethnic influences and filtered the effects of extractive capitalism, colonial control, and exploitation of the environment.

Where Markandaya reworks colonial ideas of the pastoral through a subtly ambivalent view of landscape and agricultural practices in the colonial context, Anita Desai's *Fire on the Mountain* challenges the discourse of the picturesque that continues to adhere to hill stations in the postcolonial era and explores its relation to the ongoing destructive effects of deforestation and extractivism on the local environment. Set in the hill station of Kasauli, Desai's novel traces how the "slow violence" (Nixon, *Slow Violence* 2) of colonial deforestation, overpopulation, and tourism has led to environmental degradation and drought-like conditions that plague the region in the postcolonial period. Within this context of increased environmental precarity, Desai explores how the picturesque setting of Kasauli serves as a distraction for the central character, Nanda Kaul, from her role in reproducing patriarchal power relations in her extended family. Drawn to the picturesque aesthetics associated with hill station environments, Nanda retreats to her summer cottage, Carignano, in an attempt to forget her unhappy marriage and the cycle of domestic violence that troubles the family life of her great-granddaughter, Raka. The droughtlike conditions in the region, hinted at in the novel's title, are brought to the fore when Raka, sent to spend the summer with Nanda, asks about forest fires that are visible in the hills surrounding Kasauli. Instead of enjoying the hill station's picturesque setting, Raka spends her time visiting burned-out houses. She is frightened by stories of animal research carried out at the nearby Pasteur Institute and haunted by memories of her mother's physical abuse at the hands of her father. Desai's novel thus explores the entanglement of the droughtlike conditions and the aesthetics of the picturesque in hill station settings as blunting social critique and links it to the ongoing effects of intergenerational colonial and patriarchal violence in the present (see Didur, "Guns").

Reading for the Environmental Picturesque

The subversion of picturesque discourse—or the environmental picturesque—associated with India's hill stations and Himalayan landscapes in Kiran Desai's *The Inheritance of Loss* is instrumental to the novel's critique of the ongoing effects of colonialism on the environment and marginalized communities in postcolonial India (see Didur, "Cultivating Community"). By introducing students to the friction Desai sets up between colonial and postcolonial ways of looking at the Himalayan landscape, I am able to help students recognize how the novel links the unequal effects of globalization to environmental concerns. Desai's *Inheritance* explores how the picturesque mode has shaped the landscape and human communities in the Himalayas under colonialism and suggests a more complicated understanding of the history of this setting is needed to break with this legacy and its influence on postcolonial culture, politics, and ecology in the region. The colonial legacy of environmental refashioning of the Himalayan landscape as picturesque is rendered unstable even as it is shown to be taken for granted by most of the postcolonial inhabitants of Kalimpong. Darjeeling (and nearby Kalimpong) first attracted the attention of the East India Company in 1827, when company representatives recommended it as an ideal spot for a sanitarium, later built and named Eden Sanitarium (Kennedy 22). Annexed by the British from the Kingdom of Sikkim in 1835, the Darjeeling area was viewed by the British as an ideal location for retreat from the heat of the plains, something that in the first half of the nineteenth century was believed to have serious health consequences for Europeans and was equated with "disease, decay and death" (19). Retreat to the cooler climate associated with places like the Eden Sanitarium in Darjeeling was seen as "especially suited for patients suffering from [what an army medical officer described as] 'general debility, whether arising from a long residence in the plains or depending on tardy convalescence from fevers and other acute disease'" (29). Apart from health and strategic political reasons, the other key attraction hill stations held for colonial subjects was their perceived adaptability of the environment to notions of the picturesque, a trope that pervades nineteenth-century travel writing when these areas were first explored and then settled by the British.

Throughout *Inheritance*, nostalgia for the picturesque aesthetic and European architecture associated with the built environment of Darjeeling and Kalimpong is evoked but then quickly undermined by related details of colonial exploitation of the environment and local communities. The retired judge Jemubhai's house, for example, is described as a grand building, reminiscent of a Scottish hunting lodge, with a magnificent view and a "fireplace made of silvery river stone [that] sparkled like sand" (28). "[B]uilt long ago by a Scotsman" whose "true spirit had called to him . . . and refused to be denied the right to adventure," the narrator notes, "As always, the price for such romance had been high and paid for by others. Porters had carried boulders from the riverbed—legs growing bandy, ribs curving into caves, backs into U's, faces being bent slowly to look always at the ground—up to this site chosen for a view that could raise the human heart to spiritual heights" (12).

Desai's narrator contrasts the forgotten physical labor of colonial subjects with the transcendent and self-absorbed outlook of the colonizer, whose fireplace made with "silvery river stone" adds to the picturesque romance of the house. The discourse of human ascendency that drives the colonizer's relation to the environment is challenged in the postcolonial context when the judge's man-made house is figured as under threat and decaying, while trees, plants, insects, and the natural elements appear to slowly reclaim the colonized space. The first night Jemubhai's granddaughter Sai spends in the house, for instance, the narrator observes that "she could sense the swollen presence of the forest, hear the hollow-knuckled knocking of the bamboo, the sound of the *jhora* that ran deep in the décolleté of the mountain" (34). Not only does the narrator personify the forests, plants, and waterfalls of the Himalayan landscape that surround Jemubhai's house, but the house is also described as "fragile in the balance of this night—just a husk." The fragility of the house is contrasted with the flourishing of the nonhuman when Sai becomes "aware of the sound of microscopic jaws slowly milling the house to sawdust" (34). Representations of human and nonhuman interaction in the landscape of Kalimpong and Darjeeling highlight the overlapping spheres of "the biotic, the public, and the private" and align Desai's novel with what Aarthi Vadde has described elsewhere as "narratives of connection" that criticize "humanism as an epistemology of ascendancy" (525).[1]

In addition to challenging ways of perceiving the landscape, Desai's environmental picturesque further undercuts colonial modes of inhabiting Kalimpong and nearby Darjeeling by choosing to set her novel in the mid-1980s during the violent uprising of the GNLF. Sai's math tutor and love interest, Gyan, is part of the Indian Nepali community that refers to its members as "Gorkhas." Gorkhas are a majority population with a long history in the region who are in a subordinate economic and social status in relation to a minority of elite Indians such as Sai's grandfather, her Bengali neighbors Lola and Noni, and expatriates like Father Booty. Referring to the Darjeeling region as a "shadow place," Besky argues the GNLF's assertion that the region is the Gorkhas' homeland and elite Indians' assumption that they are "at home" in the hill station share a common origin in the colonial history. "Shadow places," as Besky explains (following Val Plumwood) are "places materially and imaginatively oriented to the sustenance and enjoyment of others." "Darjeeling is a shadow place," according to Besky, "in the sense that much of its landscape is devoted to high-intensity plantation agriculture" (19). On the one hand, the novel portrays the GNLF having internalized colonial stereotypes of Nepalis as warlike and masculine, leveraging essentialist ideas of their community as a "martial race" to strengthen their cause for statehood. On the other hand, elite figures like Lola and Noni have internalized the colonial Edenic and picturesque discourses that have shaped hill station culture and are blind to the history of Gorkha economic exploitation and the effects of deforestation and tea plantation culture on the local environment. As Besky points out, Darjeeling is a place where "the cultivation of plants and the accumulation of capital have gone hand in hand with the production of identities since the annexation of the region from the Kingdom of Sikkim in 1835" (22). Thus, like most Indian Nepalis, Gyan's ancestors have lived for generations in the region, and like the exotic tea plants they have cultivated over many generations, they are now adapted to the new conditions of their home. However, unlike the *Camellia sinensis* or Darjeeling teas that have acquired the status of a PDO (protected designation of origin), the members of the Gorkha community in Desai's novel continue to be viewed as "exotic outsiders" (Besky 22), which deflects their claims for social justice.

These divergent modes of inhabiting the hill station that paradoxically share a common origin in the "ruins of empire" (Stoler 196) come to a head in the novel when followers of the GNLF build huts on the grounds of Lola and Noni's property, and Lola visits Pradhan, the leader of the Gorkha political movement in Kalimpong, to ask him to have them removed.[2] Not only does Pradhan refuse to intervene, he humiliates Lola in front of his followers, drawing attention to her precarious status as an elderly widow without patriarchal patronage in a shifting political landscape. Suddenly made to feel vulnerable to the masculinist culture of GNLF and as an interloper in the shifting power relations between Nepali and Indian communities in Kalimpong, Lola later curses her dead husband Joydeep's blindness to their neocolonial position in the hills. "Bastard!" Lola thinks. "Never a chink in his certainty, his poise. Never the brains to buy a house in Calcutta—no. No. Not that Joydeep, with his romantic notions of countryside living; with his Wellington boots, binoculars, and birdwatching book; with his Yeats, his Rilke (in German), his Mandelstam (in Russian); in the purply mountains of Kalimpong with his bloody Talisker and his Burberry socks" (244).

Joydeep's mimicry of English pastoral attitudes, love of Scotch whisky, and cosmopolitan cultural affinities are cursed by Lola for lulling her into a false sense of belonging in the anglophilic and picturesque hill station setting. After learning about her sister's humiliation in the meeting with Pradhan, Noni also chastises herself: "The real place has evaded them," she thinks. "The two of them had been fools feeling they were doing something exciting just by occupying this picturesque cottage, by seducing themselves with those old travel books in the library, searching for a certain angled light with which to romance themselves, to locate what had been conjured only as a tale to tell before the Royal Geographic Society" (247). Where Lola and Noni's mode of inhabiting the Himalayan region is mediated by picturesque discourse that frames the surrounding landscape as comfortably familiar and foreign, when they feel their property is threatened by squatters and landslides, they quickly recognize Kalimpong is really their "center . . . but they had never treated it as such" (247).

The idea of the Himalayas as an exclusive homeland for the Gorkhas as well as a space for retreat and recreation for elite cosmopolitan Indians is further complicated in the novel through references to the indigenous Lepcha population. As Kennedy has argued, colonial portraits of indigenous communities such as the Paharis near Shimla and Lepchas in Darjeeling as "nature's children" worked to enhance the Edenic qualities the British associated with hill station locations, while also neutralizing the threat these indigenous groups might have posed to the fantasy of "escape" that hill stations represented to colonial administrators (63). The short story "Lispeth," from Rudyard Kipling's *Plain Tales from the Hills*, for example, invokes these stereotypes through an account of an indigenous Pahari woman, Lispeth, hailing from the hill station of Kotgarh, who falls in love with an Englishman who "had come from Dehra Dun to hunt for plants and butterflies among the Simla hills" (9). The story conforms in many ways to the colonial practice of idealizing indigenous communities as innocent, childlike, and innately in tune with nature; Lispeth is described as "very lovely"; as possessing "eyes that were wonderful" (7), a ruddy complexion, and a hearty constitution; and as behaving in a truthful and loving manner in contrast to the threatening and deceptive character of Indian populations of the plains. In Desai's novel, a man who is known as "a miserable drunk" in the town and is later identified as Lepcha is wrongly arrested for the robbery at Cho Oyu and then severely beaten by the local police—a stark contrast to colonial representations of Lepchas as "tokens of the secluded and Edenic character of the places they inhabited" (Kennedy 227). The narrator of *Inheritance* describes how the police "reduced [the man] to a pulp, bashed his head until blood streamed down his face, knocked out his teeth, kicked him until his ribs broke" (226). When the wife of the beaten man visits Jemubhai to plead for charity (her husband is left blind by the police beating), she asks, "What will we do? . . . We are not even Nepalis, we are Lepcha" (263). The Lepcha woman emphasizes her family's marginal status in relation to the Gorkhas and reliance on the benevolence of the elite Indian residents like the judge. The childlike innocence and trustworthiness associated with colonial perceptions of indigenous figures is further challenged when, after the judge refuses to extend any charity to the tortured man's family, the wife later returns with her father to steal the judge's dog with the desperate hope of later selling it in the market (283).

Kiran Desai's use of the environmental picturesque to articulate a postcolonial double consciousness about the aesthetic, material, and colonial practices that have molded hill station ecologies foregrounds the relation between the natural world and social inequality in India today. *Inheritance* explores extractive landscapes in the Darjeeling region to reveal the entanglement of patriarchal, colonial, and capitalist modes of viewing and interacting with the environment. While the novel suggests that human ascendency continues to dominate the political and cultural dynamics of the Himalayan region and beyond, its attention to the coimplication of human and nonhuman agency in shaping hill station landscapes points to alternative modes for framing the pursuit of social justice in the postcolonial context. Teaching students to read for the environmental picturesque allows instructors to highlight how South Asian women's writing explores the entanglement of nature and culture and the enduring effects of colonialism and globalization on the environment in the present.

Notes

1. Roy's novel *The God of Small Things* also shares a focus on the entanglement of nature and culture in the Indian context. Kerala, as Vadde points out, "has historically been a crucial center of India's environmentalism versus development debate" (523). Roy's oeuvre as a whole (including her political writing), Vadde argues, "challenges institutions [that] wield power through the creation and subjugation of human and non-human others" (522). See also Didur's "Walk This Way" for a discussion of Roy's *Walking with the Comrades*. Scholarly monographs that significantly engage with South Asian women's writing and the environment include Mukherjee (for more on *The God of Small Things*) and Carrigan

(for a discussion of Lokugé's *Turtle Nest*). Anam explores environmental themes related to shipbreaking in Bangladesh and marine paleontology (*Bones of Grace*), and she has written about the link between climate change and catastrophic flooding in Bangladesh ("Losing").

2. Lola also raises the threat of landslides being precipitated by overbuilding on her property. Pretending to speak only broken English to try to hide her cosmopolitan identity and the fact that she had never learned Nepali, she tells Pradhan, "Have cut into the hill, land weak, landslides may occur." Pradhan, however, deflects this concern and suggests, "In fact, it's your house that might cause a landslide. Too heavy, no? Too big?" (244). See Ferguson for a discussion of landslides as symbolically disrupting normalized notions of belonging from various subject positions in the novel.

Works Cited

Anam, Tahmima. *The Bones of Grace*. Canongate, 2016.

———. "Losing the Ground beneath Their Feet." *The Guardian*, 3 Sept. 2008, www.theguardian.com/environment/2008/sep/04/climatechange.flooding.

Besky, Sarah. "The Land in Gorkhaland: On the Edges of Belonging in Darjeeling, India." *Environmental Humanities*, vol. 9, no. 1, 2017, pp. 18–39.

Carrigan, Anthony. *Postcolonial Tourism: Literature, Culture, and Environment*. Routledge, 2010.

Casid, Jill H. *Sowing Empire: Landscape and Colonization*. U of Minnesota P, 2005.

Desai, Anita. *Fire on the Mountain*. 1977. Random House India, 2008.

Desai, Kiran. *The Inheritance of Loss*. Atlantic Monthly Press, 2006.

Didur, Jill. "Cultivating Community: Counter Landscaping in Kiran Desai's *The Inheritance of Loss*." *Postcolonial Ecologies: Literature of the Environment*, edited by Elizabeth DeLoughrey and George B. Handley, Oxford UP, 2011, pp. 43–61.

———. "Guns and Roses: Reading the Picturesque Archive in Anita Desai's *Fire on the Mountain*." *Textual Practice*, vol. 27, no. 3, 2013, pp. 499–522.

———. "Walk This Way: Postcolonial Travel Writing of the Environment." *The Cambridge Companion to Postcolonial Travel Writing*, edited by Robert Clarke, Cambridge UP, 2018, pp. 33–48.

Ferguson, Jesse Patrick. "Violent Dis-placements: Natural and Human Violence in Kiran Desai's *The Inheritance of Loss*." *The Journal of Commonwealth Literature*, vol. 44, no. 2, June 2009, pp. 35–49.

Ghose, Indira. *Women Travellers in Colonial India: The Power of the Female Gaze*. Oxford UP, 1998.

Kennedy, Dane Keith. *The Magic Mountains: Hill Stations and the British Raj*. U of California P, 1996.

Kipling, Rudyard. "Lispeth." *Plain Tales from the Hills*, Penguin, 1990.

Lokugé, Chandani. *Turtle Nest*. Penguin, 2003.

Markandaya, Kamala. *Nectar in a Sieve*. 1954. Signet, 1982.

Mitter, Partha. *Much Maligned Monsters: A History of European Reactions to Indian Art*. U of Chicago P, 1992.

Mount, Dana C. "Bend Like the Grass: Ecofeminism in Kamala Markandaya's *Nectar in a Sieve*." *Postcolonial Text*, vol. 6, no. 3, 2011, www.postcolonial.org/index.php/pct/article/view/1189/1208.
Mukherjee, Upamanyu Pablo. *Postcolonial Environments: Nature, Culture and the Contemporary Indian Novel in English*. Palgrave Macmillan, 2010.
Nixon, Rob. "Environmentalism and Postcolonialism." *Postcolonial Studies and Beyond*, edited by Ania Loomba, Duke UP, 2005, pp. 233–51.
———. *Slow Violence and the Environmentalism of the Poor*. Harvard UP, 2011.
Plumwood, Val. "Shadow Places and the Politics of Dwelling." *Australian Humanities Review*, vol. 44, 2008, pp. 139–50.
Roy, Arundhati. *The God of Small Things*. Random House, 1997.
———. *Walking with the Comrades*. Penguin, 2012.
Shiva, Vandana. *Staying Alive: Women, Ecology and Development*. Zed Books, 1988.
Stoler, Ann Laura. "Imperial Debris: Reflections on Ruins and Ruination." *Cultural Anthropology*, vol. 23, no. 2, May 2008, pp. 191–219.
Vadde, Aarthi. "The Backwaters Sphere: Ecological Collectivity, Cosmopolitanism, and Arundhati Roy." *Modern Fiction Studies*, vol. 55, no. 3, Fall 2009, pp. 522–44.

Filippo Menozzi and Deepika Bahri

South Asian Women's Poetry as World Literature

In this essay we discuss the relevance of teaching poetry by the contemporary writers Meena Alexander, Meena Kandasamy, Rupi Kaur, and Raman Mundair in courses on world literature in order to pose questions about language, distant versus close reading, and the place of poetry in a conversation dominated largely by the novel. The concluding section of the essay suggests that the world literature debate also needs to contend with the potentially revolutionary impact of born-digital texts by addressing the Indian Canadian Instapoet and writer Kaur's unprecedented success in the literary marketplace. The courses and approaches described in this essay accomplish multiple objectives: they introduce students to debates on world literature, test its parameters through a focus on poetry, and explore questions of language, translation, canonicity, and the global marketplace of literature.

Since its first emergence in nineteenth-century Europe in writings by Goethe, Karl Marx, and Friedrich Engels, the concept of world literature corresponded to an emerging consciousness of the interconnectedness produced by modernity as a global system of exploitation and exchange. In their *Communist Manifesto*, Marx and Engels challenged the restriction of literatures to national spheres because, in a commodified world, texts circulate and are produced and reproduced globally (16). The world literature paradigm positions texts within the frame of what Fredric Jameson calls a "singular modernity" produced by the worldwide expansion of capitalism as an uneven and unequal mode of production. How do South Asian women writers respond to and engage with this wider field of circulation and commodification? Liverpool John Moores University, where one of the authors of this essay is based, offers an optional third-year course on world literature that includes texts by such authors as Meena Alexander, Sujata Bhatt, Meena Kandasamy, and Arundhati Roy alongside writers from other regions and languages. Teaching South Asian women's writing through the prism of world literature enables teachers to reposition writers beyond the purview of nation and cultural identity and connect their works to the historical dynamics of capitalist modernity.

The paradigm of world literature reemerged in the early 2000s after the publication of a pivotal essay by Franco Moretti, "Conjectures on World Literature." Moretti argues that the single text or literary work is an insufficient object for analyzing how literary works engage with and represent the history of a global modernity. Instead of focusing on one text, literary critics should address how literature is part of a global "world system" that has reorganized nations and economies through the expansion of capitalism as a hegemonic mode of production. According to Immanuel Wallerstein, the modern world system is the dominant form produced by capitalism since its expansion in the sixteenth century (23). This shift from text to system entails a rearrangement of traditional ways of locating and interpreting literary texts: instead of addressing national literary histories, literature should be seen as part and parcel of the world system of capitalism; instead of being read closely, texts should be read distantly, so they can disclose wider patterns and trends through an examination of large sets of written material. Moretti's claims triggered intense debates in literary studies: Emily Apter argues for a renewed attention to the "politics of untranslatability" and "close reading with a worldview" (64). Aamir Mufti questions the argument for distant reading, emphasizing the "linguistic heterogeneity" that animates literary production in the Global South instead. Mufti argues that the universalism of the world literary paradigm has to be "uncoupled from the effects of standardization and homogenization"; neither pedagogy nor criticism should invest in distant reading or close reading "for its own sake" (493).

In our view, the subject specificity of literary studies demands some kind of close reading, while attending to wider sociopolitical currents affecting literary production in global modernity. Engaging the question of linguistic transparency and translatability, for instance, must take stock of the individual experience of cultural creolization as well as the reappropriation of English as a decolonizing textual strategy. Negotiating proximity and distance in teaching these writers also raises the question of poetic language itself as a sort of capital being circulated and accumulated globally, mirroring wider dynamics proper to the process of exploitation and peripheralization of the Global South.

Reading, Language, Capital, and Translatability

A world literature perspective can raise questions about the "situation" of the writer, the text, and the reader, an issue South Asian poets themselves have been reflecting on in their works. For example, in her essay "What Use Is Poetry?," Alexander offers a striking image of "the poet in the twenty-first century as a woman standing in a dark doorway." She is an "odd" sort of "homemaker," who maintains "a home at the edge of the world." The poet speaks, indeed has to "invent a language marked by many tongues." The figurative poet described by Alexander signals her biographical trajectory. Born in Allahabad, raised in India and Sudan, and residing in New York till her death, this diasporic South Asian's life is marked by dislocation and many "fault lines," the title of her memoir. In *Poetics of Dislocation*, she writes, "[T]he internal map of place is torn . . . what we are faced with are not fixed settlements but pinhole scatterings, dismemberments, a 'line of flight,' several lines of flight" (6–7). Alexander's poetry is a lyrical representation of ontological deterritorialization mirroring the poet's attempt to rewrite and redraw the torn map of memory and a sense of the past that "chops and scatters our identity in the air, bits and pieces capable of ceaseless rearrangement" (7). While writing in English, a language of supposed global transparency and accessibility, Alexander expresses the loss of a stable sense of belonging and the metaphorical dismemberment provoked by the insecurity of diasporic lives caught in the currents of globalization.

The questions addressed by Alexander place South Asian women's writing within current debates on the use of language, the importance of critical reading, and the fact that the economic regime of global modernity has triggered a seemingly paradoxical effect: while global capitalism makes the work of anglophone South Asian women writers circulate widely, this system also reproduces forms of inequality and uprootedness. As Wai Chee Dimock puts it, going beyond the national paradigm means unsettling the "almost automatic equation between the literary and the territorial" (175). In the classroom, Alexander's claims to dislocation and uprootedness can be usefully linked to a global situation determined by the deterritorializing logic of capitalism.

Indeed, contemporary South Asian women writers are centrally preoccupied with the way linguistic heterogeneity and the worldliness of language inform the making of literary works. Kandasamy examines language as poetic medium in a poem titled "Mulligatawny Dreams." Based in Chennai, South India, Kandasamy writes about issues with urgent political valence. Her work addresses feminism, anticasteism, and anticensorship, often using social media and online platforms and requiring us to attend to new mediums of production and circulation. In "Mulligatawny Dreams" Kandasamy begins with a list of English words that derive from other languages, followed by lines that reflect on the role of English in giving shape to her poetry:

> i dream of an english
> full of the words of my language.
>
> an english in small letters
> an english that shall tire a white man's tongue

Starting with a series of untranslated words that have become part of English while being of non-European origin, the poem troubles a generic stance toward the questions of language and translatability. Kandasamy's poem starts by listing nouns such as *anaconda*, *candy*, *cash*, and *catamaran*, which arguably derive from Tamil. Most of these words refer to non-European products, commodities, and natural resources extracted from peripheral economies and distributed in the global market, suggesting that the wealth of "english" derives from a chain of global exploitation in which center and periphery are in constant interrelationship. These words embody a global history of incorporation, circulation, and appropriation that captures what Benita Parry has described as the "proximity of discordant discourses and discrete narrative registers" (39), characterizing capitalism at the periphery. Their loanword status testifies to the links between poetry in English and global capital, even suggesting that language, to an extent, is a kind of capital accumulated through the exploitation of Asian societies. Such a reading can insert South Asian women's poetry into debates on primitive accumulation along with linguistic and cognitive capitalism. These texts allow for teaching strategies moving beyond the East-West dichotomy by emphasizing the concrete realities of combined and uneven development.

Kandasamy claims that the language she is using in her poem should go beyond "white man" sensibility. The words *I* and *English* are not capitalized throughout the poem, suggesting a language in "small letters" that questions hegemonic uses of English while expanding its communicative possibilities through minority writing. In this "english," Kandasamy muses, "a pregnant woman is simply stomach-child-lady." The poet's use of kenning, a device common in Old English poetry, also suggests that the language has always harbored these possibilities, allowing the anglophone South Asian writer to repurpose the language for her own ends. In a world riven by inequality, Kandasamy seeks to level "english" to a series of infinite choices that allow for "the magic of black eyes and brown bodies."

In an undergraduate course on world literature, "Mulligatawny Dreams" promotes debate about the status of English, because the poem is not merely written in English but language is its object. Instead of reading the poem as a representation of cultural difference or Indian literature, Kandasamy's lines are connected to the use of a globally hegemonic language, English, and the practice of close reading is interrogated in relation to the global dimension of the language of the poem and its entanglements in the historical dynamics of global modernity. From this perspective Kandasamy's poem is grasped as a process of translation and self-translation responsive to the inequities, exploitations, and distances produced by global capitalism. As the Warwick Research Collective points out, the world literature debate allows critics to "grasp reading and translating as themselves social rather than solitary processes, and thereby . . . attend to the full range of social practices implicated: writing as commodity labour, the making of books, publishing and marketing, the social 'fate' of a publication" (28). These remarks complement David Damrosch's emphasis on translation as an "expansive transformation of the original, a concrete manifestation of cultural exchange" (84). Kandasamy's interventions on the status of English as a sort of poetic, linguistic capital and a symbol of the exclusions and inequalities produced by global modernity help connect South Asian poetry to some central preoccupations that currently animate the world literature debate.

Form and Medium

We now turn to the evolving digital scape of literary production to explore an unprecedented question: are new modes of producing and circulating texts using online platforms beginning to breach the canon of world literature? While questions of language, translation, distant versus close reading, uneven marketplace, and the canon have been central to discussions of world literature, the actual medium used to usher the text into the world has received less attention. B. Venkat Mani's concept of bibliomigrancy, "the material and digital circulation of books" (5), is a crucial corollary to any discussion of translation, reception, interpretation, and, indeed, the market or the canon. Mani is invested in exploring the "multiple meanings of world literature: as a philosophical ideal, a mode of reading, a pedagogical strategy, a unit of aesthetic evaluation, a strategy of affiliation, and a system of classification" (14). How do libraries, both brick and mortar and virtual, contribute to the fund of world literature? Even more crucially, in what sense does *Instagram* poetry or the video performance of a poem with a huge global audience challenge the idea of the world and of literature? In our concluding discussion of the work of Rupi Kaur and a comparative gloss on the Indian-British poet Raman Mundair, we pose the following questions for teachers invested in the material production and circulation of texts in the twenty-first century: How should we understand the born-digital text—written, aural, or audiovisual—within the context of world literature? How should we teach the born-digital text of a poet such as Kaur, unmarked as it was in its original appearance on *Instagram* by national origin, date, or the imprimatur of any publishing house? What challenges lie ahead of us as teachers confronting literary production in cyberspace, with all its contingencies and contradictions? Or, as Alexander trenchantly asked, "How to make sense of Cicero's mnemonic—the order of places securing the order of things—in a world that faces the plethora of postings in cyberspace?" (*Poetics* 7).

These questions first surfaced in a course on women's literature featuring, among others, established writers such as Kamala Das and Mundair. We had been discussing the appropriation of English by Das as personal and idiosyncratic, with self-confessed "distortions" and "queernesses" in her poem "An Introduction" (59), and Mundair's delight in the languages and Englishes she encountered from "Phagwara to Shetland (via Manchester and Glasgow)." At this point, a student asked if we could discuss Kaur, a writer who had become "a phenomenon" (Groen), particularly, but not only, among young women. Kaur began sharing her poetry on *Tumblr* around 2013, subsequently moving it to *Instagram*, an Internet-based social photo- and video-sharing application, where she now has more than 1.4 million followers worldwide.

Kaur writes candidly about rape, menstruation, and domestic abuse as well as the everyday tyranny of expectations of depilation and feminine behavior. Using text-image hybridity, Kaur adds telling illustrations to her prose and verse. One short poem suggests how a woman should respond to a tacit suggestion that she shave her legs because the hair is "growing back" : "remind / that boy your body is not his home / he is a guest." This is accompanied by the line drawing of a woman that depicts "hair" on the body as outcroppings of flowers, leaves, mushrooms, and other flora of the natural world. In 2014 she gathered these online poems and prose pieces and used Amazon's self-publishing platform for a collection titled *Milk and Honey*.[1] The rest, as the saying goes, is history: "*Milk and Honey* landed on the Amazon top seller list for Canadian literature, alongside literary icons such as Margaret Atwood. It also made it to the second spot on the Amazon bestseller list for poetry" (Jain). A year later "*Milk and Honey* was snapped up by American publisher Andrews McMeel." Packed "with deeply personal poems that sweep from heartache and trauma to recovery and resilience," it garnered "more than a million copies in print," stayed on *The New York Times* best-seller list for over seven months, and led to a two-book deal to be published in five countries (Groen).

In March 2015, when Kaur posted a photo of herself with a bloodstain on her pajamas and a coin-sized patch of menstrual blood on her bed as part of a visual rhetoric project, *Instagram* removed the post "because it doesn't follow our Community Guidelines." Kaur reposted the photo, berating a society that publishes "countless photos" of underage women who "are objectified. pornified. and treated less than human" (qtd. in Jain). Her post went viral; *Instagram* reinstated her photo with an apology. This photograph prompted a master's thesis using "Kaur's Instagram controversy as a case study to examine mainstream news media responses to Kaur's period photograph published on Instagram" (Lese 11). Kaur has been pronounced "the voice of her generation" (Groen) and extolled by the *HuffPost* contributor Erin Spencer as "the poet every woman needs to read." Although many readers question the quality of the writing, the disconcerting conclusion is that Kaur's writing resonates with an impressively large readership not only despite but because of writing that is "raw, unpolished, strikingly direct" (Jain).

Bypassing the usual gatekeepers of the world literature canon—publishing houses, prizes, critical responses, and syllabi that draw upon these resources—digital publications that resonate with millennials and younger audiences exert new pressure on teachers to formulate meaningful pedagogic responses. Groen's article comes to the following unnerving conclusion: "what Kaur's success shows is that if you want to hook millennial readers, you shouldn't bother with *The New Yorker* or the Griffin Prize; instead, put that poem on Tumblr or Twitter or Facebook or Instagram—or all of them—and reach an infinitely larger audience." In lieu of scholarship in peer-reviewed journals, *eNotes.com*, which includes study guides to William Shakespeare's *Romeo and Juliet*, Robert Frost's "The Road Not Taken," and George Orwell's *1984*, offers sections titled "Summary," "Themes," "Analysis," and "Homework Help" on Kaur's *Milk and Honey*, effectively recruiting her into the same canon as long-established classics.

Defying warnings about the death of poetry, the Kaur phenomenon points to an alternative feminist public sphere on the Internet, a formidable if unacknowledged populist wing of the house of world literature. The Internet gave this unlikely sensation her voice on a platform where, the shy writer says, "I could say what I wanted to say in a way I still felt comfortable. Whenever, however I wanted to" (Jain). A twenty-first-century pedagogy will need to respond to new platforms such as *Tumblr*, *Facebook*, and *Instagram* where Instapoets such as Kaur and the Somali-British writer Warsan Shire are able to connect instantly with readers through their personal feed. These platforms allow a writer to gloss and explain her work in direct communication with her readers, while allowing writers to respond to each other. One of Kaur's poems, for instance, is written in homage to Shire. Literature emerges here not as the province of professors and published critics but as a conversation among poets, writers, and readers, who determine the world-scape of literature in an intertextual feminist weave that traverses national boundaries without losing cultural specificity or reference to experience. Kaur's followers on *Instagram* often respond with their own poems or those of other feminist poets, arguably contributing to the *Gemeingut* of a feminist digital world literature.

The unexpected inclusion of Instapoetry in the classroom forces a confrontation with the implicit elitism, Anglo-European bias, and possible masculism of the paradigm of world literature. It also poses a more politically charged question: Is South Asian women's writing, even that of established writers, much less that of an Instapoet (albeit well published since her debut on a humbler, easily dismissed platform), fated to be consigned to peripheral aesthetic zones? Does the boundary between world and global literature, even more preciously global anglophone literature, tacitly privilege circulation and marketplace at the expense of equal footing in terms of quality? Kaur's poetry, typified by an impressive market share in the privileged medium of print despite modest beginnings on the leveled playing field of the Internet and a large following online, points to a global readership, something like community consensus, and a markedly feminist framework, all of which potentially broach and breach the hallowed order of things in discussions of world literature. Contemporary South Asian women writers are not simply products of globalization, but they also demand recognition of new networks of affiliation paradoxically produced by dislocations, alternative linguistic possibilities that tax and challenge what Kandasamy calls the "white man's tongue," and digital horizons of expression that test the hegemony of the canon and its gatekeepers.

Note

1. Kaur chose to self-publish *Milk and Honey* against the advice of her college professor, who warned her that she might be excluding herself from literary circles. "I sat with myself one day and asked: Who is in those prestigious literary circles? Do they represent me? Do they appreciate the topics I write about and the style in which I write? Do those gatekeepers let a demographic like mine through the door? And the answer was no. I was already barred from those literary circles, so self-publishing wouldn't make a difference" (qtd. in Jain).

Works Cited

Alexander, Meena. *Poetics of Dislocation.* U of Michigan P, 2009.

———. "What Use Is Poetry?" *World Literature Today*, Sept. 2013, www.worldliteraturetoday.org/2013/september/what-use-poetry-meena-alexander.

Apter, Emily. *The Translation Zone: A New Comparative Literature.* Princeton UP, 2006.

Damrosch, David. *How to Read World Literature.* Wiley-Blackwell, 2008.

Das, Kamala. "An Introduction." *Summer in Calcutta: Fifty Poems*, by Das, Rajinder Paul, 1965, pp. 59–60.

Dimock, Wai Chee. "Literature for the Planet." *PMLA*, vol. 116, no. 1, Jan. 2001, pp. 173–88.

Groen, Danielle. "How Rupi Kaur Became the Voice of Her Generation." *Flare*, 11 Nov. 2016, www.flare.com/culture/rupi-kaur-milk-and-honey-the-voice-of-her-generation/.

Jain, Atishsa. "A Poet and Rebel: How Insta-sensation Rupi Kaur Forced Her Way to Global Fame." *Hindustan Times*, 22 Oct. 2016, www.hindustantimes.com/brunch/a-poet-and-a-rebel-how-insta-sensation-rupi-kaur-forced-her-way-into-the-global-bestseller-lists/story-DCbkk7EBMxrSjdoFsxQmDM.html.

Jameson, Fredric. *A Singular Modernity*. Verso, 2002.

Kandasamy, Meena. "Mulligatawny Dreams." *Sampsonia Way*, 31 Oct. 2009, www.sampsoniaway.org/literary-voices/2009/10/31/mulligatawny-dreams/.

Kaur, Rupi. *Milk and Honey*. Andrews McMeel, 2016.

Lese, Kathryn M. *Padded Assumptions: A Critical Discourse Analysis of Patriarchal Menstruation Discourse*. James Madison U. Master's thesis, 2016, commons.lib.jmu.edu/cgi/viewcontent.cgi?article=1104&context=master201019.

Mani, B. Venkat. *Recoding World Literature: Libraries, Print Culture, and Germany's Pact with Books*. Fordham UP, 2016.

Marx, Karl, and Frederick Engels. *Manifesto of the Communist Party*. 1848. *Marxists Internet Archive*, www.marxists.org/archive/marx/works/download/pdf/Manifesto.pdf.

Moretti, Franco. "Conjectures on World Literature." *New Left Review*, no. 1, Jan.-Feb. 2000, pp. 54–68.

Mufti, Aamir R. "Orientalism and the Institution of World Literatures." *Critical Inquiry*, vol. 36, no. 3, Spring 2010, pp. 458–93.

Mundair, Raman. "Scots Dialect." *Internet Archive*, web.archive.org/web/20120212122952/http:/www.friendsofscotland.gov.uk/scotlandnow/issue-11/arts/raman-mundair.html. Accessed 19 Aug. 2020.

Parry, Benita. "Aspects of Peripheral Modernisms." *ARIEL*, vol. 40, no. 1, Jan. 2009, pp. 27–56.

Spencer, Erin. "Rupi Kaur: The Poet Every Woman Needs to Read." *HuffPost*, 22 Jan. 2015, www.huffingtonpost.com/erin-spencer/the-poet-every-woman-needs-to-read_b_6193740.html.

Wallerstein, Immanuel. *World-Systems Analysis: An Introduction*. Duke UP, 2004.

Warwick Research Collective. *Combined and Uneven Development: Towards a New Theory of World-Literature*. Liverpool UP, 2015.

Part V

Resources

Selected Resources for South Asian Women's Writing

These resources are meant to supplement materials provided in the lists of works cited in individual essays. The scholarly literature on this subject is so vast as to defy any attempts at a comprehensive bibliography. Instead, we offer a selective curated list and recommend a keyword search on the *MLA International Bibliography* as the volume of scholarship continues to grow.

Historical and Literary Contexts

Ali, Tariq, et al. *Kashmir: The Case for Freedom.* Verso, 2011.

Bose, Sugata, and Ayesha Jalal. *Modern South Asia: History, Culture, Political Economy.* Routledge, 2004.

Burton, Antoinette M. *Dwelling in the Archive: Women Writing House, Home, and History in Late Colonial India.* Oxford UP, 2003.

Butalia, Urvashi. *The Other Side of Silence: Voices from the Partition of India.* Penguin, 2000.

Chawla, Devika. *Home, Uprooted: Oral Histories of India's Partition.* Fordham UP, 2014.

Jaffrelot, Christophe. *A History of Pakistan and its Origins.* Anthem, 2002.

Johnson, Gordon, editor. *The New Cambridge History of India.* Cambridge UP, 1988–2013. 24 vols.

Loomba, Ania, and Ritty Lukose, editors. *South Asian Feminisms.* Duke UP, 2012.

Mann, Michael. *South Asia's Modern History: Thematic Perspectives.* Routledge, 2015.

Mehrotra, Arvind Krishna. *A History of Indian literature in English.* Columbia UP, 2003.

Menon, Ritu, and Kamla Bhasin. *Borders and Boundaries: Women in India's Partition.* Rutgers UP, 1998.

Metcalf, Barbara, and Thomas Metcalf. *A Concise History of Modern India.* 3rd ed., Cambridge UP, 2012.

Pandey, Gyanendra. *Remembering Partition: Violence, Nationalism and History in India.* Cambridge UP, 2004.

Talbot, Ian. *A History of Modern South Asia: Politics, States, Diasporas.* Yale UP, 2016.

———. *Pakistan: A New History.* Columbia UP, 2012.

Thapar, Romila. *A History of India*. Penguin, 1990.

Van Schendel, Willem. *A History of Bangladesh*. Cambridge UP, 2009.

Visweswaran, Kamala, editor. *Perspectives on Modern South Asia*. Blackwell, 2011.

Whelpton, John. *A History of Nepal*. Cambridge UP, 2005.

Wickramasinghe, Nira. *Sri Lanka in the Modern Age: A History*. Oxford UP, 2014.

Theoretical and Literary Criticism

Agarwal, Nilanshu Kumar. *Arundhati Roy's* The God of Small Things. Roman Books, 2012.

Alam, Fakrul. *Bharati Mukherjee*. Twayne, 1996.

Anantharam, Anita. *Bodies That Remember: Women's Indigenous Knowledge and Cosmopolitanism in South Asian Poetry*. Syracuse UP, 2012.

Anwar, Nadia. *Aesthetics of Displacement in Jhumpa Lahiri's Fiction*. Anchor Academic Publishing, 2015.

Bahri, Deepika, and Mary Vasudeva. *Between the Lines: South Asians and Postcoloniality*. Temple UP, 1996.

Basu, Lopamudra, and Cynthia Leenerts, editors. *Passage to Manhattan: Critical Essays on Meena Alexander*. Cambridge Scholars, 2009.

Bhalla, Amrita. *Shashi Deshpande*. Northcote House, 2006.

Bharat, Meenakshi, editor. *Desert in Bloom: Contemporary Indian Women's Fiction in English*. Pencraft International, 2004.

Brinks, Ellen. *Anglophone Indian Women Writers, 1870–1920*. Ashgate, 2013.

Chanda, Geetanjali Singh. *Indian Women in the House of Fiction*. Zubaan, 2008.

Crane, Ralph J. *Ruth Prawer Jhabvala*. Twayne, 1992.

Das, Nigamananda. *Jhumpa Lahiri: Critical Perspectives*. Pencraft International, 2012.

De Mel, Neloufer. *Women and the Nation's Narrative: Gender and Nationalism in Twentieth-Century Sri Lanka*. Rowman and Littlefield, 2001.

De Mel, Neloufer, and Minoli Samarakkody, editors. *Writing an Inheritance: Women's Writing in Sri Lanka, 1860–1948*. Women's Education and Research Centre, 2002.

Dhawan, R. K., editor. *Indian Women Novelists*. Prestige, 1991.

Dhingra, Lavina, and Floyd Cheung, editors. *Naming Jhumpa Lahiri: Canons and Controversies*. Lexington Books, 2012.

Gooneratne, Yasmine. *Silence, Exile, and Cunning: Fiction of Ruth Prawer Jhabvala*. Sangam Books, 1991.

Gopal, N. R. *A Critical Study of the Novels of Anita Desai*. Atlantic, 1999.

Gulati, Varun, and Mythili Anoop. *Contemporary Women's Writing in India*. Lexington Books, 2014.

Hassan, Mushirul. *Sarojini Naidu: Her Way with Words*. Niyogi Press, 2012.

Hazarika, Nikara, et al., editors. *Contemporary Indian Women Writers in English: Critical Perspectives*. Pencraft International, 2015.

Ho, Elaine Yee Lin. *Anita Desai*. Northcote House, 2005.

Hussain, Sofia, and Munazza Yaqoob. *Muslim Women Writers of the Subcontinent (1870–1950)*. Emel Publications, 2014.

Hussain, Yasmin. *Writing Diaspora: South Asian Women, Culture, and Ethnicity*. Ashgate, 2005.

Jackson, Elizabeth. *Feminism and Contemporary Indian Women's Writing*. Palgrave Macmillan, 2010.

Joseph, Clara A. B. *The Agent in the Margin: Nayantara Sahgal's Gandhian Fiction*. Wilfrid Laurier UP, 2008.

Joseph, Margaret Paul. *Jasmine on a String: A Survey of Women Writing English Fiction in India*. Oxford UP, 2014.

———. *Kamala Markandaya*. Arnold-Heinemann, 1980.

Jussawalla, Feroza F., and Deborah Fillerup Weagel, editors. *Emerging South Asian Women Writers: Essays and Interviews*. Peter Lang, 2015.

Kafka, Phillipa. *On the Outside Looking In(dian): Indian Women Writers at Home and Abroad*. Peter Lang, 2003.

Kamala, N. *Translating Women: Indian Interventions*. Zubaan, 2010.

Kohli, Devindra. *Kamala Das: Critical Perspectives*. Pencraft International, 2010.

Kohli, Devindra, and Melanie Maria Just, editors. *Anita Desai: Critical Perspectives*. Pencraft International, 2008.

Kundu, Rama. *Anita Desai's* Fire on the Mountain. Atlantic, 2005.

Kuortti, Joel. *Writing Imagined Diasporas: South Asian Women Reshaping North American Identity*. Cambridge Scholars, 2007.

Kuortti, Joel, and Rajeshwar Mittapalli, editors. *Indian Women's Short Fiction*. Atlantic, 2007.

Mahabir, Joy, and Mariam Pirbhai, editors. *Critical Perspectives on Indo-Caribbean Women's Literature*. Routledge, 2013.

Mandal, Somdatta. *Bharti Mukherjee: Critical Perspectives*. Pencraft International, 2010.

Menon, Ritu. *Women Writers on the Partition of Pakistan and India*. Vanguard Books, 2006.

Morton, Stephen. *Gayatri Chakravorty Spivak: Routledge Critical Thinkers*. Routledge, 2003.

Mullaney, Julie. *Arundhati Roy's* The God of Small Things*: A Reader's Guide.* Continuum, 2005.

Naik, Chanchala K., editor. *Writing Difference: The Novels of Shashi Deshpande.* Pencraft International, 2005.

Nimsarkar, P. D., editor. *Kiran Desai, the Novelist: An Anthology of the Critical Essays.* Creative Books, 2008.

Palade, Roxana. *South Asian Women Writers: Breaking the Tradition of Silence.* Anchor Academic Publishers, 2015.

Paranjape, Makarand R. *Sarojini Naidu.* Rupa, 2010.

Prasad, Murari, editor. *Arundhati Roy: Critical Perspectives.* Pencraft International, 2006.

Priskil, Peter. *Taslima Nasrin: The Death Order and Its Background.* Ahriman International, 1997.

Rajan, Rajeswari Sunder. *Real and Imagined Women: Gender, Culture, and Postcolonialism.* Routledge, 1993.

Ray, Mohit Kumar, and Rama Kundu, editors. *Studies in Women Writers in English.* Atlantic, 2006. 10 vols.

Ray, Sangeeta. *Gayatri Chakravorty Spivak: In Other Words.* Wiley-Blackwell, 2009.

Rege, Sharmila. *Writing Caste/Writing Gender: Narrating Dalit Women's Testimonies.* Zubaan, 2006.

Sen, Nandini. *Mahasweta Devi: Critical Perspectives.* Pencraft International, 2011.

Sen, Nivedita, and Nikhil Yadav, editors. *Mahasweta Devi: An Anthology of Recent Criticism.* Pencraft International, 2008.

Shahane, Vasant Anant. *Ruth Prawer Jhabvala.* Arnold-Heinemann, 1976.

Sharma, Radhe Shyam. *Anita Desai.* Arnold-Heinemann, 1981.

Shimla, Malashri Lal. *The Law of the Threshold: Women Writers in Indian English.* Indian Institute of Advanced Study, 1995.

Singh, Jaspal Kaur, and Rajendra Chetty. *Indian Writers: Transnationalisms and Diasporas.* Peter Lang, 2010.

Sinha, Sunita, and Bryan Reynolds, editors. *Critical Responses to Kiran Desai.* Atlantic, 2009.

Stoican, Adriana Elena, and Mădălina Nicolaescu. *Transcultural Encounters in South-Asian American Women's Fiction: Anita Desai, Kiran Desai and Jhumpa Lahiri.* Cambridge Scholars, 2015.

Sucher, Laurie. *Ruth Prawer Jhabvala: The Politics of Passion.* Macmillan, 1989.

Tejero, Antonia Navarro. *Gender and Caste in the Anglophone-Indian Novels of Arundhati Roy and Githa Hariharan.* Edwin Mellen Press, 2005.

Tickell, Alex. *Arundhati Roy's* The God of Small Things*: A Routledge Study Guide.* Routledge, 2007.

Vijayasree, C. *Suniti Namjoshi: The Artful Transgressor.* Rawat, 2001.

Watkins, Alexandra. *Problematic Identities in Women's Fiction of the Sri Lankan Diaspora.* Brill Rodopi, 2015.

Yadav, Nikhil, editor. *Mahasweta Devi: An Anthology of Recent Criticism.* Pencraft International, 2008.

Comparative Contexts

Aftab, Tahera. *Inscribing South Asian Muslim Women: An Annotated Bibliography and Research Guide.* Brill, 2008.

Amireh, Amal, and Lisa Suhair Majaj. *Going Global: The Transnational Reception of Third World Women Writers.* Garland, 2000.

Conway, Jill K. *Written by Herself: Women's Memoirs from Britain, Africa, Asia, and the United States.* Vintage, 2011.

Ponzanesi, Sandra. *Paradoxes of Postcolonial Culture: Contemporary Women Writers of the Indian and Afro-Italian Diaspora.* State U of New York P, 2004.

Singh, Jaspal Kaur. *Representation and Resistance: South Asian and African Women's Texts at Home and in the Diaspora.* U of Calgary P, 2008.

Anthologies

Butalia, Urvashi, and Ritu Menon, editors. *In Other Words: New Writing by Indian Women.* Westview Press, 1994.

George, Annie, and S. N. Sandhya, editors. *Roots and Wings: An Anthology of Indian Women Writing in English.* Roots and Wings, 2011.

Kapur, Manju, editor. *Shaping the World: Women Writers on Themselves.* Hay House, 2014.

Paranjape, Makarand R., editor. *Sarojini Naidu: Selected Letters, 1890s to 1940s.* Kali for Women, 1996.

Tharu, Susie J., and K. Lalita, editors. *Women Writing in India.* Feminist Press, 1991–93. 2 vols.

Vadgama, Kusoom, editor. *An Indian Portia: Selected Writings of Cornelia Sorabji, 1866 to 1954.* Zubaan, 2011.

Memoirs, Biographies, and Interviews

Memoirs

Afzal-Khan, Fawzia. *Lahore with Love: Growing Up with Girlfriends, Pakistani-Style*. Syracuse UP, 2010.

Alexander, Meena. *Fault Lines: A Memoir*. Feminist Press at the City U of New York, 1993.

Chughtai, Ismat. *A Life in Words*. Translated by M. Asaduddin, Penguin, 2012.

Das, Kamala. *A Childhood in Malabar: A Memoir*. Penguin, 2003.

———. *My Story: The Compelling Autobiography of a Most Controversial Indian Writer*. Sterling, 1996.

De, Shobha. *Selective Memory: Stories from My Life*. Penguin, 2015.

Devidayal, Namita. *The Music Room: A Memoir*. Thomas Dunn Books, 2009.

Gooneratne, Yasmine. *Relative Merits: A Personal Memoir of the Gooneratnes of Sri Lanka*. C. Hurst, 1986.

Haldar, Baby. *A Life Less Ordinary: A Memoir*. Translated by Urvashi Butalia, HarperCollins, 2007.

Lahiri, Jhumpa. *In Other Words*. Knopf, 2016.

Nasrin, Taslima. *Meyebela: My Bengali Girlhood*. Steerforth Press, 1998.

Pritam, Amrita. *The Revenue Stamp: An Autobiography*. Times Group Books, 2015.

Sorabji, Cornelia. *India Calling: The Memories of Cornelia Sorabji, India's First Woman Barrister*. Oxford UP, 2001.

Suleri, Sara. *Excellent Things in Women: A Memoir of Postcolonial Pakistan*. U of Chicago P, 2013.

Umrigar, Thrity. *First Darling of the Morning: Selected Memories of an Indian Childhood*. Harper, 2008.

Biographies

Dhawan, R. K. *Arundhati Roy: The Novelist Extraordinary*. Sangam Books, 1999.

Ho, Elaine Yee Lin. *Anita Desai*. Atlantic, 2010.

Menon, Ritu. *Out of Line: A Personal and Political Biography of Nayantara Sahgal*. HarperCollins, 2014.

Ray, Bharati. *Early Feminists in Colonial India: Sarala Devi Chaudhurani and Rokeya Sakawat Hossain*. Oxford UP, 2002.

Weisbord, Merrily. *The Love Queen of Malabar: My Friendship with Kamala Das*. McGill-Queens UP, 2010.

Interviews

Joseph, Ammu, editor. *Just between Us: Women Speak About Their Writing.* Women Unlimited, 2004.

———, editor. *Storylines: Conversations with Women Writers.* Women Unlimited, 2003.

Kuortti, Joel, editor. *Tense Past, Tense Present: Women Writing in English.* Stree, 2003.

Meena Alexander

Maxey, Ruth, interviewer. "Interview: Meena Alexander." *MELUS*, vol. 31, no. 2, 2006, pp. 21–39.

Tharu, Susie, interviewer. "Susie Tharu Interviews Meena Alexander." *Journal of South Asian Literature*, vol. 21, no. 1, 1986, pp. 11–14.

Kamala Das

Raveendran, P. P., interviewer. "Of Masks and Memories: An Interview with Kamala Das." *Indian Literature*, vol. 36, no. 3, May–June 1993, pp. 144–61.

Anita Desai

Bliss, Corinne Demas, interviewer. "Against the Current: A Conversation with Anita Desai." *The Massachusetts Review*, vol. 29, no. 3, 1988, pp. 521–37.

Menozzi, Filippo, interviewer. "The Art of the Custodian: Interview with Anita Desai." *Wasafiri*, vol. 30, no. 1, 2015, pp. 29–34.

Ram, Atma, interviewer. "Interview with Anita Desai." *World Literatures Written in English*, vol. 16, no. 1, 1977, pp. 95–103.

Mahasweta Devi

Asokan, Anu T., interviewer. "Reflections on Adivasi Silence: An Interview with the Eminent Activist for Tribal Rights and Environmental Crusader Mahasweta Devi." *Asiatic*, vol. 7, no. 1, June 2013, pp. 154–62.

Chakraborty, Madhurima, interviewer. "'The Only Thing I Know How to Do': An Interview with Mahasweta Devi." *Journal of Postcolonial Writing*, vol. 50, no. 3, July 2014, pp. 282–90.

Chitra Banerjee Divakaruni

Aldama, Frederick Luis, interviewer. "Unbraiding Tradition: An Interview with Chitra Divakaruni." *Journal of South Asian Literature*, vol. 35, no. 1/2, 2000, pp. 1–12.

Zupančič, Metka, interviewer. "The Power of Storytelling: An Interview with Chitra Banerjee Divakaruni." *Contemporary Women's Writing*, vol. 6, no. 2, 2011, pp. 85–101.

Gita Hariharan

Kuorrti, Joel, interviewer. "'The Double Burden: The Continual Contesting of Tradition and Modernity': Githa Hariharan Interviewed by Joel Kuorrti." *The Journal of Commonwealth Literature*, vol. 36, no. 1, 2001, pp. 7–26.

Jhumpa Lahiri

Leyda, Julia, interviewer. "An Interview with Jhumpa Lahiri." *Contemporary Women's Writing*, vol. 5, no. 1, 2011, pp. 66–83.

Bharati Mukherjee

Carb, Alison B., interviewer. "An Interview with Bharati Mukherjee." *The Massachusetts Review*, vol. 29, no. 4, 1988, pp. 645–54.

Chen, Tina, and Sean X. Goudie, interviewers. "Holders of the Word: An Interview with Bharati Mukherjee." *Jouvert: A Journal of Postcolonial Studies*, vol. 1, no. 1, 1997, legacy.chass.ncsu.edu/jouvert/v1i1/bharat.htm.

Desai, Shefali, and Tony Barnstone, interviewers. "A Usable Past: An Interview with Bharati Mukherjee." *Manoa*, 1998, pp. 130–47.

Edwards, Bradley C., editor. *Conversations with Bharati Mukherjee*. UP of Mississippi, 2009.

Arundhati Roy

Abraham, Taisha, interviewer. "An Interview with Arundhati Roy." *ARIEL*, vol. 29, no. 1, 1998, pp. 89–92.

Barsamian, David, interviewer. *The Checkbook and the Cruise Missile: Conversations with Arundhati Roy: Interviews*. South End Press, 2004.

Roy, Arundhati. *The Shape of the Beast: Conversations with Arundhati Roy*. Hamish Hamilton, 2008.

———. *The Shape of the Beast: Conversations with Arundhati Roy*. Penguin India, 2008.

Kamila Shamsie

Cilano, Cara, interviewer. "'In a World of Consequences': An Interview with Kamila Shamsie." *Kunapipi*, vol. 29, no. 1, 2007, p. 150.

Bapsi Sidhwa

"Interview: Bapsi Sidhwa." *Dawn*, 15 April 2013, www.dawn.com/news/802298.

Montenegro, David, interviewer. "Bapsi Sidhwa: An Interview." *The Massachusetts Review*, vol. 31, no. 4, 1990, pp. 513–33.

Moza, Raju, interviewer. "Interview: Bapsi Sidhwa on Growing Up in Pakistan, Writing and the Future of the Parsi Community." *HuffPost*, 27 July 2015, www.huffingtonpost.in/raju-moza/interview-bapsi-sidhwa-on_b_7847946.html.

Periodicals

ARIEL: A Review of International English Literature is a quarterly journal devoted to the critical and scholarly study of new and established literatures in English around the world.

The Asian Writer aims to provide a platform for new and emerging writers of South Asian origin.

Asiatic, housed at the International Islamic University, Malaysia, is the first international journal on Asian Englishes and English writings by Asian and Asian diasporic writers. It aims to publish high-quality research articles and outstanding creative works combining the broad fields of literature and linguistics within its focus area.

The Bombay Review is a bimonthly online literary magazine publishing short fiction and poetry, with annual print anthologies. With a readership in more than 120 countries, *TBR* is based out of New York City, Mumbai, and Jeddah.

Commonwealth Essays and Studies is a peer-reviewed journal of criticism devoted to the study of postcolonial literatures in all periods and genres. The Société d'Étude des Pays du Commonwealth (Society for the Study of Commonwealth Countries) at the University Sorbonne Nouvelle publishes two issues of the journal per year.

Contemporary South Asia. Focused on cross-regional and multidisciplinary research on the countries of South Asia—Bangladesh, Bhutan, India, Maldives, Nepal, Pakistan, and Sri Lanka—this journal highlights the internal diversity of the region and encourages the development of new perspectives on the study of South Asia from across the arts and social sciences disciplines.

Economic and Political Weekly, published in Mumbai, is a prestigious forum for debates straddling economics, politics, sociology, culture, literature, the environment, and numerous other disciplines.

Frontline, a fortnightly English magazine from India, covers a range of topics from politics, economics, and social issues to the environment, nature, culture, cinema, and literature.

Indian Literature, Sahitya Akademi's bimonthly journal, is India's oldest journal and features translations of poetry, fiction, drama, and criticism from twenty-three Indian languages into English besides original writing in English. There is hardly any significant Indian author who has not been featured in the pages of this journal.

Interventions: An International Journal of Postcolonial Studies, a specialist peer-reviewed journal focusing on postcolonial research, theory, and politics.

Journal of Commonwealth Literature is internationally recognized as the leading critical and bibliographic forum in the field of Commonwealth and postcolonial literatures.

Journal of Postcolonial Writing is an academic journal devoted to the study of literary and cultural texts produced in various postcolonial locations around the world. The journal seeks to promote diasporic voices, as well as creative and critical texts from various national or global margins.

Journal of South Asian Literature. Formerly known as *Mahfil* (1963–72) and discontinued in 2000, the journal was published by the Asian Studies Center at Michigan State University and included creative writing as well as rich discussions of South Asian literature in English and vernacular languages.

Kunapipi: Journal of Postcolonial Writing and Culture was a biannual arts magazine with special, but not exclusive, emphasis on new literatures written in English.

Modern Language Quarterly publishes scholarly essays and book reviews pertaining to literary history. The journal is published by Duke University Press and housed at the University of Washington, Seattle.

Pakistaniaat: A Journal of Pakistan Studies is a refereed, multidisciplinary, and open access academic journal offering a forum for scholarly and creative engagement with various aspects of Pakistani history, culture, literature, and politics.

Postcolonial Text is a refereed open-access journal that publishes articles, book reviews, interviews, poetry, and fiction on postcolonial, transnational, and indigenous themes.

South Asian Review, the refereed journal of the South Asian Literary Association affiliated with the MLA, is a scholarly forum for the examination of South Asian languages and literatures in a broad cultural context.

South Asian Studies, journal of the British Association of South Asian Studies (BASAS), publishes original research in the arts and humanities of South Asia and from across the South Asian diaspora. Articles explore the historical, visual, and literary cultures of South Asia. The geographical focus of the journal is that of BASAS: India, Pakistan, Bangladesh, Afghanistan, Sri Lanka, Nepal, Bhutan, Maldives, and the South Asian diaspora.

Wasafiri has become the United Kingdom's leading magazine for international contemporary writing. Launched in 1984, it is renowned for publishing some of the world's most distinguished writers including Anita and Kiran Desai and Nayantara Sahgal, among others.

World Literature Today is an international literary magazine that publishes contemporary interviews, essays, poetry, fiction, and book reviews from around the world.

Selected Journal Articles

Alexander, Meena. "Outcaste Power: Ritual Displacement and Virile Maternity in Indian Women Writers." *The Journal of Commonwealth Literature*, vol. 24, no. 1, 1989, pp. 12–29.

Alonso-Breto, Isabel. "'Enormous Cracks, Towering Mountains': The Displacement of Migration as Intimate Violence in Sri Lanka–Australia Migration Narratives." *South Asian Review*, vol. 33, no. 3, 2012, pp. 125–38.

Anderson, Jean. "Lost Oceans: Indian and Pacific Ocean Women Writers." *Dalhousie French Studies*, vol. 94, 2011, pp. 1–164.

Apap, Christopher. "Jhumpa Lahiri's 'Sexy' and the Ethical Mapping of Subjectivity." *MELUS*, vol. 41, no. 2, 2016, pp. 55–75.

Bagchi, Barnita. "Fruits of Knowledge: Polemics, Humour and Moral Education in the Writings of Rokeya Sakhawat Hossain, Lila Majumdar and Nabaneeta Dev Sen." *Asiatic*, vol. 7, no. 2, Dec. 2013, pp. 126–38.

Behera, Guru Charan. "Development and Welfare Discourses, Marginality and Cultural Interventions in Mahasweta Devi's *Aajir*." *Asiatic*, vol. 10, no. 1, June 2016, p. 54.

Boehmer, Elleke. "Without the West: 1990s Southern African and Indian Woman Writers—A Conversation?" *African Studies*, vol. 58, no. 2, Dec. 1999, pp. 157–70.

Bowers, Maggie Ann. "Asia's Europes: Anti-Colonial Attitudes in the Novels of Ondaatje and Shamsie." *Journal of Postcolonial Writing*, vol. 51, no. 2, May 2015, pp. 184–95.

Chae, Youngsuk. "Postcolonial Ecofeminism in Arundhati Roy's *The God of Small Things*." *Journal of Postcolonial Writing*, vol. 51, no. 5, Dec. 2015, pp. 519–30.

Dasgupta, Shumona. "Interrogating the 'Fourth Space': Re-Imagining 'Nation,' 'Culture' and 'Community' in South Asian Diasporic Fiction." *South Asian Review*, vol. 24, no. 1, 2003, pp. 116–29.

Dora-Laskey, Prathim-Maya. "Bodies as Borderwork: From Cartographic Distance to Cosmopolitan Concern in Bapsi Sidhwa's *Ice-Candy-Man* and Amitav Ghosh's *The Shadow Lines*." *South Asian Review*, vol. 36, no. 3, Dec. 2015, pp. 33–50.

Farrier, David. "Disaster's Gift: Anthropocene and Capitalocene Temporalities in Mahasweta Devi's *Pterodactyl, Puran Sahay, and Pirtha*." *Interventions*, vol. 18, no. 3, 2016, pp. 450–66.

Farshid, Sima, and Somayeh Taleie. "The Fertile 'Third Space' in Jhumpa Lahiri's Stories." *International Journal of Comparative Literature and Translation Studies*, vol. 1, no. 3, 2013, pp. 1–5.

Feng, Pin-chia. "Birth of Nations: Representing the Partition of India in Bapsi Sidhwa's *Cracking India*." *Chang Gung Journal of Humanities and Social Sciences*, vol. 4, no. 2, Oct. 2011, pp. 225–40.

Fernandez, Jean. "Graven Images: The Woman Writer, the Indian Poetess, and Imperial Aesthetics in L.E.L.'s 'Hindoo Temples and Palaces and Madura.'" *Victorian Poetry*, vol. 43, no. 1, 2005, pp. 35–52.

Ganapathy-Doré, Geetha. "A Mouthful of Stones in a Mango Leaf: History, Womanhood and Language in Sara Suleri's *Meatless Days, a Memoir*." *Commonwealth Essays and Studies*, vol. 24, no. 1, 2001, pp. 31–40.

Gargey, Amita Raj. "Search for Identity and Self in Indian Poetry in English by Women Writers." *Language in India*, vol. 9, no. 5, May 2009, pp. 60–65.

Gee, Maggie. "Anita and Kiran Desai in Conversation: Writing Across the Generations." *Wasafiri*, vol. 25, no. 3, 2010, pp. 30–37.

Ghosh, Shoba Venkatesh. "Refiguring Myth: Draupadi and Three Indian Women Writers." *New Quest*, vol. 116, Mar. 1996, pp. 91–98.

Grobin, Tina. "The Development of Indian English Post-colonial Women's Prose." *Acta Neophilologica*, vol. 44, nos. 1–2, 2011, p. 93.

Gunew, Sneja. "'Mouthwork': Food and Language as the Corporeal Home for the Unhoused Diasporic Body in South Asian Women's Writing." *The Journal of Commonwealth Literature*, vol. 40, no. 2, June 2005, pp. 93–103.

Gupta, Pragya. "'Rudali': From Mahasweta Devi to Kalpana Lajmi." *Creative Forum*, vol. 21, nos. 1–2, 2008, pp. 15–25.

Hai, Ambreen. "Adultery behind Purdah and the Politics of Indian Muslim Nationalism in Zeenuth Futehally's *Zohra*." *Modern Fiction Studies*, vol. 59, no. 2, 2013, pp. 317–45.

———. "(Re)Reading Fawzia Afzal-Khan's *Lahore with Love*: Class and the Ethics of Memoir." *Pakistaniaat: A Journal of Pakistan Studies*, vol. 3, no. 2, 2011, pp. 29–51.

Haider, Nishat. "Reading 'The Endless Female Hungers': Love and Desire in the Poems of Kamala Das." *South Asian Review*, vol. 31, no. 1, 2010, p. 277.

———. "Voices from behind the Veil: A Study of Imtiaz Dharker's *Purdah and Other Poems*." *South Asian Review*, vol. 30, no. 1, 2009, p. 246.

Hasan, Md. Mahmudul. "Muslim Bengal Writes Back: A Study of Rokeya's Encounter with and Representation of Europe." *Journal of Postcolonial Writing*, vol. 52, no. 6, Dec. 2016, pp. 739–51.

Hasanat, Fayeza. "Sultana's Utopian Awakening: An Ecocritical Reading of Rokeya Sakhawat Hossain's *Sultana's Dream*." *Asiatic*, vol. 7, no. 2, Dec. 2013, pp. 114–25.

Heinze, Ruediger. "A Diasporic Overcoat? Naming and Affection in Jhumpa Lahiri's *The Namesake*." *Journal of Postcolonial Writing*, vol. 43, no. 2, Aug. 2007, pp. 191–202.

Herbert, Caroline. "Lyric Maps and the Legacies of 1971 in Kamila Shamsie's *Kartography*." *Journal of Postcolonial Writing*, vol. 47, no. 2, May 2011, pp. 159–72.

Herrick, Margaret. "New Ways of Thinking Recovery from Trauma in Arundhati Roy's *The God of Small Things* and Two Other South Indian Narratives of Caste-Based Atrocity." *Interventions*, vol. 19, nos. 3–4, 2017, pp. 583–98.

Hirsiaho, Anu. "Devouring Grief: Mourning and the Embodied Politics of Memory in Sara Suleri's *Meatless Days*." *Atlantic Literary Review*, vol. 3, no. 2, Apr. 2002, pp. 188–209.

Jackson, Elizabeth. "Globalization, Diaspora, and Cosmopolitanism in Kiran Desai's *The Inheritance of Loss*." *ARIEL*, vol. 47, no. 4, Oct. 2016, pp. 25–43.

———. "Transcending the Politics of 'Where You're From': Postcolonial Nationality and Cosmopolitanism in Jhumpa Lahiri's *Interpreter of Maladies*." *ARIEL*, vol. 43, no. 1, Oct. 2012, p. 109.

Jayaraman, Uma. "John Peter Peterson or Jemubhai Popatlal Patel? 'The Uncanny' Doubleness and 'Cracking' of Identity in Kiran Desai's *Inheritance of Loss*." *Asiatic*, vol. 5, no. 1, June 2011, pp. 54–68.

Johnson, Alan. "Sacred Forest, Maternal Space, and National Narrative in Mahasweta Devi's Fiction." *ISLE: Interdisciplinary Studies in Literature and Environment*, vol. 23, no. 3, 2016, pp. 506–25.

Khan, Nyla Ali. "Inevitable Multiplicity of Subject Positions in Fawzia Afzal Khan's *Lahore with Love: Growing Up with Girlfriends, Pakistani-Style*." *Pakistaniaat: A Journal of Pakistan Studies*, vol. 3, no. 2, 2011, pp. 23–28.

King, Bruce. "Kamila Shamsie's Novels of History, Exile and Desire." *Journal of Postcolonial Writing*, vol. 47, no. 2, May 2011, pp. 147–58.

Koshy, Susan. "Minority Cosmopolitanism." *PMLA*, vol. 126, no. 3, May 2011, p. 592.

Lau, Lisa. "Making the Difference: The Differing Presentations and Representations of South Asia in the Contemporary Fiction of Home and Diasporic South Asian Women Writers." *Modern Asian Studies*, vol. 39, no. 1, Feb. 2005, pp. 237–56.

Le Guellec, Anne. "Strategies of Colour, Mysticism of Form in Anita Desai's *In Custody*." *Commonwealth Essays and Studies*, vol. 32, no. 2, 2010, pp. 75–86.

Lemaster, Tracy. "Influence and Intertextuality in Arundhati Roy and Harper Lee." *Modern Fiction Studies*, vol. 56, no. 4, 2010, pp. 788–814.

Lobnik, Mirja. "Sounding Ecologies in Arundhati Roy's *The God of Small Things*." *Modern Fiction Studies*, vol. 62, no. 1, 2016, pp. 115–35.

Machwe, Prabhakar. "Prominent Women Writers in Indian Literature after Independence." *Journal of South Asian Literature*, vol. 12, nos. 3–4, 1977, pp. 145–49.

Majithia, Sheetal. "Rethinking Postcolonial Melodrama and Affect." *Modern Drama*, vol. 58, no. 1, 2015, pp. 1–23.

Malik, Surbhi. "Homelessness as Metaphor and Metonym: Transatlantic Geopolitics in Jhumpa Lahiri's Fiction and Kiran Desai's *The Inheritance of Loss*." *South Asian Review*, vol. 37, no. 2, 2016, pp. 47–70.

Mann, Harveen Sachdeva. "'Cracking India': Minority Women Writers and the Contentious Margins of Indian Nationalist Discourse." *The Journal of Commonwealth Literature*, vol. 29, no. 2, 1994, pp. 71–94.

Marino, Alessandra. "'Where Is the Time to Sleep?' Orientalism and Citizenship in Mahasweta Devi's Writing." *Journal of Postcolonial Writing*, vol. 50, no. 6, Dec. 2014, pp. 688–700.

Matthew, Jibu George. "Multiple Temporalities: The Aesthetics and Politics of Time in Arundhati Roy's *The God of Small Things*." *South Asian Review*, vol. 37, no. 2, 2016, pp. 97–108.

Menozzi, Filippo. "Beyond the Rhetoric of Belonging: Arundhati Roy and the Dalit Perspective." *Asiatic*, vol. 10, no. 1, June 2016, pp. 66–80.

———. "'Too Much Blood for Good Literature': Arundhati Roy's *The Ministry of Utmost Happiness* and the Question of Realism." *Journal of Postcolonial Writing*, vol. 55, no. 1, 2019, pp. 20–33.

———. "Tracking Down Ruins: Anita Desai and the Ethics of Postcolonial Writing." *Journal of Postcolonial Writing*, vol. 52, no. 3, July 2016, pp. 319–30.

Mirza, Maryam. "Female Relationships across Class Boundaries: A Study of Three Contemporary Novels by Women Writers from the Indian Sub-continent." *Sri Lanka Journal of the Humanities*, vol. 36, nos. 1–2, 2010, pp. 11–18.

Mody, Naman. "Author-Activism: Philosophy of Dissent in the Writings of Arundhati Roy." *Asiatic*, vol. 7, no. 1, June 2013, pp. 56–72.

Nandi, Miriam. "Longing for the Lost (M)other: Postcolonial Ambivalences in Arundhati Roy's *The God of Small Things*." *Journal of Postcolonial Writing*, vol. 46, no. 2, May 2010, pp. 175–86.

Parinitha, Shetty. "'Re-Formed' Women and Narratives of the Self." *ARIEL*, vol. 37, no. 1, Jan. 2006, pp. 45–60.

Poon, Angelia. "In a Transnational World: Exploring Gendered Subjectivity, Mobility, and Consumption in Anita Desai's *Fasting, Feasting*." *ARIEL*, vol. 37, nos. 2–3, Apr. 2006, pp. 33–48.

———. "(In)visible Scripts, Hidden Costs: Narrating the Postcolonial Globe in Kiran Desai's *The Inheritance of Loss*." *Journal of Postcolonial Writing*, vol. 50, no. 5, Sept. 2014, pp. 547–58.

Qureshi, Irna, and Naiza Khan. "Women Artists and Male Artisans in South Asia." *South Asian Popular Culture*, vol. 9, no. 1, 2011, pp. 81–88.

Rani, N. Jamuna. "Mode of Assertion Adopted by the Woman Protagonist in Arundhati Roy's *The God of Small Things*." *New Academia: An International Journal of English Language Literature and Literary Theory*, vol. 3, no. 3, July 2014, pp. 30–36.

Rastogi, Pallavi. "Pedagogical Strategies in Discussing Chitra Banerjee Divakaruni's *Arranged Marriage*." *Asian American Literature: Discourse and Pedagogies*, vol. 1, 2010, pp. 35–41.

Ray, Sangeeta. "Memory, Identity, Patriarchy: Projecting a Past in the Memoirs of Sara Suleri and Michael Ondaatje." *Modern Fiction Studies*, vol. 39, no. 1, 1993, pp. 37–58.

Ross, Oliver. "'Other Creatures That Have Their Own Identities': Strategic Essentialism in Sunita Namjoshi's Fables." *South Asian Review*, vol. 37, no. 1, 2016, pp. 179–96.

Roye, Susmita. "'Sultana's Dream' vs. Rokeya's Reality: A Study of One of the 'Pioneering' Feminist Science Fictions." *Kunapipi*, vol. 31, no. 2, 2009, pp. 135–46.

Salma, Umme. "Displacement of Desire in Kiran Desai's *Inheritance of Loss*." *Asiatic*, vol. 9, no. 1, June 2015, pp. 122–36.

Seyhan, Azade. "'World Literatures Reimagined': Sara Suleri's *Meatless Days* and A. H. Tanpınar's *Five Cities*." *Modern Language Quarterly*, vol. 74, no. 2, June 2013, pp. 197–215.

Singh, Harleen. "Insurgent Metaphors: Decentering 9/11 in Mohsin Hamid's *The Reluctant Fundamentalist* and Kamila Shamsie's *Burnt Shadows*." *ARIEL*, vol. 43, no. 1, Oct. 2012, p. 23.

Singh, Jaspal. "Representing the Poetics of Resistance in Transnational South Asian Women's Fiction and Film." *South Asian Review*, vol. 24, no. 1, 2003, pp. 202–19.

Singh, Julietta. "'Between Food and the Body': Sara Suleri's Edible Histories." *Journal of Commonwealth and Postcolonial Studies*, vol. 16, no. 1, 2009, pp. 26–44.

Stähler, Axel. "The Holocaust in the Nursery: Anita Desai's *Baumgartner's Bombay*." *Journal of Postcolonial Writing*, vol. 46, no. 1, Feb. 2010, pp. 76–88.

Subramanian, Shreerekha Pillai. "Diasporic Memories, Dissident Memoirist." *Pakistaniaat: A Journal of Pakistan Studies*, vol. 3, no. 2, 2011, pp. 6–22.

Tilby, Michael. "Baudelaire through Bengali Eyes: Toru Dutt's Translations from *Les Fleurs du Mal* in Context." *Comparative Critical Studies*, vol. 12, no. 3, Oct. 2015, pp. 333–55.

Twidle, Hedley. "Rachel Carson and the Perils of Simplicity: Reading *Silent Spring* from the Global South." *ARIEL*, vol. 44, no. 4, Oct. 2013, pp. 49–88.

Vadde, Aarthi. "The Backwaters Sphere: Ecological Collectivity, Cosmopolitanism, and Arundhati Roy." *Modern Fiction Studies*, vol. 55, no. 3, 2009, pp. 522–44.

Watkins, Alexandra. "The Diasporic Slide: Representations of Second-Generation Diasporas in Yasmine Gooneratne's *A Change of Skies* (1991) and in Chandani Lokugé's *If the Moon Smiled* (2000) and *Softly as I Leave You* (2011)." *Journal of Postcolonial Writing*, vol. 52, no. 5, 2016, pp. 581–94.

Weedon, Chris. "Migration, Identity, and Belonging in British Black and South Asian Women's Writing." *Contemporary Women's Writing*, vol. 2, no. 1, June 2008, pp. 17–35.

Williams, Délice. "Figuring Resistance: Abject Temporality and Subaltern Agency in Mahasweta Devi's Short Fiction." *South Asian Review*, vol. 37, no. 2, 2016, pp. 9–28.

Zubair, Shirin. "Women, English Literature and Identity Construction in Southern Punjab, Pakistan." *Journal of South Asian Development*, vol. 1, no. 2, 2006, pp. 249–71.

Web Sites and Databases

Alexander Street Press, alexanderstreet.com/products/south-and-southeast-asian-literature-english

Alexander Street Press publishes *South and Southeast Asian Literature*, a subscription-based searchable collection of fiction and poetry written in English by authors from South and Southeast Asia and their diasporas.

Focusing on works composed during the late-colonial and postcolonial eras, the collection features author interviews and manuscript materials that shed additional light on the rich literary heritage and emerging traditions of this region. New content is uploaded on a biweekly basis, giving users immediate access to a steadily growing treasury of classic, rare, and contemporary literature.

A Celebration of Women Writers: Writers from India, digital.library.upenn.edu/women/_generate/INDIA.html
A page provided by the digital library at the University of Pennsylvania.

Center for South Asian Studies Archive, www.s-asian.cam.ac.uk/archive/
The University of Cambridge Center for South Asian Studies Archive is a collection of private papers, photographs and drawings, books, ciné film, and tape recordings covering a period of over 200 years and includes 600 written collections, 900 maps, 100,000 photographs, and 80 collections of ciné films. Together they paint a rich and unique picture of the Raj and the early decades of postcolonial South Asia.

Emory University Scholar Blogs, scholarblogs.emory.edu/postcolonialstudies/tag/south-asia/
This site includes short articles on women writers and filmmakers of South Asian origin.

Literature Written by South Asian Women, guides.lib.uw.edu/c.php?g=341864&p=2301846, and *Poetry Written by South Asian Women*, guides.lib.uw.edu/c.php?g=341864&p=2301848
Useful bibliographies compiled by Irene Joshi, the former librarian at the University of Washington. These useful databases do not feature more recent information.

SASIALIT, sasialit.org
The *SASIALIT* mailing list is for the discussion of contemporary literature of South Asia (Bangladesh, India, Nepal, Pakistan, and Sri Lanka), including works by authors of South Asian origin throughout the world.

South Asian Literature: Some Primary Sources, www.columbia.edu/itc/mealac/pritchett/00litlinks/index.html
Compiled by Professor Fran Pritchett of Columbia University, this page provides a very useful list of online literary sources featuring writing by women.

South Asian Women's Creative Collective, www.sawcc.org
The South Asian Women's Creative Collective (SAWCC) provides women of South Asian descent with links to various communities and encourages their growth as artists by providing a venue to exchange ideas and feedback

on their creative work and network with other South Asian women artists, educators, community workers, and professionals.

Women in Pre-Independent India, www.lib.umn.edu/ames/women-pre-independent-india

A page of works by or about women, chiefly by women travelers to India, supported by the University of Minnesota.

Notes on Contributors

Deepika Bahri is professor of English at Emory University. She specializes in postcolonial literature and theory, critical theory, race studies, political aesthetics, and philosophical discourses of utopia and the good life. She has secondary interests in human health. Her publications include *Postcolonial Biology: Psyche and Flesh after Empire* (2017); *Native Intelligence: Aesthetics, Politics, and Postcolonial Literature* (2003); and two edited books and more than thirty articles and chapters.

Nilufer E. Bharucha is director of the Diasporic Constructions of Home and Belonging Indian Diaspora Centre and former senior professor of English, University of Mumbai. She has written and edited six books and published more than sixty essays in national and international journals and anthologies in the areas of postcolonial Indian writing, diasporic Indian literature and cinema, and the writing of the Parsis. Bharucha has served on the jury for the Commonwealth Literature Prize and for the English literature award of the Sahitya Akademi, Delhi. She has been a DAAD Visiting Professor at German universities and the Indian Council of Cultural Relations Rotating Chair at Muenster University, Germany.

Sushmita Chatterjee is associate professor and director of gender, women's, and sexuality studies in the Department of Interdisciplinary Studies at Appalachian State University. She received her PhD in political science and women's studies from Pennsylvania State University. Her research and teaching interests focus on postcolonial studies, feminist-queer theory, democratic theory, visual politics, and animal studies.

Cara Cilano is professor and chair of English at Michigan State University. She is author of *Post-9/11 Espionage Fiction from the US and Pakistan: Spies and "Terrorists"* (2014), *Contemporary Pakistani Fiction in English: Idea, Nation, State* (2013), and *National Identities in Pakistan: The 1971 War in Contemporary Pakistani Fiction* (2011). Cilano's current project examines the spatialization of Islam and representation of non-Muslim minorities in Pakistan through the Cold War period.

Kavita Daiya is director of the women's, gender, and sexuality studies program and associate professor of English at George Washington University. She specializes in postcolonial literature and cinema, Asian American studies, migration and race, and gender and sexuality studies. Her publications include *Violent Belongings: Partition, Gender, and National Culture in Postcolonial India* (2008) and *Graphic Migrations: Precarity and Gender in India* *and the Diaspora* (2020). She edited *Graphic Narratives from South Asia and South Asian America: Aesthetics and Politics* (2019).

Jill Didur is professor of English at Concordia University in Montreal. Her research addresses critical concerns in South Asian literature and culture, globalization studies, the environmental humanities, postcolonial and diasporic theory, critical posthumanism, and literature and media. She is author of *Unsettling Partition: Literature, Gender, Memory* (2006) and coeditor of *Global Ecologies and the Environmental Humanities: Postcolonial Approaches* (with Elizabeth DeLoughrey and Anthony Carrigan, 2015).

Gurleen Grewal is associate professor of English at the University of South Florida, Tampa. She specializes in postcolonial literature and theory, American multiethnic literature, feminist studies, and critical race theory. She has contributed numerous book chapters on diasporic South Asian and American women writers. Her book *Circles of Sorrow / Lines of Struggle: The Novels of Toni Morrison* won the Toni Morrison Society book award in 2000. She has an appreciation for holistic epistemologies and continues to pursue her study of Indian nondual philosophical traditions. She expects to soon complete and publish her work of creative nonfiction, "One River."

Ambreen Hai is professor of English language and literature at Smith College. In addition to her book *Making Words Matter: The Agency of Colonial and Postcolonial Literature* (2009), she has published essays on South Asian anglophone fiction by writers such as Rudyard Kipling, E. M. Forster, Salman Rushdie, Bapsi Sidhwa, Daniyal Mueenuddin, and Thrity Umrigar, among others. She is currently working on a manuscript titled "Postcolonial Servitude: Domestic Servants in Contemporary Transnational and South Asian English Fiction."

Reshmi Hebbar is associate professor of English at Oglethorpe University. Her book *Modeling Minority Women: Heroines in African and Asian American Fiction* was reprinted in 2010, and her essay "Bharati Mukherjee's *Jasmine* and the Romance of the Refugee Governess" was published in *Diaspora Poetics and Homing in South Asian Women's Writing* in 2018. She writes and produces *Sweet Om Atlanta*, a collaborative podcast about fictional South Asians.

Nalini Iyer is professor of English at Seattle University, where she teaches postcolonial literatures. She is the coeditor of *Other Tongues: Rethinking the Language Debates in India* (2009), coauthor of *Roots and Reflections: South Asians in the Pacific Northwest* (2013), and coeditor of *Revisiting India's Partition: New Essays in Memory, Culture, and Politics* (2016). She has published numerous articles in journals such as *ARIEL*, *South Asian Review*, and *Alam-e-Niswan: Pakistan Journal of Women Studies.*

Pranav Jani is associate professor of English at Ohio State University. Pranav's research and teaching is in postcolonial studies and critical ethnic studies, with a focus on South Asian writing, nationalism, and Marxism. He is author of *Decentering Rushdie* (2010), and has published in journals like *Critical Sociology, Postcolonial Studies,* and *South Asian Review,* and collections like *Marxism, Modernity, and Postcolonial Studies*; *Tracing the New Indian Diaspora*; and *Marxism, Postcolonial Theory, and the Future of Critique.* Pranav's current research is on the shifting narratives of the 1857 Rebellion in British India in anticolonial, nationalist, and Marxist texts.

Maryse Jayasuriya is associate professor of English and associate dean of the College of Liberal Arts at the University of Texas, El Paso. She is author of *Terror and Reconciliation: Sri Lankan Anglophone Literature, 1983–2009* (2012). She has published articles on South Asian and Asian American literature in such venues as *South Asian Review, Journeys, Margins,* and *Journal of Postcolonial Cultures and Societies.*

Joel Kuortti is professor of English at the University of Turku, Finland. His major research interests are in postcolonial theory, anglophone Indian literature, transnational identity, diaspora, hybridity, gender, and cultural studies. His publications include *Fictions to Live In: Narration as an Argument for Fiction in Salman Rushdie's Novels* (1998); *Tense Past, Tense Present: Women Writing in English* (2003); *Writing Imagined Diasporas: South Asian Women Reshaping North American Identity* (2007); *Reconstructing Hybridity: Post-colonial Studies in Transition* (coedited with J. Nyman, 2007); *Changing Worlds, Changing Nations: The Concept of Nation in the Transnational Era* (coedited with O. P. Dwivedi, 2012); *Critical Insights: Midnight's Children* (2014); *Transculturation and Aesthetics* (2015); *Manju Kapur, the Indian Novelist: A Bibliography* (2017); and *Thinking with the Familiar in Contemporary Literature and Culture "Out of the Ordinary"* (coedited with Kaisa Ilmonen, Elina Valovirta, and Janne Korkka; 2019).

Lisa Lau is lecturer at Keele University in the United Kingdom and a postcolonialist working on South Asian literature in English. The pioneer of re-orientalism theory and discourse, she works on issues of narrative, gender, class, power, and identity. Her research on representation also includes issues of precarity, hospitality, commercial surrogacy, anger, and urban Indian issues. Her publications include *Re-Orientalism and South Asian Identity Politics: The Oriental Other Within* (2011), *Re-Orientalism and Indian Writing in English* (2014), and *Indian Writing in English and Issues of Visual Representation* (2015).

Aruni Mahapatra is assistant professor of English at the University of Alabama, Birmingham. His first book project is titled *Irreverent Reading:*

Nations, Books and Communities in the Postcolonial Novel (1897–1997) and examines novels as a means of public education in colonial and postcolonial India. His research has appeared, most recently, in the *Cambridge Journal of Postcolonial Literary Inquiry.*

Shane A. McCoy (they/them/theirs) is lecturer in the Department of English at Middle Tennessee State University. Their work has appeared in *Radical Teacher*, *Writing from Below*, the *CEA Critic*, and the *Journal of the African Literature Association.* Their research focuses on transnational women's literature, critical and feminist pedagogies, social justice, and pedagogies of empowerment. Their courses have focused on contemporary transnational literature, women of color and black feminisms, Hurricane Katrina, and comedy as social and cultural critique. They are currently at work on a book manuscript that weds contemporary transnational women's literature to feminist affect studies.

Roger McNamara is associate professor in the English department at Texas Tech University. His book *Secularism and the Crisis of Minority Identity in Postcolonial Literature* was published in 2018. His current research project examines the role of religious and secular enchantment in postcolonial literature. He teaches courses in postcolonial literature, South Asian literature in translation, and secularism, religion, and cosmopolitanism.

Filippo Menozzi is lecturer in postcolonial and world literature at Liverpool John Moores University. He is the author of *Postcolonial Custodianship: Cultural and Literary Inheritance* (2014) and *World Literature, Nonsynchronism, and the Politics of Time* (2020). His work has appeared in journals such as *New Formations, ARIEL*, *Wasafiri*, *Journal of Postcolonial Writing*, *Interventions*, *College Literature*, and *Historical Materialism.* In 2019 he was awarded an LJMU Teaching Excellence Award.

Indrani Mitra is professor and chair of the Department of English at Mount St. Mary's University in Maryland. Her scholarly interests include postcolonial literatures of India, Africa, and the Caribbean; literature and secularism; and religion and sexuality. Her articles have appeared in journals such as *Modern Fiction Studies* and *Tulsa Studies in Women's Literature.*

Padmini Mongia teaches literature in English at Franklin and Marshall College in Lancaster, Pennsylvania. She edited *Contemporary Postcolonial Theory* (1996) and has published numerous articles on Joseph Conrad as well as on contemporary Indian writing in English. Her current research is on popular fiction written in English in India. A picture book, *Pchak! Pchak!*, appeared in 2008, and a book for young readers, *"Baby Looking Out" and Other Stories*, in 2018.

Stephen Morton is professor of English and postcolonial literatures at the University of Southampton. His publications include *States of Emergency: Co-*

lonialism, Literature, and Law (2013), *Terror and the Postcolonial* (coedited with Elleke Boehmer, 2009), *Foucault in an Age of Terror* (coedited with Stephen Bygrave, 2008), *Salman Rushdie: Fictions of Postcolonial Modernity* (2007), *Gayatri Spivak: Ethics, Subalternity and the Critique of Postcolonial Reason* (2006), and *Gayatri Chakravorty Spivak* (2003), as well as articles in *Textual Practice*, *Public Culture*, *New Formations*, *Parallax*, *The Journal of Commonwealth Literature*, *Cultural Studies*, and *Interventions*.

Antonia Navarro-Tejero is professor of English at Universidad de Córdoba, Spain, where she chairs a seminar on India studies. She has written *Gender and Caste in the Anglophone-Indian Novels of Arundhati Roy and Githa Hariharan* (2005) and *Talks on Feminism: Indian Women Activists Speak for Themselves* (2008) and coedited *Globalizing Dissent: Essays on Arundhati Roy* (2009), *India in the World* (2011), *India in Canada, Canada in India* (2013), and *Revolving around India(s): Alternative Images, Emerging Perspectives* (2020). She was a Fulbright Scholar at the University of California, Berkeley, and is president of the Spanish Association for Interdisciplinary India Studies.

Pushpa Parekh is professor of English and director of the African Diaspora and the World program at Spelman College. Her publications include *Response to Failure: Poetry of Gerard Manley Hopkins, Francis Thompson, Lionel Johnson, and Dylan Thomas* (1998), *Postcolonial African Writers: A Bio-Bibliographical Critical Sourcebook* (1998), and *Intersecting Gender and Disability Perspectives in Rethinking Postcolonial Identities* (2008), an edited special issue of *Wagadu*.

Ruvani Ranasinha is reader in postcolonial literature at King's College London; author of *Hanif Kureishi* (2002), *South Asian Writers in Twentieth-Century Britain: Culture in Translation* (2007), and *Contemporary Diasporic South Asian Women's Fiction* (2016); and editor of *South Asians Shaping the Nation, 1870–1950* (2012). She is associate editor of the *Journal of Postcolonial Writing* and on the editorial board of the feminist digital humanities Orlando Project.

Josna E. Rege is professor of English at Worcester State University, where she teaches the modern novel and South Asian, British, postcolonial, and world literatures and participates in the interdisciplinary programs of ethnic, global, and women's, gender, and sexuality studies. Her book *Colonial Karma: Self, Action, and Nation in the Indian English Novel* was published in 2004. More recently she has examined women's engagement with transnational cultural forms such as digital archives; her current project explores questions of migration, exile, and citizenship.

Susmita Roye is associate professor of English at Delaware State University. She has published widely in women and gender studies, postcolonial literature, and cultural history. She edited *Flora Annie Steel: A Critical Study of an Unconventional Memsahib* (2017) and coedited *The Male Empire under the Female Gaze: The British Raj and the Memsahib* (2013); a monograph on early Indian women's writing in English is forthcoming.

Cecile Sandten is professor of English literatures at Chemnitz University of Technology, Germany. She is the author of a monograph on Sujata Bhatt (1998) and of *Global Shakespeares: Transcultural Adaptations of Shakespeare in Postcolonial Literatures* (2015). She has published numerous articles on Indian English poetry and coedited volumes on the representation of the postcolonial metropolis, the notion of home, detective fiction, and, most recently, crisis, risks, and new regionalisms.

Henry Schwarz is professor emeritus of English at Georgetown University, where he was director of the Program on Justice and Peace from 1999 to 2007. His books include *Writing Cultural History in Colonial and Postcolonial India* (1997) and *Constructing the Criminal Tribe in Colonial India: Acting Like a Thief* (2010) and the coedited volumes *Reading the Shape of the World: Toward an International Cultural Studies* (1996) and *A Companion to Postcolonial Studies* (2000). He was co–general editor of *The Encyclopedia of Postcolonial Studies* (2017). He has also produced four documentary films on underclass culture in India.

Krupa Shandilya is associate professor of sexuality, women's, and gender studies at Amherst College. She is the author of *Intimate Relations: Social Reform and the Late Nineteenth-Century Novel in South Asia* (2017). She has published widely on South Asian cinema, postcolonial literature, and feminist theory in a range of journals, including *Signs: Journal of Women in Culture and Society*, *Modern Fiction Studies*, and *New Cinemas*.

Alpana Sharma is professor and chair of English at Wright State University. Her articles on South Asian writers, postcolonial literature, and Indian cinema have appeared in book chapters and academic journals such as *Modern Fiction Studies* and *Quarterly Journal of Film and Video*. She edited *New Immigrant Literatures in the United States: A Sourcebook to Our Multicultural Literary Heritage* as well as a special issue of the journal *South Asian Review* on South Asian modernism.

Harleen Singh teaches literature, South Asian studies, and women's studies at Brandeis University. Her book *The Rani of Jhansi: Gender, History, and Fable in India* was published in 2014. Her interests lie in the postcolonial novel, film and music from India, women's literature and history, and narratives of the South Asian diaspora. Her articles and reviews have appeared in the *South Asian Review*, *ARIEL*, *The American Historical Review*, and *BIBLIO*, among others.

Rajini Srikanth is professor of English at the University of Massachusetts, Boston. Her publications include the award-winning book *The World Next Door: South Asian American Literature and the Idea of America* (2004) and *Constructing the Enemy: Empathy/Antipathy in US Literature and Law* (2012). She coedited, among other collections, *The Cambridge History of Asian American Literature* (2015) and a special issue on Islamic feminisms for the *International Feminist Journal of Politics* (2008). Her teaching and research interests are in human rights, global anglophone literatures, and comparative race and ethnic studies.

Ragini Tharoor Srinivasan is assistant professor of English at the University of Arizona, where she teaches cultural theory and contemporary literature. Her current project examines diasporic nonfictions on an emergent New India in the twenty-first century. Recent scholarship has appeared in venues including *ARIEL*, *Feminist Formations*, *Comparative Literature Studies*, *GLQ*, and the collection *The Critic as Amateur*. Srinivasan edited a special issue, *From Postcolonial to World Anglophone*, for *Interventions* (2018) and is coediting a book on interdisciplinary accent studies. She is also an award-winning journalist with bylines in more than two dozen publications.

Ruth Vanita, former reader at Delhi University, is professor of English at the University of Montana. The founding coeditor of *Manushi* (1978–90), she is the author of many books, most recently *Dancing with the Nation: Courtesans in Bombay Cinema* (2017). She is an acclaimed translator from Hindi and Urdu to English. Her first novel, *Memory of Light*, appeared from Penguin in 2020.